Neurodivergence and the Criminal Justice System

This book explores key topics in the area of neurodivergence and the criminal justice system (CJS) of England and Wales, encompassing a synopsis of up-to-date academic literature, key challenges in the area, and the practical implications for fair and effective justice processes.

Neurodivergent individuals are more likely to encounter the CJS as victims and accused persons, in addition to being more likely to face barriers and adverse outcomes associated with CJS involvement. It is increasingly recognised that specifically adapted approaches are required to address this at all stages of the CJS, from policing through to prisons. This book explores and critically appraises existing scholarship and practices in this context, signposting areas for further research and policy development, and highlighting best practice approaches which have demonstrated potential in England and Wales. Whilst there are books that touch on neurodivergence generally, or specific forms of neurodivergence (e.g., autism or developmental language disorder) and the CJS, this will be the first to deal specifically with neurodivergence as a broader phenomenon in justice processes, providing a novel contribution to the field. Each chapter includes recommendations and tips for practice with a focus on pragmatic application for practitioners.

This book will appeal to anyone working in the fields of neurodiversity or criminal justice, as well as those working therapeutically with offenders. It will also appeal to researchers, policy makers, and academic faculty.

Tom Smith, LLB, PhD, is Associate Professor in Law at the University of the West of England (UWE), UK, specialising in criminal justice, fair trial, and neurodivergence.

Roxanna Dehaghani, LLB, LLM, PhD, is Reader in Law at Cardiff University, UK, specialising in vulnerability in the criminal process.

Blánaid Gavin, PhD, is Associate Professor at University College Dublin, Ireland, and a Consultant Child and Adolescent Psychiatrist. She is the co-founding editor of the journal *Neurodiversity*.

Etain Quigley, PhD, is Lecturer in Law at Maynooth University, Ireland. Her research specialisms are neurodiversity and mental health. She is the co-founding editor of the journal *Neurodiversity*.

Emma Smith, PhD, received her Doctorate in Communication and Culture from Toronto Metropolitan University and York University, Canada. She is an independent researcher and consultant in Toronto.

Neurodiversity: International Perspectives on Theory Policy and Practice

Series Editors

Andrew Eddy, Timothy Frawley, Blánaid Gavin, Etain Quigley and Charlotte Valeur

About the Series

This five-book series explores neurodiversity across important and interconnected domains – mental health, higher education, the criminal justice system, gender, and relationships. The series grew from a series of annual international online conferences organised by University College Dublin, Maynooth University, ADHD Ireland, ION and the Neurodiversity Hub. The conference sparked significant interest and dialogue, leading to a series of follow-up masterclasses, and eventually, this book series.

At its core, this series seeks to push beyond traditional academic boundaries by creating a platform for neurodivergent and neuro-mixed voices to share research, lived experience, and critical reflections. Contributors were invited for their scholarly expertise, but also for their capacity to bring authentic, engaged, and at times challenging perspectives to the forefront. The resulting volumes reflect an inclusive and dialogic approach that takes on complexity, fosters respectful disagreement, and centres empowerment for those often marginalised by dominant systems and narratives.

The books are underpinned by a neurodiversity-affirmative framework, which seeks to move away from deficit-based thinking and clinical labelling, and instead recognises and values neurological variation as part of human diversity. While clinical terminology (such as "Autism Spectrum Disorder" or "ADHD") is used where chosen by authors, the editorial team encouraged contributors to adopt affirming, identity-respecting language and to situate their work within the broader goals of inclusivity and transformation.

Each book in this series focuses on a distinct yet overlapping domain in which neurodivergent individuals often experience systemic barriers, exclusion, and misunderstanding. These volumes seek to shift the paradigm:

- from assimilation to authentic inclusion;
- from pathologisation to validation;
- from silencing to co-production of knowledge.

The first book addresses the critical link between neurodiversity and mental health, where masking, marginalisation, and social exclusion can lead to significant distress. The second book turns its attention to higher education, interrogating how inclusive practices can be implemented and reimagined through neurodivergent-led scholarship. Future volumes will examine how neurodiversity intersects with the criminal justice system, with gendered experiences, and within the context of interpersonal relationships, bringing fresh perspectives to policy, practice, and daily life.

The editorial approach has been both rigorous and reflexive. Contributors were encouraged to draw on both empirical research and theoretical frameworks, while also writing in a style and structure that best reflected their message. In doing so, this series fosters an academic space that honours diversity not only in neurological profile but also in scholarly voice.

This series is grounded in the principle of 'nothing about us without us'. It champions a rights-based, community-led approach to knowledge and advocacy, promoting systemic change through informed dialogue and shared vision. It aims not only to advance academic and policy discourse, but to support a growing movement that reclaims space, agency, and dignity for neurodivergent individuals around the world.

This series is, unapologetically, part of a wider paradigm shift — one that affirms neurodivergent lives, challenges institutional norms, and creates space for critical and collaborative transformation.

Books in this Series

Neurodiversity and Mental Health
Andrew Eddy, Timothy Frawley, Blánaid Gavin, Etain Quigley and Charlotte Valeur

Neurodiversity and Higher Education
Andrew Eddy, Timothy Frawley, Blánaid Gavin, Etain Quigley and Charlotte Valeur

Neurodivergence and the Criminal Justice System
Tom Smith, Roxanna Dehaghani, Blánaid Gavin, Etain Quigley, and Emma Smith

Neurodivergence and the Criminal Justice System

Edited by
Tom Smith, Roxanna Dehaghani,
Blánaid Gavin, Etain Quigley, and
Emma Smith

Routledge
Taylor & Francis Group
LONDON AND NEW YORK

Designed cover image: Caelestiss © Getty Images

First published 2027
by Routledge
4 Park Square, Milton Park, Abingdon, Oxon OX14 4RN

and by Routledge
605 Third Avenue, New York, NY 10158

Routledge is an imprint of the Taylor & Francis Group, an informa business

British Library Cataloguing-in-Publication Data
A catalogue record for this book is available from the British Library

ISBN: 978-1-041-07086-3 (hbk)
ISBN: 978-1-041-07085-6 (pbk)
ISBN: 978-1-003-63874-2 (ebk)

DOI: 10.4324/9781003638742

Typeset in Times New Roman
by Deanta Global Publishing Services, Chennai, India

Contents

About the Editors

Tom Smith is Associate Professor in Law at the University of the West of England (UWE), UK. His research focuses on suspect and defendant rights, pre-trial detention and bail, open justice, and neurodivergence in the criminal justice system. He is the founder and joint coordinator of the Neurodivergence in Criminal Justice Network (NICJN): a group of academics, practitioners, and community members promoting research and knowledge exchange, and evidence-led practice. He has undertaken funded projects on pre-trial detention and criminal defence lawyers' representation of autistic suspects and defendants and provided training for criminal justice institutions and professionals, including the College of Policing, Judicial College, HM Inspectorate of Constabulary & Fire and Rescue Services, and lawyers in Australia and Canada. He has spoken at national and international conferences, including the European Society of Criminology Annual Conference and published extensively on his areas of specialism in peer-reviewed journals. He has edited two books covering disclosure of evidence in criminal proceedings and autism in the criminal justice system.

Roxanna Dehaghani is Reader in Law, at Cardiff University, UK. Roxanna is a socio-legal researcher who works at the intersections of criminal justice, human rights, and legal psychology. Her research focuses on understanding and improving the vulnerable position of the accused, particularly pre-trial. She has written extensively on measures and safeguards for vulnerable suspects, including three books and one edited collection, and her research has resulted in changes to policy and practice in England and Wales, including to national codes of practice for the police. With Tom Smith, she has a forthcoming book examining criminal defence effectiveness for autistic people accused of crime. She is co-founder and Chair of the British Society of Criminology Vulnerability Research Network.

Blánaid Gavin is Associate Professor at University College Dublin, Ireland, and a Consultant Child and Adolescent Psychiatrist. She works clinically with children who experience mental health difficulties and sub-specialises in ADHD treatment. She is also involved in teaching, training, and research in the field of child and adolescent psychiatry. Dr Gavin has led training developments to heighten awareness of children and young people's mental health across a variety of sectors, including health and education. She has co-written guidelines for GPs, a book for teachers, and multiple peer-reviewed papers in national and international journals. She led the development of the first interdisciplinary research in Ireland exploring the experiences of young people attending mental health services and led the foundation of the first special interest group in Youth Mental Health in Ireland, which led to the development of the International Declaration in Youth Mental Health. She is Chair of the university EDI working group on *Neurodiversity* and is co-lead of the research programme on Making UCD a Neurodiversity Friendly Campus. She is also the joined module coordinator of the Certificate and Diploma in Neurodiversity. She is a co-founder of the new SAGE journal *Neurodiversity*. She works with a variety of voluntary organisations to support collaborative models of awareness and system development.

Etain Quigley is Lecturer in Law at Maynooth University, Ireland. She teaches and conducts research in the areas of neurodiversity, mental health, youth justice, and criminological theory and has been appointed and reappointed to sit on mental health tribunals for over a decade. Dr Quigley completed her PhD and postdoctoral work at University College Dublin, Ireland. She was successful in her application for the Irish Research Council Government of Ireland Postdoctoral Scholarship. She was also successful in receiving a Teaching and Learning Fellowship and two Irish Research Council New Foundations awards. Moreover, she has worked on an Fp7 and an H2020 research project. Finally, she is a co-founding editor of the Sage journal *Neurodiversity*.

Emma Smith is a cultural criminologist, independent researcher, and consultant whose work explores media representations of crime, community policing, and inclusive and ethical learning in higher education. She earned her PhD in Communication and Culture from Toronto Metropolitan University and York University, where her research examined how news coverage of serial violence transforms tragedy into spectacle. Her work brings together critical criminology, pedagogy, and community engagement, with a focus on accessibility, neurodiversity, and equitable, evidence-informed practices. She has taught undergraduate courses in research design, gender studies, sociology, and criminology, and contributes to international initiatives such as the *Affirming and Inclusive Engaged Learning for Neurodivergent Students* seminar series hosted by Elon University. Since 2021, Dr. Smith has collaborated with the Toronto Police Service through the Neighbourhood Community Officer Program (NCOP), serving as a Co-Investigator on a multi-method evaluation and contributing to broader conversations on community-centered and evidence-informed approaches to public safety and justice. Her work bridges scholarship, practice, and system changes across education and criminal justice contexts.

About the Authors

Clare S. Allely is Professor of Forensic Psychology at the University of Salford and an affiliate member of the Gillberg Neuropsychiatry Centre, Gothenburg University. She is also an Honorary Research Fellow at the University of Glasgow. Clare holds a PhD in Psychology from the University of Manchester and multiple postgraduate degrees in psychology and forensic psychology. She acts as an expert witness in criminal cases involving defendants with autism spectrum disorder and contributes to the evidence base on psychology and law through her research. Clare is the author of *The Psychology of Extreme Violence* (2020) and *Autism Spectrum Disorder in the Criminal Justice System* (2022), both published by Routledge. She is a key member of the FASD research team, supporting prevalence studies, intervention development (SPECIFiC), and serving as co-investigator on the NIHR/Oglesby Charitable Trust-funded feasibility trial of SPECIFiC.

Victoria Bell is Senior Lecturer in Policing and Criminology at the Institute of Policing at Staffordshire University, a Fellow of the Higher Education Academy, and an External Examiner for Criminological and Sociological undergraduate and postgraduate degrees. Victoria's current role as course leader for the Police Constable Degree Apprenticeship includes supporting our diverse range of policing students who are currently employed as police officers and studying part time. Victoria oversees the policing students' research projects whereby they are presented to force evidence-based policing boards across force partnerships. Victoria has an extensive academic background in both criminology and policing, as well as practitioner experience in the criminal justice system. Victoria is also a PhD candidate researching the role of higher education in professionalising the police service. The research includes working with the police service, academic institutes, policymakers and the public. With a specialist area in research and evidence-based policing, Victoria has experience in conducting research of mixed methodologies and disseminating findings to a range of audiences, in both public and private sectors. Victoria also has over 15 years of experience in the youth justice sector, working on prevention and rehabilitation programmes with young people. Her additional research interests are centred around identifying the youth voice and developing aspirations and opportunities for young people. She is currently undertaking research in the youth work sector working to identify the youth voice in Stoke-on-Trent and pathways to higher education.

Eddie Chaplin is Professor of Mental Health in Neurodevelopmental Conditions at the Institute of Health and Social Care, London South Bank University. He originally studied Mental Health Interventions, completing his MSc at Middlesex University, followed by a PhD in Health Services Research at the Institute of Psychiatry, Psychology, and Neuroscience at King's College London. His main research interests include the identification and understanding of neurodevelopmental conditions in the Criminal Justice System, an over-represented and largely unrecognised group with high rates of need who are often unable to access treatment or diversion to more suitable services. He is interested in co-produced research around self-help and peer mentoring strategies for improving mental health. He is currently Head of the Scientific Committee for the European Association of Mental Health in Intellectual Disability and the Editor for the journal *Advances in Autism*. He has published extensively in peer-reviewed journals and authored several books and training packs.

Penny A. Cook is Professor of Public Health and Associate Dean for Research and Innovation in the School of Health and Society at the University of Salford. She leads the UK's largest academic research group focused on Fetal Alcohol Spectrum Disorders (FASD), specialising in prevalence, impact, and effective interventions. Working with the National FASD Clinic and Professor Raja Mukherjee, she has contributed key evidence suggesting that 2–4% of UK children may be affected. Penny leads the SPECIFiC project, funded by major research bodies, to develop and evaluate a parenting intervention for families living with FASD. Her wider research portfolio includes alcohol harm reduction, where she led the NIHR-funded Communities in Charge of Alcohol programme, training community volunteers as alcohol health champions. Penny's interdisciplinary work extends to sexual health, health inequalities, and the benefits of green spaces. She is also a co-investigator on GreenME, a Horizon Europe project examining nature-based therapies for mental health and wellbeing.

Anne-Marie Day is Senior Lecturer based at the Centre for Youth Justice Research at Manchester Metropolitan University. She has conducted research on children in care and neurodivergent children's experiences in the youth justice system, and more recently conducted research exploring racial disparities in youth justice diversion. Anne-Marie has many years' experience as a practitioner and policy maker within criminal justice. She is a qualified Probation Officer and has worked in the community, courts, and prison. Anne-Marie has also worked as a youth justice manager and for the Youth Justice Board as a Senior Policy

Adviser. Anne-Marie is a trustee of both the Alliance for Youth Justice and the Michael Sieff Foundation.

Andrew Forrester is Professor of Forensic Psychiatry at Cardiff University. Andrew trained in psychiatry at the Royal Edinburgh Hospital and the Maudsley Hospital, London, and has worked as a Consultant Forensic Psychiatrist for 20 years. During that time, he has worked in London, Melbourne, Cornwall, Liverpool, Manchester, and Cardiff. Clinically, his main interest has been in prison psychiatry, from which he developed an interest in other parts of the criminal justice system (police custody, the criminal courts, and probation), and people who are detained in other settings (e.g., immigration removal centres). He collaborates widely and has a broad interest in mental health conditions as they arise in the criminal justice system in Wales, the wider UK, and internationally, with a focus on vulnerability and marginalisation. His interests are underpinned by a focus on fair and equal treatment for people in the criminal justice system, taking into consideration human rights obligations and issues in respect of social justice.

Mo Foster is the Head of the London Prison Group Director's Office with oversight of six London Prisons. She has extensive experience working across the prison estate and supporting neurodivergent individuals, having previously been the Head of Young People and Services at HM YOI Feltham where she oversaw the implementation of the autism standards and was part of the Sternberg award-winning team. Mo's current work area includes HMP Pentonville, which has established one of the first neurodivergent units in the country, and HMP Wandsworth which has recently opened their own neurodivergent unit.

David Junior Gilbert is an interdisciplinary researcher and University Fellow in the School of Health and Society. Dr Gilbert's research is focused on investigating the vulnerabilities of individuals with FASD to and within the justice system. Some of the vulnerabilities Gilbert researches include impulsivity, suggestibility, compliance, confabulation, and acquiescence in the FASD population. Currently, Gilbert is further investigating these vulnerabilities in six countries including the UK, Canada, Australia, New Zealand, Ireland and the US. Gilbert (as he prefers to be called) is a member of the academic network of Her Majesty's Prisons and Probation Service (HMPPS), Society for Evidence-Based Policing, Neurodivergence in the Criminal Justice Network, and Salford FASD research group. Gilbert is passionate about increasing the knowledge, understanding, and awareness surrounding the vulnerabilities of individuals with fetal alcohol spectrum disorders (FASD) to and within criminal justice system (CJS) encounters. FASD is a condition that impacts individuals exposed to alcohol in the womb.

Tania Goddard is a PhD student in the School of Health and Society at the University of Salford. A UK-qualified solicitor with a master's in psychology, she has extensive experience in the criminal justice system, including roles as a Magistrates' Court Clerk and Local Authority Prosecutor. Tania also worked in legal publishing in New Zealand, editing major law reviews. After returning to the UK, she supported students with autism, ADHD, and FASD, deepening her interest in neurodevelopmental vulnerabilities. Her research focuses on whether FASD constitutes a barrier to justice under the common law doctrine of fitness to plead in England and Wales. She highlights gaps in training and awareness among legal professionals and aims to improve understanding of FASD within forensic psychology and law. Tania is a member of the Law Society, British Psychological Society, JUSTICE, and the Criminal Justice Alliance.

Adam Greenslade is Senior Lecturer in Policing with the Institute of Policing in Staffordshire University, a Senior Fellow of the Higher Education Academy, and a former police officer with a long career that has included many specialist leadership roles across the UK criminal justice system. As a course leader for the MSc in Disaster Management and the degree holder entry pathway for student police officers in the Midlands, and a research supervisor for both undergraduate and postgraduate students, he is responsible for the day-to-day ongoing support and development of neurodivergent students and student officers across the many pedagogical areas and has worked in the field of Higher Education (HE) since 2019. He is currently undertaking a professional doctorate in education with a research focus on the influence of police culture on neurodivergent officers undertaking police education programmes in the UK, which builds on his earlier MA thesis "'Fit for Duty, Supported to Learn?' A mixed-methods exploration of student experience and perceptions of specific learning differences (SpLD) support in Higher Education (HE) police entry pathways," which is currently in the process of publication. His doctoral research builds on this early study and forms a comprehensive investigation into the influence of police culture on supporting neurodivergent students pursuing HE police entry pathways in the UK. It explores the relevance and significance of police culture in shaping the experiences and success of neurodivergent students, fills gaps in existing literature, and addresses the pressing need for fostering inclusivity and diversity within police education.

Todd Hogue is Emeritus Professor at the University of Lincoln. Todd moved to the UK from Canada in 1985 and worked for eight years as a psychologist in HM Prison Service, mainly specialising in the assessment and treatment of sexual offenders. He then spent a year in the community providing a sexual offending treatment service and the following year working with adolescents in secure care before joining Rampton High Security Hospital in 1995. He was initially Lead Psychologist in developing a specialist service for complex needs and from 2001 was Lead Psychologist on the development of The Peaks, a specialist unit for people diagnosed with Dangerous and Severe Personality Disorder (DSPD). Todd has been at the University of Lincoln since 2006 and undertakes research on a range of forensic and clinical topics. Since joining Lincoln, Todd established and was the initial Programme Lead for the BSc in Psychology with Forensic Psychology and MSc in Forensic Psychology Programmes. From 2017, he was Director of Research for the College of Social Science and returned in 2022 to the School of Psychology to focus on developing a research programme related to forensic psychology.

Mel Jordan is Associate Professor in Criminology at the University of Nottingham who publishes work on criminal justice settings and the social justice agenda broadly defined, often with a health harms and medical sociology angle.

Emma Joyes is Lecturer in Forensic Psychology at Newcastle University. Emma successfully completed her PhD at the University of Nottingham in 2019, exploring mental health recovery through ethnography within forensic mental health. Emma has a degree in Psychology (BSc Hons) and a masters in Research Methods (MSc). Since 2012, Emma has worked on a range of criminal justice research and evaluation projects, including academic, NHS, and governmental projects. Emma joined the School of Psychology in June 2022 and contributes towards teaching Forensic Psychology at both undergraduate and postgraduate levels. Academic fields and areas of interest include Forensic Mental Health Services, Offender Mental Health, Health Inequalities, Sexual Offending, Violence Against Women and Girls, and Research Methods (qualitative, participatory methods). Emma's research interests include Forensic Mental Health, Sexual Offending Treatment, including Feminist Perspectives.

Niko Kargas is Associate Professor of Psychology at the University of Lincoln. Niko's vision as an academic is to make a significant contribution to society by translating research and expertise in clinical audit, service evaluation, and quality improvement into social and economic development. His goal is to promote an inclusive society by creating easy-to-implement and effective person-centred approaches. These approaches assist professionals across the criminal justice system, employment, education, health, and social services in enhancing the quality of life for neurodivergent individuals and their families, including autistic people and those with learning disabilities. Niko is also the founder and director of the Autism Research Innovation Centre (ARIC), which is focused on strengthening the broader autism community through participatory action research. The mission of the group is to foster a diverse and inclusive environment in which community knowledge and academic expertise converge to generate evidence-based, innovative, professional approaches and services. These endeavours aim to enrich the lives of autistic individuals and those who support them throughout their lifespan.

Alexandra Lewis is a consultant psychiatrist trained in both forensic psychiatry and child and adolescent psychiatry and has particular expertise in autism and attention deficit hyperactivity disorder. She has over 25 years of experience working across the criminal justice system, including in the children and young persons secure estate, in the male and female adult estate, in criminal justice liaison and diversion services, and as an expert witness in court. She worked with the other authors to develop the world's first autism-sensitive prison at HMYOI Feltham. This work subsequently acted as a catalyst for change across the criminal justice system and led to increased awareness of how simple adaptations can make a meaningful difference for autistic individuals. She was an expert witness to the All-Party Parliamentary Group for Autism for the Access to Justice session of the ten-year review of the Autism Act. Dr Lewis works as a clinical adviser to the Health & Justice team at NHS England and regularly delivers training to staff working with justice-involved neurodivergent individuals.

Rachael Mason is Senior Lecturer in the School of Health and Social Care at the University of Lincoln. Her undergraduate degree is in Psychology and Criminology, and her master's degree is in Forensic Psychology. Rachael has worked for HMPPS delivering accredited Offender Behaviour Programmes for substance users. Following this, Rachael worked in a residential housing project as a Duty Officer and Training Coordinator, supporting young people aged 16–25 years to develop life skills and help them prepare to live independently. Rachael's main research interests include emergency responses to substance use and the health and wellbeing of people in the criminal justice system, including issues related to substance use. She is a member of the Combating Drugs Partnership/Substance Misuse Core Priority Group for Lincolnshire (UK).

Jane McCarthy is Divisional Clinical Director for Specialist Services & Consultant Psychiatrist for the Intellectual Disability Service at Sussex Partnership NHS Foundation Trust, Visiting Senior Lecturer at the Department of Forensic & Neurodevelopmental Sciences, King's College London, UK, and Honorary Associate Professor in Psychological Medicine, University of Auckland, New Zealand. Dr McCarthy has over 30 years of experience as Consultant Psychiatrist working with people with intellectual disability and/or autism spectrum disorders presenting across inpatient services, forensic services, prisons, courts, and community-based services. She has over 100 publications in peer-reviewed journals and has been an editor of six textbooks, including a textbook titled *Forensic Aspects of Neurodevelopmental Disorders: A Clinician's Guide*.

Raja A.S. Mukherjee is Adult Learning Disability Consultant Psychiatrist at Surrey and Borders Partnership NHS Foundation Trust, specialising in developmental disorders across the lifespan. In 2009, he founded the first NHS-based Fetal Alcohol Spectrum Disorders (FASD) behavioural clinic, providing over 250 specialist second opinions nationally. He completed his PhD on Fetal Alcohol Syndrome in 2014 and has advised the BMA, Department of Health, and WHO on FASD. He contributed evidence to the first All-Party Parliamentary Group on FASD and serves on the NICE quality standards group. Professor Mukherjee is the UK representative for a US NIH initiative on FASD research criteria and volunteers as a medical adviser to FASD charities globally. Honorary Professor at the University of Salford since 2021, he leads adult neurodevelopmental services and holds executive roles within RCPsych. In June 2023, he was awarded an MBE for his work on FASD.

Uzma Naseem is a UK-qualified lawyer with over 15 years' experience in commercial and not-for-profit sectors and currently serves as Head of Legal for a commercial company. She holds an LLB from King's College London and an LLM in Public International Law (Distinction) from LSE, where she received multiple academic prizes. Uzma trained at Clifford Chance LLP, including a secondment to Liberty, and has worked with UNHCR and the UN International Criminal Tribunal. She volunteers as a researcher on international children's rights and sits on adoption panels, alongside a part-time judicial appointment. As an adopter and caregiver for a child with FASD, Autism, and ADHD for 17 years, Uzma's research explores protective and risk factors for individuals with FASD encountering the criminal justice system, particularly in sexual offence cases. Her work aims to inform strategies and interventions to improve outcomes for those affected by FASD.

Alan D. Price is Lecturer in Psychology at the University of Salford, specialising in fetal alcohol spectrum disorder (FASD). His PhD examined how childhood trauma further affects cognitive and behavioural functioning in children with FASD. He works with colleagues in academia, the NHS, and the charity sector to develop and evaluate SPECIFiC, a training programme for parents and carers of children with FASD. Alan contributed to the first UK study estimating FASD prevalence, conducted in Greater Manchester, and is a founding member of the UK FASD Research Collaboration. He serves on the Professional Advisory Panel for the Irish charity EndPAE and frequently delivers talks and training on FASD to academics, professionals, families, and students. Alan is also part of the team delivering a regular Royal College of Paediatrics and Child Health one-day training course for paediatricians, supporting improved understanding and practice in the clinical management of FASD.

Jim Rogers is Honorary Senior Fellow at the University of Lincoln. Jim has taught at the university since 2000, on a variety of health and social care programmes, largely those relating to social work. He is currently programme leader for professional postgraduate courses relating to mental health and mental capacity. Following a social science degree, Jim had a career in mental health nursing for 11 years before moving into the voluntary sector for several years. In terms of research activity, Jim has published systematic reviews in the following areas: complementary therapies, substance misuse during the COVID pandemic, primary care and gambling, and gambling and suicide. He has conducted primary research with care homes, homelessness services, and mutual help groups. He has led or been part of teams conducting several service reviews. He has co-authored two social work textbooks. In 2012, with Sue Watling, *Social Work in a Digital Society* was published, and in 2015 with colleagues from the university, he authored *Social Work with Adults*.

Alice Siberry is Specialist Criminal Justice Neurodiversity Consultant at Creased Puddle. Her primary role is to deliver neurodiversity training to police practitioners. She also conducts Workplace Needs Assessments for neurodivergent (diagnosed and undiagnosed) police practitioners. Alice received her PhD in Criminology and Law from the University of Sheffield in July 2021. She also holds a first-class degree in Counselling, Coaching, and Mentoring and an MSc Psychology degree. Throughout her studies, Alice continued to gain experience in the criminal justice field and the neurodiversity sector. She has worked with North and West Yorkshire Police, and the Independent Office of Police Conduct. She also lectured at the University of Sheffield and York St John University, where she worked primarily with neurodivergent students. Alongside her work at Creased Puddle, Alice continues her academic practice. She is currently in the final stages of publishing her book *Neurodiversity in British Policing*, which will be the first to explore neurodiversity as a wider concept within police organisations. Furthermore, Alice has recently been awarded the Translational Fellowship from the Vulnerability and Policing Futures Research Centre to conduct research into algorithm-based radicalisation and how Counter-Terrorism practitioners can support neurodivergent people who may be affected by this. Alice considers herself to be neurodivergent, and therefore has a personal passion towards neuroinclusion, and given her experience, particularly police workspaces.

Lauren Smith is Lecturer in Psychology at the University of Lincoln. Prior to joining the University in 2020, Lauren worked in voluntary sector services supporting people in the Criminal Justice System for 14 years. Her roles included performance and development of services, delivery of resettlement support services in prisons, development and delivery of support services for people transitioning from the community into prison, delivery of services to families of people in prison, and work within a supported accommodation provider for families and young people. She is now Senior Lecturer, and her research interests are centred around the rehabilitation and reintegration of people with convictions, including the complex relationships between homelessness, employment, health, addictions, and (re)offending. Lauren utilises a variety of qualitative and quantitative methods to undertake her work. She is a member of the Reducing Offending Core Priority Group for Lincolnshire (UK).

James Tangen is Assistant Professor in Criminology at the University of Nottingham. James joined the National Probation Service in 2001 as a Trainee Probation Officer in the Nottinghamshire area. During his training and immediately following his qualification as a Probation Officer in 2003, James was seconded to Youth Offending Teams and spent over two years delivering the Intensive Supervision and Surveillance Programme (ISSP) to prolific and otherwise Priority Young Offenders (PYOs). James has also worked in a variety of courts and has experience in supervising adult offenders. In 2006, James was promoted to Senior Probation Officer of an inner-city team in Nottingham, following which he moved to supervising a community supervision team in Newark and Sherwood, a rural district of Nottinghamshire. Consequently, James has been responsible for the delivery of all aspects of probation services, from Magistrates' Court liaison to Unpaid Work. In 2010, James took the difficult decision to leave his career with Nottinghamshire Probation Trust to pursue a long-held ambition of an academic career. Following the completion of an MA in Research Methods (Public Policy & Management), James undertook his doctoral research at the University of Nottingham. In 2015, James joined De Montfort University as Lecturer in Probation. Over the next seven years, James developed his academic experiences to become Senior Lecturer in Criminology; during his tenure at DMU, James was responsible for coordinating two large programmes at DMU: the Professional Qualification in Probation (2017–2018) and the BA Criminology (2018–2022). In 2022, James returned to his academic home at the University of Nottingham.

Victoria Turley is an expert by experience and visiting lecturer at Birmingham City University. She is also a performer and is currently training for her BA in Acting at Performers College in BIMM University. Victoria focuses on neurodiversity and the effects and impacts of living with it. She has also trained Sandwell Youth Justice Service in neurodivergent-affirming practice and has a strong interest and belief in feminism, neurodivergent pride, and support for LGBTQIA+ people and those with mental illnesses.

Kim Turner is Senior Lecturer in the Faculty of Health and Education at Manchester Metropolitan University. She is a qualified speech and language therapist with over 20 years' clinical experience in the fields of mental health and criminal justice. In 2010, she moved to work at HM YOI Feltham with male young offenders and developed the service there. In 2016, the service won the RCSLT's Sternberg Award for Clinical Innovation after becoming the first prison in the world to gain autism accreditation with the National Autistic Society. Kim is passionate about supporting those with speech, language, and communication needs to have equity of access to justice and rehabilitation. She has worked with the Government, Royal College of Speech and Language Therapists, The Communication Trust, ICAN, Royal College of Paediatrics and Child Health, Disability Matters, Unlocked Grads, and NICE to develop resources and standards in this area.

Gina Vale is Lecturer in Criminology at the University of Southampton. She is also Associate Fellow of the International Centre for Counter-Terrorism (ICCT) and Member of the Vox-Pol Network of Excellence. Her research takes a feminist, intersectional approach to studying terrorism and extremist violence, primarily focusing on the organisational roles and experiences of women and children. Gina is the author of *The Unforgotten Women of the Islamic State* (2024) and has published in the *British Journal of Criminology*, *Terrorism and Political Violence*, *Studies in Conflict & Terrorism*, and *Critical Studies on Terrorism*, among others.

Craig Webber is Associate Professor of Criminology in the Department of Sociology, Social Policy and Criminology at the University of Southampton. Between 2020 and 2024, he was Head of Department. Craig's research applies the lessons of critical criminology to the practical problems through active engagement with those whose job it is to deal with them. Craig's research allows for the sensitive application of critical analysis to better define the limits of what is possible, and more importantly, what is desirable or ethically accountable. His work explores the interaction of technology and crime, utilising transdisciplinary research methods that cross and embrace the boundaries of varied disciplines, notably criminology, psychology, and computer science. He is the author of *Psychology and Crime: Transdisciplinary Perspectives* (2021, 2nd Edition) and *Precarious Futures: Crime, Technology, and the Web* (with Christopher Hamerton, 2027, forthcoming). He has published in *Theoretical Criminology*, *Crime Media Culture*, *Policing and Society*, and *American Behavioural Scientist*, among others.

Claire Westwood is a Designated Clinical Officer for SEND in the NHS and a Speech and Language Therapist (SLTs) by background. Her clinical work spans health, education and justice systems, with a particular focus on equitable communication access in youth justice and school exclusion. Claire has led specialist services within youth justice, alternative provision and SEMH settings, held positions in academia and co-founded the Homelessness Clinical Excellence Network for SLTs. She is Lead Author for the Royal College of Speech and Language Therapists' guidance on supporting disabled students, contributes to national policy and has published and presented internationally on communication access, disability and criminal justice.

Bobbie Jay White is currently working on completing her PhD at Birmingham City University. She has previously completed a Psychology with Criminology BSc and Forensic Psychology MSc at this institution. Importantly to both her work and approach is the fact that she is AuDHD (someone who is Autistic and diagnosed with ADHD) and as such her work is rooted in the social paradigm of disability. In addition to this, she aims to highlight difficulties faced by Neurodiverse people living in a society which is not always conducive to their needs.

Michelle White is a Lecturer of Law and PhD student at Teesside University. Her research takes a multi-disciplinary approach, considering the relationship of law, psychology, and criminal justice, with a particular interest in the psychology of the criminal justice system and considering proposals for reform.

David Wilkin is an independent researcher, self-funded campaigner and activist, and supporter of victims of disability hate crime. He was an Honorary Fellow at the University of Leicester is an Associate Lecturer at the Open University. David is autistic, with an early life involving victimisation of what latterly became known as Disability Hate Crime. After leaving school without qualifications and being unable to properly read and write until his mid-20s, David acquired undergraduate, master's, and PhD qualifications. He has published widely on his area of injustice toward disabled people, is a lead coordinator for the Disability Hate Crime Network, a steering group member of the British Society of Criminology Hate Crime Network, and a consultant to various agencies and the UK government. In 2022, he co-directed the world's first international conference on disability hate.

Abbreviations

AA	Appropriate Adult
AAA	Ambitious about autism
ADHD	Attention Deficit Hyperactivity Disorder
APP	Authorised Professional Practice
ASC	Autism Spectrum Condition
ASD	Autism Spectrum Disorder
ATR	Alcohol Treatment Requirement
CJS	Criminal Justice System
CSTR	Community Sentence Treatment Requirement
DRR	Drug Rehabilitation Requirement
EST	Enhanced Support Teams
ESU	Enhanced Support Unit
E&W	England and Wales
FASD	Foetal Alcohol Spectrum Disorder
HMP	Her/His Majesty's Prison
GSS	Gudjonsson Suggestibility Scale
HMPPS	Her/His Majesty's Inspectorate of Prison and Probation Services
HM YOI	Her/His Majesty's Young Offender Institution
ID	Intellectual Disability
L&D	Liaison and Diversion
MDS	Memory Distrust Syndrome
MHTR	Mental Health Treatment Requirement
NAS	National Autism Society
NDD	Neurodevelopmental Disorders and Difficulties
NDM	National Decision Model
NDU	Neurodivergent Unit
NHS	National Health Service
NPCC	National Police Chiefs' Council
NPPF	National Police Promotion Framework
OCD	Obsessive-Compulsive Disorder
PACE	Police and Criminal Evidence Act
PAE	Prenatal Alcohol Exposure

PCC	Police and Crime Commissioner
PCER	Police Constable Entry Routes
PEACE	Planning and Preparation, Engage and Explain, Account, Closure, and Evaluation
PEQF	Policing Education Qualifications Framework
POM	Prison Offender Manager
PTSD	Post-Traumatic Stress Disorder
RAP	Reasonable Adjustment Passports
RSD	Rejection Sensitive Dysphoria
SOTP	Sex Offender Treatment Programme
TBI	Traumatic Brain Injury
WKS	Wernicke-Korsakoff syndrome

Introduction

This book is the first of two collections focusing on neurodivergence in the criminal justice system, with this collection addressing England and Wales specifically. Neurodivergence collectively describes a range of neuro-developmental differences that are atypical, which primarily affect cognitive processes such as social communication, learning and memory, and sensory processing. The term embraces a cluster of medically defined conditions such as autism, ADHD, dyslexia, and a variety of others. Whilst the importance of neurodivergence – including understanding of and responding to the needs of neurodivergent individuals – has been emphasised by practitioners and researchers for decades (Debbaudt, 2002; Cashin and Newman, 2009), it has only been more recently that policy consideration has emerged, most notably, in England and Wales through the Criminal Justice Joint Inspection (2021). This Inspection offered a wide-ranging view of neurodivergence in the criminal justice system, underpinned by research. Not only did this catalyse various policy responses (see Ministry of Justice Action Plan (2022)), it also appears to have provided impetus for further research on neurodivergence and criminal justice. Therefore, the way in which criminal justice systems, processes, and institutions (including policing, courts, and prisons) engage with neurodivergent individuals is an emerging priority for policymakers, legal and clinical practitioners, and academics.

Notwithstanding the now extensive body of scholarship on neurodivergence and criminal justice, literature on the subject is diffuse, fragmented, and (to some extent) siloed. Much of the scholarship focuses on single forms of neurodivergence (such as autism or ADHD) or at specific points of the criminal process, rather than neurodivergence as a broader concept. Thus, the benefits (and challenges) of bringing together such insights in the context of neurodivergence are that they primarily allow for reflection between different forms of neurodivergence and at different stages of the criminal process. The criminal process can be bewildering, overwhelming, and stressful for most, if not all, lay people engaging with it. Such challenges may be more pronounced for neurodivergent people given their differences in, for example, cognitive and sensory processing, receptive and expressive

DOI: 10.4324/9781003638742-1

communication, executive functioning, and ability to cope with change and uncertainty. The current criminal justice system is not always well-equipped to meet the needs of neurodivergent people who encounter it as victims, suspects, and defendants. Rather, neurodivergent people may have their needs entirely neglected because of deficiencies in training, funding, systems, and processes, as well as laws and other frameworks. This collection aims to identify common and divergent experiences, acknowledge aspects of good and improving practice, and critique areas where practice is failing neurodivergent people. In doing so, it aims to identify shared experiences, challenges, and changes in this vital area that can be built on by the next generation of scholars and practitioners. It also seeks to significantly contribute to socio-legal, psychological, and criminological literature on criminal justice and procedure.

Edited by an international team of interdisciplinary experts in the field, the collection showcases a variety of unique scholarly perspectives in a variety of legal contexts, shedding light on existing challenges for neurodivergent individuals – including suspects, defendants, and victims of crime – as well as best practice in ensuring fair and effective justice processes. Contributions were sought via convenience and purposive selection – principally through an open call for abstracts issued by the Editors. Taken together (and in isolation), these contributions offer original and unique perspectives on a fairly well-established topic in forensic and developmental psychology but one that is nascent within socio-legal and criminological scholarship – that is, how (and whether) neurodivergence is identified, acknowledged, and accommodated in a variety of criminal justice contexts such as prisons, police detention and interviews, and youth justice.

From its inception, the ethos of this book was one of inclusivity, respect for others' opinions and perspectives, and empowerment of those who are often disempowered and marginalised by systems and processes. The collection therefore aims to allow for contemplation of often complex ideas that transcend the boundaries of long-standing biomedical perspectives. Central to this book, therefore, was that it should – in the spirit of 'nothing about us without us' – include the perspectives and experiences of neurodivergent people. Without excluding neurotypical authors from contributing, we were keen to include perspectives from those with lived experience as neurodivergent people. This was achieved in a variety of ways – principally by including neurodivergent authors with criminal justice user experience, practice experience, and/or academic research experience, as well as by having neurodivergent representation on the editorial team.

To provide a safe space for dialogue and discourse on neurodivergence, we also acknowledged the different perspectives on the appropriate terminology and language relating to neurodivergence across the academic and non-academic community. Our aim was, moreover, to allow authors to determine the authorial style best suited to their writing. We did not therefore restrict the authors' ability to reflect their reasonable preferences in terms of language, including whether authors used an identity-first (e.g., autistic person) and a person-first (e.g., person with autism) construction. We also provided a broad scope for first- and third-person writing to permit authors to use the conventions which they felt were most suited to their (sub)field generally and their work specifically. In this sense, this book, building on an earlier collection on Neurodiversity and Mental Health (Quigley et al., 2025), seeks to continue to challenge conventions in typical academic research and allow authors, particularly those who are neurodivergent, significant latitude when articulating their message. That said, there were clear guidelines for all contributors around being evidence-led and adhering to established theoretical frameworks and ethical protocols. Doing so, we felt, allowed us to continue with our ethos of flexibility whilst also maintaining scholarly authenticity and robustness.

We also considered it important to adopt neuro-affirmative language where possible, as doing so emphasises respect for and validation of neurological differences among individuals and seeks to eschew othering or marginalisation. We did, however, recognise the importance of academic freedom when engaging with language conventions. Thus, we asked that authors avoid using clinical and diagnostic language as much as possible, whilst acknowledging that, at times, such language may be necessary to make a particular point or to be consistent with how the research evidence is articulated. Where authors wished to use clinical and diagnostic language, we requested that they explain their approach to language such that the rationale is clear to the reader. As such, each chapter contains a brief rationale for language choices. Ultimately, we wished to foster understanding and acceptance and to honour neurodevelopmental diversity. We were therefore – as with *Neurodiversity and Mental Health* (Quigley et al., 2025) – guided by three key principles:

1. **Respect for Individual Experiences**: Acknowledging that everyone has their own way of processing and interacting with the world.
2. **Avoiding Pathologising Terms**: Using language that doesn't frame neurominority traits as deficits or disorders.
3. **Empowerment**: Encouraging self-advocacy and valuing diverse ways of thinking and being.

References

Cashin, A., Newman, C. (2009) Autism in the criminal justice detention system: A review of the literature. *Journal of Forensic Nursing*, 5(2), 70–75. https://doi.org/10.1111/j.1939-3938.2009.01037.x.

Criminal Justice Joint Inspection. (2021) Neurodiversity in the criminal justice system: A review of the evidence. Available at https://cloud-platform-e218f50a4812967ba1215eaecede923f.s3.amazonaws.com/uploads/sites/43/2024/09/2021-07-15-Neurodiversity-in-the-Criminal-Justice-Sustem-a-review-of-evidence.pdf (Accessed: 26/11/25).

Debbaudt, D. (2002) *Autism, Advocates, and Law Enforcement Professionals: Recognizing and Reducing Risk Situations for People with Autism Spectrum Disorders*. Jessica Kingsley.

Ministry of Justice. (2022) *Action Plan: A Response to the Criminal Justice Joint Inspection: Neurodiversity in the Criminal Justice System, A Review of Evidence*. Available at https://assets.publishing.service.gov.uk/media/62bd9c26e90e075f2ac6045d/MoJ_Neurodiversity_Action_Plan_30_06_2022__001_.pdf (Accessed: 26/11/25).
Quigley, E., Eddy, A., Frawley, T., Valeur, C., Gavin, B. (2025) *Neurodiversity and Mental Health*. Routledge.

Chapter 1

Neurodivergent Perspectives in Policing

Embracing Diversity for an Inclusive Criminal Justice System

Victoria Bell, Adam Greenslade, and Alice Siberry

1.1 Introduction

The narrative of policing and neurodiversity reflects broader societal attitudes towards difference, disability, and justice. Therefore, when reviewing the landscape of police attitudes towards neurodivergence,[1] it is important to recognise that these perspectives do not exist in isolation but rather function as an echo chamber of societal views related to neurodiversity. Explicit discussions on this topic are limited; however, existing literature on policing and neurodiversity implies that England and Wales (E&W) policing, like many institutions, operates within a predominantly neurotypical framework (Siberry, 2025). This framework often fails to fully acknowledge or accommodate the unique needs, strengths, and contributions of neurodivergent people. As a result, neurodivergent people may encounter significant barriers, not only in their interactions with the police but also in seeking and sustaining careers within the police organisation itself. Issues surrounding recruitment, retention, disclosure of neurodivergence, and further workplace experiences of neurodivergent police employees remain underexplored (Macdonald and Cosgrove, 2019), highlighting a critical gap in both research and policy. Addressing these challenges requires a deeper examination of institutional attitudes and practices, and ways to create a shift towards a more inclusive and informed approach to neurodiversity within the police organisation. Such a shift is not only essential to fulfilling legal and ethical obligations around equality but also holds the potential to foster a more inclusive workforce; one that leverages the unique strengths of neurodivergent individuals and aims to promote more empathetic, innovative, and effective policing practices, particularly when policing neurodivergent members of society.

1.2 Policing a Neurodiverse Society

Neurodiversity is considered both a social concept and political movement (Walker, 2014), established in the 1990s, that encompasses a variety of diagnosable differences that affect how individuals perceive, process, and interpret information and their environment. These diagnosable differences often refer to autism, dyslexia,

DOI: 10.4324/9781003638742-2

dyscalculia, and attention deficit hyperactivity disorder (ADHD), though they stretch beyond a variety of neurodivergent differences, sometimes collectively known as neurodivergence or 'neurodivergent conditions'. This terminology is typically used in contrast to the experience of neurotypical individuals, who are considered to represent the societal majority. The term neurotypical refers both to individuals who do not exhibit characteristics of diagnosable neurodivergent conditions and to the processes and procedures traditionally designed to serve the majority population. Historically, neurodiversity was understood through the lens of the medical model of disability, which frames people who 'diverge' from societal norms as disordered or deficient, as having 'conditions' that need to be cured or corrected (Baker, 2006). This perspective has deeply influenced societal attitudes, institutional practices, and cultural norms, reinforcing the belief that neurodivergence is a problem to be fixed or requiring an intervention, rather than recognising it as a natural and valuable part of human diversity (Crow, 1996).

Since the emergence and adoption of a more 'social' model of disability (Kirby, 2021), which developed between the 1970s and 1980s, perceptions of neurodiversity have shifted significantly. The neurodiversity movement followed in the late 1990s and early 2000s, moving from the view that neurodivergence is a problem to be eradicated or cured, to recognising that many challenges faced by neurodivergent individuals arise from societal barriers rather than neurological differences themselves (Beardon, 2017). This evolving perspective promotes acceptance of neurodiversity as a natural and valuable aspect of human diversity, highlighting the importance of inclusive environments that actively support and accommodate neurodivergent experiences. Though there is increasing awareness of the damaging impact the pathologising of neurodivergence can have as a result of the social model, the medical model of disability continues to run deeply within most of the main sources of diagnostic criteria used in the UK, such as the *Diagnostic and Statistical Manual* (see American Psychiatric Association, 2022). As such, a pervasive, more medicalised impact remains regarding how neurodiversity is understood and perceived within society.

Progress in understanding neurodiversity appears to have been slower within policing, though there are continuing efforts in raising awareness and recognition, particularly through initiatives led by employee resource groups or staff associations (Tromans et al., 2023). However, there remains a significant need for a more fundamental shift in how the police service approaches neurodiversity. Greater awareness has not yet translated into full acceptance, meaningful integration, or systemic change. Many neurodivergent officers and staff still report encountering barriers rooted in outdated attitudes, inconsistent support, and inflexible structures (Tromans et al., 2023). This lack of meaningful change is particularly concerning given the dynamic and impactful nature of police work; failure to fairly and effectively address neurodiversity can result not only in harm to the wellbeing and careers of neurodivergent employees, but also in compromised interactions with the public, particularly when neurodivergent people are involved. Though it is important to recognise that there are other organisations that require reform in relation to neurodiversity (for example, within the education system), policing arguably continues to remain behind wider societal progress, where sectors are beginning to fully embrace neurodiversity as a strength rather than perceiving neurodivergence as something that simply requires accommodation, or even more concerningly, as a hindrance. For genuine inclusion to be achieved, a cultural transformation is needed, one that not only recognises but actively values the diverse skills and perspectives neurodivergent individuals bring to the profession.

Traditionally, the criminal justice system, including the police organisation, approached neurodivergence primarily through institutionalisation, seeking to remove neurodivergent people from society by placing them in asylums and other facilities designed for those deemed mentally unwell (see Dyck and Russell, 2020; Hutson et al., 2022). This approach aligned strongly with the medical model of disability and was largely punitive, serving the interests of a particular view of what broader society should be rather than addressing the needs of neurodivergent individuals. There was little to no consideration of how neurodivergent people could be supported or integrated, reinforcing the perception that these individuals were inherently problematic or even disordered or dangerous. As the frontline enforcers of laws and public order, police were, and remain in many ways, the most visible agents of this punitive framework, often responsible for the initial detention of neurodivergent and potentially vulnerable people. Although societal attitudes towards neurodivergence have evolved significantly, remnants of these historical perspectives continue to shape criminal justice policies and practices today. Their central role has contributed to a deeply embedded institutional culture that associates neurodivergence with risk, disorder, and even potential deviance.

The criminal justice system continues to operate mostly within a neurotypical framework, meaning its structures, systems, and decision-making processes often fail to accommodate neurodivergent ways of thinking and behaving (Siberry, 2025). This is particularly evident in the over-representation of neurodivergent people within the criminal justice system. Kirby (2021) suggests that at least one in three individuals within the criminal justice system may be neurodivergent. Furthermore, a review commissioned by the Chief Inspector of Prisons suggests that up to half of those incarcerated could be neurodivergent (Taylor et al., 2021). This over-representation raises significant concerns about how neurodivergent people engage with criminal justice processes and whether the system is adequately equipped to meet the needs of those with fluctuating vulnerability (Siberry, 2025).

1.2.1 The Role of Police: Beyond Punishment, towards Social Work

Looking more closely at interactions between police and neurodivergent people, particularly during the pre-modern and early modern eras, there appears to be limited awareness and understanding of neurodiversity, often placing neurodivergent individuals at greater risk of criminalisation (Hepworth, 2017). Police officers continued to receive inconsistent training in recognising and appropriately responding to neurodivergent people, leading to frequent misinterpretations of neurodivergent traits as suspicious, deviant, or even criminal (Crane et al., 2016; Lim et al., 2022). This lack of awareness can result in escalation of situations, unnecessary arrests, distressing encounters, and unjust outcomes for neurodivergent people. While awareness of neurodiversity has increased within the police organisation, these historical patterns have left a lasting impact on policing practices, such as within the construction and implementation of provisions in the Mental Health Act (1983), including powers to involuntarily detain individuals; and within warning markers for 'Mental Health' and 'Ailments' (Siberry, 2025). This necessitates a critical examination of how the system can become more inclusive and responsive to neurodivergent needs, both for neurodivergent members of the public and for those who work within policing.

The shift towards community care in the 1980s and 1990s could account for the increased encounters between police and neurodivergent people in everyday situations (Hutson et al., 2022). This major social policy reform aimed to move people with mental health conditions, learning disabilities, and other support needs out of long-stay institutions (like hospitals) and into community-based living. This had a significant impact on policing, particularly in how the police interacted with vulnerable populations, including neurodivergent individuals. Whilst the intent of the reform was to promote dignity and integration, a lack of adequate infrastructure led to policing inheriting a major public safety and welfare responsibility for which they were not prepared (Scull, 2021; Barker, 2013). The reform of policing and policy indirectly redefined the role of the police in relation to vulnerability, and subsequently neurodiversity. However, it has also unintentionally increased demands on officers, exposing significant gaps in training and awareness.

These gaps help explain why policing practices around neurodivergence remain inconsistent across police organisations. Researchers and practitioners continue to highlight the lack of sufficient training in recognising and appropriately responding to neurodivergence (Dickie, Reveley and Dorrity, 2018; Hepworth, 2017), and while discussions around these shortcomings have led to the gradual introduction of neurodiversity awareness training (Hepworth, 2017), these efforts often remain surface-level. A Freedom of Information request from 34 of the 43 E&W police forces identified that only 16 police organisations had had some form of awareness or training, which was specifically in reference to autism (Beardon, Chown and Cossburn, 2018). Subsequent appeals to mandate training have not come to fruition (Ministry of Justice, 2022), and it appears that consistent, more general, education packages about neurodivergence are limited. Despite the College of Policing efforts to increase the levels of education about neurodiversity within policing, gaps appear to remain. As such, there is a pressing need for police training to go beyond basic awareness, incorporating practical tools such as tailored communication strategies and de-escalation techniques to support meaningful, compassionate engagement with neurodivergent individuals.

The response from police organisations in addressing neurodiversity internally also remains uneven and inconsistent (Police Federation, 2023). While some forces have developed specialist training programmes, internal support networks, and partnerships with organisations such as Creased Puddle, others have yet to adopt comprehensive strategies for supporting neurodivergent police practitioners. The College of Policing has issued national guidelines and toolkits to support forces in addressing neurodiversity, including advice on legal obligations, workplace adjustments, and case study examples (see, for example, College of Policing 2025a). However, these remain non-mandatory and often framed more as tools for legal compliance than as instruments of genuine cultural change. Crucially, there is a growing recognition of the need to equip line managers with the training and confidence to support neurodivergent colleagues in the workplace. This includes understanding how to implement reasonable adjustments, provide flexible support, and foster an inclusive team culture. Without investing in line manager training as a core component of organisational change, police organisations risk undermining the very inclusion strategies they aim to promote, both internally and in their engagement with the public.

1.3 A Neurodiverse Police Workforce

There is much focus on developing understanding of the police service in relation to neurodiversity, particularly in terms of interactions with neurodivergent individuals (such as witnesses, victims, and suspects). What is often overlooked is the need to adequately support neurodivergent individuals in their role as police officers and fulfilling this role in line with the expectations of the public, as well as in terms of maintaining the standards related to their legal powers and obligations. Some neurodivergent officers require support with their adaptive communication techniques; for example, they may interpret social cues, body language, and facial expressions from members of the public differently and thus respond in ways that could be misinterpreted as unempathetic, aggressive, or dismissive. An autistic or ADHD officer may appear distracted or overly blunt in public interactions, potentially leading to public dissatisfaction or formal complaints, particularly in sensitive or emotionally charged situations. This carries particular weight considering the intense scrutiny police officers face as public-facing figures of authority; public perceptions of professionalism, empathy, and fairness are critical to maintaining trust. Without adequate organisational understanding and support, interactions between neurodivergent officers and others can be compromised, not because of individual shortcomings, but due to a lack of shared understanding and practical tools for support and adaptation. For instance, witnesses may disengage if they perceive an officer as inattentive, while suspects may become uncooperative, defensive, or even hostile. Research suggests that in investigative interview settings, neurodivergent people may be particularly vulnerable to acquiescence or suggestibility, especially when eager to exit a stressful situation, potentially undermining the accuracy and quality of evidence gathered (Gudjonsson et al., 2008; Maras et al., 2020). When neither party is equipped to recognise or appropriately respond to neurodivergence, there is increased risk of miscommunication (in short, the 'double empathy problem' (Milton et al., 2022)). Such risks are increased where line managers and supervisors are equally unaware of neurodivergence.

Over the years, policing as an institution has evolved into a modern, professionalised public service, with a variety of societal changes requiring significant adaptation. A key part of this evolution has been increased expectations surrounding diversity. However, despite an increased awareness in wider society of neurodiversity and the work of organisations such as the National Police Autism Association (NPAA), Police National Dyslexia Association (PNDA), ADHD Alliance, and the Disabled Police Association (DPA) to advance understanding, the experiences of neurodivergent practitioners within the police service remain underexplored. Historical underrepresentation of neurodivergent individuals in policing is an institutional design that has failed to accommodate cognitive diversity. Such design has been shaped by multiple factors, including recruitment processes that historically favour conformity over difference, internal cultures that often prize uniformity and predictability, and a persistent assumption that accommodating neurodivergent needs might compromise operational standards or efficiency (Tromans et al., 2023). These elements collectively contribute to a police culture that inadvertently excludes those who process, communicate, or engage with the world differently. However, in recent years, the police service has shown a gradual shift in its approach to inclusion and representation, with notable efforts to diversify its workforce to reflect a true representation of the society it polices. Traditionally, this focus has been on gender and racial diversity, driven by broader societal movements advocating equality in relation to these demographics. In particular, longstanding evidence of racial disproportionality and discrimination within policing and the wider criminal justice system has catalysed policy attention and reform efforts. A similar recognition is now emerging in relation to neurodivergence, where disproportionate outcomes, exclusion and misrecognition are beginning to be identified as systemic rather than incidental. This growing awareness may be contributing to a broader diversification agenda that now increasingly includes neurodiversity as a critical dimension of inclusion.

While these efforts have achieved varying degrees of success, neurodiversity (and disability more generally) has been largely overlooked in inclusivity initiatives to date (Siberry, 2025). As Doyle (2020) estimates 15–20 per cent of the UK population are neurodivergent, it is expected that this will be represented in those who work for the police organisation. This is particularly important given the unique and public-facing nature of policing. Police officers are not only representatives of the law but also symbols of fairness and accountability in the eyes of the public. Failure to uphold internal equity, particularly in the treatment of neurodivergent employees, risks undermining public confidence and trust, especially when these same organisations are responsible for enforcing legal standards of equality in wider society. For police professionals who are neurodivergent, it is important to note that legal frameworks such as the Equality Act 2010 impose significant duties on policing as an organisation. Specifically, the public sector equality duty (s.149) mandates support for employees with disabilities (and subsequently neurodivergence). Ensuring genuine inclusivity within the police organisation is therefore not only a legal and moral obligation but a critical step in modelling the values that underpin effective, trusted public service. Yet, significant barriers remain in practice. As will be explored below, disclosure of neurodivergence, whether formally diagnosed or self-identified, does not always guarantee access to appropriate support or fair treatment in the workplace.

1.4 Exploring the Barriers Experienced by Neurodivergent Police Practitioners

1.4.1 Recruitment

Challenges for neurodivergent people often begin at the outset of a career in policing, stemming from systemic barriers in recruitment, institutional inflexibility, and cultural norms that favour neurotypical working styles. As such, this amounts to indirect discrimination against neurodivergent applicants for a job in policing, reflecting broader societal trends. For example, the Buckland Report (2024) highlighted that only three in ten autistic adults are in employment generally, with 'unfair hiring practices' and inaccessible processes impacting employment opportunities. Vague job descriptions, unclear questions, and sensory challenges can make the process overwhelming, leading some to feel they must mask their traits to be considered (Buckland, 2024). In the context of policing, the application process for roles is often complex and multi-staged, creating substantial barriers for neurodivergent candidates. In addition to navigating intricate forms and socially intensive interview formats, applicants must often make early decisions about entry routes, such as the various degree-based pathways now utilised in the UK, each with its own academic and procedural demands. These layers of complexity can be particularly challenging for individuals who process information differently or require clear, structured guidance. While reasonable adjustments are often offered, many neurodivergent candidates are reluctant to disclose their needs for fear it will be seen as a marker of reduced competence or unsuitability for the role (Hunter and Hunter, 2022). This concern is heightened for police officers, who operate under constant public scrutiny and are expected to perform consistently in high-pressure environments. This is further reinforced by persistent cultural assumptions within policing that conflate neurodivergence with limitation, rather than recognising it as a form of cognitive diversity that can strengthen the profession.

Hesketh and Stubbs (2023) highlight the challenges of implementing more inclusive recruitment processes in the police force, identifying how several utilised initiatives have, paradoxically, created long-term disadvantages. For example, they outline how positive action initiatives designed to level the recruitment playing field for marginalised individuals may inadvertently contribute to disparities.

Candidates benefiting from these initiatives often lack the informal social networks that provide ongoing support and identity reinforcement, potentially leading to challenges in their professional socialisation and career progression within the police force, as the recruitment initiatives support entry but not longevity, making them a temporary benefit. In relation to neurodivergent candidates, social network dependence could be a significant barrier as applicants may not only lack access to such networks but find social navigation more challenging, compounding exclusion. Whilst practical help (such as coaching and feedback) may be available, it does not always accommodate different learning styles and communication requirements, thus impacting social bonding. There is a risk of feeling isolated or alienated, even while technically being supported. This has led organisations such as the NPAA to argue that whilst there is no formal, automatic bar to the police profession for neurodivergent people, being autistic 'would be an additional hurdle to overcome during the assessment process and initial training, which are significant challenges in themselves' (NPAA, n.d.). Notwithstanding legal requirements around equality, this demonstrates that there is, in practice, an initial barrier to entry into a policing career for neurodivergent individuals and that addressing systemic and cultural barriers is essential not only for ensuring fair access to policing careers but also for fostering a more diverse, capable, and representative workforce.

1.4.2 Entry Routes

As part of a drive to further professionalise policing, the College of Policing introduced the Policing Education Qualifications Framework (PEQF) in 2016, including a requirement (from 2020) for all new police officers in England and Wales to have a policing degree level qualification (Watkinson-Miley et al., 2022). Though not initially considered, reflecting on the introduction of these entry routes reveals an additional layer of challenge for some neurodivergent individuals whilst also identifying a crucial support gap that exists between policing and higher education institutes. Degree-entry routes require academic study alongside frontline policing. For neurodivergent individuals, the dual demands of academic work and operational duties can be overwhelming without tailored support, as evidenced by the increasing numbers of neurodivergent student officers on regulatory reviews for perceived 'underperformance' either academically or operationally. Despite the PEQF's stated intentions of professionalisation, the police education sector still faces increased scrutiny regarding diversity, recruitment, and retention. National debates on improving inclusivity, professional standards, and training frameworks have increasingly questioned the effectiveness and accessibility of higher education degree-entry routes for would-be officers (Feilzer and Loftus, 2024).

While the framework aspires to modernise the profession, it risks reinforcing structural inequalities if it fails to accommodate a wider range of cognitive, cultural, and socio-economic experiences. Neurodiversity is emerging as a critical area in broader education, yet scrutiny around the inclusivity of police training and recruitment has been slow to adopt inclusive strategies for neurodivergent recruits.

Indeed, an illustrative example is found in the official guidance on police entrance medicals, which continues to describe some neurodivergent conditions as rendering an officer unfit for service (Home Office, 2004). This guidance has remained unchanged for over two decades, despite widespread clinical, social, and legal shifts in understanding neurodivergence. Such policies sit uncomfortably alongside the stated goals of reform and risk undermining public trust in policing as an equitable and progressive career path. The lack of updated criteria also exposes a deeper tension within the professionalisation agenda: while seeking to elevate standards, it may inadvertently narrow the definition of who is considered 'fit' to serve.

PEQF programmes are co-delivered by police and university staff across academic and workplace settings, presenting two very distinct occupational cultures for student officers to navigate: the hierarchical, militaristic structures of traditional police training and the critical, reflective environment of higher education (Charman, 2018). Police trainers prioritise operational competence and adherence to procedures, while university lecturers place greater emphasis on theoretical understanding and critical evaluation of those same procedures, requiring student officers to frequently switch between different communication styles, learning approaches, and professional expectations, sometimes within the same day.

Support structures within these professional contexts are similarly divided; university student inclusion teams typically focus on academic accommodations within classroom and assessment settings, such as extra time in exams, alternative formats, or private rooms for tests, while police support tends to emphasise operational adjustments, which are limited in their application by the day-to-day realities of policing. Such dichotomy often leaves neurodivergent student officers caught between competing systems with differing disclosure processes, accommodation procedures, and support policies (Tromans et al., 2023; O'Reilly et al., 2024). There is also often a gap in communication between the academic provider and the police organisation regarding student officer support needs, causing students to have a disjointed inclusive experience and in turn affecting completion rates and retention.

For some recruits, particularly those with undiagnosed neurodivergent profiles, the academic demands, such as essay writing, managing deadlines, and theoretical learning, can highlight cognitive differences they may not have previously recognised. Some neurodivergent adults are not diagnosed during childhood, and this makes awareness in adulthood more difficult (Butcher and Lane, 2024). As student police officers balance operational and academic demands, undiagnosed traits often become more noticeable. In some cases, the academic pressures have prompted individuals to seek formal assessment and diagnosis, enabling access to appropriate support. In this way, the introduction of degree-entry routes into policing has had a positive impact by directing recruits into institutions, such as universities, where structured support services are more readily available. However, it is also arguable that this shift introduces a double disadvantage for neurodivergent student police officers, who must navigate the expectations and systems of two complex institutions, higher education and policing, both of which have historically struggled to provide effective and consistent support for neurodivergent individuals.

However, in 2022 the mandatory degree requirement was removed by the College of Policing (at the request of the then Home Secretary) and replaced with the Police Constable Entry Routes (PCER). This shift in recruitment strategy now allows police forces to recruit into non-degree pathways, justified based on widening access and increasing flexibility. While this move promotes broader inclusion by allowing candidates from diverse educational backgrounds to enter policing, it raises critical concerns regarding support. Under degree-based routes, neurodivergent recruits often benefited from university support structures which complemented or even compensated for gaps within police organisations. The non-degree pathways, however, risk creating a support poverty for neurodivergent individuals, as policing organisations have historically failed to maintain progress in relation to providing equivalent, consistent support systems. This disparity could therefore widen inequalities, where only those on academic pathways gain access to comprehensive neurodiversity support, while others are left without necessary accommodations. While intended to democratise entry routes into policing, this change risks unintentionally disadvantaging neurodivergent recruits unless policing institutions invest meaningfully in equivalent internal support frameworks. Nevertheless, this shift also offers neurodivergent individuals the flexibility to choose the pathway that best suits their needs, potentially improving access to a career in policing.

1.4.3 Cultural and Institutional Challenges

Whilst there has been progress in supporting the neurodiversity agenda within the police workforce, with an increase in internal training and audits of recruitment, retention, and promotion processes, significant inconsistencies remain across E&W police organisations, specifically in relation to accommodations and adjusted working practices. One barrier appears to be the persistence of stigma surrounding neurodivergence and specific diagnosable neurodivergent differences, which discourages individuals from disclosing their diagnosis or seeking support (Tromans et al., 2023). Police officers and staff may be unaware that they are neurodivergent, which can prevent disclosure, despite still requiring support for challenges. Under Section 6 of the Equality Act 2010, there is no requirement for a disabled person to 'prove' their need for reasonable adjustments by obtaining a formal diagnosis of any specific medical condition or illness. Yet, there are neurodivergent police practitioners who may feel—due to fear of stigma or disbelief—that they do not 'qualify' for adjustments as they do not have a diagnosis, further complicating access to resources. O'Reilly et al. (2025) found that some police forces wanted proof of a diagnosis which provides further barriers to support.

These disparities in accessing support can lead to differing experiences for neurodivergent officers and staff. One of the most significant challenges is that support is often led by managerial discretion. This then adds a level of knowledge and awareness required by those in senior ranks. Instead of receiving proactive support, neurodivergent employees in policing who encounter difficulties in the workplace are often misunderstood or perceived as underperforming by their managers. Rather than being offered tailored adjustments to help them thrive, they are usually referred (sometimes appropriately) to Occupational Health, or placed on performance development plans, which can be stressful and demoralising. In some cases, persistent challenges, often stemming from a lack of reasonable adjustments rather than genuine misconduct, can escalate to formal disciplinary action or even misconduct measures. This process can lead to forced disclosure, exacerbating workplace stress, and in some cases contributing to negative outcomes such as restricted duty, lack of access to promotion, or dismissal.

It is reported that individuals who have had a neurodivergent difference diagnosed prior to joining the police are more likely to disclose this to the organisation compared to those who receive a diagnosis during their service (Tromans et al., 2023), suggesting that they are more confident to do so and less fearful of stigma. However, disclosure does not always lead to support. Hill (2024) identified that police officers who disclosed that they were dyslexic often faced negative experiences, characterised by a lack of institutional support and understanding. These challenges were particularly evident during the recruitment process, where officers reported difficulties in accessing adjustments, faced stigmatisation, and were perceived as less capable because of their neurodivergence (Hill, 2024). These findings are particularly surprising given the College of Policing's stated commitment to increasing diversity within police recruitment, notably during the 20,000-officer uplift initiative in 2019 (see College of Policing, 2021). Despite these goals, the lived experiences of neurodivergent police practitioners suggest that recruitment and workplace practices may not yet fully align with the principles of inclusion and accessibility required by law and sought by various initiatives and reforms. Moreover, while the College of Policing has engaged in discussions about reasonable adjustments, there are concerns regarding the implementation and consistency of these adjustments across different police organisations. In many cases, the strategic direction set by senior leadership has not fully filtered down through the organisational structure, resulting in limited impact at the rank-and-file level. Without clear and enforceable policies, neurodivergent police practitioners may continue to face systemic barriers and a postcode lottery regarding the support they receive.

The disconnect between diversity policies and the lived experiences of neurodivergent officers and staff highlights the need for consistent, stigma-free support mechanisms across all police organisations to ensure neurodivergent employees are supported at all stages of their careers, from recruitment and onboarding, through to progression and promotion. The lack of adequate support structures has profound consequences. Neurodivergent employees may experience increased absenteeism, difficulties meeting rigid performance expectations (including policing targets), and higher attrition rates. More broadly, the failure to accommodate neurodivergent police practitioners means that police organisations risk overlooking the valuable skills and perspectives that neurodivergent officers and staff can bring to their roles. There is also potential to further miss opportunities for the police organisation to develop a workforce that reflects the community it serves, which mirrors a similar logic in the context of ethnic and gender diversity. Recognising such skillsets could improve police interactions with neurodivergent members of the public (an issue which has been increasingly highlighted as a problem in recent years) and ultimately improve the trust and confidence in policing.

Notwithstanding the above criticisms, in recent years, significant strides have been made towards making policing a more inclusive workplace for neurodivergent people. Many officers have shared positive experiences, particularly regarding access to support and suitable adjustments, such as the use of Reasonable Adjustment Passports (RAP). There is also evidence to suggest there has been an increase in the number of police practitioners who feel confident not only in sharing their neurodivergence but also in becoming advocates for change, offering support to colleagues and championing inclusivity (O'Reilly et al., 2024). The establishment of key organisations, such as the PNDA in 2010, the NPAA in 2015, and more recently, the development of the ADHD Alliance, marked significant milestones in supporting neurodivergent practitioners within E&W policing. These organisations are committed to providing resources, advocacy, and support for neurodivergent police staff while promoting greater awareness and understanding of neurodiversity across all emergency services. However, despite the positive intentions behind such networks, their effectiveness is often limited by structural constraints. Many of these networks are run by individuals who take on the responsibility in addition to their primary roles, usually on a volunteer basis. The dual burden can lead to burnout and limit the consistency and availability of support, undermining the long-term sustainability of these initiatives. Without formal recognition, dedicated time, and resources, even the most well-meaning efforts risk becoming overstretched and underutilised.

British policing operates within a hierarchical and regimented framework, characterised by standardised procedures, rigid communication norms, and a strong emphasis on team-based operations. Whilst these structures may be seen by some as essential in ensuring consistency and accountability (Reiner, 2010), they often pose significant challenges for neurodivergent officers whose cognitive processes and communication styles differ from traditional expectations. For example, the College of Policing's authorised professional practices (APP) may inadvertently disadvantage neurodivergent officers by prioritising neurotypical approaches to decision-making, problem-solving, and interpersonal communication, therefore marginalising alternative cognitive approaches (See College of Policing APP, 2025b). These institutionalised norms risk overlooking the strengths that neurodivergent officers bring to policing roles, particularly in areas requiring attention to detail, pattern recognition, or innovative thinking (Krzeminska et al., 2019). It is crucial to emphasise that supporting neurodivergent police practitioners is not about lowering standards or changing goalposts for the sake of diversity. Police officers in particular carry immense responsibility in maintaining public safety; however, all individuals, regardless of role, face challenges, and policing is no exception. Recognising and responding to those challenges through appropriate support and inclusive practices is not a compromise on quality, but rather an investment in a more resilient and effective workforce. It could be argued that rigid, centralised approaches—such as standardised communication protocols based on neurotypical norms—limit officer discretion and, in doing so, reduce opportunities for neurodivergent strengths to complement or address the blind spots often present in neurotypical ways of working.

Further day-to-day challenges for neurodivergent officers lie in navigating routine internal interactions, such as shift handovers and briefings, as well as the informal communication networks that underpin everyday policing. These practices are embedded within a culture that prioritises teamwork and often demands seamless collaboration in high-pressure, dynamic environments. For neurodivergent individuals, engaging in these socially nuanced contexts, particularly where unspoken norms, non-verbal cues, or unstructured group discussions prevail, can be cognitively and emotionally taxing. Difficulties in interpreting these expectations may contribute to feelings of exclusion, marginalisation, or social disconnection within the policing environment. O'Reilly et al. (2024) found that some autistic people and/or those with ADHD often had difficulty with expected social interactions with colleagues. Furthermore, given the highly visible and public nature of most policing roles, many neurodivergent officers face the additional challenge of balancing their professional duties while masking or compensating for traits that may be misunderstood or stigmatised by both colleagues and the public. This masking demands significant cognitive and emotional effort, often at the expense of authenticity, wellbeing, and optimal professional performance. For instance, an autistic officer might feel pressure to consciously adjust their tone, facial expressions, and body language to fit perceived expectations, distracting from their operational focus. Similarly, an officer with ADHD may rely heavily on intricate time-management strategies (efforts that are often invisible to others) to navigate administrative tasks that pose particular difficulties due to executive functioning differences.

The cultural environment within policing plays a critical role in shaping the experiences of neurodivergent officers. Traditionally, police culture has been underpinned by values such as uniformity, emotional resilience, and a 'can-do' attitude, traits considered essential for managing the demands of high-risk and unpredictable situations (Reiner, 2010). While these characteristics have been argued to contribute to operational cohesion and performance, they can also create a rigid normative framework that inadvertently marginalises those who think or behave differently. For neurodivergent officers, this cultural pressure often manifests as a need to 'mask', a coping strategy involving the suppression or modification of one's natural behaviours to align with perceived neurotypical social or professional expectations (Hull et al., 2017). Masking is an especially prevalent coping strategy used by neurodivergent individuals, and is frequently used to avoid stigma, navigate social interactions, or meet institutional expectations (Milton and Sims, 2016). However, this behavioural adaptation comes at a cost. Sustained masking has been linked to increased levels of anxiety, emotional exhaustion, and decreased self-esteem, and can undermine an individual's sense of authenticity and belonging in the workplace (Cage and Troxell-Whitman, 2019).

1.4.4 Environmental and Operational Challenges

The sensory environment within modern police stations can significantly intensify the challenges experienced by neurodivergent officers, particularly those with sensory processing sensitivities. Police stations are often designed as open-plan environments to encourage visibility, communication, and team cohesion. However, such layouts can be overstimulating, characterised by persistent noise, fluorescent lighting, frequent movement, and minimal opportunities for quiet retreat. For individuals with heightened sensory sensitivities, these environments may lead to cognitive overload, anxiety, and difficulties concentrating, impairing task performance and wellbeing. These challenges are particularly pronounced in specialist operational areas such as custody suites, where officers are required to manage detainees in enclosed, high-stress environments. Custody settings are often loud, unpredictable, and emotionally charged, with detainees sometimes exhibiting volatile or aggressive behaviour. For neurodivergent officers, the combination of sensory intensity and limited physical escape from these secure spaces can significantly increase the risk of sensory overwhelm, emotional distress, and burnout (Crane et al., 2020). Despite growing recognition of neurodiversity in the workplace, the physical design of police stations and the operational demands placed on officers frequently remain misaligned with inclusive practice, highlighting the need for more adaptive environments and occupational adjustments.

Standard-issue operational equipment, though essential for officer safety and communication, can pose significant sensory challenges for neurodivergent officers. Items such as Airwave radios, body armour, and high-visibility uniforms are not only physically restrictive but can also contribute to heightened sensory discomfort. The tactile sensation of heavy, tight-fitting gear and synthetic fabrics may be distressing and distracting, negatively impacting comfort and performance. Airwave radio transmissions can be intrusive and unpredictable; officers may receive urgent, high-volume communications (often involving colleagues shouting for assistance) which can contribute to auditory overstimulation and emotional dysregulation in already intense operational contexts. Additionally, police vehicles introduce further layers of sensory complexity. Flashing blue lights, rapidly alternating sirens, and multiple simultaneous radio channels can combine into a sensory-rich environment. For some neurodivergent officers, particularly those with heightened sensory sensitivity, these working conditions may create difficulties in processing information efficiently, not due to a lack of capability, but because the environment itself is not designed with diverse sensory needs in mind.

While certain equipment and uniform standards are essential for operational safety and consistency, inclusive occupational health practices should consider adaptable, evidence-based solutions. For example, some forces have explored the use of softer, breathable uniform fabrics, noise-dampening earpieces, or customisable lighting options in control rooms. Sensory-aware protocols—such as allowing optional use of tinted lenses or permitting the adjustment of radio earpiece volume and positioning—could make environments more accessible without compromising safety. These factors highlight the importance of inclusive occupational health practices and the need for sensory-aware equipment protocols within police forces to ensure that working environments are accessible to all.

Beyond the physical workspace, the outward-facing demands of the British model of policing by consent present further challenges (see Home Office, 2021). This model requires officers to manage unpredictable and emotionally charged public interactions, drawing heavily on social adaptability, emotional regulation, and rapid decision-making (Jackson et al., 2012). These expectations often reflect neurotypical norms and can marginalise officers whose cognitive strengths lie elsewhere. For instance, officers with ADHD may be better suited to dynamic, fast-paced tasks but may require additional support during extended or repetitive duties such as report writing or updating tasks. Similarly, autistic officers may bring valuable precision and integrity to community engagement but may benefit from clearer communication structures or alternative approaches to interpersonal interactions. Again, these are not specifically deficits in ability, but differences in cognitive processing that require a more flexible and inclusive operational framework, which could bring significant benefits and strengths to policing. The introduction of the National Decision Model (NDM) was intended to provide a structured and ethical framework for decision-making (College of Policing, 2013). While its structured approach aligns well with some neurodivergent thinking styles, the expectation to rapidly weigh complex situational, legal, and ethical factors in high-stress contexts can impose a significant cognitive load. This risk of cognitive overload not only affects operational effectiveness but may also contribute to increased levels of work-related stress and burnout among neurodivergent police practitioners, without sufficient support or adaptations. Supporting neurodivergent officers must therefore be understood not as a question of individual limitation but as an organisational responsibility to design working conditions that enable all officers to thrive.

1.4.5 Career Progression

Career progression in policing often presents barriers for neurodivergent officers, particularly due to the nature of selection processes for specialist roles or promotions. These processes typically rely on competency-based interviews, written exercises, and assessment centres that privilege conventional forms of verbal reasoning, social fluency, and normative decision-making styles (see the College of Policing, national police promotion framework (NPPF), 2025c). For neurodivergent officers, whose strengths may lie outside these frameworks, these formats can obscure their true capabilities and potential for leadership or specialist contribution. The rigid and formalised design of these assessments often fails to recognise alternative cognitive approaches that are well-suited to key policing functions, including pattern recognition, attention to detail, and lateral thinking, skills that are frequently found in neurodivergent individuals. As a result, highly capable officers may find themselves overlooked for advancement, not due to a lack of competence, but because the selection criteria and evaluative mechanisms do not align with their communication styles or strengths (O'Reilly et al., 2024). This misalignment not only perpetuates disparities in career progression but may also contribute to reduced morale and underutilisation of diverse talent within the policing workforce and ultimately impact attrition.

Promotion and selection processes could also have far-reaching implications for leadership pipelines within police forces. Neurodivergent individuals often possess strategic thinking abilities, systems-level insight, and a capacity for innovative problem-solving. These qualities are invaluable in leadership contexts, particularly in senior roles navigating complex organisational challenges or engaging with diverse communities, often in time-critical or adversarial contexts. However, Tromans et al. (2023) found that some neurodivergent individuals chose not to disclose their differences due to the potential impact on their career and lack of support to apply for promotion.

In policing, where conformity, professionalism, and emotional regulation are heavily emphasised, neurodivergent officers often feel compelled to mask consistently—suppressing behaviours such as stimming, rehearsing social interactions, or forcing eye contact—to appear 'neurotypical'. The paramilitary and hierarchical nature of police culture tends to valorise uniformity, composure, and social fluency, which can create an implicit expectation to downplay or conceal traits such as atypical communication styles, sensory sensitivities, or executive functioning differences. This persistent masking carries a significant psychological toll, with research linking it to chronic stress, burnout, and a diminished sense of authenticity, all of which can erode confidence and self-advocacy (Bradley et al., 2021; Cage et al., 2018). These factors not only reduce job satisfaction but can also undermine long-term retention and impede career progression. Studies further suggest that without a formal diagnosis, neurodivergent individuals may feel even less able to 'unmask' in professional settings, resulting in cycles of invisibility and unmet support needs (Pryke-Hobbes et al., 2023). These challenges are compounded by the limited presence of neurodivergent officers in leadership and specialist roles, as well as a lack of neuro-inclusive mentorship and organisational cultures that routinely overlook cognitive diversity. In the absence of visible role models and structural support, neurodivergent police practitioners may struggle to envision a viable path for advancement, reinforcing patterns of underrepresentation and disengagement across the service.

1.5 Employing the Strengths of Neurodivergent Police Practitioners

Although awareness of neurodiversity is gradually increasing within wider society and public sector employment, policing remains a domain where considerable progress is still needed. The College of Policing toolkit mentioned earlier aimed to better support neurodivergent individuals but fails to resolve the gaps in the training and a lack of consistency nationally, and in individual police forces, which can result in a disparity of support available, with there being a reliance on support networks rather than a cultural shift. Addressing these issues requires a multifaceted strategy that includes enhanced training, adaptive recruitment and promotion processes, workplace adjustments, and a genuine cultural shift towards valuing difference. Without such change, the police service risks not only the loss of talented individuals but also the perpetuation of environments that are misaligned with the diverse society they are supposed to serve.

Whilst recognising that there are challenges faced by neurodivergent police practitioners, it is equally important to acknowledge the strengths and skill sets that neurodivergent people can bring to the policing organisation, and how a strength-based approach to neurodivergence can enhance both individual and organisational outcomes. The 'spiky profile' is a concept that is often used to illustrate how the skill sets of neurodivergent people vary from neurotypical people (Doyle, 2020). The skills of neurotypical people more frequently fall within a perceived acceptable range, meaning their skills are neither exceptionally high nor significantly disabling. In contrast, neurodivergent people often demonstrate skills and experience challenges that extend beyond this accepted range, making them more noticeable (Doyle, 2020). The 'spiky profile' could explain why there has often been greater focus on the challenges experienced by neurodivergent police practitioners, with these challenges typically being cited on performance improvement plans and other regulatory actions, following traditional deficit-focused approaches to difference. However, there is typically less attention given to the strengths of neurodivergent people. Efforts often focus on aligning those whose challenges fall outside the normatively acceptable performance (as defined from a neurotypical perspective); yet when strengths exceed the typical range, they are sometimes labelled as 'superpowers', a term that has been regarded as infantilising the skill sets of neurodivergent professionals and creating unreasonable expectations. These strengths are a natural part of the person's abilities and deserve recognition as such.

It is important to contextualise neurodivergence not solely as a matter of individual difference but as an organisational opportunity for innovation and improvement. Police organisations provide complex services that depend on a diverse range of cognitive and emotional skills; when appropriately aligned with roles, these skills can drive innovation, resilience, and trust. Neurodivergent officers can bring fresh perspectives to entrenched problems, challenge assumptions and foster reform in ways that neurotypical colleagues may overlook (O'Reilly et al., 2025).

As E&W policing faces increasing scrutiny and the demand for reform intensifies, leveraging neurodivergent strengths can only contribute towards an inclusive workforce representative of the wider community and form a pathway towards improving public confidence.

Crucially, recognising neurodivergence as a strength must go beyond policy and translate into established practice. Strength-based language without structural change risks tokenism; celebrating an officer's hyper-focus or intense drive for fairness means little if those same qualities are penalised through rigid processes or misunderstood by line managers. To unlock these strengths, policing must reimagine everything from recruitment to role assignment, from leadership development to support mechanisms. Rather than asking neurodivergent officers and staff to adapt continually to neurotypical expectations, police organisations should consider how their frameworks might evolve to accommodate, and benefit from, cognitive difference. To achieve this, police organisations must cultivate 'neuro-inclusive leadership', a commitment not only to inclusion, but to transformation (Bernard et al., 2024). Neuro-inclusive leaders recognise the value of divergent perspectives, particularly in roles such as financial investigation or intelligence, and promote psychological safety and intentionally dismantle structural barriers that hinder neurodivergent practitioners (Kuzmanov, 2025). By embedding neurodivergence into strategic priorities, workforce planning, and performance metrics, police organisations can not only support current neurodivergent officers and staff but also attract and retain future talent that might otherwise be excluded.

1.5.1 Specialists in a Generalist Framework

The concept of 'spiky profiles' is particularly relevant in understanding neurodivergent police practitioners' strengths. Unlike neurotypical people, who may display more evenly distributed cognitive strengths and challenges, neurodivergent people often exhibit areas of exceptional ability alongside disabling challenges not normally experienced by their neurotypical counterparts. It is important to note that neurodivergent people are not a homogenous group, and it is critical to recognise the dangers of over-generalisations and stereotyping about the traits and characteristics of different diagnosable differences. There are, however, examples of increased strengths dependent on a person's neurodivergence. For example, autistic police practitioners may excel in roles requiring attention to detail and pattern recognition, such as forensics, data analysis, or even within detective departments, while those with ADHD might thrive more in fast-paced, response-based roles where their energy and stimulation-driven brains are an advantage.

A further element of this dynamic is the reality that police organisations are notoriously conservative and resistant to change, tending to reward conformity and consistency over divergence and innovation, particularly in performance evaluation criteria, promotion pathways, and the day-to-day expectations placed on officers. Neurodivergent officers whose skillsets flourish in unconventional ways may find difficulty with rigid assessment benchmarks, even when their contributions are valuable and impactful. For example, the officer who excels in long-term case analysis, unravelling complex evidence chains over weeks or months, may not be seen as 'high performing' within a culture that places emphasis on short-term, reactive accomplishments such as direct arrests or swift clear-up rates.

However, an area of systemic disadvantage within policing that has yet to be explored in relation to neurodivergent police practitioners is that police organisations and routes to recruitment typically emphasise generalist capabilities, requiring (specifically) new recruits to demonstrate a broad range of skills before focusing on more specialised departments such as investigations or intelligence teams. This approach may be disadvantageous for neurodivergent people, whose potential may be best realised in specialist and/or specific policing roles.

To address these barriers, a reframing of what constitutes 'competence' for policing roles is needed, incorporating neurodiversity-informed assessment models into student officer pathways that value depth of knowledge and aptitude in specific domains, rather than broad generalist traits. Some police organisations have already begun experimenting with such alternative assessment frameworks for student officers; for example, workplace portfolios of evidence, operationalised problem-solving scenarios, or structured interviews that allow for processing time and clarity of expectation. These methods not only make the entry routes to police careers more equitable for neurodivergent applicants but may also attract a broader range of talents overall, diversifying the pool of future police officers available for specific specialist roles within the organisation.

1.5.2 Utilising Strengths in Policing Contexts

Though there are limited studies exploring the strength-based profiles of neurodivergent police practitioners, there is a plethora of lived-experience evidence that has been presented by the increasing number of workplace needs assessments accessed by police practitioners, as well as neurodiversity-based police support groups such as the ADHD Alliance and the NPAA. The n-POLICE study (O'Reilly et al., 2024), which involved the latter police association, found that neurodivergent police practitioners often perceived their traits as advantageous. For instance, autistic practitioners noted their ability to focus on detail, whilst those with ADHD valued the variability and stimulation provided in police work. Neurodivergent police practitioners also highlighted a desire to help people and to serve justice. These strengths align with a variety of neurodivergent qualities, including justice sensitivity, high emotional intelligence, and a desire for meaningful work, all of which are essential for police work.

Justice sensitivity is a frequently observed trait in many neurodivergent individuals, particularly those who are autistic (Al-Attar and Worthington, 2024). This heightened sensitivity can manifest as a profound commitment to fairness and a refusal to accept unethical or unjust actions, even in the face of institutional pressure. In the context of policing, this can translate into officers who are less prone to corruption, more likely to advocate for marginalised victims, and more diligent in ensuring procedural fairness. While this trait may create tensions within the hierarchical, compliance-culture environment of policing, it also positions neurodivergent officers as internal catalysts for ethical improvement. In addition, the keen sense of mission and craving for meaningful, high-impact work often found among those with ADHD enable them to bring high levels of energy, spontaneity, and interpersonal connection to frontline response policing roles. Such officers possess skills to build strong rapport with victims and community members, especially in high-stress or emotionally charged environments where empathy and an ability to adapt dynamically can be an enormous asset in de-escalating situations and preventing harm.

Similarly, Tromans et al. (2023) identified that 81 per cent of autistic police practitioners and 78 per cent of ADHD practitioners believed their neurodivergent traits benefited their policing work. These strengths included heightened observational skills and innovative problem-solving. Practitioners also cited personal rewards in the role, such as their contribution to societal wellbeing and helping victims of crime, underscoring the alignment between neurodivergent values and policing objectives. These strengths are seldom explored and discussed in conjunction with the many challenges that are cited for neurodivergent police practitioners. The impact of this is that police organisations fail to fully leverage the potential of their talent pool, thereby limiting their opportunities to enhance overall effectiveness and performance within their police work.

1.5.3 The Role of Workplace Environment and Support

The ability of neurodivergent police practitioners to demonstrate their skills is influenced by the environment and operational demands they face. For instance, while autistic police practitioners may excel in structured tasks requiring intense focus, excessive workloads and stressful sensory environments such as open-plan offices can hinder their performance. Similarly, practitioners with ADHD may thrive in dynamic environments but may struggle with administrative tasks if not adequately supported. Thematic understandings from police workplace needs assessments continue to emphasise the importance of workplace adjustments to enable neurodivergent officers to access the 'top half' of their spiky profile by enabling environments that amplify strengths without pathologising variability. Simple measures such as acknowledging and giving equal attention to both strengths and challenges, providing appropriate role placements which can be tailored collaboratively through workplace needs assessments and line manager consultation, along with making slight adjustments to working practices can significantly enhance outcomes for neurodivergent police practitioners (Tromans et al., 2023). Furthermore, neurodiversity training for managers and revised recruitment practices are essential to mitigate biases and create a more inclusive workplace culture (O'Reilly et al., 2024).

Encouragingly, there are signs of positive change with some E&W police forces establishing neurodivergent peer networks and embedding screening assessments in their initial recruit training programmes. These measures not only benefit neurodivergent officers but also foster a systemic cultural shift that promotes understanding and inclusivity across policing; that adopts strengths-based competencies; encourages specialised role assignments; and proactively builds supportive work environments (O'Reilly et al., 2024).

1.6 Conclusion

This chapter has examined the complex and often contradictory position of neurodivergent police practitioners within modern policing. While neurodivergent individuals bring distinctive strengths that can significantly enhance policing outcomes, these contributions often go unrecognised or are undervalued within the current cultural and structural framework of police organisations. Barriers in recruitment, progression, and access to support and accommodations continue to create environments where neurodivergent police practitioners must navigate added layers of challenge simply to be accepted or understood. Without deliberate, systemic efforts to transform workplace culture and dismantle the stigma surrounding neurodivergence, the police service risks alienating not only its own workforce, but also the neurodivergent public it seeks to serve. Mirroring the negative experiences reported by neurodivergent communities more broadly, many police practitioners face similar marginalisation within their own institution.

Creating a truly neuro-inclusive police organisation is essential for operational effectiveness, workforce wellbeing, and public trust. By embracing neurodivergent skillsets and perspectives, policing can evolve into a more adaptive, empathetic, and ultimately effective service. The strengths of neurodivergent police practitioners, ranging from analytical and observational skills to 'thinking outside the box', offer invaluable contributions to police culture. Rather than being seen solely through the lens of requiring accommodation or support, neurodivergent individuals should be recognised as assets to the workforce. By embracing neurodiversity, operational effectiveness within police work would not only be enhanced but would also align more closely with the desired values of inclusivity and equity most workplaces strive to achieve, progressing towards police practitioners who reflect the communities they serve.

Note

1 In this chapter, we have chosen to use identity-first language when referring to neurodivergent experiences (e.g., autistic person). This approach reflects a commonly expressed preference within parts of the neurodivergent community, which is towards identity-first language, though individual preferences do vary. Our intention is to use terminology that is respectful, inclusive, and non-ableist. Clinical or diagnostic language has been used only where necessary for context, and efforts have been made to frame discussions through a 'differences' lens, as opposed to a 'deficit' lens, or with a focus on individual skillsets.

References

Al-Attar, Z. and Worthington, R. (2024) Moral distress and moral injury in the context of autism. *Advances in Autism*, 10(3): 200–219. https://doi.org/ 10.1108/AIA-05-2023-0025.

American Psychiatric Association (2022) *Diagnostic and statistical manual of mental disorders (DSM-5)*. 5th ed.

Baker, D. L. (2006) Neurodiversity, neurological disability, and the public sector: Notes on the autism spectrum. *Disability & Society*, 21(1): 15–29. https://doi.org/10.1080/09687590500373734.

Barker, J. (2013) Police encounters with the mentally ill after deinstitutionalization. *Psychiatric Times*, 30(1): 9.

Beardon, L. (2017) *Autism and Asperger syndrome in adults: An up-to-date overview*. London: Sheldon Press.

Beardon, L., Chown, N. and Cossburn, K. (2018) First responders and autism. In: Volkmar, F. (Ed.), *The encyclopaedia of autism spectrum disorders*. New York: Springer.

Bernard, A., Brooks-Cleator, L., De Raaf, S. and Fraser, N. (2024) *Neuroinclusive employment knowledge synthesis*. Ottawa: Social Research and Demonstration Corporation. Available at: https://www.srdc.org/wp-content/uploads/2024/06/Sinneave-Knowledge-Synthesis-2024.pdf (Accessed: 8 April 2025).

Bradley, L., Shaw, R., Baron-Cohen, S. and Cassidy, S. (2021) Autistic adults' experiences of camouflaging and its perceived impact on mental health. *Autism Adulthood*, 1;3(4): 320–329. https://doi.org/10.1089/aut.2020.0071.

Buckland, R. (2024) Department for work and pensions. *The Buckland Review of Autism Employment: Report and Recommendations.* Available at https://www.gov.uk/government/publications/the-buckland-review-of-autism-employment-report-and-recommendations/the-buckland-review-of-autism-employment-report-and-recommendations (Accessed 5th March 2025).

Butcher, L. and Lane, S. (2024) Neurodivergent (Autism and ADHD) student experiences of access and inclusion in higher education: An ecological systems theory perspective. *The International Journal of Higher Education Research.* https://doi.org/10.1007/s10734-024-01319-6.

Cage, E., Di Monaco, J. and Newell, V. (2018) Experiences of autism acceptance and mental health in autistic adults. *Journal of Autism Developmental Disorders*, 48(2): 473–484. https://doi.org/10.1007/s10803-017-3342-7.

Cage, E. and Troxell-Whitman Z. (2019) Understanding the reasons, contexts and costs of camouflaging for autistic adults. *Journal of Autism Development Disorders*, 49(5), 1899–1911. https://doi.org/10.1007/s10803-018-03878-x.

Charman, S. (2018) *Police socialisation, identity and culture*. 2nd edn. London: Palgrave MacMillan.

College of Policing (2013) *National decision model, college of policing*. Available at: https://www.college.police.uk/app/national-decision-model (Accessed 24 April 2025).

College of Policing (2021) *Discovery report into workplace adjustments*. Available at: https://assets.college.police.uk/s3fs-public/2021-08/discovery-report-workplace-adjustments.pdf (Accessed 18th December 2024).

College of Policing (2025a) Workplace adjustments toolkit. Available at: https://www.college.police.uk/support-forces/diversity-and-inclusion/workplace-adjustments-toolkit (Accessed July 2025).

College of Policing (2025b) APP (authorised professional practice). Available at: https://www.college.police.uk/app (Accessed 23rd February 2025).

College of Policing (2025c) National Police promotion framework (NPPF). Available at https://www.college.police.uk/career-learning/national-police-promotion-framework (Accessed July 2025).

Crane, L., Maras, K.L., Hawken, T., Mulcahy, S. and Memon, A. (2016) Experiences of autism spectrum disorder and policing in England and Wales: Surveying police and the autism community. *Journal of Autism Development Disorder,* 46, 2028–2041. https://doi.org/10.1007/s10803-016-2729-1.

Crane, L., Adams, F., Harper, G., Welch, J. and Pellicano, E. (2020) Something needs to change': Mental health experiences of young autistic adults in England. *Autism*, 24(4), 768–783.

Crow, L. (1996) Including all of our lives. In: Morris, J. (Ed.), *Encounters with strangers: Feminism and disability*. London: The Women's Press.

Dickie, I., Reveley, S. and Dorrity, A. (2018) The criminal justice system and people on the autism spectrum: Perspectives on awareness and identification. *Journal of Psychology and Social Sciences*, 4(1): 1–21.

Doyle, N. (2020) Neurodiversity at work: A biopsychosocial model and the impact on working adults. *British Medical Bulletin,* 135(1), 108–125.

Dyck, E. and Russell, G. (2020) Challenging psychiatric classification: Healthy autistic diversity and the neurodiversity movement. In: Taylor, S. J. and Brumby, A. (Eds.), *Health minds in the twentieth century. Mental health in historical perspective*. Cham: Palgrave Macmillan. https://doi.org/10.1007/978-3-030-27275-3_8.

Equality Act (2010) Available at: https://www.legislation.gov.uk/ukpga/2010/15/contents.

Feilzer, M., and Loftus, B. (2024) Scrutiny of Police Institutions and the Spectre of Culture. *The Political Quarterly*, 95 (2), 514–522. https://doi.org/10.1111/1467-923X.13434.

Gudjonsson, G. H., Sigurdsson, J. F., Bragason, O. O., Newton, A. K. and Einarsson, E. (2008) Interrogative suggestibility, compliance and false confessions among prisoners and their relationship with attention deficit hyperactivity disorder (ADHD) symptoms. *Psychological Medicine*, 38(7): 1037–1044. https://doi.org/10.1017/S0033291708002882.

Hepworth, D. (2017) A critical review of current police training and policy for autism spectrum disorder. *Journal of Intellectual Disabilities and Offending Behaviour*, 8(4): 212–222. https://doi.org/10.1108/JIDOB-06-2017-0011.

Hesketh, I. and Stubbs, G. (2023) Positive action paradox in UK police recruitment: A critical perspective. *The Police Journal*, 97(2), 315–335. https://doi.org/10.1177/0032258X231172030.

Hill, A. P. (2024) Being a dyslexic police officer in England and Wales: Identity, disability, and disclosure. *The Police Journal: Theory, Practice and Principles.* https://doi.org/10.1177/0032258X241280197.

Home Office (2004) National recruitment standards - medical standards for police recruitment. Available at https://www.gov.uk/government/publications/national-recruitment-standards-medical-standards-for-police-recruitment (Accessed 24th February 2025).

Home Office (2021) FOI release: Definition of policing by consent. Available at https://www.gov.uk/government/publications/policing-by-consent/definition-of-policing-by-consent (Accessed 25th November 2025).

Hull, L., Petrides, K. V., Allison, C., Smith, P., Baron-Cohen, S., Lai, M. C. and Mandy, W. (2017) "Putting on my best normal": Social camouflaging in adults with autism spectrum conditions. *Journal of Autism and Developmental Disorders*, 47(8): 2519–2534. https://doi.org/10.1007/s10803-017-3166-5.

Hunter, S. T. and Hunter, M. D. (2022) Performance management and career development for employees with autism. Uncovering hidden requirements. In Bruyere, S.M (Ed). *Neurodiversity in the workplace, interests, issues, and opportunities.* Routledge. New York.

Hutson, T. M., McGhee Hassrick, E., Fernandes, S., Walton, J., Bouvier-Weinberg, K., Radcliffe, A. and Allen-Handy, A. (2022) "I'm just different–that's all–I'm so sorry ... ": Black men, ASD and the urgent need for DisCrit Theory in police encounters. In *Policing: An International Journal*, 45(3).

Jackson, J., Bradford, B., Hough, M., Myhill, A., Quinton, P. and Tyler, T. R. (2012) Why do people comply with the law?: Legitimacy and the influence of legal institutions. *British Journal of Criminology*, 52(6), 1051–1071. https://doi.org/10.1093/bjc/azs032.

Kirby, A. (2021) *Neurodiversity – a whole-child approach for youth justice.* HM Inspectorate of Probation Academic Insights. Available at: https://www.justiceinspectorates.gov.uk/hmiprobation/wpcontent/uploads/sites/5/2021/07/Neurodiversity-AI.pdf (Accessed 15th November 2024).

Krzeminska, A., Austin, R., Bruyere, S. and Hedley, D. (2019) The advantages and challenges of neurodiversity employment in organizations. *Journal of Management & Organization*, 25, 453–463. https://doi.org/10.1017/jmo.2019.58.

Kuzmanov, I. (2025) Strategic need for talent: Neurodiversity and the future of leadership. *Journal of Novel Research and Innovative Development*, 3(2): 113–142. Available at: https://doi.org/10.1729/Journal.43722.

Lim, A., Young, R. L. and Brewer, N. (2022) Autistic adults may be erroneously perceived as deceptive and lacking credibility. *Journal of Autism Development Disorder*, 52, 490–507. https://doi.org/10.1007/s10803-021-04963-4.

Macdonald, S. J. and Cosgrove, F. (2019) Dyslexia and policing: Understanding the impact that dyslexia has in the police service in England and Wales. *Equality, Diversity and Inclusion: An International Journal*, 38(6): 634–651. Available at: https://doi.org/10.1108/EDI-11-2018-0218.

Maras, K., Dando, C., Stephenson, H., Lambrechts, A., Anns, S. and Gaigg, S. (2020) The Witness-Aimed First Account (WAFA): A new technique for interviewing autistic witnesses and victims. *Autism*, 24(6): 1449–1467. https://doi.org/10.1177/1362361320908986.

Mental Health Act (1983) c. 20. Available at: https://www.legislation.gov.uk/ukpga/1983/20/contents.

Milton, D. and Sims, T. (2016) How is a sense of well-being and belonging constructed in the accounts of autistic adults? *Disability & Society*, 31(4): 520–534. https://doi.org/10.1080/09687599.2016.1186529.

Milton, D., Gurbuz, E. and López, B. (2022) The 'double empathy problem': Ten years on. *Autism*, 26(8), 1901–1903. https://doi.org/10.1177/13623613221129123.

Ministry of Justice (2022) *Neurodiversity in the criminal justice system action plan.* Available at https://www.gov.uk/government/publications/a-response-to-the-criminal-justice-joint-inspection-neurodiversity-in-the-criminal-justice-system-action-plan.

NPPA (n.d.) *Recruitment Q&A.* Available at https://www.npaa.org.uk/recruitment/ (Accessed 5th March 2025).

O'Reilly, M., Tromans, S. J. and Drewett, A. (2024) *The n-POLICE study: Neurodiverse police officers and staff - Learning information about their career experiences* (University of Leicester). Available at: https://le.ac.uk/-/media/uol/docs/academic-departments/criminology/exploring-neurodiversity-in-the-police-workforce-qual-report-final-share.pdf (Accessed 26th March 2026)

O'Reilly, M., Kiyimba, N., Tromans, S. and Drewett, A. (2025) The experiences of mid-career disclosure of autism and ADHD diagnosis by UK police officers and staff. *Policing: An International Journal.* https://doi.org/10.1108/PIJPSM-03-2025-0047.

Police Federation (2023) Set standards needed so forces can support neurodiverse officers, says Fed chair. Available at: https://www.polfed.org/suffolk/news/2023/set-standards-needed-so-forces-can-support-neurodiverse-officers-says-fed-chair/ (Accessed 13th March 2025).

Pryke-Hobbes, A., Davies, J., Heasman, B., Livesey, A., Walker, A., Pellicano, E. and Remington, A. (2023) The workplace masking experiences of autistic, non-autistic neurodivergent and neurotypical adults in the UK. *PLoS One*, 6;18(9): e0290001. https://doi.org/10.1371/journal.pone.0290001.

Reiner, R. (2010) *The politics of the police* (4th ed.). Oxford University Press.

Scull, A. (2021) 'Community care': Historical perspective on deinstitutionalization. *Perspectives in Biology and Medicine*, 64(1): 70–81.

Siberry, A. (2025) *Diversity, difference or disorder: Neurodiversity in British policing.* White Rose University Press

Taylor, C., Russell, J. and Winsor, T. (2021) *Neurodiversity in the criminal justice system a review of evidence.* Available at: https://www.justiceinspectorates.gov.uk/cjji/wp-content/uploads/sites/2/2021/07/Neurodiversity-evidence-review-web-2021.pdf (Accessed 14th November 2024).

Tromans, S., Drewett, A., Lee, P. and O'Reilly, M. (2023) A survey of the workplace experiences of police force employees who are autistic and/or have attention deficit hyperactivity disorder. *British Journal of Psychiatry Open*, 9(4), e123.

Watkinson-Miley, C., Cox, C. and Deshpande, M. (2022) A new generation of police officers: Experiences of student officers undertaking the police constable degree apprenticeship in one UK police force. *Policing: A Journal of Policy and Practice*, 16(1): 122–134. https://doi.org/10.1093/police/paab062.

Walker, N. (2014) *Neurodiversity: Some basic terms and definitions.* Neuroqueer: The Writings of Dr Nick Walker. Available at: https://ndclibrary.sjc1.vultrobjects.com/NEURODIVERSITY_%20SOME%20BASIC%20TERMS%20%26%20DEFINITIONS%20•%20NEUROQUEER.pdf.

Chapter 2

Autistic and Under Arrest

Challenges Faced by Autistic Suspects

Bobbie Jay White

2.1 Introduction

There are many challenges facing Autistic people in the criminal justice system (CJS). It is important to understand that when it comes to Autistic people, we are much more likely to be the victims of crime than perpetrators of it. Nevertheless, there remains a paucity of information regarding the difficulties Autistic people face as suspects. Daily, our existence as Autistic people results in us dealing with additional pressures that those who are neurotypical may not. These include, but are not limited to, masking, social exclusion and being subjected to preconceived notions of what Autism is (and is not), which hampers our ability to thrive. According to White, O'Neill and Griffin (2024, p. 66), masking refers to the performance of neurotypical actions and behaviours. They note that whilst performative normalcy offers a level of protection, it comes at a cost to the masked individual. There are few occasions as stressful as when one is engaged with the CJS, and under these circumstances, the existing pressures on an Autistic person can intensify. In this chapter, I will examine the difficulties that Autistic people encounter, the ways in which these may manifest during arrest and subsequent processing, and measures that may be implemented to support Autistic people.

Moreover, this chapter elaborates nuances otherwise absent in well-intentioned official guidance. Autistic people and behaviours come in many shapes and forms and should not be reduced to simple archetypes. For example, an Autistic person who is verbose and able to understand complex theories and texts in one moment can also be a person in need of a high level of support when distressed. It is important that both the individual who presents in a manner recognised as Autistic is as supported as the individual who does not, in appearance, behaviour or actions, conform to preconceived notions of what Autism is. In this respect, this chapter aims to clarify the importance of treating individuals in accordance with their needs, especially when it comes to the police and broader CJS. Finally, it is important to recognise that some of the concerns highlighted in this chapter cannot be adequately addressed by individual actors. Systemic issues require systemic reforms for effective changes to be achieved. In this way, an additional aim of this chapter is to shed light on these issues in the hope that active steps can be taken

DOI: 10.4324/9781003638742-3

by larger authorities to address these concerns. Finally, as an Autistic woman, the approach I try to take when discussing these issues is rooted in the social model of disability. Such looks beyond individual 'impairments' or conditions and focuses on broader societal factors that act to disable individuals (Scope, n.d., para. 1; and Spectrum, 2018, pp. 3–4). As such, I do not consider Autism to be a disability in and of itself; rather, the extent to which it is disabling emerges from existing in a world that is hostile to neurodivergence. The following chapter attempts to avoid the pathologising language often employed when discussing Autism and instead to focus on the consequences of misunderstanding between Autistic people and a CJS reflective of dominant neurotypical norms and expectations.[1] This chapter aims to:

- encourage a deeper understanding of Autism and Autistic people;
- identify issues faced by Autistic people before, during and after arrest;
- highlight, where possible, solutions to these issues.

2.2 Suspicion

Before considering the difficulties faced by Autistic people when being arrested, it is important to consider factors which instigate an arrest. At first glance it may be obvious—that is, an officer suspects that an individual has, is or will commit a crime (as per s.24 Police and Criminal Evidence (PACE) Act 1984). However, on closer inspection it quickly becomes apparent that there are larger societal issues at play. For example, the National Autistic Society (NAS) (2020a, para. 2) notes that in certain circumstances factors associated with Autism may lead to involvement with the CJS. These include difficulties with social cues, leading to 'inappropriate' responses perceived as threatening (i.e., making too much eye contact), difficulty with change resulting in anxious and possibly aggressive behaviour, naivety leading to involvement with criminality, and misunderstanding implications of their behaviour. Further investigation into Autistic people's experiences with the police highlights additional factors which may initiate suspicion or arrest. Research conducted by Rava et al. (2017) examined the experiences of Autistic youth with the CJS. Conducted in the American context, their work held several key findings. By the time they had reached their 20s, 19.5 per cent of Autistic people had been stopped by the police, with 4.7 per cent facing arrest (p. 343). Males were more likely to be stopped than females, alongside those who showed 'externalising' behaviours. In explaining externalising behaviours, Rava et al. (2017, p. 342) seemingly referred to upset, distress and anger displayed by Autistic individuals under various circumstances. It is important to note here that having behavioural responses to being upset and distressed is not inherently an Autistic phenomenon—although the pathologisation and criminalisation of such may be. As highlighted by the NHS (n.d., para. 2), when overwhelmed or anxious, Autistic individuals may enter a state of fight, flight or freeze. The difference here from neurotypicals may lie in how this distress is expressed by Autistic people. The NHS (n.d., para. 1) notes that some Autistic people may enter either a state of 'meltdown' or a 'shutdown'. Unfortunately, there is a real paucity of academic literature on these phenomena—especially from the perspectives of Autistic people (Phung et al., 2021, p. 2). As such, examinations of these phenomena are often described from a neurotypical perspective and, at times, in pathologising language that implicitly reproduces the harms it seeks to address.

Whilst different in their expression, shutdowns and meltdowns appear to have common causes. They are responses to being overwhelmed—whether due to unexpected change, sensory distress or social exhaustion (Autistica n.d., para. 3). Meltdowns result in a loss of control and can be expressed physically, through lashing out, and/or verbally (NAS, 2020b, para. 2). The exact behaviour differs, but in certain instances meltdowns can result in injury to the Autistic person or others (Ambitious about Autism (AAA), n.d., para.1). Comparatively, shutdowns may be less noticeable and are marked by withdrawal. Whilst dealing with a shutdown, an Autistic person may experience some reduced cognitive capacity and struggle with communication (AAA, n.d., para. 3). Communitive disfluency may be seen both in verbal expression, as well as in the capacity to receive and process information. Jones (2021, p. 62) notes there is little to be gained from asking more from an Autistic individual in this state. Instead, they emphasise the importance of time for recuperation. For children, meltdowns and shutdowns risk being misconstrued as 'tantrums' and may result in punishment. For Autistic children who then grow into adults, experiencing a shutdown or meltdown may be associated with feelings of shame, anxiety and fear, amplifying the intensity of these episodes.

As such, if an Autistic person is visibly experiencing a meltdown or shutdown, their distress is already overwhelming. At this point, following the orders of or engaging politely with an officer may not be possible. At times, an Autistic person may be accompanied by someone familiar with them, who can act as an advocate. Here, escalation can be avoided more easily. This is not always the case, however, and without the ability to self-advocate or be advocated for, a distressed Autistic person is beholden to the knowledge of officers. Avoiding escalation here requires officers to recognise these episodes as distress and not label them as purposeful disobedience or criminality. Recognising someone as Autistic may help with this, but expecting officers to do this based on limited contact with the individual during arrest is impractical. If Autism is considered by officers, they then need to have an adequate understanding of such to respond appropriately. Crane et al. (2016) considered the experiences of E&W police officers, Autistic people and their families regarding knowledge of Autism. They found a little less than half of the officers indicated that they were 'fairly knowledgeable' about Autism and felt able to work with Autistic people. This was not the perspective of Autistic people, nor their families (p. 2037). Comparatively, most described their experiences with officers as 'unsatisfactory'—with open responses identifying officers' lack of knowledge and understanding of the needs of Autistic people (p. 2036). Clearly, there is a gulf between the knowledge of Autism purported by officers and the consequences of that knowledge for Autistic people and their families.

2.3 Arrest

Being arrested is stressful. This is true regardless of an individual's neurotype, but for Autistic people, our behavioural and social differences mean that we are more vulnerable during these events (Hepworth, 2017, p. 4). Being overwhelmed often means a reduction in our function and ability to advocate for ourselves. Even if not overwhelmed initially, the process of arrest involves many discomforting experiences. Indeed, even the presence of a police officer can sometimes create anxiety for Autistic people (NAS, 2020a). Such is not necessarily an indication of guilt, but instead arises from preconceptions of the police, their associations and insecurities around 'doing something wrong'. Indeed, fear of being perceived as 'abnormal' and subsequent micromanagment of our own behaviour is a common experience for us as Autistic people—as is described frequently in Price's (2022) work. As such, coming face-to-face with officers in uniform can inadvertently be a jarring experience. One example I have found useful when explaining this phenomenon is that of the supermarket. If the alarms sound when exiting a supermarket, many individuals can empathise with a feeling of fear and self-doubt. Although you know you have not stolen anything, the alarm and presence of a security guard can easily spark anxiety that you have done something wrong or illegal. As a result, when an Autistic person is stopped by the police, feelings of anxiety and fear may result in behaviours officers consider 'difficult', even when this is not the intent of the individual (Brown and Kennedy, 2022, pp. 53–54).

Being arrested also comes with overwhelming sensory input. Most overtly, officers may employ emergency lights and sirens. This form of signalling can overstimulate an Autistic person and can undermine their ability to articulate themselves. Some individuals may flee to get away from the sensory distress, others may freeze and not engage with communication (shutdown), and some may outwardly withstand the noise but be battling overstimulation (masking). 'Fleeing' (i.e. attempting to escape a distressing sensory stimulus) can lead to an Autistic individual being chased or subjected to force, whilst in the case of a shutdown or masking, there is a wider range of outcomes. Depending on the individual, they may appear dazed, standoffish, or fine for a time. Regardless of the immediate behaviour shown, being over-stimulated will be distressing for the individual and impact their ability to communicate and be communicated with. In this respect, even before an individual has been directly communicated with, the sensory circumstances of arrest may have acted to aggravate the situation. This situation may not always be avoidable, but its impact and prevalence can be mitigated.

If an officer is aware of, or suspects, a suspect to be Autistic, lights and sirens should be avoided where possible. Where such isn't known and sirens have been deployed, there are behaviours that may indicate a sensory overload. Covering ears, shutting eyes, attempts at distraction such as humming, tapping or self-harm or signs of anxiety can all indicate sensory distress (Steel, 2024, para. 4). Additionally, in E&W, officers may benefit from looking for a sunflower lanyard. Such indicates a 'hidden' disability, where an individual may require additional support or understanding (Hidden Disabilities, n.d., para. 1). As soon as sirens are no longer necessary, they should be shut off, and the individual given a moment to self-regulate. Importantly, this approach is beneficial to a range of individuals, Autistic or not. Those with learning disabilities, mental health conditions, even members of the public that do not fit any of these categories. Reducing cognitive demand allows for better comprehension and engagement. In the case of Autism, this approach may allow an individual the time they need to re-regulate and better engage with the legal process. In cases where the individual has not committed a crime or has been wrongly identified, a calmer approach may prevent escalation and unnecessary arrest.

Due to the dynamic nature of police work, officers will not necessarily know at this stage if an individual is Autistic or not. As noted, however, this more neuro-affirmative approach benefits all. All elements of the public can benefit from people-centred policing. On the other hand, not taking this approach can be devastating to the lives of Autistic and other neurodiverse individuals. Starting off with an individual in distress is not likely to result in a productive or fair experience for either the Autistic individual or investigating officers. The difference in the impact of best practice for those who are and are not neurodiverse can be further seen in terms of volume and tone. For example, the Metropolitan Police (2021, p. 11) note that speaking in a soft and calm manner is considered best practice. It shows respect for citizens and can reduce ill-will. An individual who is not Autistic can see shouting as aggressive but ultimately may be able to engage with officers and entertain grievances later. For an Autistic person, shouting can be frightening and physically painful. Such behaviour risks a meltdown, shutdown or other state of distress which ultimately leads to a breakdown in communication and trust.

2.4 Issuing a Caution and Restraint

Decisions made at the initial point of contact between officers and the Autistic individual have consequent effects for everything that follows. This is seen clearly when considering the decision to arrest, or when using force. When it comes to arrest, an Autistic person's understanding of what is happening and why will be influenced by how overwhelmed they feel. Once the decision to arrest is made, officers must inform the suspect they are being arrested, why, and shortly thereafter issue an official caution (PACE 1984; PACE Code G 2023). At this point, even an Autistic person who was previously communicative may struggle with the significance of arrest, sensory distress arising from such and the duration of the process. Here, language may become more unclear and difficult to grasp. As such, an Autistic person may struggle to understand both the caution and the arrest. Furthermore, there could be the pretence of understanding from the Autistic individual to expedite the sensorily distressing process of arrest or, as Hepworth (2017, p. 5) notes, because it is felt that such is the desired response. It is important, in moments like these, for officers to remain compassionate and attentive to the individual they are arresting.

In cases where an officer is aware or suspects an individual is Autistic, this means giving the individual the best chance at understanding what is being said, what is going on and what will be expected of them. What is best for the individual can vary, but there are some general approaches that can be beneficial.

- Ensure information is communicated in a calm environment where possible; or reinstate it in a calmer environment later where it is not.
- This may mean moving the individual to a quieter area, or reinstating information once in the arrest vehicle.
- Speak calmly, clearly and directly, whilst allowing the individual additional time to process and respond to what is being said or asked (NAS, 2020a).
- Slow compliance with orders is not automatically disobedience, but instead may be the result of delayed processing.
- Questions should be asked one at a time, and by one officer at a time (Brown and Kennedy, 2022, p. 54).
- Be mindful that too much verbal information here could be overwhelming and lead to misunderstandings.

During arrest, officers may decide reasonable force is necessary (Section 117, PACE 1984), including use of handcuffs. The use of handcuffs is at the discretion of the arresting officer, and as a form of force, officers must justify their decision (The Metropolitan Police, 2024, p. 1; College of Policing 2023, para. 10). The College of Policing (2023, para. 5) outlines behaviours that may be indicative of someone who is about to commit violence. These include but are not limited to:

- facial expressions;
- increased restlessness;
- pacing or bodily tension;
- increased volume;
- erratic movements;
- refusal to communicate;
- withdrawal, fear or irritation;
- unclear thought processes;
- poor concentration.

Here, many Autistic people are disadvantaged by comparison to neurotypical standards of behaviour. Many of these behaviours are reminiscent of Autistic behavioural expressions—especially when distressed or attempting to self-regulate. Not making eye contact, engaging with repetitive movements, appearing withdrawn, agitated or reacting in a manner deemed unexpected could be used as grounds for mistrust on behalf of an officer without suitable knowledge of Autism. To manage what may be perceived as risk, officers could be inclined to engage with some form of use of force to maintain control over an Autistic suspect. Unfortunately, the increased contact and restraint used as part of use of force is likely to only further overwhelm the Autistic individual and risk either a meltdown or shutdown. Being restrained by handcuffs, for example, creates discomfort and may inhibit self-soothing behaviours such as stimming. Stimming differs from person to person but can often include repetitive movements (flapping hands) or behaviours (touching items or fabrics) (NAS, 2020c, para. 1–2). Naturally if an individual is handcuffed, engaging in these self-soothing behaviours may no longer be practical. In this way, restraint not only causes distress but also acts to prevent attempts at self-regulation. Unfortunately, under the current policing guidelines, officers may have little room for discretion if aggression has already been present. According to CoP (2024, para. 10), if there is violent struggle at the time of an arrest, suspects must not be left alone or unrestrained when being transported. As such, even when violence was the result of significant distress stemming from 'disability', officers may have no choice but to restrain an individual.

2.5 Booking In

If Autism has not been recognised beforehand, it may be recognised on arrival at police custody during the 'booking in' process. Booking in involves questioning, including about welfare and medical concerns. Unfortunately, a lack of specificity hampers disclosure. Holloway et al. (2020) considered Autistic experiences of the custody process, with their work highlighting several concerns. Communication difficulties between Autistic participants and officers were notable (pp. 6–10). Disclosure of Autism and medical information was hampered by reliance on verbal communication (p. 9). Moreover, the use of open-ended and ambiguous questions catalysed anxiety and fuelled miscommunication (p. 6). Ultimately, Holloway et al. (2020) noted that both Autistic individuals and police officers did not feel that the existing questions allowed for or encouraged the disclosure of an Autism diagnosis (p. 9). This is concerning as it leaves potentially vulnerable Autistic adults without the chance for support and guidance in circumstances that have considerable consequences. Not recognising an individual as Autistic results in their rights and needs not being met and may act to frustrate interactions between officers and the individual. For example, in Holloway et al.'s (2020) work, an Autistic participant responded literally to an ambiguous question, giving the name of their city as opposed to their address when asked where they lived (p. 6). This simple miscommunication has ramifications in the legal context. Officers may misconstrue such responses as defiance or obstruction. Where Autism is known and understood, officers may draw more favourable conclusions. Unfortunately, a formal diagnosis of Autism may not necessarily be present and ambiguous booking in questions hamper disclosure when it is.

Moreover, there are larger societal concerns at play when it comes to disclosure. Crane et al. (2016) found that Autistic people did not always disclose their neurotype to the police. They found 39 per cent always disclosed, 36 per cent never did and 25 per cent sometimes did. The decision to disclose was often related to fear—either of discrimination or victimisation by officers (p. 2036). Wider reading into Autistic experiences provides further insight. Huang et al. (2022, p. 5304) found that avoiding stigmatisation is a common reason for non-disclosure among Autistic adults, though their research focused on educational and work environments. This familiar rationale is rooted in common Autistic experiences. Prior experiences of disclosure impact future behaviour, as highlighted in Vincent and Fabri's (2022) work. Considering Autistic people's experiences of the job market, they noted that past incidences of discrimination following disclosure resulted in a reticence for Autistic people to disclose their diagnosis (p. 1831). Further, White, O'Neill and Griffin (2024, p. 70) recount how Autistic disclosure in academic settings can be met with doubt and dismissal. These attitudes minimise Autistic struggles and experiences, with White, O'Neill and Griffin (2024, p. 70) adding that these interactions disincentivise discussions about Autism with colleagues. Huang et al.'s (2022, p. 5305) work reflects these experiences, with dismissive, negative judgements and misunderstandings being common negative experiences following Autistic disclosure. If these are the reactions Autistic people face daily, in familiar environments, among those from whom we would expect support, why then should we expect disclosure when under arrest? Placing the onus on the individual to disclose their struggles to those they do not know, in a hostile environment, whilst distressed, is unrealistic and arguably a failure of the CJS.

2.6 Encouraging Disclosure and Autism Alert Cards

When it comes to encouraging disclosure at booking in, there is a somewhat simple solution. Notably, such will not work in all instances for the reasons noted above, but regardless, it may still be beneficial. This is to ask an individual directly and unambiguously, 'Are you diagnosed with, or suspected of having, Autism or an Autistic Spectrum Condition?' Asking about medical conditions or disabilities is not direct enough, as was seen in Hollway et al.'s (2020, p. 9) work. As was seen there, Autistic people do not consider Autism to be a medical condition or a disability. It is simply who we are. Moreover, diagnosis is a privilege (Jones, 2021, p. 29) that not all autistic people are lucky to have. As such, a direct question may have the best chance of eliciting disclosure.

Another solution to disclosure comes in the form of autism alert cards. Charities such as the NAS and Autism West Midlands offer downloadable card templates, aimed at notifying others that an individual is Autistic, alongside emergency contact information. Indeed, the National Police Autism Association (2025) highlights related schemes on their website—noting that such cards or documents can help to communicate needs to officers or other officials. Research into these schemes is limited, but Edwards et al.'s (2025) work did consider the effectiveness of a similar scheme in the Australian context. Whilst the cards were rarely used, most participants indicated that the cards were carried either in a wallet or their personal bag (p. 677). As such, whilst infrequently used, those involved with the scheme ensured the cards were kept close (p. 677). Edwards et al.'s. (2025) work further highlighted themes of facilitation, with both carers and Autistic people noting how the cards helped to aid understanding about Autism (pp. 677–678). One individual noted how the card helped to explain sensory difficulties to an authority figure on public transport—allowing for greater empathy and support (p. 678). Indeed, several autistic participants emphasised the importance of the cards when they were overwhelmed, or where emergency services were involved—with one individual noting how the card relieved the pressure of verbal communication (p. 678).

Whilst more research is needed, particularly in the legal context, it appears that alert cards could be useful for facilitating communication. Nevertheless, it is hard to know the uptake rate for such in E&W nor how police officers respond to them. As such, we cannot assume that everyone who needs these cards will have them, nor that every officer will know how to respond appropriately. Even in Edwards et al. (2025) work it was noted that the cards' use was limited by societal attitudes (p. 678). Ignorance around Autism and a lack of consideration hampered card users. One participant noted how, when dealing with a police officer, little attention was paid to the card, and their repeated disclosure of autism was dismissed (p. 678). It is important that mitigation methods such as these do not stand in for wider societal and institutional change. The onus for facilitating communication cannot be placed solely on the shoulders of the Autistic individual. Instead, as suggested by Holloway et al. (2020, p. 10) police forces would benefit from implementing direct questioning around Autism and neurodiversity.

2.7 Appropriate Adults

If an individual is known to be Autistic, there is a framework in E&W which may support, specifically Appropriate Adults (AAs). AAs are available for children and vulnerable adults with impaired communication or understanding (Para. 1.13(d), PACE Code C). AAs' work is complex, but according to the National Appropriate Adult Network (NAAN) (n.d., para. 8) and the Home Office (2024, para. 3) such includes:

- advising individuals of their rights;
- helping them use such;
- observing that officers are acting accordingly;
- observing changes or deterioration in an individual's state;
- ensuring that any issues are recorded;
- aiding communication between officers and those suspected of a crime.

Unfortunately, a considerable barrier is the assessment of vulnerability. Even when Autism is disclosed, officers may fail to appreciate vulnerability. Nelson (2019, para. 4) highlights, irrespective of officer training or an individual's intelligence or independence, social difficulties associated with Autism may result in nuance being missed or disclosures made that have significant consequences. As such, regardless of opinion, Autistic adults should be offered an AA.

The usefulness of the AA regarding Autism is unknown. The limited research available indicates once more how Autistic people are hindered by preconceptions. Richards and Milne (2020) considered knowledge of Autism among AAs. Whilst most showed knowledge of traits associated with autism, some drew on stereotypes—i.e., regarding memory and aggression (pp. 4–5). Richards and Milne (2020, p. 9) note that this may hamper productive engagement, but more than this, it leaves Autistic people in an all too familiar situation—where those supposed to advocate for us do not fully understand our behaviour and struggles. Moreover, AA efficacy likely varies due to who can take the role and the knowledge they bring. Where the AA is a 'professional', their understanding of the CJS and their role may be good, but not so their understanding of Autism, or the needs of the Autistic person they're entrusted to support. When the role is adopted by someone known to the Autistic person, they may have good knowledge of that individual's needs, but not the requisite understanding of the role of an AA. As such, Autistic people may be forced to decide between those who understand their needs as an Autistic person, or a professional AA. Arguably then, a single individual is not enough to meet both the needs of the Autistic person and ensure their rights are met.

2.8 Detention

Having been arrested and booked in, an Autistic person will then face time in the station's custody suite. The National Police Chief's Council (2022, p. 7) highlights the multiple purposes of custody, among such being the facilitation of investigations and maintenance of public safety. Further, they aim to ensure individuals leave custody in a better condition, or circumstances, than they arrived. It is an unfortunate reality then, that for many Autistic people custody suites are seldom conducive to their wellbeing. Instead, these spaces may act to the detriment of an Autistic person and their ability to engage with the investigative process. Such can be seen most overtly in regard to the physical custody environment and the impact such has on Autistic suspects.

Research has highlighted how the environment of custody is likely to cause considerable sensory distress for Autistic detainees (Crane et al., 2016, pp. 2032, 2039, Hepworth 2017, p. 6, Hollway et al., 2020, pp. 4, 6–7, and Fisher, 2024, p. 2). In their participatory walkthrough, Hollway et al. (2020) emphasised how the potential for distress was made clear by participants. They noted increased anxiety with the small spaces, closed-off areas, brightness of lights and lack of privacy (p. 9). As such, following the distressing events of arrest and booking in, Autistic suspects are faced with lock-up in an environment unsuitable to their sensory needs. Similarly, whilst some suspects may be able to use their time in the custody suite to decompress and reconstitute themselves, this is not the case for Autistic people. Instead, individuals are left in an environment harmful to their wellbeing and must simply await the next step in the custody process. As a result of this, it can be argued that custody neither effectively facilitates investigation, nor do Autistic individuals leave better than they entered.

A compassionate and understanding custody officer may be able to mitigate some distress, but they are hampered by systemic barriers. For example, fluorescent lighting may be a source of pain for an Autistic person. An officer may wish to rectify this, but without alternative lighting or a dimmer switch, there is little that can be done. Indeed, in Crane et al.'s (2016) work police officers noted that they were not ignorant of the needs of Autistic people but were hampered by systematic barriers—such as outdated facilities and lack of suitable alternatives (pp. 2032, 2036–2037). As such, there are elements of custody that will continue to be an issue for Autistic people until larger scale changes are implemented. In these circumstances, and when already overworked, officers may feel at a loss as to how to handle these situations. Nevertheless, acknowledging an individual's distress and keeping such in mind during interactions (particularly if faced with 'challenging behaviour') may go a long way.

In addition to the sensory distress of custody, the symbolic element of arrest and detention can also be the cause of distress for Autistic people. Skinns and Wooff (2021, p. 246) argue that in many ways police custody is a transitory space for individuals—with few means by which the discomfort of such is compensated for. The instability associated with these spaces may have a significant impact on the mental health of Autistic people, for whom routine and predictability are grounding rods in an uncertain world. Through interviews with those detained in custody, Skinns and Wooff (2021) highlight stressors associated with custody. For participants, fear stemmed from both isolation and the notion of being separated from their loved ones and the outside world. These concerns were further exacerbated by the designs of detention cells, with specific note made of heavy doors and the noises they made when closed. This environment can be immensely suffocating for anyone, but especially for Autistic people who are dealing with the stress of arrest whilst being separated from external support systems. Importantly, those Autistic individuals who, through extreme effort, blend into neurotypical society are at significant risk here. These individuals often have complex coping mechanisms and important support systems on which they rely to get through each day. In custody, routines cannot be followed, coping mechanisms not employed and assistance from friends and family are impossible to reach.

Further, Price (2022, pp. 180–181) notes that not only do Autistic people expend significant energy on finding and creating coping mechanisms, but often we hide our reliance on such. Price (2022, pp. 101–102) notes how for them masking Autisim was often the result of shame and misunderstandings between themselves and those around them. They expand, adding how experiences likes theirs are common amongst Autistic people. As such, an Autistic suspect who complies and asks for little may seem at a lower risk, but in reality, may require considerable support and is scared to or unable to communicate their needs. Finally, Fisher (2024, p. 1) notes that for those who are neurodiverse, the context for their custody may include a range of negative experiences, from trauma, exploitation and restraint to unmet needs and bullying. Autistic people are thus placed in an unsuitable environment, with prior experience that indicates their needs will remain unmet. As such, it is understandable that even when in significant distress an Autistic individual may be reluctant to highlight their struggles to the officers who they do not know. It is these individuals who, in some ways, may be at additional risk. This is because their distress may not always be clear to officers, who, without adequate understanding of the nature of autism, may not be proactive in taking additional actions that could mitigate distress. Not only is this a failure of care for a vulnerable individual in custody, but it is liable to impact on an Autistic person's ability to provide their best evidence when later questioned by officers.

According to Skinns and Wooff (2021, pp. 250, 255), isolation in custody resulted in reflection and distress for some individuals. They highlight the inner conflict felt, with the weight of being seen as 'criminal' and its social and moral implications. This internal distress can be utterly devastating for Autistic people. Commonly considered amongst Autistic communities is rejection sensitive dysphoria (RSD). While RSD is widely discussed in autistic communities, empirical research remains nascent and should be interpreted cautiously pending further validation. Nevertheless, there is a consistency surrounding RSD and its impact on Autistic people. RSD is marked by intense emotional upset when failing to meet the expectations of oneself or others, or rejection more generally—whether such is actual or perceived (Bedrossian, 2021, p. 4 and Bercovici, 2024, para. 1). In Lin et al.'s (2022) work, they assessed Autistic traits in regard to RSD and psychological distress. They found that traits of Autism resulted in increased sensitivity to distress stemming from negative social assessment, though not to non-social assessment (pp. 291–292) Further experimentation showed that those with higher traits of Autism had higher levels of distress due their increased levels of rejection sensitivity (pp. 294–296). These findings highlight the nuances in RSD, its distinctive impact on those with higher traits of Autism, and its relationship to distress. When in police custody, these feelings of RSD are likely to be intense—regardless as to whether an Autistic person has committed a crime or not. Feelings of shame and fear will only compound such feelings, ultimately leading to a state of emotional exhaustion.

The additional weight custody places on Autistic people is clear, though solutions to such are less so. Logistical and legal demands make supporting Autistic people in these circumstances difficult. Much top-down change needs to happen before there can be a level of equality in this aspect of the CJS. A potential solution to some of the issues presented may be to allow the involvement of an Autistic suspect's wider support system where appropriate. Bringing in a trusted individual to support the Autistic person has many potential benefits. Firstly, if an Autistic person cannot or is fearful of advocating for themselves, this trusted individual may be able to provide officers with necessary sensory and medical information, which, if acted on, can create a safer custody environment. Secondly, knowing a member of their support system is near and is able to act on their behalf may significantly reduce the pressure and stress felt by an Autistic suspect. Finally, this individual is likely to have greater knowledge regarding how this Autistic person may act when under distress. They may be able to inform officers that 'challenging behaviour' is a response to overstimulation or anxiety and the means by which to mitigate this. Such may then reduce tensions on both sides. The reduction of pressure and explanation of potential misunderstandings can allow for the Autistic individual to better respond to the custody process and act in a manner more beneficial to their best interest. Although this is in part the role of an AA, it could be argued that such a role is better suited to multiple individuals: one who understands the legal process and one with knowledge of the Autistic individual.

2.9 Investigative Interviews

Following arrest and custody, an Autistic suspect is finally faced with the investigative interview. At this stage, and without appropriate support, it is likely that an Autistic person is utterly exhausted. Further, if vulnerability has not been recognised prior to this point, it is unlikely that appropriate adaptations will be made regarding questioning (Hepworth, 2017, p. 11). Lack of appropriate support can have significant consequences here, especially when considering misunderstandings of Autistic behaviour. When exhausted, masking Autistic traits can become a near impossible burden, resulting in behaviour which may be misconstrued as indicative of guilt. An Autistic person's voice may become monotone, with little emotion displayed. Eye contact could falter completely, with the Autistic person not even looking in the direction of officers. Responses may be over-literal, with further questioning met with little response. Once an individual has hit this point of exhaustion, it becomes a Sisyphean challenge to act in accordance with one's best interests—regardless of guilt or innocence. Viewing this behaviour as indicative of exhaustion and a sign to stop the interview requires an understanding of Autism uncommon among the public.

Furthermore, the actual methodology involved in investigative interviewing is unfavourable to Autistic suspects. The College of Policing (2022, para. 30) advocates for open-ended questions as a means of extracting information during an interview. For example, 'tell me everything that happened when you left home this morning'. Whilst useful in eliciting recall from neurotypical people, such is too broad a question for Autistic people for whom filtering relevant and irrelevant information can be difficult (Price, 2022, pp. 24–25, Hepworth, 2017, p. 13). For someone who is neurotypical, it is simply a case of recalling their day, considering the question and its context. For an Autistic person, this process is much more manual. Firstly, the question must be processed and initial literal responses considered. Responses may then branch; an individual may verbally recall everything from their day, including non-relevant details, they may become overwhelmed by the question and struggle to give a response, or mentally investigate the question further with consideration of their audience. In the latter case, this means translating a literal response into one that considers what the officer may want from the question. Such requires perspective taking in a stressful environment, for which the wrong response may have significant consequences. How successful they are in this regard will differ from individual to individual, but regardless of the exact response, this is a process which is much more demanding in nature.

Work by Bagnall et al. (2025) further highlights issues with police interviewing. Conducting mock interviews with Autistic participants, they identified various challenges. Whilst participants understood questions asked throughout interviews, they did have difficulty understanding what was expected of their answers. Moreover, in one instance, an officer involved in the research doubted the completeness of a response given, indicating that information was possibly being withheld (pp. 10–12). If not understood in the context of Autism, such a situation could escalate to distress and frustration. Indeed, the College of Policing (2022, para. 67) encourages persisting with questioning if a suspect avoids or refuses to answer. With an Autistic suspect, avoidance may not be a purposeful attempt at deceit, but instead the result of misunderstanding what is expected of them. Repeated questioning in this circumstance may only create fear and frustration.

2.10 Recommendations

The paucity of research on suspect interviews of Autistic people means there is still much we do not know. Regardless, there are actions officers can take to encourage a fairer process. Firstly, it is important to consider the physical environment of the interview room. If an Autistic person is to be able to respond to questioning, their sensory needs must be considered. In Bagnall et al.'s (2025, p. 9) work, Autistic participants noted issues with sound bleeding from adjacent rooms and lights having the potential to cause discomfort in the long-term. Maras (2022, para 5) suggests conversing with the Autistic person (and relevant support persons) about sensory sensitivities in advance and making adaptations where possible. They note that such may involve removing ticking clocks, allowing for stimming behaviours or moving the interview to a more familiar environment. Understandably, the latter may not be appropriate when interviewing a suspect, but even moving an interview to a quiet part of the station would be preferable to overstimulation.

The Police Federation (2010, p.2) outlines some useful guidance for officers when communicating with Autistic individuals. They note the importance of questions being direct and focused, alongside officers remaining patient and granting the time needed for an Autistic person to process a question and offer a response. If a question has not been fully answered or officers are not satisfied with the response, it may be worth reconsidering the question asked. It may be that the Autistic individual is not certain what is expected of their response. In this instance, identifying where there is a misunderstanding and rephrasing a question is beneficial to both the Autistic person and the investigative process. Ultimately, an over-stimulated and frustrated Autistic person will not be able to provide the information needed in an interview setting. Forcing this process or doggedly following a line of questioning to the distress of the suspect benefits neither the criminal justice process, the interviewing officer nor the Autistic interviewee.

With open questions, it is important that officers formulate such questions carefully and prompt appropriately. For example, Maras (2021, p. 2) suggests setting parameters or focusing on specifics when interviewing Autistic people. This can be in terms of time frames, specific locations or by focusing on the who, the what, or the where, for example. In this way, a broad question such as that mentioned before can be narrowed, i.e., 'Tell me where you went after you left the house this morning'. Officers should also be mindful that Autistic participants may not respond in specificity without support and prompting. Research conducted by Norris, Crane and Maras (2020) looked at Autistic responses to open questions. They found that, in general, Autistic people produced less specific information from their recall as compared to non-autistic people (pp. 1507, 1511–1512). However, they also found that visual-verbal prompting could be used to increase specificity (pp. 1511–1512). In this case, prompting included the use of a pie chart with the following sections: 'objects', 'when', 'people', 'actions' and 'setting'(p. 1510). Aiding Autistic people in the interview setting can not only help prevent misunderstandings and communications but is also vital in ensuring equality within the CJS.

2.11 Conclusion

In conclusion, Autistic people's experience of the CJS is routinely one of disadvantage. Dominant neurotypical standards of behaviour result in the misunderstanding of Autistic people—with distress being viewed under the guise of suspicion, criminality and risk. Ultimately, such can result in escalation and arrest when de-escalation and compassion are needed most. Moreover, throughout and following arrest, the sensory, cognitive and emotive needs of Autistic individuals are either not being met or are actively agitated by the arrest process—leaving individuals in intensely vulnerable positions. In addition to this, there is neither an understanding of the complexity of Autism disclosure, nor adequate procedures to facilitate such. Indeed, the booking in process in E&W is ineffective when it comes to identifying if an individual is Autistic, ultimately leaving such individuals without the appropriate support during the custody and questioning process.

Finally, whilst this chapter has attempted to highlight issues and offer potential solutions where possible, change cannot be limited to individual officers or CJS representatives. Systemic issues require systemic solutions, and the best will in the world will not resolve issues of unsuitable custody suites or ineffective booking in procedures. Moreover, whilst means of mitigation and potential solutions to common issues have been offered throughout this piece, their utility, practical application and effectiveness cannot fully be known at this stage. Instead, much more collaboration is needed between police forces, researchers, and most importantly Autistic people and their families, to identify, articulate and advocate for effective CJS reforms.

Note

1 In line with my approach to Autism and my perspective as an Autistic person, I use identity-first language. Autism is fundamental to my being as a person, not something that can (nor would I wish it to) be separated from myself. It is the basis of my experiences in this world and that of many others. As such, for myself, there is a strength and community to be found through this identification.

References

Ambitious about Autism (n.d.). Meltdowns and shutdowns. [online] *Ambitious about Autism*. Available at: https://www.ambitiousaboutautism.org.uk/understanding-autism/behaviour/meltdowns-and-shutdowns [Accessed 25 Mar. 2026].

Autistica (n.d.). Supporting autistic people who are overwhelmed or having a meltdown. [online] *Autistica*. Available at: https://www.autistica.org.uk/what-is-autism/supporting-meltdowns [Accessed 24 Feb. 2025].

Bagnall, R. et al. (2025) 'I'm listening to you, but I can't hear you': Perspectives of autistic adults, investigators and support staff on police suspect interviews. *Psychology, Crime & Law*, pp. 1–28. https://doi.org/10.1080/1068316X.2025.2486411.

Bedrossian, L. (2021). Understand and address complexities of rejection sensitive dysphoria in students with ADHD. *Disability Compliance for Higher Education*, 26(10), p. 4. https://doi.org/10.1002/dhe.31047.

Bercovici, D. (2024). Rejection Sensitive Dysphoria in ADHD & autism | Embrace Autism. [online] *Embrace Autism*. Available at: https://embrace-autism.com/rejection-sensitive-dysphoria-in-adhd-and-autism/ [Accessed 25 Jun. 2025].

Brown, D. and Kennedy, S. (2022). Stop and Search guidance for autistic people. [online] Available at: https://www.met.police.uk/SysSiteAssets/foi-media/metropolitan-police/priorities_and_how_we_are_doing/corporate/stop-search-guidance-autistic-people-police-officers-large-print.pdf [Accessed 19 May 2025].

College of Policing (2022). Investigative interviewing. [online] *College of Policing*. Available at: https://www.college.police.uk/app/investigation/investigative-interviewing/investigative-interviewing [Accessed 14 Jul. 2025].

College of Policing (2023). Control, restraint and searches. [online] *College of Policing*. Available at: https://www.college.police.uk/app/detention-and-custody/control-restraint-and-searches [Accessed 2 Jun. 2025].

College of Policing (2024). Moving and transporting detainees. [online] *College of Policing*. Available at :https://www.college.police.uk/app/detention-and-custody/moving-and-transporting-detainees [Accessed 5 Mar. 2025].

Crane, L., Maras, K.L., Hawken, T., Mulcahy, S. and Memon, A. (2016). Experiences of autism spectrum disorder and policing in England and Wales: Surveying police and the autism community. *Journal of Autism and Developmental Disorders*, [online] 46(6), pp. 2028–2041. https://doi.org/10.1007/s10803-016-2729-1.

Edwards, C., Love, A.M., Flower, R.L., Ying Cai, R. and Gibbs, V. (2025). 'Just knowing it's there gives me comfort': Exploring the benefits and challenges of autism alert cards. *Autism*, 29(3). https://doi.org/10.1177/13623613241286025.

Fisher, L. (2024). Understanding the needs of autistic people in police custody A step-by-step approach for custody visitors. [online] *ICVA*. Available at: https://icva.org.uk/wp-content/uploads/2024/12/Understanding-the-needs-of-autistic-people-in-police-custody-a-step-by-step-guide-for-ICVs.pdf [Accessed 15 Jul. 2025].

Hepworth, D. (2017). *A critical review of current police training and policy for autism spectrum disorder*. [Online] *Salford Repository*. Available from: https://salford-repository.worktribe.com/output/1564572/a-critical-review-of-current-police-training-and-policy-for-autism-spectrum-disorder [Accessed 20 April 2026].

Hidden Disabilities (n.d.). *What is the Hidden Disabilities Sunflower?* [online] Hdsunflower.com. Available at: https://hdsunflower.com/uk/ [Accessed 7 Jul. 2025].

Holloway, C.A., Munro, N., Jackson, J., Phillips, S. and Ropar, D. (2020). Exploring the autistic and police perspectives of the custody process through a participative walkthrough. *Research in Developmental Disabilities*, [online] 97, p. 103545. https://doi.org/10.1016/j.ridd.2019.103545.

Home Office (2024, December 18). Being an appropriate adult. *GOV.UK*. https://www.gov.uk/government/publications/guidance-for-appropriate-adults/being-an-appropriate-adult.

Huang, Y., Hwang, Y.I., Arnold, S.R.C., Lawson, L.P., Richdale, A.L. and Trollor, J.N. (2022). Autistic adults' experiences of diagnosis disclosure. *Journal of Autism and Developmental Disorders*, 52(12). https://doi.org/10.1007/s10803-021-05384-z.

Jones, C. (2021). *Safeguarding Autistic Girls*. Jessica Kingsley Publishers.

Lin, X., Zhuo, S., Liu, Z., Fan, J. and Peng, W. (2022). Autistic traits heighten sensitivity to rejection-induced social pain. *Annals of the New York Academy of Sciences*, 1517, pp. 286–299. https://doi.org/10.1111/nyas.14880.

Maras, K. (2021). Conducting an investigative interview with an autistic person. Available at: https://www.bath.ac.uk/publications/conducting-an-investigative-interview-with-an-autistic-person-handbook/attachments/conducting-an-investigative-interview-with-an-autistic-person-handbook.pdf [Accessed 14 July 2025].

Maras, K. (2022). Police interviewing of autistic people. [online] www.autism.org.uk. Available at: https://www.autism.org.uk/advice-and-guidance/professional-practice/police-interviews [Accessed 20 April 2026].

Metropolitan Police (2021). *MPS Use of Handcuffs Policy* – Version 5.0. MPS.

Metropolitan Police (2024). *Handcuffing FAQ*. Available at: https://www.met.police.uk/SysSiteAssets/foi-media/metropolitan-police/disclosure_2024/may_2024/handcuffing-procedures-policy-faq.docx [Accessed 02 Jun. 2025].

National Appropriate Adult Network (n.d.). What is an appropriate adult? Www.appropriateadult.org.uk. https://www.appropriateadult.org.uk/information/what-is-an-appropriate-adult.

National Autistic Society (2020a). Criminal Justice – A guide for police officers and professionals. [online] *www.autism.org.uk*. Available at: https://www.autism.org.uk/advice-and-guidance/topics/criminal-justice/criminal-justice/professionals [Accessed 26 May 2025].

National Autistic Society (2020b). Meltdowns – A guide for all audiences. [online] *National Autistic Society*. Available at: https://www.autism.org.uk/advice-and-guidance/topics/behaviour/meltdowns/all-audiences [Accessed 7 Aug. 2025].

National Autistic Society (2020c). Stimming – A Guide for all audiences. [online] *National Autistic Society*. Available at: https://www.autism.org.uk/advice-and-guidance/topics/behaviour/stimming/all-audiences [Accessed 3 Mar. 2025].

National Police Autism Association (2025). Alert card schemes. [online] *National Police Autism Association*. Available at: https://www.npaa.org.uk/alert-card-schemes/ [Accessed 31 Mar. 2025].

National Police Cheif's Council (2022). National strategy for police custody. [online] *NPCC*. Available at: https://www.npcc.police.uk/SysSiteAssets/media/downloads/publications/publications-log/criminal-justice/2023/national-strategy-for-police-custody.pdf [Accessed 19 May 2025].

Nelson, J. (2019, October 14). Disordered, vulnerable – or autistic? *National Police Autism Association*. https://www.npaa.org.uk/disordered-vulnerable-autistic/.

NHS (n.d.). Meltdowns and shutdowns | Autism space. [online] *Leicestershire Partnership NHS Trust*. Available at: https://www.leicspart.nhs.uk/autism-space/health-and-lifestyle/meltdowns-and-shutdowns/ [Accessed 30 Jan. 2025].

Norris, J.E., Crane, L. and Maras, K. (2020). Interviewing autistic adults: Adaptations to support recall in police, employment, and healthcare interviews. *Autism*, 24(6), pp. 1506–1520 doi:https://doi.org/10.1177/1362361320909174.

Phung, J., Penner, M., Pirlot, C. and Welch, C. (2021). What i wish you knew: Insights on burnout, inertia, meltdown, and shutdown from autistic youth. *Frontiers in Psychology*, 12(12). doi:https://doi.org/10.3389/fpsyg.2021.741421.

Police Federation (2010, September 22). *Dealing with Victims / Witnesses or Suspects who have an Autistic Spectrum Condition.*

Price, D. (2022). *Unmasking Autism: Discovering the New Faces of Neurodiversity.* Harmony Books.

Rava, J., Shattuck, P., Rast, J., and Roux, A. (2017). The prevalence and correlates of involvement in the criminal justice system among youth on the autism spectrum. *Journal of Autism and Developmental Disorders*, 47(2), 340–346. https://doi.org/10.1007/s10803-016-2958-3.

Richards, J. and Milne, R. (2020). Appropriate adults: Their experiences and understanding of Autism Spectrum Disorder. *Research in Developmental Disabilities*, 103, 103675. https://doi.org/10.1016/j.ridd.2020.103675.

SCOPE (n.d.). Social model of disability | Disability charity scope UK. [online] *Scope*. Available at: https://www.scope.org.uk/social-model-of-disability [Accessed 29 Aug. 2025].

Spectrum (2018, pp.3-4). *What is 'The Social Model of Disability'?* [online]. Available at: https://spectrumcil.co.uk/wp-content/uploads/2018/02/ULO17-What-is-the-Social-Model-of-Disability.pdf [Accessed 29 Aug. 2025].

Steel, C. (2024). Sensory overload and autism: A guide for parents. [online] *Ambitious about Autism*. Available at: https://www.ambitiousaboutautism.org.uk/about-us/media-centre/blog/sensory-overload-and-autism-guide-parents [Accessed 29 Aug. 2025].

Vincent, J. and Fabri, M. (2022) The ecosystem of competitive employment for university graduates with autism, *International Journal of Disability, Development and Education*, 69(5), 1823–1839. https://doi.org/10.1080/1034912X.2020.1821874.

White, B.J., O'Neill, C., and Griffin, C.J. (2024). A mask that eats the face. Neurotypicality and autistic doctoral researchers. Chapters, in: M.S. Edwards, A.J. Martin, N.M. Ashkanasy and L.E. Cox (Eds.), *Research Handbook of Academic Mental Health*, chapter 3, pages 64–77. Edward Elgar Publishing.

Skinns, L. and Wooff, A. (2021). Pain in police detention: a critical point in the 'penal painscape'? *Policing & Society*, 31(3), 245–262.

Chapter 3

Confabulation

Considering Neurodivergence and Confession Credibility

Michelle White

3.1 Introduction

Regarded as one of the most powerful forms of evidence in criminal proceedings, the impact of confession evidence cannot be overstated (Kassin and Neumann, 1997). In a legal context, a confession is "any statement wholly or partly adverse to the person who made it" (s.82, Police and Criminal Evidence Act (PACE) 1984). The evidential worth of such a confession is considered invaluable to the prosecution and can strongly prejudice the perspectives of both judge and jury, even where the confession has later been recanted (Leo, 2009; Drizin and Leo, 2004). The impact upon both judge and jury is greater than other evidential factors, with studies determining that the impact of confession evidence (however lacking in substance) is often enough to secure a conviction (Appleby, Hasel and Kassin, 2011). This reflects a common assumption that no rational person would falsely confess to their own detriment. However, a substantial body of research demonstrates that individuals may confess falsely for a variety of reasons. Consequently, Shifton (2019) argues that the potential implications of such are so significant that they should be supported by expert testimony to ensure the jury understands the evidential limitations and the potential for unreliability.

According to data from the Innocence Project (IP) (2020), false confessions contribute to 12-27% of wrongful convictions in the United States alone, with an estimated 9% of those having mental health or capacity issues at the time of the trial. Research from the IP, however, does not distinguish between facets of false confession. Contemporary literature has advanced our understanding of false confessions yet remains focused on intentional untruths from the accused. Deliberate confessions may be provided to evade oppression or coercion during questioning, safeguard the actual perpetrator, or even seek notoriety. There is a significant amount of literature surrounding the vulnerable suspect and the predisposition to falsely confess, and it is accepted that several vulnerabilities can cause the suspect to profess guilt for a crime they did not commit (Gudjonsson et al., 2021). Albeit much of the current discourse centres upon the accused being aware of their innocence yet nonetheless confessing. Yet, there remains less discussion regarding the confabulated confession. Referring to the unintentional

DOI: 10.4324/9781003638742-4

fabrication or distortion of memories, confabulation is seemingly under-recognised in legal contexts (Brown et al., 2017). Emerging research indicates that the risk of confabulation is prominent among individuals with neurodivergent conditions, including autism (often referred to as Autism Spectrum Disorder (ASD in the literature), attention deficit hyperactivity disorder (ADHD), and Foetal Alcohol Spectrum Disorder (FASD), etc.

This chapter critically examines confabulation in the context of false confession, exploring its prevalence, aggravating factors, and potential for legal reform. Integrating legal, psychological, and neuroscientific scholarship, with a particular focus on the English legal system, this chapter considers how memory distortion, particularly among neurodivergent populations, can contribute to false confessions and wrongful convictions, and the implications for miscarriages of justice, and the necessity for legal reform. The chapter first examines the three established categories of false confessions: voluntary, coerced-compliant, and coerced-internalised confessions. It then specifically considers coerced-internalised confessions, aka confabulations, within the framework of neurodivergence and the criminal justice system (CJS). The chapter then explores the development and definition of confabulation, distinguishing it from deliberate deception. It proceeds to analyse the neurological, psychological, and situational factors that contribute to the formation of false memories, with respect to neurodivergent individuals.

Following this, the chapter considers the evidential and procedural challenges that confabulated confessions pose within the current legal framework, particularly under PACE 1984. Finally, it presents a series of proposed reforms, including enhanced police training, improved screening protocols, and the statutory recognition of confabulation, aimed at safeguarding cognitively vulnerable suspects. Ultimately, the chapter contends that confabulation represents a critical and underexplored area in the CJS, one that, without urgent recognition and reform, risks allowing genuine but false memories to continue contributing to miscarriages of justice.

3.2 Categories of False Confession

Scholars have identified distinct categories of false confession, each underpinned by differing psychological and situational mechanisms (Norris, 2017). Such differentiation has been refined by Kassin and Wrightsman (1985), establishing that there are three mechanisms of false confession: "voluntary", "coerced-compliant", and "coerced-internalised". Coerced-compliant confessions are typically elicited from individuals who have a cognitive awareness of their innocence. Responses to the stimuli of pressurised interrogation or incentives, such confessions are often recanted once the external stimuli are removed. Coerced-compliant confessions also elicit more understanding from observers; for example, jurors may find it viable that a false confession was made if the suspect believed it would be beneficial to them, or if they were trying to avoid a lengthy, oppressive interrogation (Kassin, 2007).

The coerced-compliant confession is easier to identify within England and Wales as a result of the PACE 1984. With Code E of the Codes of Practice mandating that all interviews are subject to audio recording and Code F allowing for visual recording, the provision of recordings allows for any procedural irregularities or misconduct contributing to a confession to be identified, which may lead to the confession being regarded as inadmissible (s76 PACE 1984).

In contrast, voluntary false confessions arise spontaneously (Leo, 2009). They will occur without stimulus and can be difficult to challenge, even where the suspect later attempts to retract their admission. Voluntary false confession may be the result of a pathological desire for notoriety; the need for atonement for another unrelated event; or to protect another perpetrator (Hillier and Dingwall, 2021). The lack of elicitation in these cases makes voluntary false confessions problematic from an evidential perspective, as it is difficult to prove that the confession had been obtained by "circumstances that make it unreliable" (s76 PACE 1984).

The focus of this chapter is on coerced-internalised confession, an area widely perceived to be the most complex and problematic (Hillier and Dingwall, 2021). Suspects, who are potentially vulnerable, can (mistakenly) conclude that they have committed the offence they have been accused of. The suspect's belief in their culpability may also be accompanied by the formation of vivid but fabricated memories, or confabulations. Kassin (2007) describes confabulated confession as:

> Statements made by an innocent but vulnerable person who, as a result of exposure to highly suggestive and misleading interrogation tactics, comes to believe that he or she may have committed the crime- a belief that is sometimes supplemented by false memories [confabulations]

Generally, false confessions attract some scepticism and critique (Bernhard, 2004). Consequently, the notion that an individual would harbour a genuine (yet incorrect) belief in their own guilt seems completely implausible and outside the innate drive for self-preservation (Kassin, 2007). Furthermore, research conducted by White (2003, p.139), found that jurors in a murder trial could not conceptualise the idea that someone would confess to a crime they did not commit.

Yet, there is growing evidence that not only are coerced-internalised confessions possible, but that they are more prevalent than originally conceptualised. Examples of coerced-internalised false confessions include Peter Reilly[1] (Kassin and Gudjonsson, 2005); Oliver Campbell[2] (Campbell v R [2024]); and Andrew Evans[3] (University of Exeter, n.d.). Considering those examples, the potential for other historic confession cases being unreliable is concerning.

This chapter contends that the phenomenon of confabulated confession is both underexplored and underappreciated within legal practice. Given the potential of false confession to distort the evidential process, a deeper evaluation of this issue is essential. Confabulation represents a critical factor in assessing the reliability and admissibility of confession evidence within the CJS. As such, this chapter will evaluate the validity of existing definitions of confabulation and propose a legal definition of confabulation before examining its underlying causes.

3.3 Defining Confabulation

Whilst understanding of confabulation has significantly increased over time, it is still denied the notoriety of its cognitively aware counterparts. Further, whilst there is a volume of research on the issue, it exists within psychological and neuroscientific academia, yet there is clearly a need for legal recognition, given the weight afforded to confession evidence in court.

Although there is no official legal definition, the Oxford Dictionary of Psychology (2009) defines confabulation as:

> a memory disorder related to amnesia but involving the generation of fabricated accounts of events, experiences, or facts, either deliberately or without conscious intent, to compensate for memory loss.

This definition provides a basis for academic discussion, however, it requires further refinement to apply within a legal context. Gudjonsson (2003) observed that confabulation can equate to "problems in memory processing where people replace gaps in their memory with imaginary experiences that they believe to be true". Wiggins and Bunin (2021) proffer confabulation to be "a neuropsychiatric disorder wherein a patient generates a false memory without the intention of deceit". Whereas Moscovitch and Melo (1997) simply define the condition to be "honest lying".

Burgess and Shallice (1996) recognised several key factors in their definition of confabulation, namely that confabulations are typically coherent accounts given when "autobiographical recollection" is required; the memory is false in context and/or detail; the content is usually derived from personal experience; it occurs as a result of impaired memory processes; and, "confabulators are unaware that they are confabulating". This definition emphasises some of the more problematic elements of the condition, namely that confabulated accounts are generally coherent (thus more believable), and that the confabulator is unaware that they are confabulating, thus making false recollections difficult to detect.

The perplexing nature of confabulation inevitably leads to cynicism and accusations of lying or malingering. Nevertheless, there is a fundamental differentiation between falsely believing in one's own guilt and a deliberate falsehood (Brown et al., 2017). To lie, one must have an awareness of the falsehood of their statements (Brown et al., 2013). Additionally, malingering or exaggeration still requires a "conscious" fraud. Whilst there are numerous issues with the reliability of confession evidence in relation to intentional deception, this is outside the scope of this chapter.

The common underpinning factor across the multitude of definitions is the generation of a false memory or recollection, with a genuine belief in that fabrication. Therefore, for the purposes of this chapter, the term confabulation will be representative of a genuine belief of false recollection, resulting from a number of causes and/or vulnerabilities (which will be discussed in the next section).

3.4 Causes of Confabulation

3.4.1 Fallibility of Memory

Most people do not possess eidetic memory, and discrepancies can occur during both the memory encoding and retrieval process (Lentoor, 2023). Furthermore, Lentoor (2023) states that the acquisition of new memory is highly dependent on both pre-existing knowledge and external influences; therefore, it is susceptible to "biases, distortions, or errors".

Therefore, it can be assumed that there are concerns about the validity of memory across the general population. However, this chapter specifically considers the correlation between specific neurodivergent groups and the potential increased impairment to memory function and/or accuracy.

3.4.2 A Neurological Approach

There is a substantial body of scientific research establishing direct correlations between specific neurological conditions and the risk of confabulation.

One leading theory is that confabulation relates to dysfunction of both the frontal lobe (Turner et al., 2008), and the prefrontal cortex (Cooper et al., 2016) of the brain. Specifically, the frontal lobes are associated with memory and executive function, and the prefrontal cortex is responsible for decision-making and reasoning. Studies have found confabulation to occur where an individual has suffered frontal lobe damage (Turner et al., 2008). Additionally, Gilboa and Moscovitch (2002) report that 81% of confabulators in their study had damage to the prefrontal cortex.

There is a growing body of evidence suggesting that the tendency to confabulate is more prevalent among some populations. However, the research undertaken has been limited in scope thus far. What has been determined, though, is that confabulation is typified into spontaneous and provoked confabulation (Gudjonsson et al., 2021). With both types linking to a range of mental health conditions or disorders, cognitive impairments, and, as an extension of normal memory processing, respectively (Schneider, 2018).

Spontaneous (or voluntary) confabulation was identified by Kopelman (1987), as the development of a false memory because of a "superimposition of frontal dysfunction on an organic amnesia" and is widely acknowledged to be voluntarily proffered, as opposed to prompted or instigated (Coltheart, 2017). Whereas provoked confabulation typically occurs in response to a trigger factor, for example, a prompt or leading question, provoked confabulation can also be prompted by lapses or flaws in a person's memory (Kopelman, 1987).

Statistics demonstrate that an inclination to confabulate is exacerbated by a range of mental and/or neurological conditions or vulnerabilities. Furthermore, it has transpired that exposure to the early criminal justice process can act as a catalyst for confabulations (Gudjonsson, 2016), with provoked confabulations being elicited by specific stimuli (Brown et al., 2017), which may occur during questioning, interrogation and cross-examination.

3.5 The Nexus of Confabulation, Cognitive Function, and Neurodivergence: Why Is Confabulation a Problem across the Neurodivergent Population?

3.5.1 Defining Neurodivergence

There is considerable academic discussion about the extent to which neurology drives confabulation; confabulations can occur in neurotypical or "non-impaired individuals" (Brown et al., 2017). Yet, a significant volume of research suggests that there is a tendency towards confabulation within neurodivergent populations (Gudjonsson, Young and Bramham, 2007; Spitzer, White and Burgess, 2017; Asperger, 1944). With recognition that a range of neurological conditions may link to a predisposition for confabulation including, (but not exclusively limited to): traumatic brain injury (TBI), Foetal Alcohol Spectrum Disorder (FASD), Wernicke-Korsakoff Syndrome (WKS), Post Traumatic Stress Disorder (PTSD), Alzheimer's disease, Anosognosia, Anton's Syndrome, Schizophrenia, bipolar disorder, anterior communicating artery aneurysms etc. (Wiggins and Bunin, 2021; Brown et al., 2017).

There is, however, some debate regarding the classification of neurodivergence.

Coined by Kassiane Asasumasu in the early 2000s, neurodivergence is an umbrella term encompassing a divergence from typical neurology and encompasses a broad range of conditions, including:

> Autistic people. ADHD people. People with learning disabilities. Epileptic people. People with mental illnesses. People with MS [Multiple Sclerosis] or Parkinsons or apraxia or cerebral palsy or dyspraxia or no specific diagnosis but wonky lateralization or something.
>
> (Armstrong, 2021)

Yet, there is academic disagreement regarding the use of the term and specific conditions. The term is typically used to categorise conditions such as autism, ADHD, OCD, Tourette's, dyspraxia, dyslexia etc (Resnick, 2024). Researchers have debated different models of neurodivergence and neurodiversity, ranging from disability vs disorder arguments, genetic vs acquired neurodivergence, medical vs social models etc. (Goldberg, 2023).

For the purposes of this chapter, a broad, inclusive definition of neurodivergence is applied, encompassing applied, genetic, and acquired neurodivergence. This aligns with the College of Policing definition (2021) and the User Voice report

(2021), widening the scope to include conditions such as TBI, PTSD, Obsessive Compulsive Disorder (OCD), neurogenetic disorders, intellectual disabilities, and neurological damage (Purcell, n.d.), ensuring that there is a comprehensive application of neurodivergence.

3.5.2 Prevalence

This chapter specifically examines the risks of confabulation within the neurodivergent population, on the basis that proportionately, neurominorities are over-represented in the CJS, and there have been clear links established with numerous neurodivergent conditions and false confessions.

In terms of specifying the percentage of neurodivergent individuals within the CJS, there are practical difficulties in doing so. There is no centrally verified database documenting that percentage across the United Kingdom (Criminal Justice Joint Inspection Report, 2021). Academic studies have, however, made attempts to estimate the prevalence of neurodivergent conditions within the CJS. The Criminal Justice Joint Inspection Report (2021) estimated that within the UK adult population, 4% have ADHD, 1–2% have autism, and 10% have dyslexia. It also drew upon existing research, indicating that between 8.5 and 12% of adults have a TBI. It also found there to be a general consensus among professionals that between 15 and 20% of the population have a neurodivergent condition (including TBI) and made a working assumption that up to half of the adult prison population may experience neurodivergence. Young et al. (2018), undertook a study in a UK prison and found there to be 33% of inmates sampled who met the criteria for neurodevelopmental disorders (namely ADHD, ASD and intellectual disability (ID)), with a breakdown of 24.6% for ADHD, 8.5% for ASD and 9% for ID, estimated to be disproportionately high compared to the general population. Headway, the brain injury association, estimates that around 50% of the prison population have suffered a TBI (n.d., from The Criminal Justice Joint Inspection Report, 2021, see also Headway. (n.d.). *Effects of Brain Injury*. Available at: https://www.headway.org.uk/aboutbrain-injury/individuals/effects-of-brain-injury/ (Accessed 31 March 2021)).

As demonstrated, there is an established link between neurodivergent conditions and disproportionate representation within the CJS.

With approximately 15–20% of the general population currently identified as neurodivergent, estimates of neurodivergent people making up 33–50% of the prison population suggest a significant level of disproportion within the prison system. The level of disparity evidenced is disconcerting and is exacerbated further when it is considered that the comorbidity rates for neurodivergent individuals are extremely high (e.g., it is estimated that the prevalence of ADHD among autistic people is around 40% (Apperly et al., 2024)). Furthermore, there is a potential significant percentage of individuals who have undiagnosed neurodivergence[4] (UserVoice, 2021), therefore the estimates of neurodivergent representation within the CJS could be significantly underestimated.

3.5.3 *Why Is Confabulation More Prevalent in Neurodivergent Populations?*

Historic studies (Asperger, 1944) identified confabulating behaviours in a study of children with autism, and more contemporary research also recognises the links between neurodivergence, memory, and confabulation. Lyons and Fitzgerald (2013) examined issues around problematic memory recall and autism, contemplating Millward's et al. (2000) theory that individuals on the Autism Spectrum incur recall issues due to a lack of 'experiencing self'. A lack of clarity of memory in the autistic community could infer that there is a greater need to confabulate (particularly in line with Malle's theory of an inherent drive to formulate answers—see Section 3.3.1). Similarly, Lind et al. (2014) found memories of an autistic individual to be "less salient and coherent" than their neurotypical peers, which could infer a link to distortion of memory, again linking to the potential to confabulate to formulate answers.

It has also been established that there is a relationship between ADHD and confabulation, with studies reporting a correlation between allegations of false confession and ADHD. Gudjonsson et al. (2008) reported that their study found 41% of participants with ADHD to falsely confess, as opposed to 18% of other non-ADHD participants. That is not to say that there is a higher degree of susceptibility present in individuals with ADHD, but rather, that they had more of an inclination to respond with perceived evasive replies, which Gudjonsson et al. (2007) argued may be misconstrued by the interviewing officers. It has further been recognised that the mannerisms and responses of ADHD suspects may be a corroborating factor, again resulting in being misconstrued by interviewing officers, subconsciously impacting upon interview technique. Additionally, it has been observed that individuals with ADHD may have poor emotional regulation and issues with behaviour inhibition, which may impair capacity to cope with interrogation (Gudjonsson et al., 2009).

3.6 How Do We Measure a Risk of Confabulation?

To review an individual's risk of confabulation, across a potentially inexhaustive group of conditions constituting neurodivergence, and with the vast volume of individuals potentially undiagnosed or misdiagnosed, it would be nigh impossible to consider the risk of confabulation on a condition-specific basis. Thus, risk should be measured by shared characteristics of the neurodivergent population. As such, this section will focus on measuring the risk of confabulation, considering psychological characteristics that would make an individual more predisposed to confabulate.

3.6.1 *Interrogative Suggestibility*

One of the most recognised underpinning causes of confabulation is that of interrogative suggestibility. According to Gudjonsson (1986), suggestibility can be defined as "the extent to which persons 'come to accept and subsequently incorporate post-event information' into their recollections of memory". Interrogative suggestibility is, however, different from compliance, which (in the context of the CJS) is the tendency to acquiesce to suggestions/accusations of culpability for personal benefit (Gudjonsson, 2003). Gudjonsson's theory of suggestibility was later refined (Gudjonsson and Clark, 1986) denoting the concept of interrogative suggestibility as the:

> Extent to which, within a closed social interaction, people come to accept messages communicated during formal questioning, as the result of which their subsequent behavioural response is affected.

Gudjonsson identified two components: "yield", a tendency to submit to leading questions, and "shift", a tendency to alter responses following feedback (Szpitalak, 2020). Both components are problematic in the scope of a police interview, given the nature of the transaction is that the individual is usually suspected of the commission of a crime and will be questioned about their recollection of a specific event, which undoubtedly can create the potential for officers to be both leading and/or reactive, based on their expectations.

The College of Policing (2022) warns that leading questioning can undermine the reliability of evidence and should be used with caution; however, it is allowed, creating a risk of "yield" responses (i.e., submissions). Furthermore, even subconscious reactions can also be problematic. Both Kassin and Gudjonsson (2004) and Clarke and Milne (2001) found there to be an adverse effect on the reliability of evidence, where the interviewing officer reacted negatively to statements made, resulting in a "shift" response (i.e., the suspect tailoring their response to meet the expectations of their interviewer). In circumstances of interrogation or questioning, subconscious cues can be expressed by the interviewer (Snook et al., 2020), relating to what their expectation of the "correct" answer may be, potentially creating a latent "shift" response from the interviewee. Therefore, even the most innocuous or subconscious behaviour of an interviewing officer can be prejudicial.

The link between neurodivergence and interrogative suggestibility is well established, with a significant volume of research identifying links to ADHD (Gudjonsson et al., 2008 and Young and Bramham, 2007), autism (North, Russel and Gudjonsson, 2008), FASD (Gilbert et al., 2024), intellectual disability (Gudjonsson et al., 1993), TBI (Brown, n.d.), mental disorder (Geijsen, Ruiter and Kop, 2018), and WKS (Kopelman, 1987).

The link of suggestibility and confabulation has proven difficult to verify on a practical level. But there have been varying levels of success in smaller scale studies. Otgaar et al. (2021) reaffirmed the connection between high levels of suggestibility and (to a lesser degree) compliance, with false confession, in a number of studies observed; however, the study was limited in establishing a link specifically with internalised false confession, as it considered false confession as a wider concept. Kassin (2007) noted a correlation between high levels of suggestibility in "false confessors" and a corresponding lower level across those maintaining innocence. Gudjonsson and Young (2010) also note that there is a link between confabulation and suggestibility. Furthermore, there is a connection between interrogative suggestibility and confabulation, and that connection is more prevalent within certain vulnerable populations (Clare and Gudjonsson, 1993).

3.6.2 Memory Function and Memory Distrust Syndrome

Another potential indicator for confabulation is that of memory distrust syndrome (MDS). First identified by Gudjonsson and MacKeith (1982), MDS occurs where an individual develops a significant distrust in their own recollections and becomes more susceptible to suggestion. MDS leads to pressured-internalised confession/confabulation (Gudjonsson, 2003). MDS has been established to be more present within vulnerable populations (Gudjonsson et al., 2021). Again, reaffirming the theory that a risk of confabulation is more prevalent in vulnerable populations.

In terms of neurodivergence, there is a lack of literature directly linking MDS to neurodivergence; however, there are parallels in memory processing, inferring a connection. For example, Rabiee et al. (2020) identify clear deficits in working memory in autistic populations; Kofler et al. (2020) determined marked executive working memory deficits linked to ADHD; Saarinen et al. (2015) found links with ODD and visuospatial working memory deficits in children; and Brown et al. (2017) clarified the link with frontal lobe damage, memory processing, and confabulation. Thus, supporting the theory that there is a substantial link between memory function issues and neurodivergent conditions, which, as highlighted above, increase the risk of confabulation.

Gudjonsson identifies two forms of MDS. Firstly, it can occur when an individual has no actual memory of the event in question and comes to believe they must have committed the offence simply because they are being accused. Secondly, an individual may initially recall not committing the offence, but through certain interrogative techniques, they begin to doubt their own memory and accept the version of events presented to them, leading to MDS.

There are also some contextual risk factors for confabulation with respect to memory distrust namely: social isolation, persuasive interrogation, and high emotional intensity (Gudjonsson, 2016), all of which may be present during police custody and interview. Where there are faults or limitations in memory processing, and subsequently a lack of trust in an individual's own memory, that person is much more inclined to rely on cues and external information to reconstruct their memory (Zhang, Otgaar, and Wang, 2022). The combination of memory deficit and lack of trust creates the perfect storm for confabulation when the individual is exposed to the right triggers (see Section 3.4.1).

3.6.3 Additional Underpinning Factors

Interrogative suggestibility and memory processing are some of the more established causal factors that contribute to confabulation. However, there are several other elements that have been linked to both confabulation and neurodivergence, including: reality monitoring, credulity, and gullibility, which will be discussed in the sections below.

Reality monitoring is another associated characteristic of confabulation and has been linked to neurodivergence. Reality monitoring is:

> The act or process of discriminating between genuine memories that are acquired through perception from external reality and apparent memories that are generated internally by imagination.
>
> (Oxford Dictionary of Psychology)

It provides a substantial influence on the credibility of confession evidence. If there are impairments in reality monitoring capabilities, this can increase the likelihood of memory distortion and/or confabulation. There is no specific research that links reality monitoring impairment and neurodivergence; however, there are several studies that have linked the issue to specific neurodivergent conditions. For example, autism (Cooper et al., 2016); TBI (Bajo et al., 2017); and neurological impairment following aneurysm (Schneider, 2001). These findings indicate that difficulties with reality monitoring may play a significant role in the occurrence of confabulation among individuals across various neurodivergent populations. Johnson et al. (2000) proposed a correlation between confabulation and deficits in reality monitoring, suggesting that individuals who confabulate often struggle to differentiate between real and imagined experiences. Although the relationship between reality monitoring and confabulation is not consistently supported in isolation (Spitzer et al., 2017), further research may help to clarify and strengthen the evidence for this connection.

Credulity and gullibility are additional factors that correlate with confabulation and neurodivergence. Credulity refers to a person's inclination to accept information as true and correct despite a lack of believability or evidence, whereas gullibility refers to "a person's susceptibility to be manipulated or tricked" (Brown et al., 2020). Brown's research examines the link between credulity and gullibility, suggesting that the former can be used to exploit the latter. Both traits are strongly associated with increased suggestibility and a heightened risk of confabulation. While Brown highlights the association between these traits and FASD, other studies have also linked both to autism (Williams et al., 2018) and damage to the prefrontal cortex (Asp et al., 2012). This further reinforces concerns about the reliability of confessions among certain neurodivergent populations and may point to a broader issue related to neurodivergence.

3.7 How Confabulation Occurs and Its Challenges within the Criminal Justice System

3.7.1 Provocation and Triggers

Although confabulation can occur spontaneously without external provocation, there is compelling evidence that negative interactions with the CJS can trigger such responses, especially in individuals who are predisposed to confabulate. Gudjonsson (2016) proposes that confabulation usually unfolds through a five-stage sequential process:

1. *Trigger* (e.g., an arrest, police interview, leading questioning, and even dreams), making the suspect distrust his/her own memory.
2. *Plausibility* (for example, whilst in a confused state, the suspect is persuaded that the material event could have happened or may be given a narrative of how it could have viably occurred).
3. *Acceptance* (i.e., the suspect accepts that the event may have happened). This occurs when the suspect has abandoned his own belief or memory of innocence. Gudjonsson notes that the more plausible the accusation, the more likely the acceptance.
4. *Memory reconstruction.* Once accepting their guilt, the suspect will try to reconstruct the events in their imagination to determine their plausibility. This can be exacerbated by the interviewers' affirmations or external sources of information.
5. *Resolution* (when the suspect becomes aware of the true events). This can happen sometime after the original confession and is likely to be received with scepticism from authorities.

Those with conditions such as ASD, ADHD, and FASD may be particularly vulnerable due to such factors as impaired executive functioning, low memory confidence, and difficulty distinguishing between fictional thoughts and external reality (Rabiee et al., 2020; Kofler et al., 2020; Brown et al., 2020). Similarly, individuals with TBI may experience impaired executive function and memory recall, making them more prone to confabulation under stress (Bajo et al., 2017). This is highly relevant in the context of the CJS, as it emphasises the need for greater awareness of neurocognitive vulnerabilities that may affect the reliability of testimony and confession evidence.

What is evident is that specific behaviours during the interview can exacerbate an existing tendency to confabulate. One such example occurs when suggestions are introduced during the interview process. Pezdek et al. (2009) refer to this as "other-generated confabulation", where the false memory is suggested by a third party, typically the interviewing officer.[5]

Whilst research on suggestive questioning has primarily focused on witnesses, it raises important evidential concerns when similar techniques are used with suspects, particularly given the added stress and vulnerability suspects may experience during an investigation. The study by Pezdek et al. (2009) found that when confabulation is introduced by a third party, it is more likely to be incorporated into an individual's memory than if the false information is self-generated.

Another problematic element is the posing of the impossible or unanswerable question. With our inherent drive to find solutions (see Section 3.3.1), when pressured to answer an "unanswerable question" (being one that is factually impossible), human beings are predisposed to create a reasonable answer (Gombos et al., 2012). Similarly, another influential factor may be the investigating officer's presumption of guilt. Kassin et al. (2003) found that when an investigating officer believed a suspect to be guilty, it influenced the officer's behaviour, shaped the suspect's responses, and negatively impacted the overall outcome of the investigation. Kassin's research correlates with that of Gudjonsson et al. (2007), regarding interviewing suspects with ADHD, noting that their tendency to provide evasive responses (i.e. "don't know") acted as a trigger for interviewing officers, resulting in a change of interview style and consequently a reduction in the reliability of confession evidence.

Brown et al. (2017) asserted that provoked confabulations are elicited by specific stimuli. In the context of this chapter, such stimuli exist within the parameters of questioning, interrogation, and cross-examination. The interview process for a neurodivergent suspect requires significant caution and an understanding of the potential impact of different interview techniques on these individuals.

3.7.2 Clarifying the Boundary between False Confession and Confabulation

False or inaccurate admissions of guilt are well recognised within the CJS, which may prompt the reader to question the necessity for further research in a field that has already been extensively studied. In cases of provoked false confessions, a suspect may knowingly admit guilt due to interrogational pressure or perceived incentives (e.g., being told, "if you admit to doing XYZ, you can go home"). However, once these stressors or incentives are removed, such confessions are often quickly recanted. Whilst this recalled confession can still be influential, the fact that the confession has been recalled allows for a reasoned challenge of innocence. Yet, when experiencing a confabulation, the suspect assimilates the false information as an actual memory, internalising it without recognising it to be fictional. Confabulated confessions can be particularly difficult to challenge, especially when the suspect holds a vivid but false memory of having committed the offence.

Once a confession is made, regardless of its reliability or eventual admissibility, it has a lasting and prejudicial impact, particularly in the context of jury decision making. Kassin and Sukel (1997) demonstrated that even confessions deemed inadmissible by a judge can influence jurors and stigmatise the accused.

Although confabulation falls within the broader category of false confessions, it is important to consider why distinguishing between the two is necessary.

There are several fundamental reasons to make this distinction, the first being the differing psychological impacts. For instance, an innocent suspect who falsely confesses for notoriety or in response to incentives typically retains cognitive awareness of their innocence. Likewise, if a suspect confesses under pressure, they may be able to recognise the falsity of their admission once those pressures are removed and may subsequently retract the confession. In contrast, a suspect who confabulates genuinely believes in their own guilt. This false belief can be profoundly psychologically damaging and may also have a significant emotional and social impact on their family (Brown et al., 2017b).

Identifying a confabulating suspect can be challenging. While many officers rely on reading body language or detecting signs of deception, a confabulating individual is unlikely to display such cues, as they genuinely believe the false information that they are providing. Unlike knowingly false confessions, which may involve coercion or undue pressure that can be identified through custody recordings in accordance with PACE 1984, confabulated confessions can occur in the absence of any overt misconduct or procedural irregularity. As a result, the absence of visible external triggers makes cases of confabulated false confession significantly harder to detect and evaluate.

3.7.3 A "PEACE-ful" Resolution in England and Wales?

While this chapter has highlighted the serious risk of injustices associated with confabulated confessions, significant improvements have been made within the CJS in England and Wales.

PACE 1984 was introduced in England and Wales to standardise policing practices, balance police powers with civil liberties, and establish safeguards for individuals in police custody (Poyser and Milne, 2021). The provisions of PACE 1984 have proven invaluable, particularly through the accompanying Codes of Practice, which set out key safeguards, such as the mandatory recording of interviews (Codes E and F) and the requirement for an "appropriate adult" to support vulnerable suspects (Code C).

PACE 1984 also introduced several safeguards to prevent the use of psychological manipulation in interviews, for example, "No interviewer may try to obtain answers or elicit a statement by the use of oppression" (PACE Code C, 11.5). This provision is a clear improvement on interview techniques utilised on the accused, for both neurodivergent and neurotypical suspects alike; with a marked reduction in police impropriety in interviews (Sanders et al., 2010). However, PACE fell short of explicitly prohibiting more subtle forms of inducement, such as minimisation and maximisation techniques used to elicit confessions.

In 1992, the PEACE model of investigative interviewing was also introduced. This model represented a systematic shift away from interrogative and coercive techniques towards a non-confrontational, information-gathering approach grounded in psychological principles. The PEACE framework, comprising

Planning and Preparation, Engage and Explain, Account, Closure, and Evaluation, was built upon two core principles:

(1) "The purpose of investigative interviewing is to obtain accurate and reliable information from suspects, witnesses or victims in order to discover the truth about matters under investigation".
(2) "Interviews should be approached with an open mind. Information obtained from the person who is being interviewed should always be tested against what the investigator already knows or what can reasonably be established" (Bull, 2018).

PEACE has significantly contributed to a reduction in miscarriages of justice and has been adopted in various jurisdictions, earning recognition from the UN Special Rapporteur (Bull, 2018). However, criticisms remain, particularly concerning police interviewer training and the influence of pre-existing biases held by police (Poyser and Milne, 2021). Poyser and Milne also identify the difficulty of ensuring a consistent application of best practice models and in detecting and managing cognitive bias of the interviewing officers. There is also a strong argument that many police officers still lack sufficient awareness of key concepts such as vulnerability, neurodivergence, false confessions, and confabulation.

Woodhouse et al. (2024) highlight the challenges police face in appropriately identifying and screening autistic individuals. Although the study primarily focuses on autism, the findings likely apply to other forms of neurodivergence. This assertion is further reinforced by the Criminal Justice Joint Inspection Report, *Neurodiversity in the Criminal Justice System* (2021), which found that although a "wide range of screening tools" exist, none were used consistently, and in many cases, no screening was conducted at all. The Criminal Justice Joint Inspection Report (2021) indicated that the effectiveness of vulnerability screening often depended on the individual custody sergeant's experience and persistence, rather than on systematic processes. Despite guidance issued by the College of Policing (2021), only 28% of respondents to the call for evidence reported having received any training on neurodiversity, though it should be noted this figure reflects the wide CJS, not just frontline policing at the point of arrest or interview. The report also noted that where training had been provided, it predominantly focused on autism, with limited attention given to other forms of neurodivergence.

Notably, there appears to be a lack of published research examining police awareness or understanding of confabulation at the time of writing. This is significant because it reveals a lack of consistent, informed practice in recognising and supporting neurodivergent individuals during engagement with the CJS. Given the heightened vulnerability of such individuals, gaps in training and awareness may contribute to miscarriages of justice. The absence of research on confabulation is especially concerning, as this memory phenomenon can be particularly misunderstood and is not recognised in existing police training or protocols.

The level of inconsistency of knowledge demonstrated across professionals within the CJS highlights an acute problem. The failure to accurately identify neurodivergence and vulnerability within the system fundamentally undermines the implementation of safeguards designed to prevent false and confabulated confessions.

3.8 Potential Reforms to Reduce the Risk of Confabulation

The pivotal questions that need to be answered are, firstly, how the issue of confabulated testimony can be resolved and secondly, how we make the system more equitable for neurodivergent suspects. Although progress has been made in aligning policing practices with psychology-informed research, significant systemic gaps persist, particularly in areas such as data collection, early identification, interview techniques, officer training, and evidentiary procedures. Thus, a multi-faceted reform approach is required, considering several aspects within the CJS, including a more comprehensive data collection system, improvements to identification and screening processes, improved police training, and greater strength of legislative provision.

3.8.1 National-Level Data Collection

The Criminal Justice Joint Inspectorate (2021) critically observed:

> [T]here is no reliable, consistent or systematic data collection, either within individual services or across the CJS as a whole...This is a serious and fundamental failing with wide-ranging implications for the commissioning of services and support.

Given the current lack of statistical evidence concerning neurodivergence available within the CJS, a simple administrative improvement would be the development of a national process for data collection and monitoring, extending beyond the prison service, to encompass all stages of criminal justice engagement.

Implementation of data collection systems should incorporate the recording of relevant personal data, including self-reported neurodivergent or neurological conditions, behavioural observations made during custody, and any formal professional assessments. This approach would enable a more accurate and comprehensive analysis of the neurodivergent population within the system. Crucially, it would provide the empirical foundation necessary to assess the prevalence of confabulation among neurodivergent individuals in police custody, thereby informing evidence-based policy reform.

Until we have accurate data on the prevalence of neurodivergent individuals across the CJS, the capacity to implement strategic reform is significantly constrained. It is subsequently proposed that there should be a statutory duty to record data about individuals, such as neurodivergence, disability, and mental health problems. Once such comprehensive data is available, more pragmatic and strategic improvements can be considered.

3.8.2 Mandatory Screening and Early Identification

A more robust and standardised screening process for neurodivergence and vulnerability is urgently needed. Currently, there is no assurance that such needs will even be recognised when an individual encounters the CJS (Criminal Justice Joint Inspection Report, 2021). This creates a problematic situation in which appropriate support cannot be provided, simply because vulnerable individuals are not being adequately identified from the outset.

At a practical level, mandatory screening protocols should be introduced at the first point of contact with police, aimed at either identifying specific neurodevelopmental conditions or recognising characteristics that may contribute to confabulation, such as suggestibility, memory distrust, or cognitive vulnerability, particularly in individuals suspected of committing an offence. Early identification would allow for suitable support mechanisms to be employed from the outset, such as the provision of an Appropriate Adult. Timely identification would enable officers to adjust their interview style to ensure that they are not increasing the risk of confabulation. Similarly, prompt detection of such vulnerability would inform officers of expected neurodivergent traits, which could be misinterpreted. Not only would early mandatory screening protocols ensure equity for the neurodivergent suspect, but they would also improve the measure of credibility for any confession evidence appropriately obtained, as safeguards would have been implemented from the outset.

Early screening protocols could utilise existing tools, such as the Gudjonsson Suggestibility Scale (GSS) or other neurodevelopmental frameworks, which would serve to identify a quantifiable risk of the suspect to confabulate. It would also be beneficial to employ neurodivergent specialists within custody suites to ensure the screening is properly implemented and that support is available as needed.

3.8.3 Psychological Best Practice and the PEACE Model

Psychological research has significantly influenced the improvement of police interview and interrogation practices in England and Wales, particularly through the introduction of PACE, its associated Codes of Practice, and the development of psychology-informed models such as the PEACE framework. However, the effectiveness of these advances is undermined by inconsistent training and variable levels of awareness among some police officers.

Whilst the work of many academics in challenging and preventing the use of oppressive or manipulative interview techniques has been substantial, the College of Policing's *Investigative Interviewing* guidelines (n.d.) continue to emphasise the benefits of early admissions of guilt for all parties involved. This suggests that securing confessions remains a central focus, contradicting the psychology-led, information-gathering principles underpinning the PEACE model.

In order to resolve the inconsistency between the College of Policing and psychology-informed research, formally enshrining the PEACE methodology into legislation would reinforce its significance and afford it the protection of statutory authority.

3.8.4 Policing Education and Training

In terms of police training, current academic discourse suggests that the resolution lies in education and awareness of key authorities, such as the police (Brown et al., 2017). Training should emphasise an avoidance of closed and suggestive questioning, repetitive questioning, and negative reinforcement during interviews. Research also suggests that interviewers should avoid giving overtly positive or negative feedback during the interview process, as such responses may distort a suspect's recollection or, more problematically, reinforce confabulated memories (Tata and Gudjonsson, 1990; Kassin et al., 2010). This could be achieved by giving the PEACE model a statutory footing, thus embedding research-informed safeguards into law.

Fundamental components of police training, particularly for officers involved in suspect interviews, should include specific instruction on the risks and recognition of false confessions and confabulation, alongside ongoing training on neurodivergence.

3.8.5 Legal Reform

S.76 of PACE 1984 allows for the exclusion of confession evidence obtained by means of oppression, or other circumstances rendering it unreliable. While s.76 PACE does offer a degree of legal protection, this is insufficient with respect to the specific risk of confabulation among neurodivergent populations. Allegations of oppression must be proven beyond reasonable doubt, and thus far a narrow interpretation of "oppression" has been utilised. This was considered in *R v Fulling* [1987], whereby the Court of Appeal held it to mean harsh, unjust or cruel treatment, deriving from impropriety by the interrogator. There was some evolution of the meaning of oppression in *R v Paris (and others)* [1992], where excessively lengthy and hostile interrogations were deemed oppressive, and there was discussion of mental capacity levels and the benchmarks for oppression. However, fundamentally, the courts have fallen short of creating precedent that oppression is subjective, and in cases of neurodivergence a standard interview process could potentially be oppressive to the individual.

Neurodivergent individuals, particularly those with conditions such as ASD, ADHD, intellectual disability, or memory-related conditions may be more prone to suggestibility, acquiescence, and confabulation during police interviews. These individuals might not perceive questioning as coercive, even when it produces unreliable responses. In such cases, the standard under s.76 may not be triggered, leaving vulnerable suspects unprotected.

There is some legal protection in place by virtue of s.77 PACE 1984, which allows for judicial direction to the jury advising caution on reliance of the confession whereby:

1. The court is satisfied that the accused is "mentally handicapped".
2. The case against him depends "wholly or substantially on a confession by him".
3. The "confession was not made in the presence of an independent person".

The terminology "mentally handicapped" used in PACE is archaic and stigmatising,[6] and does not adequately encapsulate the experience of the neurodivergent individual. Similar protections afforded under PACE Code C use the term "vulnerability"; however, the term remains unclear, referring to a person who:

> 1.13(d) because of a mental health condition or mental disorder…
>
> (i) may have difficulty understanding or communicating effectively about the full implications for them of any procedures and processes connected with:
>
> • their arrest and detention

Code C also refers to vulnerability incorporating confusion, unwittingly providing unreliable or incriminating information, or accepting suggestions from others. Whilst this is a more contemporary interpretation than its 1984 parent legislation, future revision of the definition to recognise neurodivergence would be significant.

3.9 Conclusion

This chapter has examined the under-recognised phenomenon of confabulated confessions, genuine but false admissions of guilt, arising from distortion of memory. Drawing upon psychological, neuroscientific, and legal scholarship, it has argued that confabulation is a distinct form of false confession that is often overlooked in legal proceedings and policy reform. Unlike other forms of false confession, confabulated statements are not prompted by motivation or incentive but are a result of cognitive vulnerabilities. This presents a profound challenge for both legal interpretation and evidential reliability.

The evidence presented has demonstrated that neurodivergent individuals, particularly those with autism, ADHD, FASD, intellectual disabilities, or brain injuries, are particularly vulnerable to suggestibility, memory distrust, and impaired reality monitoring. These cognitive vulnerabilities, when exposed to the stressors of the CJS, can lead to the creation of vivid but inaccurate memories. Current legal safeguards within the English CJS, such as PACE 1984 and the PEACE model of interviewing, offer important protections. Yet they are undermined by outdated terminology, a lack of legislative reinforcement, and inadequate training for key personnel.

Reform must be multifaceted, including a statutory framework for neurodivergence screening; mandatory training for interviewers on the nature and signs of confabulation; and enhanced evidential safeguards for confession admissibility. Fundamentally, formal recognition of confabulation within legal frameworks is long overdue. Equally, legal terminology must be modernised to reflect inclusive, socially informed definitions of cognitive diversity and vulnerability.

Ultimately, memory is a construct, subjective and shaped by perception; it is not an eidetic recollection. It is fallible, and under the right circumstances can even betray our own innocence. Einstein was believed to have opined, "memory is deceptive because it is coloured by today's events", and this applies particularly felicitously to the issue of the vulnerable suspect. Fundamentally, the CJS must codify relevant guidelines, as failing to do so risks continuing to perpetuate injustice for the most marginalised in society.

Notes

1 Reilly created his own false narrative explaining the brutal murder of his mother.
2 Campbell was a 19-year-old pressured into believing he fired a fatal gunshot.
3 Evans falsely confessed to murder following a dream that he had about the victim.
4 A study from UserVoice (2021) suggests up to 66% of service users within the CJS were not screened for neurodivergence.
5 In this instance, the question posed was "The other eyewitness said that the car at the end of the alley was white. What colour do you think the car was?"
6 The use of "mental handicap" is actively discouraged in the Office for Disability Issues and Department for Work and Pensions guidance (2021).

References

Apperly, I.A., Lee, R., van der Kleij, S.W. and Devine, R.T. (2024). 'A transdiagnostic approach to neurodiversity in a representative population sample: The N+4 model', *JCPP Advances*, 4(2), p. e12219. https://doi.org/10.1002/jcv2.12219.

Appleby, S.C., Hasel, L.E. and Kassin, S.M. (2011). 'Police-induced confessions: An empirical analysis of their content and impact', *Psychology Crime and Law*, 19(2), pp. 111–128. https://doi.org/10.1080/1068316x.2011.613389.

Armstrong, T. (2021). 'Negotiating the neurodiversity concept', *Psychology Today*, 24 August. Available at: https://www.psychologytoday.com/us/blog/neurodiverse-age/202108/negotiating-the-neurodiversity-concept (Accessed 6 March 2025).

Asp, E., Manzel, K., Koestner, B., Cole, C.A., Denburg, N.L. and Tranel, D. (2012). 'A neuropsychological test of belief and doubt: Damage to ventromedial prefrontal cortex increases credulity for misleading advertising,' *Frontiers in Neuroscience*, 6, p. 100.

Asperger, H. (1944). 'Die Autistischen Psychopathen im Kindesalter', *Archiv f. Psychiatrie*, 117. https://doi.org/10.1007/BF01837709.

Bajo, A., Fleminger, S., Metcalfe, C. and Kopelman, M. D. (2017). 'Confabulation: What is associated with its rise and fall? A study in brain injury', *Cortex*, 87, pp. 31–43.

Bernhard, A. (2004). 'Justice still fails: A review of recent efforts to compensate individuals who have been unjustly convicted and later exonerated', *Drake Law Review*, 52, p. 716.

Bering, J.M. and Shackelford, T.K. (2005). 'Evolutionary psychology and false confession', *American Psychologist,* 60(9), pp. 1037–1038

Brown, J. (n.d.). *Traumatic Brain Injury and Confabulation in Criminal Justice and Legal Settings: A Brief Review for Caregivers and Professionals.* Brain Injury Association of America. Available at: https://biausa.org/public-affairs/media/traumatic-brain-injury-and-confabulation (Accessed 28 May 2025).

Brown, J., Asp, E., Carter, M.N., Spiller, V. and Bishop-Deaton, D. (2020). 'Suggestibility and confabulation among individuals with Fetal Alcohol Spectrum Disorder: A review for criminal justice, forensic mental health, and legal interviewers', *International Journal of Law and Psychiatry*, 73, p. 101646.

Brown, J., Long-McGie, J., Oberoi, P., Wartnik, A., Wresh, J., Weinkauf, E. and Falconer, G. (2013). 'Confabulation: Connections between brain damage, memory, and testimony', *Journal of Law Enforcement*, 3(5), p. 1.

Brown, J., Huntley, D., Asp, E.W., Wiley, C.R., Cich, J. and Morgan, S. (2017). 'Confabulation: Implications for criminal justice, forensic mental health, and legal professionals', *Journal of Neurology and Neuroscience*, 8(5), p. 2.

Brown, J., Huntley, D., Morgan, S., Dodson, K.D. and Cich, J. (2017b). 'Confabulation: A guide for mental health professionals', *International Journal of Neurology and Neurotherapy*, 4, p. 070. Available at: https://doi.org/10.23937/2378-3001/1410070.

Bull, R. (2018). 'PEACE-ful Interviewing/interrogation: What research can tell us', in Shigemasu, K., Kuwano, S., Sato, T. and Matsuzawa, T. (eds.), *Diversity in Harmony – Insights from Psychology: Proceedings of the 31st International Congress of Psychology.* 1st edn. Chichester: John Wiley & Sons, pp. 191–206.

Burgess, P.W. and Shallice, T. (1996). 'Response suppression, initiation and strategy use following frontal lobe lesions', *Neuropsychologia*, 34(4), pp. 263–272. Available at: https://doi.org/10.1016/0028-3932(95)00104--2 (Accessed 3 June 2022).

Cambridge University Press. (n.d.). *Credulity*. Cambridge Dictionary. Retrieved 29 April, 2025, from https://dictionary.cambridge.org/dictionary/english/credulity

Campbell v R [2024] EWCA Crim 1036.

Clare, I.C.H. and Gudjonsson, G.H. (1993). 'Interrogative suggestibility, confabulation, and acquiescence in people with mild learning disabilities (mental handicap): Implications for reliability during police interrogations', *British Journal of Clinical Psychology*, 32(3), pp. 295–301.

Clarke, C. and Milne, R.J. (2001). *National Evaluation of the PEACE Investigative Interviewing Course* (PRAS No. 149). London: Home Office.

Coleman, A.M. (2009). *A Dictionary of Psychology*. 3rd edn. Oxford: Oxford University Press.

College of Policing. (2021). *Neurodiversity Glossary of Terms*. Available at: https://www.college.police.uk/support-forces/diversity-and-inclusion/neurodiversity-glossary-terms (Accessed 7 June 2022).

College of Policing. (2021). *Professional Development*. Available at: https://www.college.police.uk/guidance/vulnerability-related-risks/professional-development#982906ac-ecce-4eb4-807b-ea6ec43bc4ba (Accessed 7 June 2022).

College of Policing. (2022). *Investigative Interviewing*. [online] Available at: https://www.college.police.uk/app/investigation/investigative-interviewing/investigative-interviewing (Accessed 7 June 2022)

Coltheart, M. (2017). 'Confabulation and conversation', *Cortex*, 87, pp. 62–65.

Cooper, R.A., Plaisted-Grant, K.C., Baron-Cohen, S. and Simons, J.S. (2016). 'Reality monitoring and metamemory in adults with autism spectrum conditions', *Journal of Autism and Developmental Disorders*, 46, pp. 2186–2196.

Criminal Justice Joint Inspection. (2021). *Neurodiversity in the Criminal Justice System: A Review of Evidence*. London: Criminal Justice Joint Inspection. Available at: https://www.justiceinspectorates.gov.uk/cjji/inspections/neurodiversity-in-the-criminal-justice-system-a-review-of-evidence.

Drizin, S.A. and Leo, R.A. (2004). 'The problem of false confessions in the post-DNA world', *North Carolina Law Review*, 82, pp. 891–1007.

Evidence-Based Justice Lab. (n.d.). *Andrew Evans*. University of Exeter. Retrieved 11 December, 2024, from Evidence-Based Justice Lab website: https://evidencebasedjustice.exeter.ac.uk/case/andrew-evans/

Geijsen, K., de Ruiter, C. and Kop, N. (2018). 'Identifying psychological vulnerabilities: Studies on police suspects' mental health issues and police officers' views', *Cogent Psychology*, 5(1). https://doi.org/10.1080/23311908.2018.1462133.

Gilboa, A. and Moscovitch, M. (2002). 'The cognitive neuroscience of confabulation: A review and a model', in Baddeley, A.D., Kopelman, M.D. and Wilson, B.A. (eds.), *Handbook of Memory Disorders*, 2nd edn. London: John Wiley and Sons, pp. 315–342.

Gilbert, D.J., Gudjonsson, G.H., Cook, P., Mukherjee, R.A.S. and Allely, C.S. (2024). 'Immediate and repeat interrogative suggestibility in a sample of adolescents with fetal alcohol spectrum disorder,' *Diversity & Inclusion Research*, 1(1), p. e12007.

Goldberg, H. (2023). 'Unraveling neurodiversity: Insights from neuroscientific perspectives', *Encyclopedia*, 3(3), pp. 972–980.

Gombos, V., Pezdek, K. and Haymond, K. (2012). 'Forced confabulation affects memory sensitivity as well as response bias,' *Memory & Cognition*, 40(1), pp. 127–134. https://doi.org/10.3758/s13421-011-0129-5.

Gopnik, A. (2000). 'Explanation as orgasm and the drive for causal understandings: The evolution, function and phenomenology of the theory-formation system', in Keil, F. and Wilson, R. (eds.), *Cognition and Explanation*. Cambridge, MA: MIT Press, pp. 299–323.

Gudjonsson, G. (2016). 'Memory distrust syndrome, confabulation and false confession', *Cortex*. Advance onlinepublication. https://doi.org/10.1016/j.cortex.2016.06.013.

Gudjonsson, G.H. (1986). 'The relationship between interrogative suggestibility and acquiescence: Empirical findings and theoretical implications', *Personality and Individual Differences*, 7(2), pp. 195–199.

Gudjonsson, G.H. (2003). *The Psychology of Interrogations and Confessions: A Handbook*. Chichester: John Wiley & Sons Ltd.

Gudjonsson, G.H. and Clark, N.K. (1986) 'Suggestibility in police interrogation: A social psychology model', *Social Behaviour: An International Journal of Applied Social Psychology*, 1, pp. 83–103.

Gudjonsson, G.H., Clare, I.C.H., Rutter, S.C. and Pearse, J. (1993). 'Interrogative suggestibility, confabulation, and acquiescence in people with mild learning disabilities (mental handicap): Implications for reliability during police interrogations', *British Journal of Clinical Psychology*, 32(3), pp. 295–301.

Gudjonsson, G.H., Heaton-Armstrong, A., Griffiths, T., Justice, L., Rumbold, J. and Wolchover, D. (2021). 'The impact of confabulation on testimonial reliability', *Criminal Law Review*, 10, pp. 828–850.

Gudjonsson, G.H. and MacKeith, J.A.C. (1982). 'False confessions: Psychological effects of interrogation', in Trankell, A. (ed.), *Reconstructing the past: The role of psychologists in criminal trials*. Stockholm: P. A. Norstedt and Söners Förlag, pp. 253–269.

Gudjonsson, G.H., Sigurdsson, J.F., Bragason, O.O., Newton, A.K. and Einarsson, E. (2008). 'Interrogative suggestibility, compliance and false confessions among prisoners and their relationship with attention deficit hyperactivity disorder (ADHD) symptoms', *Psychological Medicine*, 38(7), pp. 1037–1044.

Gudjonsson, G.H., Sigurdsson, J.F., Young, S., Newton, A.K. and Peersen, M. (2009). 'Attention Deficit Hyperactivity Disorder (ADHD): How do ADHD symptoms relate to personality among prisoners?' *Personality and Individual Differences*, 47(1), pp. 64–68.

Gudjonsson, G.H., Sigurdsson, J.F., Sigurdardottir, A.S., Steinthorsson, H. and Sigurdardottir, V.M. (2014). 'The role of memory distrust in cases of internalised false confession', *Applied Cognitive Psychology*, 28(3), pp. 336–348.

Gudjonsson, G.H. and Young, S. (2010). 'Does confabulation in memory predict suggestibility beyond IQ and memory?', *Personality and Individual Differences*, 49, pp. 65–68.

Gudjonsson, G.H., Young, S. and Bramham, J. (2007). 'Interrogative suggestibility in adults diagnosed with attention-deficit hyperactivity disorder (ADHD): A potential vulnerability during police questioning', *Personality and Individual Differences*, 43(4), pp. 737–745. Available at: https://doi.org/10.1016/j.paid.2007.01.014 (4th April 2023).

Hillier, T. and Dingwall, G. (2021). *Criminal Justice and the Pursuit of Truth*. Bristol: Bristol University Press.

Innocence Project (2020). 'DNA evidence in the United States'. Available at: https://innocenceproject.org/dna-exonerations-in-the-united-states/ (Accessed 15 May 2023).

Johnson, M.K., Hayes, S.M., D'Esposito, M. and Raye, C. (2000). 'Confabulation', in Boller, F. and Grafman, J. (eds.), *Handbook of Neuropsychology*. 2nd edn. Vol. 2, *Memory and its Disorders*. Amsterdam: Elsevier Science, pp. 383–407.

Kassin, S.M. (2007). 'Internalized false confessions', in Toglia, M.P., Read, J.D., Ross, D.F. and Lindsay, R.C.L. (eds.), *The Handbook of Eyewitness Psychology, Vol. 1: Memory for Events*. Mahwah, NJ: Lawrence Erlbaum Associates Publishers, pp. 175–194.

Kassin, S.M., Drizin, S.A., Grisso, T., Gudjonsson, G.H., Leo, R.A. and Redlich, A.D. (2010). Police-induced confessions: Risk factors and recommendations. *Law and Human Behavior*, 34(1), 3–38. https://doi.org/10.1007/s10979-009-9188-6.

Kassin, S.M., Goldstein, C.C. and Savitsky, K. (2003). 'Behavioral confirmation in the interrogation room: On the dangers of presuming guilt', *Law and Human Behavior*, 27(2), pp. 187–203. https://doi.org/10.1023/A:1022599230598.

Kassin, S.M. and Gudjonsson, G.H. (2004). 'The psychology of confessions', *Psychological Science in the Public Interest*, 5(2), pp. 33–67. Available at: https://doi.org/10.1111/j.1529-1006.2004.00016.x.

Kassin, S.M. and Gudjonsson, G.H. (2005). 'True crimes, false confessions: Why do innocent people confess to crimes they did not commit?', *Scientific American Mind*. https://www.scientificamerican.com/article/true-crimes-false-confess/ (Accessed 27 January 2025)

Kassin, S.M. and Neumann, K. (1997). 'On the power of confession evidence: An experimental test of the fundamental difference hypothesis', *Law and Human Behavior*, 21(5), pp. 469–484. Available at: https://doi.org/10.1023/a:1024871622490.

Kassin, S. and Wrightsman, L. (eds.). (1985). 'Confession evidence', in *The Psychology of Evidence and Trial Procedure*. Beverly Hills: Sage Publications, pp. 67–94.

Kofler, M.J., Singh, L.J., Soto, E.F., Chan, E.S.M., Miller, C.E., Harmon, S.L. and Spiegel, J.A. (2020). 'Working memory and short-term memory deficits in ADHD: A bifactor modeling approach', *Neuropsychology*, 34(6), pp. 686–698.

Kopelman, M.D. (1987). 'Two types of confabulation', *Journal of Neurology, Neurosurgery, and Psychiatry*, 50, pp. 1482–1489.

Lentoor, A.G. (2023). 'Cognitive and neural mechanisms underlying false memories: Misinformation, distortion or erroneous configuration?' *AIMS Neuroscience*, 10(3), 255–268. https://doi.org/10.3934/Neuroscience.2023020.

Leo, R.A. (2009). 'False confessions: Causes, consequences, and implications', *PubMed*, 37(3), pp. 332–343.

Lind, S.E., Bowler, D.M. and Raber, J. (2014). 'Spatial navigation, episodic memory, episodic future thinking, and theory of mind in children with autism spectrum disorder: Evidence for impairments in mental simulation?' *Frontiers in Psychology*, 5, p. 1411.

Lyons, V. and Fitzgerald, M. (2013). 'Atypical sense of self in autism spectrum disorders: A neuro-cognitive perspective', in Fitzgerald, M. (ed.), *Recent Advances in Autism Spectrum Disorders: Volume one*. InTech. Available at: http://dx.doi.org/10.5772/53680.

Millward, C., Powell, S., Messer, D. and Jordan, R. (2000). 'Recall for self and other in autism: Children's memory for events experienced by themselves and their peers', *Journal of Autism and Developmental Disorders*, 30(1), pp. 15–28. Available at: https://doi.org/10.1023/A:1005455926727.

Moscovitch, M. and Melo, B. (1997). 'Strategic retrieval and the frontal lobes: Evidence from confabulation and amnesia', *Neuropsychologia*, 35(7), pp. 1017–1034.

Norris, R.J. (2017). *Exonerated: A History of the Innocence Movement*. New York: NYU Press.

North, A., Russell, A.J. and Gudjonsson, G.H. (2008). 'High functioning autism spectrum disorders: An investigation of psychological vulnerabilities during interrogative interview', *Journal of Forensic Psychiatry & Psychology*, 19(3), pp. 323–334.

Otgaar, H., Schell-Leugers, J.M., Howe, M.L., De La Fuente Vilar, A., Houben, S.T.L. and Merckelbach, H. (2021). 'The link between suggestibility, compliance, and false confessions: A review using experimental and field studies', *Applied Cognitive Psychology*, 35(2), pp. 445–456.

Office for Disability Issues and Department for Work and Pensions (2021). *Inclusive Communication: Inclusive Language – Words to Use and Avoid When Writing About Disability*. GOV.UK. Available at: https://www.gov.uk/government/publications/inclusive-communication/inclusive-language-words-to-use-and-avoid-when-writing-about-disability (Accessed 19 February 2024).

Pezdek, K., Lam, S.T. and Sperry, K. (2009). 'Forced confabulation more strongly influences event memory if suggestions are other-generated than self-generated', *Legal and Criminological Psychology*, 14(2), pp. 241–252. https://doi.org/10.1348/135532508X344773.

Poyser, S. and Milne, R. (2021). 'The time in between a case of "wrongful" and "rightful" conviction in the UK: Miscarriages of justice and the contribution of psychology to reforming the police investigative process', *International Journal of Police Science & Management*, 23(1), pp. 5–16. https://doi.org/10.1177/14613557211006134.

Purcell, R. (n.d.). *Acquired Neurodiversity: An Overview*. CareScribe. Available at: https://carescribe.io/blog/acquired-neurodiversity-an-overview/ (Accessed 18 April 2025).

Rabiee, A., Vasaghi-Gharamaleki, B., Samadi, S.A., Amiri-Shavaki, Y. and Alaghband-Rad, J. (2020). 'Working memory deficits and its relationship to autism spectrum disorders', *Iranian Journal of Medical Sciences*, 45(2), pp. 100–109.

Resnick, A. (2024). *What Does it Mean to be Neurotypical? Definition, History, Characteristics*. Updated 18 August. Medically reviewed by Block, D.B., MD. Available at: https://www.verywellmind.com/what-does-it-mean-to-be-neurotypical-5195483 (Accessed 26 April 2025).

Saarinen, S., Fontell, T., Vuontela, V., Carlson, S. and Aronen, E.T. (2015). 'Visuospatial working memory in 7- to 12-year-old children with disruptive behavior disorders', *Child Psychiatry and Human Development*, 46(1), pp. 34–43.

Sanders, A., Young, R. and Burton, M. (2010). *Criminal Justice*. 4th edn. Oxford: Oxford University Press.

Schnider, A. (2001). 'Spontaneous confabulation, reality monitoring, and the limbic system — a review', *Brain Research Reviews*, 36(2–3), pp. 150–160.

Schnider, A. (2018). *The Confabulating Mind: How the Brain Creates Reality*. 2nd edn. Oxford: Oxford University Press.

Shifton, J.J. (2019). 'How confession characteristics impact juror perceptions of evidence in criminal trials', *Behavioral Sciences & the Law*, 37(1), pp. 90–108. Available at: https://doi.org/10.1002/bsl.2398.

Snook, B., Fahmy, W., Fallon, L., Lively, C.J., Meissner, C.A., Luther, K., Barron, T. and House, J.C. (2020). 'Challenges of a "toolbox" approach to investigative interviewing: A critical analysis of the Royal Canadian Mounted Police's (RCMP) phased interview model', *Psychology, Public Policy, and Law*, 26(3), 261–273. https://doi.org/10.1037/law0000245.

Spitzer, D., White, S.J., Mandy, W. and Burgess, P.W. (2017). 'Confabulation in children with autism', *Cortex*, 87, pp. 80–95.

Szpitalak, M. and Polczyk, R. (2020). 'Reducing interrogative suggestibility: The role of self-affirmation and positive feedback', *PLOS ONE*, 15(7), p. e0236088. Available at: https://doi.org/10.1371/journal.pone.0236088.

Tata, P.R. and Gudjonsson, G.H. (1990). 'The effects of mood and verbal feedback on interrogative suggestibility', *Personality and Individual Differences*, 11(10), pp. 1079–1085. Available at: https://doi.org/10.1016/0191-8869(90)90069-M.

Turner, M.S., Cipolotti, L., Yousry, T.A. and Shallice, T. (2008). 'Confabulation: Damage to a specific inferior medial prefrontal system', *Cortex*, 44(6), pp. 637–648.

User Voice. (2021). *Neuro... What? Neurodiversity in the Criminal Justice System*. London: User Voice. Available at: https://www.uservoice.org/wp-content/uploads/2021/07/Neurodiversity-in-the-Criminal-Justice-System.pdf (Accessed 8 June 2023).

White, W.S. (2003). 'Confessions in capital cases', *University of Illinois Law Review*, 2003, pp. 979–1036.

Wiggins, A. and Bunin, J.L. (2021) 'Confabulation', in *StatPearls*. Treasure Island, FL: StatPearls Publishing. Available at: https://www.ncbi.nlm.nih.gov/books/NBK536961/.

Williams, D.M., Nicholson, T., Grainger, C., Lind, S.E. and Carruthers, P. (2018). 'Can you spot a liar? Deception, mindreading, and the case of autism spectrum disorder', *Autism Research*, 11(8), pp. 1129–1137.

Woodhouse, E., Hollingdale, J., Davies, L., et al. (2024). 'Identification and support of autistic individuals within the UK Criminal Justice System: A practical approach based upon professional consensus with input from lived experience', *BMC Medicine*, 22, p. 157. Available at: https://doi.org/10.1186/s12916-024-03320-3.

Young, S. and Bramham, J. (2007). *ADHD in Adults: A Psychological Guide*. Chichester, UK: John Wiley & Sons.

Young, S., González, R. A., Mullens, H., Mutch, L., Malet-Lambert, I. and Gudjonsson, G. H. (2018). 'Neurodevelopmental disorders in prison inmates: Comorbidity and combined associations with psychiatric symptoms and behavioural disturbance', *Psychiatry Research*, 261, pp. 109–115. https://doi.org/10.1016/j.psychres.2017.12.036.

Zhang, Y., Otgaar, H. and Wang, J. (2022). 'Memory distrust is related to memory errors, self-esteem, and personality', *Applied Cognitive Psychology*, 36(2), pp. 283–292.

Chapter 4

Understanding the Impact of FASD in Forensic Interviews

Challenges, Implications, and Recommendations

David Junior Gilbert, Uzma Naseem, Tania Goddard, Alan D. Price, Raja A. S. Mukherjee, Penny A. Cook, and Clare S. Allely

4.1 Introduction

Fetal Alcohol Spectrum Disorder (FASD) is a prevalent neurodevelopmental condition resulting from prenatal alcohol exposure (PAE).[1] Individuals with FASD are over-represented in global justice systems and may become victims of miscarriages of justice due to the low level of awareness among justice professionals. Using a vignette based on real-life stories of individuals, this chapter explores certain features of FASD which may set a context for vulnerability during forensic interviews including but not limited to interrogative suggestibility, compliance, and confabulation. Interrogative suggestibility is defined as the extent to which during formal interrogation, people accept the messages communicated by the interviewers, thereby influencing their subsequent responses. Compliance is the tendency of the individual to go along with propositions, requests, or instructions, for some immediate instrumental gain. Confabulation is the use of imaginary experiences to fill memory gaps and is considered a source of self-incrimination in suspects, victims, or witnesses of crime. Understanding these vulnerabilities is crucial for legal professionals to ensure fair and accurate handling of cases involving individuals with FASD, thereby reducing the risk of miscarriages of justice.

Our chapter starts by introducing PAE and the condition it causes—FASD. This is followed by a vignette and an exploration of the links between FASD/PAE and the justice system. We then proceed to discuss the forensic interview and how FASD may impact or present during forensic interviewing. We also include a brief delineation of vulnerabilities that may distinguish the FASD population from closely related conditions such as autism spectrum disorder (ASD) and attention deficit hyperactivity disorder (ADHD). We explore the legal implications of vulnerabilities during forensic interviews for individuals with FASD and examine why justice professionals may overlook indicators of FASD—ranging from a lack of awareness to overemphasis on intelligence quotient (IQ), co-occurring diagnoses, memory distrust syndrome, fluctuating capacity, and the frontal lobe paradox.[2] Finally, recommendations are provided for consideration by justice

DOI: 10.4324/9781003638742-5

professionals who are likely to encounter individuals with FASD during forensic interviews, followed by a summary and conclusion section.

4.2 Fetal Alcohol Spectrum Disorder

FASD describes a neurodevelopmental condition that affects individuals who have been exposed to PAE. FASD is often described as a brain and body disorder and is also a neurodivergent condition (Hoyme et al., 2016, Cook et al., 2016, Harding et al., 2019). This is because alcohol is a teratogen that has the capacity to penetrate every part of the developing foetus; teratogens are substances that can affect the development of a foetus, resulting in impairments (Alwan & Chambers, 2015). There are over 400 conditions that can coexist with FASD, ranging from mental health conditions to organ malformation, system dysfunction, and growth impairments among others (Popova et al., 2016). The severity of FASD and these coexisting conditions is dependent on many inter-related factors including genetics, maternal nutritional status, the level of PAE, timing of PAE, and frequency of PAE (Henderson et al., 2007, McQuire et al., 2020; Sulik, 2014).

Several diagnostic criteria prescribe different approaches to the diagnosis of FASD (Bower et al., 2017, Chudley et al., 2005, Hoyme et al., 2016). Currently, in settings such as England, Scotland, and Canada, the diagnostic nomenclatures are "FASD with sentinel features" and "FASD without sentinel features" (Scottish Intercollegiate Guidelines Network [SIGN], 2019). Other criteria, such as from the Institute of Medicine (Hoyme et al., 2016), or the University of Washington 4-Digit Code (Astley, 2006), may employ diagnostic labels such as Fetal Alcohol Syndrome (FAS), partial Fetal Alcohol Syndrome (pFAS), Alcohol Related Neurodevelopmental Disorder (ARND), and Alcohol Related Birth Defect (ARBD). Historically, FAS has been described as the most severe form due to its obvious physical presentation based on the sentinel features: short palpebral fissures (the opening between a person's eyelids), smooth philtrum (the ridge between the upper lip and nose), and a thin upper lip (among other characteristics). Recent research now highlights that the severity of FASD may not necessarily be related to the presence of sentinel features (Price et al., 2024, Webster et al., 2023), hence individuals without the "classic" presentation of the facial features in FASD may also present with the same level of impairments observed in individuals with the sentinel features. This means that without any obvious facial features or obvious signs, an individual may still be impacted by the effects of PAE but would be less likely to have been recognised as such.

While this chapter focuses on some of the challenges with and implications of FASD within the forensic context, we wish to acknowledge early on that many individuals with FASD possess unique strengths (Kautz-Turnbull et al., 2022, Flannigan et al., 2021, Ritter et al., 2025). Research indicates that these strengths may range from physical abilities, artistic abilities, among others, and attributes such as being kind, compassionate, and caring (Flannigan et al., 2018, Ritter et al., 2025). These strengths, as later discussed in this chapter, may sometimes mask the underlying vulnerabilities to, and within, the criminal justice system (CJS) encounters, which may later lead to self-incrimination, false confessions, and miscarriage of justice.

4.3 How Does FASD Relate to the Criminal Justice System?

Research from various countries has found that individuals with FASD are over-represented in the CJS (McLachlan et al., 2019, Popova et al., 2011, Popova et al., 2019). Before discussing this further, we wish to emphasise the importance of acknowledging this pattern, whilst avoiding reinforcing stigma or implying that contact with the CJS is an inevitable outcome for people with FASD. Many individuals with FASD do not encounter the CJS. Highlighting the issue of justice system over-representation in individuals with FASD should serve to promote better understanding and support, rather than causing further marginalisation. Evidence from a systematic review suggests that individuals with FASD are 19 to 40 times more likely to be engaged with the justice system (Popova et al., 2011). While the rate of FASD in the general population ranges between 3 and 5 per cent (McCarthy et al., 2021, May et al., 2018, Popova et al., 2019b), prevalence of FASD within the CJS is estimated to be as high as 46% in Canada (Mela et al., 2022) and 36% in Australia (Bower et al., 2018). However, the majority of countries lack prevalence data for individuals with FASD in contact with the CJS. Individuals with FASD are not inherently predisposed to criminal behaviour; the high rates of CJS contact reflect how impairments resulting from PAE can contribute to behavioural and cognitive vulnerabilities CJS engagement (Mukherjee et al., 2023, Wyper & Pei, 2015). As such, involvement with the CJS is a potential secondary outcome of FASD (Streissguth et al., 2004), that is, outcomes not directly consequential of FASD but because of environmental interactions. Corrado and McCuish (2015) found that individuals with FASD had an increased risk of early onset of offending.

Impairments experienced by individuals with FASD range from impulsive behaviour, lack of cause and effect understanding, adaptive behaviour challenges, aggressive behaviour and problems with memory (Tan et al., 2023, Crossac et al., 2023, Khalifa et al., 2022). The outcome of PAE may lead to behaviours that may generate interest from the CJS ranging from minor offending to serious criminal behaviour such as mass shootings as seen in some cases (Brown et al., 2024c, Tan et al., 2023). As will be detailed later in this chapter, individuals with FASD have a high likelihood of an ADHD diagnosis, reflecting the extent of impulsivity in this population. As detailed in the body of existing literature on ADHD and criminal justice, impulsivity can lead to high levels of engagement with the CJS.

Due to the cognitive and behavioural context, in addition to the evidence of justice system over-representation (Popova et al., 2019), there are reasonable grounds to believe that individuals with FASD are many times more likely to undergo forensic interviews compared to neurotypical individuals (Gilbert et al., 2022, Popova et al., 2019). Therefore, it is important that all forensic interviewers possess knowledge about FASD and have had opportunities to undertake the requisite training in conducting "safe interviews" (Gilbert et al., 2022, Steele, 2021)—that is, forensic interviews that take into consideration the vulnerabilities of interviewees and provide accommodations to minimise the likelihood of false confessions (Medford et al., 2003). This is important especially as research highlights the possibilities of self-incrimination within the CJS due to the vulnerabilities associated with PAE/FASD (Mukherjee et al., 2023, Gilbert et al., 2023).

4.4 The Forensic Interview and FASD

The forensic interview is a dynamic setting which typically involves the questioning of suspects, witnesses or victims of crimes; the questioning is usually about past events to obtain testimony that will aid the administration of justice (Newburn et al., 2012). For most forensic interviews, there is a dependence on the interviewee's comprehension, recollection and verbal statements to offer testimony. Testimony obtained during forensic interviews often extends beyond the interview itself, influencing subsequent stages of the criminal justice process, including decisions made up to and during sentencing. This demonstrates the implication of the verbal statements made by interviewees during such interviews, andone of the most significant and unfavourable outcomes from this process is a false confession.

It has long been established through experimental research that confession evidence remains the most potent form of evidence, followed by eyewitness and character testimony (Kassin and Neumann, 1997). For example, a recent systematic review and meta-analysis revealed the influence confessions have on jury decisions (Mindthoff et al., 2024). Drizin and Leo (2003) found that over 81% of defendants were found guilty by jurors despite evidence that their confessions were demonstrably false. Historically, it was considered counterintuitive that suspects would admit to crimes that they had not committed (Kassin, 2005). However, extensive literature and case studies show how miscarriages of justice can stem from the forensic interview stage where innocent individuals admit to crimes they have not committed (Kassin et al., 2010, Catlin et al., 2024, Gudjonsson & Pearse, 2011). Analysis of the literature in this area particularly points to duress and interview styles, reflecting coercion and its impact on confessions (Kassin et al., 2010).

There has been a noteworthy increase in understanding about how existing neurodevelopmental conditions may impact the admissibility of testimonies obtained during the interview of suspects, witnesses, and victims of crime. Some of the published studies in this area involve autistic individuals, individuals with intellectual disabilities, and Attention Deficit/Hyperactivity Disorder (ADHD), amongst others. Other chapters in this book discuss autistic individuals and individuals with ADHD alongside other neurodivergent conditions. However, very little has been studied in the FASD population despite evidence of the over-representation of individuals with FASD within the CJS (Gilbert et al., 2022). This requires research, as well as practical and professional consideration, especially since FASD is a prevalent condition within society due to the wide-ranging use and impact of alcohol (Popova et al., 2017).

The previous section in this chapter discussed the typical vulnerabilities evidenced in individuals with FASD. It is also important to mention that some of the highlighted vulnerabilities may also be seen in autism and ADHD (Mukherjee et al., 2012, Stevens et al., 2013). For example, individuals with FASD may also show communication differences (as seen in some autistic individuals) and challenges with impulse control (as seen in ADHD (Mukherjee, 2021)). Mukherjee et al. (2012) argue that the clinical features associated with FASD are mostly characteristic and not discriminatory—the latter being features peculiar to certain conditions; the former being features seen across different conditions (First & Westen, 2007, Blashfield & Draguns, 1976). From a clinical/biological standpoint, Mukherjee (2021) provide a differentiation between FASD, autism and ADHD with the argument that autism and ADHD are phenomenology-outcome-based diagnoses related to underlying neurological differences. In contrast, FASD is an aetiology-based diagnosis, i.e., the condition that has led to a classic presentation of neurological deficits. These deficits may not be uniquely seen in FASD; however, they would be expected to be seen. As Mukherjee (2021) explain, autism and ADHD are diagnoses based on behavioural presentation while FASD is a diagnosis that points to the causal agent (alcohol), hence the three conditions overlap. FASD is more comparable to other causes of neurological damage from genetic and non-genetic conditions, whereas autism and ADHD are common presentations in people with FASD (and other aetiological conditions). From a forensic standpoint, it is useful to also, where possible, delineate vulnerabilities that may be unique to the FASD population to assist forensic interviewers in practice.

There is emerging evidence that individuals with FASD may demonstrate unique vulnerabilities not typically seen in autism or ADHD. Identifying these differences can be particularly valuable in forensic settings, where understanding the specific needs and risks of the FASD population can assist in tailoring more appropriate approaches to interviewing and assessment. The next section explores suggestibility, compliance, and confabulation as potential markers of FASD-related impairments that may be especially relevant in forensic interview contexts.

4.4.1 Interrogative Suggestibility and Compliance

Interrogative suggestibility describes the extent to which individuals will accept suggestions during formal questioning and change their responses (Gudjonsson & Clark, 1986). The context of interrogative suggestibility involves a closed interaction where an interviewee is questioned about a past event, a suggestion is tendered (by the interviewer), then accepted (by the interviewee), and hence influences the behaviour of the interviewee. For an interviewee to be suggestible, the Gudjonsson and Clare (1986) model prescribes that there must be levels of uncertainty on the part of the interviewee, some expectations on the interview outcome (by the interviewee), and thirdly, some level of interpersonal trust between the interviewee and interviewer.

The assessment of interrogative suggestibility in forensic and mental health settings is currently measured using either of the two versions of the Gudjonsson suggestibility scales (GSS 1 and GSS 2) (Gudjonsson, 1987, Gudjonsson, 1984). These two parallel forms involve the reading of a short story to interviewees, after which they are asked to recall the story. The accuracy of their recall is measured, which gives a score for "immediate recall". Then, a 40-to-50-minute break is offered to interviewees where other activities are undertaken, after which 20 questions are posed, containing 15 leading questions that contain false suggestions. Once the answers to these questions are received from interviewees, regardless of performance, the interviewee is given some negative feedback: "you have made several errors. It is therefore necessary to go through the questions once more, and this time try to be more accurate". After the negative feedback, the 20 questions are repeated, and the following parameters are assessed: yield 1, which represents the number of false suggestions accepted by the interviewee; yield 2, the number of false suggestions accepted after negative feedback; shift, the number of changes in answers due to negative feedback; and total suggestibility, which defines overall susceptibility to suggestions.

Review articles and opinion pieces (Brown et al., 2015, Brown et al., 2020, Watts & Brown, 2016, Mukherjee et al., 2023) have described interrogative suggestibility in individuals with FASD, and a tendency for suggestibility has been confirmed in experimental studies (Gilbert et al., 2024a, Brown et al., 2011). These studies may provide a basis to distinguish the FASD population from conditions such as ADHD and autism where there are other causes. Using an experimental approach with the GSS 2, Brown et al. (2011) provide a foundational study of suggestibility in adults with FASD (n = 7). Participants demonstrated higher levels of suggestibility in comparison to individuals without FASD from the general population. More recently, interrogative suggestibility was studied in adolescents with FASD (n = 27) immediately and after one week of reassessment (Gilbert et al., 2024a). The FASD group evidenced higher levels of suggestibility immediately and after one week of reassessment.

With respect to suggestibility, autistic individuals and individuals with ADHD are not considered more suggestible than the neurotypical population (Maras & Bowler, 2012, North et al., 2008). However, this does not imply that autistic and ADHD groups are not vulnerable during CJS encounters. Current evidence shows that these two groups are more "compliant" than "suggestible", whereas the FASD population is typically more suggestible than neurotypical controls (Brown et al., 2011, Gilbert et al., 2024a). Although suggestibility and compliance are two closely related vulnerabilities that may impact interview outcomes, there are key differences between the two constructs. Compliance refers to admittance of false suggestions despite personal conviction that the suggestion is false (Gudjonsson, 2003, Gudjonsson, 1989). Suggestibility relates to the internalisation of false suggestions and admission to the same with the belief that the false suggestion is true (Gudjonsson, 2003, Gudjonsson, 1987).

4.4.2 Confabulation as a Vulnerability in Individuals with FASD

Confabulation is regarded as a significant "contaminant" in the testimony provided by suspects, witnesses, or victims of crime during investigative interviews (Gudjonsson, 2003). Gudjonsson (2003, 364) defines confabulation as "problems in memory processing where people replace gaps in their memory with imaginary experiences that they believe to be true". Confabulation may include portions of real events taken out of temporal context or involve the creation of a memory that never took place (Fotopoulou et al., 2007). Two of the most common types of confabulations found in the literature are provoked and spontaneous confabulation (Schnider et al., 1996). Spontaneous confabulations occur without an apparent cause and tend to be rare (Gilboa et al., 2006; Glowinski et al., 2008). In contrast, provoked confabulations occur in response to an external stimulus such as questions from a person in a position of authority (Kopelman, 1987). In some cases, the confabulated memory may be rooted in partial truth, and, in other cases, the confabulated memory may present as bizarre or delusional in nature. In these cases, only a corroborating witness such as a family member or friend may be able to confirm the veracity of the memory (Brown et al., 2017; Brown et al., 2020).

There is documented evidence of people with FASD providing narratives that are untrue (Rasmussen et al., 2008; Gilbert et al., 2025). Using the GSS 2, a recent experimental study evidenced significant confabulation in individuals with FASD when compared to neurotypical controls (Gilbert et al., 2025). The formal assessment of confabulation on the GSS 2 is based on the participants' retelling of the story that had been narrated to them earlier. Any correct fact remembered by a participant earns the participant one point while any fabrication or distortion is also noted and given one point respectively. Distortion is when the interviewee misconstrues any part of the GSS 2 story while fabrication is the addition of new items to the GSS 2 story. In the study by Gilbert et al. (2025), individuals with FASD fabricated more and had higher confabulation scores (distortion plus fabrication) after one week. Whilst this is the only experimental evidence of confabulation in individuals with FASD to date, confabulation is highlighted in reviews and expert opinion articles (Brown et al., 2020, Brown et al., 2017, Brown et al., 2022, Griffin, 2025).

Some studies have researched confabulation in autistic individuals. For instance, North et al. (2008) suggest that autistic individuals did not significantly differ in confabulation when compared to neurotypical controls. Confabulation, when studied in autistic children, was suggested to relate, in some cases, to social factors rather than poor memory (Spitzer et al., 2017). Tannock et al. (1993) in their study of a sample with ADHD, found more inaccuracies in reproducing narratives when compared to neurotypical controls. While more studies are required to delineate the difference in confabulation between the FASD, autistic and ADHD populations, the current state of evidence indicates that confabulation is significantly pronounced in individuals with FASD (Brown et al., 2017, Gilbert et al., 2025, Brown et al., 2020, Rasmussen et al., 2008), likely more so than in ADHD and autism.

4.5 Why Forensic Interviewers May Miss Signs of PAE/ FASD

The objective of this section is to present factors that may hinder the identification of PAE/FASD in impacted individuals as we try to answer the question: "why should forensic interviewers know about FASD?". Several factors may create circumstances where PAE/FASD is missed in suspects, witnesses or victims of crime and some of these are discussed below.

4.5.1 Lack of Knowledge

Arguably, lack of knowledge is the most common factor that may result in the lack of appreciation of the impact of FASD/PAE on the outcome of forensic interviews. Forensic interviewers commence their careers with the genuine intent of supporting society in resolving questionable circumstances that involve crimes. However, as knowledge advances and science progresses, there exists the challenge of keeping up to date with findings from contemporary research. Lack of knowledge about FASD in professionals working within the CJS has been identified as an issue, and this may lead to unfavourable outcomes for individuals with FASD (Hill et al., 2025, Kerimofski et al., 2024).

Several articles highlight the need for increased knowledge within the CJS (Hill et al., 2025, Brown et al., 2024a, Mukherjee et al., 2023, Passmore et al., 2018, Gilbert et al., 2024b). This is important because individuals with FASD are overrepresented within CJS settings (as discussed in section 5.2); hence, forensic interviewers may frequently engage with individuals impacted by FASD. Increased knowledge about FASD within forensic settings would serve as a protective factor against miscarriage of justice. Generally, there is also a lack of knowledge among health and social care professionals who may be able to provide documented evidence to CJS professionals (Mukherjee et al., 2015, Gilbert et al., 2021, McCormack et al., 2022).

4.5.2 Co-occurring Conditions and Trauma

In sections 1 and 2, we briefly discussed possible conditions that may exist alongside FASD. These conditions, in many cases, may mask the presence of FASD (also referred to as "diagnostic overshadowing"). ADHD and autism commonly co-occur with FASD, and the literature suggests links between PAE, autism, and ADHD (Weyrauch et al., 2017, Mukherjee et al., 2012). For example, heavy PAE was seen to be linked with autism (Mukherjee et al., 2011); a recent systematic review and meta-analysis study found that 50% of individuals with PAE had co-occurring ADHD, a rate much higher than in the general population (Clark et al., 2024). Conant et al. (2021) found that individuals with more than three neurodevelopmental diagnoses were seven times more likely to have FASD.

There is increased recognition that many individuals who encounter the CJS have significant amounts of trauma or adverse childhood experiences (ACEs). This is crucial as there is ample evidence about the links between trauma, ACEs, and vulnerabilities in forensic settings (Baglivio et al., 2014, Tan et al., 2022, Kambeitz et al., 2019). For example, studies have demonstrated vulnerability to interrogative pressure and leading questions in asylum seekers (Childs et al., 2021) and children who have experienced sexual abuse (Vagni et al., 2015). Often, individuals with FASD/PAE have experienced significant ACEs (Tan et al., 2022, Price et al., 2017). A chart review study of 196 patients found that individuals with any ACEs are nearly four times more likely to have PAE/FASD, while individuals with eight or more ACEs were six times more likely to have FASD (Conant et al., 2021). More recently, a meta-analysis of all available data showed that individuals with FASD have an average ACE score of 4.4 out of 10, which is far higher than the population average (Rockhold et al., 2025). So, there is a high level of comorbidity between FASD and ACEs. Clinical studies on the relative long-term impacts of PAE and ACEs suggest a complex picture which is not yet fully understood, but the studies show that PAE is a strong and significant predictor of many adverse developmental outcomes even when ACEs and other forms of adversity are taken into account (Astley-Hemingway et al., 2020; Price et al., 2017; Tan et al., 2022). In practice, this means that where individuals have a history of early life adversity, exposures during the prenatal stage, especially PAE, are likely to be part of the reason for any developmental, behavioural, or cognitive difficulties and should not be overlooked. In other words, we need to consider the prenatal stage whenever we are thinking about adverse childhood experiences.

4.5.3 The Emphasis on Intelligence Quotient (IQ)

IQ assessments are, in many jurisdictions, undertaken to assess the cognitive abilities of individuals who are in contact with the CJS (Katner, 2023, Beaver et al., 2013). In many instances, the assessments are conducted to rule out intellectual impairment in a bid to ensure that procedural support is offered to individuals who may be found vulnerable. The marker of vulnerability in this context refers to two standard deviations beyond the average IQ of 100 in the general population (Greenspan et al., 2015). Hence, any individual who is identified as possessing an IQ below 70 is considered vulnerable and requiring additional support. While this is useful in several respects, the literature suggests that there is an over-reliance on IQ as a marker of vulnerability (Greenspan et al., 2015, Brown et al., 2010, Brown, 2021).

It is well recognised that the results from IQ assessments are not a true marker of daily functionality. This is because IQ and adaptive behaviour are independent constructs (Arvidsson and Granlund, 2018, Tassé and Kim, 2023). Adaptive behaviour refers to the necessary daily activities required for social and personal independence (Schalock et al., 2010). Thus, the vulnerabilities that make daily functionality difficult are easily missed when IQ is completely relied upon in individuals with FASD (Brown, 2021). This is especially true for individuals with FASD where several studies have found that the average IQ of this population is above 70 (Streissguth et al., 2004, Greenspan et al., 2016). Thus, individuals with FASD may be considered capable because they possess an IQ over 70 but remain significantly vulnerable in day-to-day functionality. The term 'intellectual disability equivalence' has been applied for individuals with FASD (Greenspan et al., 2016), reflecting that while they do not meet the IQ-based criterion, they may exhibit vulnerabilities similar to individuals with intellectual disabilities, as also evidenced in a meta-analysis (Gilbert et al., 2026). It is proposed that adaptive behaviour assessment is the best indicator of daily functionality in this group (Brown, 2021). This does not diminish the importance of IQ assessments but, rather, is an argument for the use of adaptive behaviour assessments in addition to IQ results to understand underlying daily difficulties.

4.5.4 Frontal Lobe Paradox

Studies have found that some individuals with frontal lobe damage retain their language abilities (Fisher-Hicks et al., 2021, George & Gilbert, 2018, Teuber, 1964). Tuber (1964) presented the case of a man who, despite damage to his frontal lobes, retained unexpected communication abilities. With this ability, individuals with frontal lobe paradox will eloquently express themselves but show difficulties in executing what they have eloquently described (George & Gilbert, 2018). This is also seen in test situations where individuals will perform better at structured psychometric tests but struggle in daily life.

FASD can also be partially characterised as an injury to the frontal lobes, with alcohol being the reason for this injury (Hoyme et al., 2016). Recognising the concept of the frontal lobe paradox in relation to individuals with FASD is useful, as forensic interviewers will understand the link between structured test environments and real-world settings and functionality. Hence, entire dependence on results from structured assessments should be de-emphasised and a holistic approach employed to assess the vulnerabilities of individuals with FASD, referred to as a "whole-cloth" approach by Steele (2021).

4.5.5 Strengths and Fluctuating Capacity

Earlier in this chapter (section 5.1) we mentioned that individuals with FASD, despite their vulnerabilities, also possess unique strengths/abilities. These abilities range from physical agility, artistic capabilities and unique abilities to work with animals (Kautz-Turnbull et al., 2022, Ritter et al., 2025). Due to the obvious strengths displayed by many individuals with FASD, there could be an illusion of capacity leading to a tendency to overestimate abilities. In many instances, these strengths may be the markers employed to dismiss the vulnerabilities of individuals with FASD and lead to overestimation of capacity. Consequently, articles have referred to FASD as an invisible disability (Mather, 2015, Brown et al., 2024b).

Fluctuating capacity refers to the varied levels of abilities that are often seen in individuals with FASD. Referred to in some articles as a "spiky profile" (Buckard, 2021, Lehane, 2013), it is a concept that tries to explain how individuals with FASD may, for instance, demonstrate strengths in certain areas at a certain point in time but then show weaknesses in other areas or even the same area when reassessed. Temporal changes in ability may be misunderstood as malingering or an attempt to evade responsibility. This is evidenced in literature and by anecdotal evidence as a characteristic that may impact societal engagements. Dependent on the areas impacted by PAE, affected individuals may display varying levels of abilities which may exacerbate the levels of misjudgement from forensic professionals, hence leading to inappropriate approaches.

4.5.6 Memory Distrust Syndrome

Memory distrust syndrome refers to a person having low confidence in their memory, leading to a dependence on external cues (Gudjonsson, 2003). Within the context of forensic interviews, this may present as a source of self-incrimination as individuals exhibiting memory distrust syndrome become susceptible to suggestions. This syndrome is very much a proposition stemming from the literature with respect to individuals with poor memories (Gudjonsson et al., 1999). Individuals with FASD are known to possess poor memories and may experience memory distrust syndrome. Empirical studies confirm that individuals with FASD are at significant risk of memory impairments (Agnihotri et al., 2019, Flannigan et al., 2019, Mattson et al., 2019). Within CJS encounters, the possession of a good memory is considered an asset, as responses to forensic questioning require recollection from interviewees. Combined with suggestibility and low executive functioning and impaired cognitive abilities, individuals with FASD, due to distrust in their memories, may easily rely on external cues to respond. This could potentially lead to self-incrimination and ease of manipulation which forensic interviewers may miss. In the context of a qualitative exploration of vulnerabilities during CJS encounters, individuals with FASD described how they "inevitably got in trouble with the law" and they were easily "manipulated" (Gilbert et al., 2023).

4.5.7 The Impact of Misdiagnosis and Underdiagnosis

Because of under-reporting, lack of knowledge, and the overlapping symptoms seen in FASD with other neurodevelopmental conditions (among many other reasons), there is a likelihood of misdiagnosis and underdiagnosis (Chasnoff et al., 2015, Ergun et al., 2021, Morleo et al., 2011). Results from the study by Chasnoff et al. (2015) revealed a missed diagnosis rate of over 80% for FASD and misdiagnosis of 6.4%. The implications of misdiagnosis and underdiagnosis are likely to impact forensic interviews as professionals may not know about the existence of FASD in their interviewees.

4.6 Legal Implications of Missing FASD from Forensic Interviews

4.6.1 Behavioural Misinterpretation

The forensic interview is a highly dynamic process, comprising a nexus of complex interactions including verbal, body language, and eye contact, among others. Inherent in many interview techniques is the observation of body language, composure, tonality, eye contact and other cue-giving gestures (Moore & Fitzsimmons, 2011, Inbau et al., 2013). For example, in the Reid technique, which is employed in some settings, certain sub-steps in the interview technique prescribe the analysis of interviewee non-verbal and body language behaviour. In individuals with FASD, such cues may be unreliable (due to frontal lobe damage and lack of impulse control). Therefore, there is a tendency for interviewers to misinterpret these behaviours with the assumption of guilt. The assumption of guilt is identified as a potential factor that may impact interview style and hence lead to higher interrogative pressure. In turn, this may lead to a further increased risk of false confession due to the issues around suggestibility and confabulation described above (Meissner & Kassin, 2004, Ridley et al., 2012).

4.6.2 False Confessions and Miscarriages of Justice

A combination of a lack of knowledge, inappropriate identification of FASD/PAE, and consequent lack of recognition of the vulnerabilities of impacted individuals during forensic interviews may easily lead to false confessions (Douglas, 2015). FASD is broadly categorised as a psychological vulnerability within forensic contexts. Psychological vulnerabilities refer to mental conditions that may lead suspects, witnesses or victims of crime to produce inaccurate testimonies. As outlined at the outset of this chapter, the vulnerabilities evident in individuals with FASD do not suggest an inability to produce accurate testimony; however, the vulnerabilities reflect factors that may impact their testimonies. We therefore advocate for better understanding among forensic interviewers about FASD as a vulnerability, especially as the impact of PAE may lead to higher CJS interactions.

The weight of confession evidence within the CJS suggests the extent to which they may impact outcomes. If forensic interviewers fail to identify the presence of PAE/FASD and administer interviews without accommodation for the potential vulnerabilities, there are chances that unreliable testimonies may be obtained (Douglas, 2015, Gilbert et al., 2022). The courts of law mainly depend on the verbal testimonies from forensic interviews/cross-examinations alongside other evidence to administer judgement. If the obtained testimonies are impacted by the vulnerabilities identified within this chapter and beyond, this increases the chances of miscarriages of justice. This is clearly seen in the well-known case of Teina Pora from New Zealand, who was imprisoned for over 20 years for a crime he did not commit (*Pora v. The Queen* [2015] UKPC 9).

4.6.3 *Missed Opportunities for Diversion and Support*

In many jurisdictions, aside from punishment and an objective to achieve deterrence, there exists a CJS focus on rehabilitation. However, this has a mixed success rate (Cullen & Gilbert, 2012, Tonry, 2013). Often, the starting point for rehabilitation may be diversion and support, which may be initiated by forensic interviewers (Harmon-Darrow et al., 2023). However, research findings identify a lack of specialist knowledge as a barrier to the use of the diversion option by frontline officers (Green et al., 2020). Opportunities for diversion and support, and hence rehabilitation, may be missed if there is a lack of FASD knowledge within forensic interview settings. Individuals with FASD may be at risk of recidivism without the necessary rehabilitation support. Additionally, support such as the use of intermediaries may not be available if interviewers do not promptly recognise the impact of PAE/FASD.

4.7 "Matt": A Vignette Case Study for FASD/PAE in Forensic Interviews

In this section, we present a fictionalised vignette that describes "Matt" and his involvement in a forensic interview. We employ this case study to highlight the need for forensic interviewers and other professionals to investigate the potential of FASD/PAE, even if no official diagnosis is available. While "Matt" is a fictional composite of individuals that we have come across in the literature and in real-life settings, he shares many key features of FASD/PAE, including unique abilities and strengths that mask his difficulties. We estimate that there would be many undiagnosed individuals like "Matt" within the CJS.

Matt is a 35-year-old individual, with a documented history of PAE. Matt has had several encounters with the CJS, and a criminal record of over 45 offences, many of which are repeat crimes.

At first glance, Matt appeared articulate, charming, and even talented. His expressive language was strong, and his musical abilities on the piano impressed teachers and peers alike. This led to the talk of a possible audition with a national music group, with the hope that he would be admitted as part of the band. However, beneath these strengths lay a complex cognitive profile shaped by unrecognised prenatal alcohol exposure (PAE). Despite early signs of developmental difficulty, including impulsivity, memory problems, and disorganisation, his school dismissed his behaviours as deliberate. His lack of academic progress, repeated non-attendance, and exclusion only deepened the cycle of misunderstanding and punishment.

As Matt entered adolescence, his criminal record began to grow. By age 30, he had accumulated over 47 convictions. In court, professionals focused on his "knowledge of right and wrong", overlooking the more nuanced reality of his fluctuating capacity and tendency to confabulate. During interviews, Matt frequently provided inaccurate details—not to deceive, but due to his impaired memory and desire to please authority figures. He would echo suggestions or admit to offences he didn't fully understand, mirroring classic signs of suggestibility and memory distrust syndrome.

For example, during a forensic interview regarding a burglary, Matt initially denied involvement. However, when the interviewer gently suggested that others had placed him at the scene, Matt paused, became visibly anxious, and quickly changed his answer: "Yeah, maybe I was there—I can't remember, but if they said I was, I must've been". When probed further, he began to describe details that didn't align with the facts of the case—confabulating events he believed were expected of him. Despite not recalling the night clearly, Matt continued answering questions to maintain the rapport with the interviewer, often nodding and agreeing with suggestions even when they were inconsistent. He showed signs of impulsivity by interrupting questions to offer rapid, unfiltered responses, some of which contradicted his earlier statements. His eagerness to please was evident in his tone, facial expressions, and repeated attempts to "get it right", often asking the interviewer, "Is that what you meant?" or "Did I say it right this time?" No breaks were offered, and the interviewing officer, unaware of Matt's cognitive vulnerabilities, interpreted his cooperation and fluent speech as a sign of capacity and truthfulness.

The vignette offers a contextualised, narrative-based lens that illustrates how undiagnosed individuals may mask impairments through apparent strengths. This approach enhances practitioner awareness of subtle vulnerabilities. It also supports critical reflection on current interviewing practices. Ultimately, the vignette underscores the need for more inclusive, developmentally informed procedures.

4.8 Practice Recommendations

This section provides some brief recommendations that may be useful to professionals and practitioners.

4.8.1 *Continual Training on FASD*

There is a need for continual training of justice professionals on FASD. This is crucial considering the high likelihood of individuals impacted by PAE/FASD to encounter the CJS and consequently engage with forensic interviewers. With training on FASD continuously delivered to existing and new CJS professionals, the subtle signs that could serve as red flags for FASD could be easily identified before or during forensic interviews, even in the absence of a formal diagnosis.

Several authors estimate that within the CJS, there are significant cases of undiagnosed FASD; hence, training can be beneficial for forensic interviewers to identify behavioural presentations that may reflect potential PAE (Brown et al., 2015; Dunbar Winsor, 2021; Gilbert et al., 2022). Further to this, it is important that resources available to CJS professionals contain FASD-specific information; such resources include the Equal Treatment Bench Book published by the E&W Judicial College (Judicial College, 2025).

4.8.2 Screening for FASD

Screening tools have been developed which can be used within forensic settings to identify the likely existence of PAE or red flags for FASD (Jewell et al., 2024, Burd et al., 2021). Screening is different from formal diagnosis but can be beneficial in assisting forensic interviewers to conceptualise possible accommodations to ensure a fair interview for potentially impacted individuals (van Dooren et al., 2024). Recently, a systematic review (Jewell et al., 2024) found 11 existing screening tools that are applicable within forensic settings with 38 potential indicators of FASD across the screening tools. However, there are challenges in the identification of vulnerable individuals in CJS settings (Burton et al., 2006, Enang et al., 2019, Gudjonsson, 1993). Hence, the findings regarding existing screening tools for the identification of FASD demonstrate that these tools can be employed in forensic settings.

4.8.3 Interview Technique Modification

The modification of interview approaches will be useful in engagement with individuals impacted by PAE/FASD. As evidenced in the literature, individuals with FASD are vulnerable to leading questions, interrogative pressure and easily manipulated into verbalising what the interviewer wants to hear (Brown et al., 2011). There is an urgent need for recognition of FASD within the CJS and modification of interview approaches to avoid false confessions and miscarriages of justice. Some of the interview modifications that may be useful in this context include the use of simple language in structured, predictable environments; the use of open-ended questions in contrast to closed-ended questions; avoidance of leading questions as individuals with FASD may confabulate or mimic responses to please authority figures; the use of breaks and physical movement; and the use of alternative communication methods, like drawing or writing.

4.8.4 More Emphasis on Adaptive Behaviour Assessments alongside IQ Assessment

As discussed in section 5.3, there is a need for the consideration of adaptive behaviour assessments alongside IQ assessment results in forensic contexts. This is because adaptive behaviour assessments (also known as functional behaviour evaluations) offer ecologically valid insight into an individual's daily challenges (Brown, 2021). Several adaptive behaviour assessment tools are available, such as the Vineland Adaptive Behaviour Scales, which measure daily functionality across several subdomains and domains, such as socialisation, communication, and self-care (Sparrow & Cicchetti, 1989). An understanding of the daily challenges of individuals with FASD via adaptive behaviour assessments will further equip forensic interviewers with the requisite information needed to conduct interviews. Authors have also mentioned the addition of executive function assessments in addition to adaptive behaviour evaluation for individuals with FASD (Brookbanks et al., 2022, Mela et al., 2020)

4.8.5 Admission of Acquaintance Testimonies

Acquaintance testimonies—that is, reports provided by those who know an individual well, such as parents, caregivers, teachers, or support workers—are increasingly acknowledged as a practically useful approach for understanding the daily functional deficits of individuals with FASD (Brown et al., 2024c, Brown & Reynolds, 2021). Acquaintance testimonies provide context and insight into how individuals perform in real-world settings, particularly under stress or without support. Individuals with FASD may appear competent in structured environments but exhibit substantial challenges in adaptive behaviour, executive functioning, and social judgement in everyday life, as highlighted in Section 4.5.4. Acquaintance reports can help professionals understand patterns that may not be observable during brief assessments, such as repeated vulnerability to exploitation, difficulties following instructions over time, or inability to generalise learning across contexts (Stewart et al., 2018, Whitehurst, 2012). These insights are crucial for appropriate accommodations, risk management, and the prevention of miscarriages of justice. Moreover, when assessments mirror and reflect the environments in which individuals function daily, they are more realistic.

4.9 Conclusion

In this chapter, we have presented a brief insight into FASD as the direct outcome of PAE. More thoroughly, we have presented evidence of how PAE/FASD can provide a context for engagement with the CJS leading to over-representation. We further discuss the vulnerabilities that may lead to encounters with the CJS and how PAE/FASD may impact the forensic interview. PAE/FASD does not make an individual inherently criminal, but the characteristic brain impairments may lead to behaviours that are of interest to the CJS. Implications of failing to recognise FASD within forensic contexts have also been discussed.

Because forensic interviews are pivotal in the CJS, the core of our argument is that an increase in knowledge is needed for CJS professionals conducting forensic interviews who will regularly encounter individuals with FASD (diagnosed or undiagnosed) and PAE. There is an urgent need for increased awareness, screening for PAE/FASD, modification of interview approaches, and continual training of the forensic workforce in the recognition of individuals with FASD and their associated strengths and vulnerabilities.

Notes

1 Fetal and Foetal—Fetal, the American spelling variant is employed when referring to the diagnostic term of FASD. Foetus—Foetus is employed when the reference is not with respect to the diagnostic FASD term. Depending on which diagnostic framework has been used, FASD may be used as a singular diagnostic term (FASD) or a plural umbrella term (FASDs) which covers a range of specific diagnoses such as fetal alcohol syndrome and alcohol-related neurodevelopmental disorder. In this chapter, we will use the singular "FASD" as a broad term covering any diagnosis within the spectrum. We have employed the term "individuals with FASD" in accordance with the FASD preferred language guide approved and published by individuals with FASD through the National Organisation for FASD in the UK (FASD: Preferred UK Language Guide—National). FASD PAE is also used alongside FASD throughout the chapter to include individuals with undiagnosed FASD but with documented history of prenatal alcohol exposure. This is important as it represents an ecologically valid approach, as many people go undiagnosed. To ensure inclusive, respectful language we have tried to use identity-first constructions in referring to autistic individuals except in places where it is unavoidable.

2 As part of our ambition to support practising forensic interviewers to grasp the complexities that may mask PAE or FASD, the chapter includes a section entitled "Why forensic interviewers may miss signs of PAE/FASD".

References

Agnihotri, S., Subramaniapillai, S., Keightley, M., Rasmussen, C., Cameron, D., Ryan, J. & Rovet, J. 2019. Everyday memory difficulties in children and adolescents with fetal alcohol spectrum disorder. *Developmental Neurorehabilitation,* 22, 462–469.

Alwan, S. & Chambers, C. D. (2015). Identifying human teratogens: An update. *Journal of Pediatric Genetics*, 4(02), 039–041.

Arvidsson, P. & Granlund, M. 2018. The relationship between intelligence quotient and aspects of everyday functioning and participation for people who have mild and borderline intellectual disabilities. *Journal of Applied Research in Intellectual Disabilities,* 31, e68–e78.

Astley, S. J. 2006. Comparison of the 4-digit diagnostic code and the Hoyme diagnostic guidelines for fetal alcohol spectrum disorders. *Pediatrics*, 118(4), 1532–1545.

Baglivio, M. T., Epps, N., Swartz, K., Huq, M. S., Sheer, A. & Hardt, N. S. 2014. The prevalence of adverse childhood experiences (ACE) in the lives of juvenile offenders. *Journal of Juvenile Justice,* 3.

Beaver, K. M., Schwartz, J. A., Nedelec, J. L., Connolly, E. J., Boutwell, B. B. & Barnes, J. C. 2013. Intelligence is associated with criminal justice processing: Arrest through incarceration. *Intelligence,* 41, 277–288.

Blashfield, R. K. & Draguns, J. G. 1976. Evaluative criteria for psychiatric classification. *Journal of Abnormal Psychology,* 85, 140.

Bower, C., Elliott, E. J., Zimmet, M., Doorey, J., Wilkins, A., Russell, V., Shelton, D., Fitzpatrick, J. & Watkins, R. 2017. Australian guide to the diagnosis of foetal alcohol spectrum disorder: A summary. *Journal of Paediatrics and Child Health,* 53, 1021.

Bower, C., Watkins, R. E., Mutch, R. C., Marriott, R., Freeman, J., Kippin, N. R., Safe, B., Pestell, C., Cheung, C. S. C. & Shield, H. 2018. Fetal alcohol spectrum disorder and youth justice: A prevalence study among young people sentenced to detention in Western Australia. *BMJ Open,* 8, e019605.

Brookbanks, W., Mcginn, V. & Chu, J. T. W. 2022. Unfitness to stand trial and fetal alcohol spectrum disorder: Understanding and responding to FASD within the criminal justice system in New Zealand. *Behavioral Sciences & the Law,* 40, 159–169.

Brown, J., Asp, E., Carter, M. N., Spiller, V. & Bishop-Deaton, D. 2020. Suggestibility and confabulation among individuals with fetal alcohol spectrum disorder: A review for criminal justice, forensic mental health, and legal interviewers. *International Journal of Law and Psychiatry,* 73, 101646.

Brown, J., Huntley, D., Morgan, S., Dodson, K. D. & Cich, J. 2017. Confabulation: A guide for mental health professionals. *International Journal of Neurology and Neurotherapy,* 4, 133–160.

Brown, J., Jonason, A., Asp, E., Mcginn, V., Carter, M. N., Spiller, V. & Jozan, A. 2022. Fetal alcohol spectrum disorder and confabulation in psycholegal settings: A beginner's guide for criminal justice, forensic mental health, and legal interviewers. *Behavioral Sciences & the Law,* 40, 46–86.

Brown, J., Lewis, D. S., Kivisalu, T., Wartnik, A. P., Carter, M. N., Harr, D., Jozan, A. & Gilbert, D. J. 2024a. Fetal alcohol spectrum disorder (FASD) and the criminal justice system: A guide for legal professionals. *International Journal of Law and Psychiatry,* 97, 102029.

Brown, J., Russell, A., Andrews, T. & Cich, J. 2015. Fetal Alcohol Spectrum Disorder (FASD) in the criminal justice system: More common than you think. *Forensic Scholars Today*, 1(4), 9.

Brown, N. N. 2021. *Evaluating Fetal Alcohol Spectrum Disorders in the Forensic Context.* Springer.

Brown, N. N., Greenspan, S. & Steele, K. 2024b. A childhood marked by red flags. *The Parkland School Shooter: Culpability and FASD*, 19–32.

Brown, N. N., Greenspan, S. & Steele, K. 2024c. *The Parkland School Shooter*. Springer.

Brown, N. N., Gudjonsson, G. & Connor, P. 2011. Suggestibility and fetal alcohol spectrum disorders: I'll tell you anything you want to hear. *The Journal of Psychiatry & Law,* 39, 39–71.

Brown, N. N. & Reynolds, C. R. 2021. Connecting the dots: Functional behavior evaluation in fetal alcohol spectrum disorder. In *Evaluating Fetal Alcohol Spectrum Disorders in the Forensic Context: A Manual for Mental Health Practice*, 191–234. Springer International Publishing.

Brown, N. N., Wartnik, A. P., Connor, P. D. & Adler, R. S. 2010. A proposed model standard for forensic assessment of fetal alcohol spectrum disorders. *The Journal of Psychiatry & Law,* 38, 383–418.

Buckard, J. 2021. Social care issues and complex family relationships intertwined with FASD. In *Prevention, Recognition and Management of Fetal Alcohol Spectrum Disorders*, 339–357. Springer International Publishing.

Burd, L., Klug, M. G. & Husark, K. 2021. Prevalence of fetal alcohol spectrum disorder and screening in the forensic context. *Evaluating Fetal Alcohol Spectrum Disorders in the Forensic Context: A Manual for Mental Health Practice*, 59–83. Springer International Publishing.

Burton, M., Evans, R. & Sanders, A. 2006. *Are Special Measures for Vulnerable and Intimidated Witnesses Working?: Evidence from the Criminal Justice Agencies.* Citeseer.

Catlin, M., Wilson, D. B., Redlich, A. D., Bettens, T., Meissner, C. A., Bhatt, S. & Brandon, S. E. 2024. Interview and interrogation methods and their effects on true and false confessions: A systematic review update and extension. *Campbell Systematic Reviews,* 20, e1441.

Chasnoff, I. J., Wells, A. M. & King, L. 2015. Misdiagnosis and missed diagnoses in foster and adopted children with prenatal alcohol exposure. *Pediatrics*, peds–2014, 135(2), 264–270.

Childs, S., Given-Wilson, Z., Butler, S., Memon, A. & Gudjonsson, G. 2021. Vulnerability to interrogative suggestibility from negative life events. A comparison of separated asylum-seeking youth and age-matched peers. *Personality and Individual Differences,* 173, 110600.

Chudley, A. E., Conry, J., Cook, J. L., Loock, C., Rosales, T. & Leblanc, N. 2005. Fetal alcohol spectrum disorder: Canadian guidelines for diagnosis. *Canadian Medical Association Journal,* 172, S1–S21.

Clark, C. A., Nakhid, D., Baldwin-Oneill, G., Lapointe, S., Macisaac-Jones, M., Raja, S. & Mcmorris, C. A. 2024. Prevalence of co-occurring diagnoses in people exposed to alcohol prenatally: Findings from a meta-analysis. *Journal of Affective Disorders,* 358, 163–174.

Conant, B. J., Sandstrom, A., Jorda, M., Klug, M. G. & Burd, L. 2021. Relationships between fetal alcohol spectrum disorder, adverse childhood experiences, and neurodevelopmental diagnoses. *Open Journal of Pediatrics,* 11, 580–596.

Cook, J. L., Green, C. R., Lilley, C. M., Anderson, S. M., Baldwin, M. E., Chudley, A. E., Conry, J. L., Leblanc, N., Loock, C. A. & Lutke, J. 2016. Fetal alcohol spectrum disorder: A guideline for diagnosis across the lifespan. *Cmaj,* 188, 191–197.

Corrado, R. R. & Mccuish, E. C. 2015. The development of early onset, chronic, and versatile offending: The role of fetal alcohol spectrum disorder and mediating factors. *International Journal of Child and Adolescent Health,* 8, 241.

Crossac, D., Adamsab, I. & Symonsacd, M. 2023. Exploring offending characteristics of young people with foetal alcohol spectrum disorder in Western Australia.

Cullen, F. & Gilbert, K. 2012. *Reaffirming Rehabilitation,* Routledge.

Douglas, H. A. 2015. Foetal alcohol spectrum disorders: A consideration of sentencing and unreliable confessions. *Journal of Law and Medicine,* 23, 427–442.

Drizin, S. A. & Leo, R. A. 2003. The problem of false confessions in the post-DNA world. *North Carolina Law Review,* 82, 891.

Dunbar Winsor, K., 2021. An invisible problem: Stigma and FASD diagnosis in the health and justice professions. *Advances in Dual Diagnosis*, 14(1), 8–19.

Enang, I., Murray, J., Dougall, N., Wooff, A., Heyman, I. & Aston, E. 2019. Defining and assessing vulnerability within law enforcement and public health organisations: A scoping review. *Health & Justice,* 7, 1–13.

Ergun, G., Schultz, M. S. & Rettig, E. K. 2021. Fetal alcohol spectrum disorder—Issues of misdiagnosis and missed diagnosis in black youth: A case report. *Innovations in Clinical Neuroscience,* 18, 20.

First, M. B. & Westen, D. 2007. Classification for clinical practice: How to make ICD and DSM better able to serve clinicians. *International Review of Psychiatry,* 19, 473–481.

Fisher-Hicks, S., Wood, R. L. & Qc, B. B. 2021. The frontal lobe paradox. *Neuropsychological Aspects of Brain Injury Litigation.* Routledge.

Flannigan, K., Harding, K., Reid, D. & Family Advisory, C. 2018. Strengths among individuals with FASD. *CanFASD Research Network.*

Flannigan, K., Pei, J., Burke, A., Frenzel, R. & Rasmussen, C. 2019. Neurocognitive functioning in young offenders with fetal alcohol spectrum disorder. *International Journal of Law and Psychiatry,* 65, 101347.

Flannigan, K., Wrath, A., Ritter, C., Mclachlan, K., Harding, K. D., Campbell, A., Reid, D. & Pei, J. 2021. Balancing the story of fetal alcohol spectrum disorder: A narrative review of the literature on strengths. *Alcoholism: Clinical and Experimental Research,* 45, 2448–2464.

Fotopoulou, A., Conway, M. A. & Solms, M. 2007. Confabulation: Motivated reality monitoring. *Neuropsychologia,* 45, 2180–2190.

George, M. & Gilbert, S. 2018. Mental Capacity Act (2005) assessments: Why everyone needs to know about the frontal lobe paradox. *The Neuropsychologist,* 5, 59–66.

Gilboa, A., Alain, C., Stuss, D. T., Melo, B., Miller, S. & Moscovitch, M. 2006. Mechanisms of spontaneous confabulations: A strategic retrieval account. *Brain,* 129(6), 1399–1414.

Gilbert, D. J., Allely, C., Mukherjee, R., Gudjonsson, G., Novick Brown, N., Brown, J., Mcginn, V. & Cook, P. 2025. An empirical examination of confabulation in adolescents with Fetal Alcohol Spectrum Disorder (FASD). *Journal of Pediatric Neuropsychology.*

Gilbert, D. J., Allely, C. S., Gudjonsson, G., Mukherjee, R. A. S. & Cook, P. A. 2024a. Immediate and repeat interrogative suggestibility in a sample of adolescents with fetal alcohol spectrum disorder. *Diversity & Inclusion Research,* 1, e12007.

Gilbert, D. J., Allely, C. S., Hickman, N., Mukherjee, R. A. S. & Cook, P. A. 2023. 'I inevitably get in trouble… in one way or another': Qualitative exploration of the vulnerabilities and experiences of justice system encountered individuals with fetal alcohol spectrum disorder. *Forensic Science International: Mind and Law,* 100124.

Gilbert, D. J., Allely, C. S., Mukherjee, R. A. S. & Cook, P. A. 2022. Foetal alcohol spectrum disorder and Investigative interviewing: A systematic review highlighting clinical and legal implications and recommendations. *Behavioral Sciences & the Law,* 40, 170–185.

Gilbert, D. J., Azumara, S. I., Wheatcroft, J. M., Steele, K., Cook, P., Mukherjee, R., Gudjonsson, G. & Brown, N. N. 2026. FASD and intellectual disability equivalence: A meta-analysis of suggestibility during forensic interviews. *Behavioral Sciences & the Law.* https://doi.org/10.1002/bsl.70052.

Gilbert, D. J., Day, A. M., Allely, C. S. & Rowland, A. G. 2024b. Safeguarding neurodivergent children: A call to professionals.

Gilbert, D. J., Mukherjee, R. A. S., Kassam, N. & Cook, P. A. 2021. Exploring the experiences of social workers in working with children suspected to have fetal alcohol spectrum disorders. *Adoption & Fostering,* 45, 155–172.

Glowinski, R., Payman, V. & Frencham, K. 2008. Confabulation: A spontaneous and fantastic review. *Australian & New Zealand Journal of Psychiatry,* 42(11), 932–940.

Green, R., Gray, R. M., Bryant, J., Rance, J. & Maclean, S. 2020. Police decision-making with young offenders: Examining barriers to the use of diversion options. *Australian & New Zealand Journal of Criminology,* 53, 137–154.

Greenspan, S., Brown, N. N. & Edwards, W. 2016. FASD and the concept of "intellectual disability equivalence". In *Fetal Alcohol Spectrum Disorders in Adults: Ethical and Legal Perspectives,* edited by M. Nelson and M. Trussler, 241–260. Springer. https://doi.org/10.1007/978-3-319-20866-4_14.

Griffin, R. 2025. *Life in the FASD Lane: Rossi's Fabulous Guide to Navigating Your Teens and Young Adulthood.* Jessica Kingsley Publishers.

Gudjonsson, G. H. 1984. A new scale of interrogative suggestibility. *Personality and Individual Differences,* 5, 303–314.

Gudjonsson, G. H. 1987. A parallel form of the Gudjonsson Suggestibility Scale. *British Journal of Clinical Psychology,* 26, 215–221.

Gudjonsson, G. H. 1989. Compliance in an interrogative situation: A new scale. *Personality and Individual Differences,* 10, 535–540.

Gudjonsson, G. H. 1993. *Persons at risk during interviews in police custody: The identification of vulnerabilities.* Unipub.

Gudjonsson, G. H. 2003. *The Psychology of Interrogations and Confessions: A Handbook.* John Wiley & Sons.

Gudjonsson, G. H. & Clark, N. K. 1986. Suggestibility in police interrogation: A social psychological model. *Social Behaviour.*

Gudjonsson, G. H., Kopelman, M. D. & Mackeith, J. A. C. 1999. Unreliable admissions to homicide: A case of misdiagnosis of amnesia and misuse of abreaction technique. *The British Journal of Psychiatry,* 174, 455–459.

Gudjonsson, G. H. & Pearse, J. 2011. Suspect interviews and false confessions. *Current Directions in Psychological Science,* 20, 33–37.

Harding, K., Flannigan, K. & Mcfarlane, A. 2019. *Policy action paper: Toward a standard definition of fetal alcohol spectrum disorder in Canada.* CanFASD.

Harmon-Darrow, C., Afkinich, J., Franke, N. D. & Betz, G. 2023. Police diversion at arrest: A systematic review of the literature. *Criminal Justice and Behavior,* 50, 307–329.

Hemingway, S. J. A., Davies, J. K., Jirikowic, T. & Olson, E. M. 2020. What proportion of the brain structural and functional abnormalities observed among children with fetal alcohol spectrum disorder is explained by their prenatal alcohol exposure and their other prenatal and postnatal risks?. *Advances in Pediatric Research,* 7, 41.

Henderson, J., Gray, R. & Brocklehurst, P. 2007. Systematic review of effects of low–moderate prenatal alcohol exposure on pregnancy outcome. *BJOG: An International Journal of Obstetrics & Gynaecology,* 114, 243–252.

Hill, G., Gerry Kc, F., Herlihen, P., Allely, C. S. & Gilbert, D. J. 2025. *Foetal Alcohol Spectrum Disorder (FASD) and the Courts: How England and Wales Could Benefit From Following an Australian Model.* Wiley Online Library.

Hoyme, H. E., Kalberg, W. O., Elliott, A. J., Blankenship, J., Buckley, D., Marais, A.-S., Manning, M. A., Robinson, L. K., Adam, M. P. & Abdul-Rahman, O. 2016. Updated clinical guidelines for diagnosing fetal alcohol spectrum disorders. *Pediatrics,* 138, e20154256.

Inbau, F. E., Reid, J. E., Buckley, J. P. & Jayne, B. C. 2013. *Essentials of the Reid Technique: Criminal Interrogation and Confessions.* Jones & Bartlett Publishers.

Jewell, E., Dunleavy, B., Faitakis, M., Pun, J. W., Moss, S., Pei, J., Mela, M., Flannigan, K., Tremblay, M. & Mclachlan, K. 2024. Screening and identification of fetal alcohol spectrum disorder in criminal legal settings: A realist review. *Criminal Behaviour and Mental Health,* 34, 208–270.

Judicial College. 2025. *Equal Treatment Bench Book.* July 2024 edition, updated May 2025. [online] Courts and Tribunals Judiciary. Available at: https://www.judiciary.uk/about-the-judiciary/diversity/equal-treatment-bench-book/ [Accessed 18 Jul. 2025].

Kambeitz, C., Klug, M. G., Greenmyer, J., Popova, S. & Burd, L. 2019. Association of adverse childhood experiences and neurodevelopmental disorders in people with fetal alcohol spectrum disorders (FASD) and non-FASD controls. *BMC Pediatrics,* 19, 1–9.

Kassin, S. M. 2005. On the psychology of confessions: Does innocence put innocents at risk? *American Psychologist,* 60, 215.

Kassin, S. M., Drizin, S. A., Grisso, T., Gudjonsson, G. H., Leo, R. A. & Redlich, A. D. 2010. Police-induced confessions: Risk factors and recommendations. *Law and Human Behavior,* 34, 3–38.

Kassin, S. M. & Neumann, K. 1997. On the power of confession evidence: An experimental test of the fundamental difference hypothesis. *Law and human Behavior,* 21, 469–484.

Katner, D. R. 2023. Juvenile competency complications: Protocol, unmet needs, developmental immaturity, FASD, and comorbidity. *American Journal of Law & Medicine,* 49, 173–192.

Kautz-Turnbull, C., Adams, T. R. & Petrenko, C. L. M. 2022. The strengths and positive influences of children with fetal alcohol spectrum disorders. *American Journal on Intellectual and Developmental Disabilities,* 127, 355–368.

Kerimofski, K. L., Panton, K. R. & Pestell, C. F. 2024. Australian psychologists' knowledge, confidence, and practices in fetal alcohol spectrum disorder diagnostic assessment. *Alcohol: Clinical and Experimental Research,* 48, 653–666.

Khalifa, N., Magee, T., Shirazi, S., Salman, S., Yang, C. C. & Mela, M. 2022. The neurocognitive profiles of justice involved people with foetal alcohol spectrum disorder: A systematic review. *Behavioral Sciences & the Law,* 40, 87–111.

Kopelman, M. D. 1987. Two types of confabulation. *Journal of Neurology, Neurosurgery & Psychiatry,* 50(11), 1482–1487.

Lehane, T. 2013. *Educating Children and Young People with Fetal Alcohol Spectrum Disorders: Constructing Personalised Pathways to Learning.* Taylor & Francis.

Maras, K. L. & Bowler, D. M. 2012. Brief report: Suggestibility, compliance and psychological traits in high-functioning adults with autism spectrum disorder. *Research in Autism Spectrum Disorders,* 6, 1168–1175.

Mather, M. 2015. *The Invisible Disability.* SAGE Publications Sage UK.

Mattson, S. N., Bernes, G. A. & Doyle, L. R. 2019. Fetal alcohol spectrum disorders: A review of the neurobehavioral deficits associated with prenatal alcohol exposure. *Alcoholism: Clinical and Experimental Research,* 43, 1046–1062.

May, P. A., Chambers, C. D., Kalberg, W. O., Zellner, J., Feldman, H., Buckley, D., Kopald, D., Hasken, J. M., Xu, R. & Honerkamp-Smith, G. 2018. Prevalence of fetal alcohol spectrum disorders in 4 US communities. *Jama,* 319, 474–482.

Mccarthy, R., Mukherjee, R. A. S., Fleming, K. M., Green, J., Clayton-Smith, J., Price, A. D., Allely, C. S. & Cook, P. A. 2021. Prevalence of fetal alcohol spectrum disorder in Greater Manchester, UK: An active case ascertainment study. *Alcoholism: Clinical and Experimental Research,* 45, 2271–2281.

Mccormack, J. C., Chu, J. T. W., Marsh, S. & Bullen, C. 2022. Knowledge, attitudes, and practices of fetal alcohol spectrum disorder in health, justice, and education professionals: A systematic review. *Research in Developmental Disabilities,* 131, 104354.

Mclachlan, K., Mcneil, A., Pei, J., Brain, U., Andrew, G. & Oberlander, T. F. 2019. Prevalence and characteristics of adults with fetal alcohol spectrum disorder in corrections: A Canadian case ascertainment study. *BMC Public Health,* 19, 1–10.

McQuire, C., Daniel, R., Hurt, L., Kemp, A. & Paranjothy, S. 2020. The causal web of foetal alcohol spectrum disorders: A review and causal diagram. European Child & Adolescent Psychiatry, 29(5), 575–594.

Medford, S., Gudjonsson, G. H. & Pearse, J. 2003. The efficacy of the appropriate adult safeguard during police interviewing. *Legal and Criminological Psychology,* 8, 253–266.

Meissner, C. A. & Kassin, S. M. 2004. "You're guilty, so just confess!" Cognitive and behavioral confirmation biases in the interrogation room. *Interrogations, Confessions, and Entrapment*, 85–106. Springer US.

Mela, M., Flannigan, K., Anderson, T., Nelson, M., Krishnan, S., Chizea, C., Takahashi, S. & Sanjanwala, R. 2020. Neurocognitive function and fetal alcohol spectrum disorder in offenders with mental disorders. *The Journal of the American Academy of Psychiatry and the Law,* 48, 195–208.

Mela, M., Wall, L., Buttinger, P., Desroches, A. & Wrath, A. J. 2022. Rates and implications of fetal alcohol spectrum disorder among released offenders with mental disorder in Canada. *Behavioral Sciences & the Law,* 40, 144–158.

Mindthoff, A., Ferreira, P. A. & Meissner, C. A. 2024. The effect of confession evidence on jurors' verdict decisions: A systematic review and meta-analysis. *Law and Human Behavior,* 48, 163.

Moore, T. E. & Fitzsimmons, C. L. 2011. Justice imperiled: False confessions and the Reid technique. *Criminal Law Quarterly,* 57, 509.

Morleo, M., Woolfall, K., Dedman, D., Mukherjee, R., Bellis, M. A. & Cook, P. A. 2011. Under-reporting of foetal alcohol spectrum disorders: An analysis of hospital episode statistics. *BMC Pediatrics,* 11, 14.

Mukherjee, R., Cook, P. A., Gilbert, D. & Allely, C. S. 2023. Overview of offenders with fetal alcohol spectrum disorders. *Forensic Aspects of Neurodevelopmental Disorders: A Clinician's Guide*, 84.

Mukherjee, R., Wray, E., Curfs, L. & Hollins, S. 2015. Knowledge and opinions of professional groups concerning FASD in the UK. *Adoption and Fostering,* 39, 212–224.

Mukherjee, R. A., Hollins, S. & Curfs, L. 2012. Fetal alcohol spectrum disorders: Is it something we should be more aware of? *Journal of the Royal College of Physicians of Edinburgh,* 42, 143–150.

Mukherjee, R. A. S. 2021. Diagnosing FASD in the context of other overlapping neurodevelopmental presentations. In *Prevention, Recognition and Management of Fetal Alcohol Spectrum Disorders*, 157–170. Springer International Publishing.

Mukherjee, R. A. S., Layton, M., Yacoub, E. & Turk, J. 2011. Autism and autistic traits in people exposed to heavy prenatal alcohol: Data from a clinical series of 21 individuals and nested case control study. *Advances in Mental Health and Intellectual Disabilities,* 5, 42–49.

Newburn, T., Williamson, T. & Wright, A. 2012. *Handbook of Criminal Investigation.* Routledge.

North, A. S., Russell, A. J. & Gudjonsson, G. H. 2008. High functioning autism spectrum disorders: An investigation of psychological vulnerabilities during interrogative interview. *The Journal of Forensic Psychiatry & Psychology,* 19, 323–334.

Passmore, H. M., Mutch, R. C., Burns, S., Watkins, R., Carapetis, J., Hall, G. & Bower, C. 2018. Fetal Alcohol Spectrum Disorder (FASD): Knowledge, attitudes, experiences and practices of the Western Australian youth custodial workforce. *International Journal of Law and Psychiatry,* 59, 44–52.

Popova, S., Lange, S., Bekmuradov, D., Mihic, A. & Rehm, J. 2011. Fetal alcohol spectrum disorder prevalence estimates in correctional systems: A systematic literature review. *Canadian Journal of Public Health,* 102, 336–340.

Popova, S., Lange, S., Poznyak, V., Chudley, A. E., Shield, K. D., Reynolds, J. N., Murray, M. & Rehm, J. 2019b. Population-based prevalence of fetal alcohol spectrum disorder in Canada. *BMC Public Health,* 19, 1–12.

Popova, S., Lange, S., Probst, C., Gmel, G. & Rehm, J. 2017. Estimation of national, regional, and global prevalence of alcohol use during pregnancy and fetal alcohol syndrome: A systematic review and meta-analysis. *The Lancet Global Health,* 5, e290–e299.

Popova, S., Lange, S., Shield, K., Burd, L. & Rehm, J. 2019. Prevalence of fetal alcohol spectrum disorder among special subpopulations: A systematic review and meta-analysis. *Addiction.*

Popova, S., Lange, S., Shield, K., Mihic, A., Chudley, A. E., Mukherjee, R. A. S., Bekmuradov, D. & Rehm, J. 2016. Comorbidity of fetal alcohol spectrum disorder: A systematic review and meta-analysis. *The Lancet,* 387, 978–987.

Pora v The Queen [2015] UKPC 9, [2015] 2 NZLR 651.

Price, A., Allely, C. & Mukherjee, R. 2024. Fetal alcohol spectrum disorders: Where we have come from, trends, and future directions. *Minerva Pediatrics.*

Price, A., Cook, P. A., Norgate, S. & Mukherjee, R. 2017. Prenatal alcohol exposure and traumatic childhood experiences: A systematic review. *Neuroscience & Biobehavioral Reviews,* 80, 89–98.

Rasmussen, C., Talwar, V., Loomes, C. & Andrew, G. 2008. Brief report: Lie-telling in children with fetal alcohol spectrum disorder. *Journal of Pediatric Psychology,* 33, 220–225.

Ridley, A. M., Gabbert, F. & La Rooy, D. J. 2012. *Suggestibility in Legal Contexts: Psychological Research and Forensic Implications*. John Wiley & Sons.

Ritter, C., Mclachlan, K., Baig, M. F., Mcmurtry, M. & Lumley, M. N. 2025. Evaluating the role of strengths and protective factors for youth with FASD and criminal legal system involvement: A scoping review. *Psychiatry, Psychology and Law*, 1–41.

Rockhold, M. N., Handley, E. D. & Petrenko, C. L. 2025. Understanding the intersection of prenatal alcohol exposure and postnatal adversity: A systematic review from a developmental psychopathology lens. *Alcohol: Clinical and Experimental Research,* 49(1), 25–42.

Schalock, R. L., Borthwick-Duffy, S. A., Bradley, V. J., Buntinx, W. H. E., Coulter, D. L., Craig, E. M., Gomez, S. C., Lachapelle, Y., Luckasson, R. & Reeve, A. 2010. *Intellectual Disability: Definition, Classification, and Systems of Supports*. ERIC.

Schnider, A., Von Däniken, C. & Gutbrod, K. 1996. The mechanisms of spontaneous and provoked confabulations. *Brain,* 119, 1365–1375.

Scottish Intercollegiate Guidelines Network (Sign). 2019. *Children and Young People Exposed Prenatally to Alcohol: A National Clinical Guideline*. SIGN. (SIGN publication no. 156). Available at: https://www.sign.ac.uk/assets/sign156.pdf [Accessed 16 July 2025].

Sparrow, S. S. & Cicchetti, D. V. 1989. *The Vineland Adaptive Behavior Scales*. Allyn & Bacon.

Spitzer, D., White, S. J., Mandy, W. & Burgess, P. W. 2017. Confabulation in children with autism. *Cortex,* 87, 80–95.

Steele, K. A. 2021. Relevance of fetal alcohol spectrum disorder in the forensic context. *Evaluating Fetal Alcohol Spectrum Disorders in the Forensic Context: A Manual for Mental Health Practice*, 19–57.

Stevens, S. A., Nash, K., Koren, G. & Rovet, J. 2013. Autism characteristics in children with fetal alcohol spectrum disorders. *Child Neuropsychology,* 19, 579–587.

Stewart, M., Lawley, L., Tambour, R. & Johnson, A. 2018. Listening in a settler state: (Birth) mothers as paraprofessionals in response to FASD. *Imagining Child Welfare in the Spirit of Reconciliation: Voices from the Prairies*, 45–68.

Streissguth, A. P., Bookstein, F. L., Barr, H. M., Sampson, P. D., O'malley, K. & Young, J. K. 2004. Risk factors for adverse life outcomes in fetal alcohol syndrome and fetal alcohol effects. *Journal of Developmental & Behavioral Pediatrics,* 25, 228–238.

Sulik, K. K. 2014. Fetal alcohol spectrum disorder: Pathogenesis and mechanisms. *Handbook of Clinical Neurology.* Elsevier.

Tan, G. K. Y., Pestell, C. F., Fitzpatrick, J., Cross, D., Adams, I. & Symons, M. 2023. Exploring offending characteristics of young people with foetal alcohol spectrum disorder in Western Australia. *Psychiatry, Psychology and Law,* 30, 514–535.

Tan, G. K. Y., Symons, M., Fitzpatrick, J., Connor, S. G., Cross, D. & Pestell, C. F. 2022. Adverse childhood experiences, associated stressors and comorbidities in children and youth with fetal alcohol spectrum disorder across the justice and child protection settings in Western Australia. *BMC Pediatrics,* 22, 587.

Tannock, R., Purvis, K. L. & Schachar, R. J. 1993. Narrative abilities in children with attention deficit hyperactivity disorder and normal peers. *Journal of Abnormal Child Psychology,* 21, 103–117.

Tassé, M. J. & Kim, M. 2023. Examining the relationship between adaptive behavior and intelligence. *Behavioral Sciences,* 13, 252.

Teuber, H.-L. 1964. The riddle of frontal lobe function in man. *The Frontal Granular Cortex and Behavior*, 410–444.

Tonry, M. 2013. Sentencing in America, 1975–2025. *Crime and Justice,* 42, 141–198.

Vagni, M., Maiorano, T., Pajardi, D. & Gudjonsson, G. 2015. Immediate and delayed suggestibility among suspected child victims of sexual abuse. *Personality and Individual Differences,* 79, 129–133.

Van Dooren, F. E. P., Hodgson, H. H. A., Hamilton, O., Johnson, E., Fitzpatrick, J., Connor, E. & Pedruzzi, R. A. 2024. Development of a Model of Care resource for FASD in the justice system. *International Journal of Adolescence and Youth,* 29, 2368883.

Watts, E. J. & Brown, J. 2016. Interrogative suggestibility in people with fetal alcohol spectrum disorder (FASD): Neurocognitive and behavioral challenges. *Forensic Scholars Today,* 1, 1–8.

Webster, B. M., Carlisle, A. C. S., Livesey, A. C., Deeprose, L. R., Cook, P. A. & Mukherjee, R. A. S. 2023. Evaluating the difference in neuropsychological profiles of individuals with FASD based on the number of sentinel facial features: A service evaluation of the FASD UK National Clinic Database. *Children,* 10, 266.

Weyrauch, D., Schwartz, M., Hart, B., Klug, M. G. & Burd, L. 2017. Comorbid mental disorders in fetal alcohol spectrum disorders: A systematic review. *Journal of Developmental and Behavioral Pediatrics,* 38, 283–291.

Whitehurst, T. 2012. Raising a child with foetal alcohol syndrome: Hearing the parent voice. *British Journal of Learning Disabilities,* 40, 187–193.

Wyper, K. & Pei, J. 2015. Neurocognitive difficulties underlying high risk and criminal behaviour in FASD: Clinical Implications. *Fetal Alcohol Spectrum Disorders in Adults: Ethical and Legal Perspectives: An Overview on FASD for Professionals.* Springer.

Chapter 5

It Needs to Be a More Holistic Approach

Person-Centred Care to Support Autistic People and People with Learning Disabilities in Prisons

Rachael Mason, Lauren Smith, Niko Kargas, Jim Rogers, and Todd Hogue

5.1 Introduction

In 2021, the National Health Service (NHS) in England published guidance on the design and delivery of healthcare services in prisons for autistic people and people with learning disabilities, being seen as two forms of variation when considering neurodiversity. The document sets out principles for healthcare providers who support people in prison. These include the need to employ person-centred care, where the wishes of the individual are respected and upheld, and where they are actively involved in decision-making regarding their care. This chapter provides an overview of a service evaluation conducted for NHS England focused on how prisons across the Midlands region in England were implementing the guidance. The findings from the service evaluation are contextualised within the person-centred care framework (Rogers, 1942, 1967), exploring how relationships influenced the effective and humanised care of autistic people and people with learning disabilities in prison.[1]

Respect for individuals and the provision of equal opportunities, including access to healthcare, is central within current models of understanding neurodivergence. The medical model conceptualises health conditions as pathologies that need medical treatment to restore a person to "normal" functioning, and this approach dominates Western responses to health (Cleland and Cotton, 2011). Pellicano and den Houting (2022) argue that this medical model, which explains neurodivergence as arising from a person's biology and diagnosed through persistent deficits, is flawed. They argue the model employs an approach that suggests the problem is within the person who needs to be fixed, failing to account for social and environmental influences. The authors stress the need to view people as unique individuals who interact with their environments, which may present barriers for them. In addition, they state it is essential that neurodivergent people are at the centre of collaborations to drive change. This approach, often referred to as the neurodiversity model, fosters the move to a more holistic person-centred approach.

DOI: 10.4324/9781003638742-6

Despite understanding the role of other factors in relation to neurodivergence, it has been argued there is a place for the medical model, especially when research has found that early mortality rates are higher in autistic people (Hirvikoski et al., 2018) and people with attention deficit hyperactivity disorder (ADHD) (London and Landes, 2016). These studies highlighted that comorbidities were a contributing factor to mortality and concluded the need for medical interventions that considered how to support the specific health needs of neurodivergent people. More recent discussions have explored the divide between the medical and neurodiversity models and suggested there may not be a need to take sides. Knopes (2025) explored how people conceptualised their mental health, finding that participants often used both models to talk about their health. For example, some participants discussed the biomedical nature of their conditions which helped to remind them this was not their fault but were also critical of the model when there were limitations in the medicalised solutions. In addition to this medical narrative, they also described their mental health conditions as a valuable form of difference, highlighting their strengths which aligned greater with the neurodiversity model. Knopes (2025) concluded that people "tell many different kinds of stories about their lives" (p. 29) and these narratives should help create an expansive and inclusive view of health. Understanding this complexity and the nuanced way people view their health, Browning and Veit (2025) support the use of multiple models rather than seeing them in opposition. The focus should be on understanding the person and their experiences, reinforcing the importance of person-centred care and the role of relationships when providing this.

Person-centred care originated with Carl Rogers, a psychologist who believed that people are experts in their own lives and have the capacity to understand themselves better than anyone else. Rogers (1942) believed the role of a therapist or counsellor is to create the right atmosphere that allows individuals to explore and harness their own strengths and support continual growth. Central to this is the therapeutic relationship that exists between two people and where there are three core conditions: unconditional positive regard, empathy, and congruence (Rogers, 1967). Unconditional positive regard is the acceptance of a person and their worth without judgement. Empathy is a willingness to understand the person, their feelings and thoughts, from their perspective. Congruence refers to being authentic and includes the therapist/counsellor having an awareness of their own feelings and how these may present in the relationship. These core conditions have influenced the development of person-centred approaches, highlighting the importance of addressing power imbalances in relationships through open dialogue rather than providing prescriptive advice to people seeking support.

A training framework for staff in health and social care professions was devised by Health Education England, Skills for Health, and Skills for Care in 2017. It outlined what is needed to work in a person-centred way and sets out three steps for putting this into action: (1) conversations to engage with people, (2) conversations to enable and support people, and (3) conversations to collaboratively manage risk and complexity. Communication is key to this implementation plan, and the use of skills such as open questions, active listening, reflection, affirmation, and normalisation to demonstrate empathy is promoted. The training explores required knowledge such as the wider determinants of health, co-production approaches, relevant policy, and how to engage in activities such as advocacy, shared decision making, and operationalising peer support. Despite this framework, and much research and guidance into person-centred care, many autistic people and people with learning disabilities continue to not receive humanised care (Quinn et al., 2023). Turning to the prison environment, person-centred care faces further challenges. The tension between prisons being a place of custody versus providing care can prevent people working in them from showing compassion (Solell and Smith, 2019). Research by Santorso (2021) into a new regime implemented in Italy where the focus was on rehabilitation found that people in prison were treated more humanely and provided with greater agency. However, these changes shifted the power and expanded the role of the prison officer, which caused role confusion and conflicted with their professional identities. Santorso (2021) concluded that prison officers viewed the empowerment of people in prison as increasing the distance in relationships with officers, rather than building it. Nevertheless, establishing positive relationships between staff and people in prison has been found to be beneficial for both, leading to better wellbeing and improved rehabilitation efforts (Lambert et al., 2014; van Ginneken et al., 2020). This reinforces the need to continue to strive towards humanised approaches that focus on developing relationships to improve outcomes.

The service evaluation that forms the basis of this chapter has been reported in full elsewhere (Kargas et al., 2023). This chapter focuses on the qualitative data gathered using questionnaires with 175 prison staff and interviews and focus groups with 93 people detained in 24 prisons in England. It utilises the core conditions of person-centred care (unconditional positive regard, empathy, and congruence) as a lens to explore the data, enhancing the evidence base on the strengths and challenges of providing this approach to autistic people and people with learning disabilities specifically within a prison environment.

5.2 Literature Review

The extent of neurodivergence in prison is not fully understood. Due to variation in definitions and which conditions are included, screening and assessment waiting times and tools used, information sharing, and where information is kept and by whom, the ability to accurately say how many people experience neurodivergence is difficult (Criminal Justice Joint Inspectorate [CJJI], 2021; Loucks, 2007; UserVoice, 2021). However, prevalence rates have been an ongoing area of enquiry alongside the exploration of assessment, the relationship between neurodivergence and offending behaviour, and the "treatment" or support provided, demonstrating the dominance of the medicalised approach to exploring neurodivergence. A cursory exploration of associated terms relating to neurodivergence and prison[2] in EBSCOhost retrieved 206,017 entries. When changing the requirements to academic peer-reviewed journals in English, this reduced to 91,479, and when focusing these terms on the abstract, 3,677 articles were returned. This shows the depth of information and the focus that has been given to elements of neurodivergence in a prison setting over the past 100 years. An overview of key points from this research is discussed below.

The first discussion potentially linked to neurodivergence was by Martin in 1927 who published an article on the development of prison psychoses. Although not explicitly referring to neurodivergence as understood today, many of the medical symptoms described in the paper mirror those related to conditions now considered as neurodivergence, highlighting the complexity and diagnostic overshadowing of neurodivergence and other mental health conditions such as psychosis (Nikolic et al., 2024). Martin (1927) explored whether the prison environment was a factor in the development of these conditions or if they developed prior to prison. Whilst discussing chronic deteriorating psychoses, he described men who had been in repeated conflict with the discipline system resulting in punishments and had been in solitary confinement on multiple occasions. Solitary confinement was an aggravating factor in the development of the paranoid characteristic seen in the group he was describing, due to it leading to "autistic daydreaming and the intellectual deterioration" (p. 411). Therefore, the knowledge that solitary confinement is an exacerbating factor for neurodivergent people has been evident for some time. However, there are many neurodivergent people still spending time in separation units negatively impacting their mental health (Independent Monitoring Boards, 2024). For some neurodivergent people, separation from the main prison population is viewed positively as it reduces sensory overload and provides safety (Bahri et al., 2024; Vinter et al., 2023). However, this could be managed in a therapeutic way such as using specialist sensory rooms instead (ibid).

Martin (1927) described chronic cases of deteriorating psychoses as sometimes developing suddenly and that "unintelligent handling at such times precipitates an assault upon the officer" (p. 411). Martin reflected on this violence and stated that it was often an expression of inferiority and persecution that the person had been repressing. More recent work (UserVoice, 2021) similarly reported frustration felt by neurodivergent people due to not being understood and how this sometimes contributed to aggression towards others. Martin (1927) noted that during acute periods, individuals inflicted injuries upon themselves including suicide attempts. Research has continued to show that autistic people are more at risk of completing suicide, suicidal ideation, self-harm, and self-injury (Camm-Crosbie et al., 2018; Jokiranta-Olkoniemi et al., 2020; Newell et al., 2023; Oliphant et al., 2020). Martin (1927) concluded with the observation that the psychoses he witnessed were "apparently excited by the prison milieu" (p. 414), paving the way for understanding the complex interplay between neurodivergence within the prison context, with many of his findings supported in current research.

Sukhareva (1927, translated by Simmonds and Sukhareva, 2020), discussed gender differences observed between males and females with schizoid psychopathies, now understood to be autism. She reported that females presented emotional disturbances which she described as "with the stamp of vulgarity, quirkiness, and eccentricity" (p. 561) alongside experiencing both sensitivity and emotional numbness, which she described as "inner tension in combination with outward coldness" (p. 561). Males presented with "tendencies towards superfluous abstraction, absurd rumination, stereotyped movements, and motor deficiencies" (p. 561). This is possibly the first discussion of gender differences in relation to autism and helps to understand the different support needs that may be required when working with different gender identities in prisons.

In a paper exploring the benefits of milieu therapy with adolescent sociopaths, Walker (1978) refers to hyperkinetic disorder. This was a diagnosis presented in the previous edition (10th) of the International Classification of Diseases (ICD-10) (World Health Organization, 2016) and resembles the diagnosis for ADHD in the Diagnostic and Statistical Manual of Mental Disorders fifth edition (DSM-5) (Tulchinsky and Varavikova, 2014). Walker (1978) said it was obvious that "incarceration should be avoided as much as possible because it is not curative" (p. 534). Instead, she advocated for early identification and treatment of hyperkinesis including the use of medication and support for learning disabilities through literacy and maths. In addition to taking a holistic approach, Gormley and Watson (2021) also advocated for end-to-end support through the complex justice system which disadvantaged neurodivergent people.

The relationship between people providing and people receiving support has gained attention. Walker (1978) recognised the benefits of peer support; an opportunity to talk with someone who understands the difficulties, better able to employ empathy, and "is also confronted with a person whom he cannot 'con'" (p. 535). Peer support and mentor programmes continue to be viewed as an essential element of support for neurodivergent people in prison, but are not consistently employed and this still appears in recommendations to improve support (CJJI, 2021; UserVoice, 2021). The importance of the relationship between people is echoed in more recent research (Vinter et al., 2024) where it is argued that the prison climate is a social phenomenon that includes the relationship between staff and people detained. The research found a negative perception of this climate among neurodivergent people. To improve relationships, and subsequently wellbeing and readiness for treatment, Vinter et al. (2024) suggested additional neurodiversity awareness and training are needed in prisons, highlighting this is important if staff are perceiving non-engagement as a sign of defiance or anti-sociality, rather than as a coping strategy. This would help to build more empathetic and understanding relationships between people to foster effective support.

When discussing empathy in relation to neurodivergence, it is important to note the double empathy problem described by Milton (2012). When a neurotypical person engages with a neurodivergent person, they are communicating in different ways, and when trying to be empathetic towards the other person, this may be misinterpreted. Milton (2012) suggested autistic people may perceive empathy from a neurotypical person as imposing and even threatening. The problem is experienced by both people in the social interaction and is the fault of neither person. Therefore, ways to overcome the double empathy problem are required. Finke and Dunn (2023) suggest overcoming empathy disconnect takes effort, opportunity and practice; if people wish to improve the social interactions, repeated engagements are needed to learn and develop better communication and empathy.

A review exploring the relationship between learning disabilities and criminality suggested that society viewed people with learning disabilities more negatively in certain circumstances, including in relation to crime (Coons, 1982). Coons (1982) noted that assessment procedures "are in a serious state of disarray" (p. 257) and that assessment is a complex process, requiring an interdisciplinary team. More recently, Walker et al. (2025) reported the prevalence of neurodivergence in a secure psychiatric hospital in the UK, finding that many patients experienced a wide range of variations. Due to this, they argue whether the term neurodivergence is useful in this context because ultimately, different variants and people have differing needs. They raise the issue that screening is difficult in practice as there is not one tool to screen for all neurodivergent variations, and if it could, it would be lengthy. When exploring what a "neurodiverse model of care" would look like, they recommended that assessments should take place once a person is settled in the environment and should include observational assessments, for example, on "difficulties with following instructions, retaining information and any 'oddities' in behaviour" (p. 177). Slokan and Ioannou (2021) also noted difficulty in the range of variations within neurodivergence and ensuring resources are best placed in prisons to support people. They suggest instead that training should focus on developing skills in identifying people who need support, with clear pathways in place for this.

Recent research found that a combination of being neurodivergent and having exposure to adverse childhood experiences increases the risk of being arrested and incarcerated (Wilson et al., 2024). The neurodivergent population in this study experienced a high prevalence of adverse childhood experiences, and the authors suggested this may help to explain health inequalities experienced. Day (2025) suggested that neurodivergence may relate to a trauma response following childhood adversity. Her research into a family support project found that trauma-informed approaches helped deliver successful support to neurodivergent people and their families. The strengths of the family project were grounded in the relationships developed between people. This included building trust and psychological safety, collaboration, and taking a strengths-based approach, resulting in needs-led support (Day, 2025), akin to the person-centred approach.

5.3 Methods

5.3.1 Overview

The service evaluation upon which this chapter is based had 15 questions to address, set by NHS England in relation to the *Meeting the Healthcare Needs of Adults with a Learning Disability and Autistic Adults in Prison Guidance* document (NHSE, 2021). Questions included establishing the prevalence of autism and learning disabilities, screening and assessment practices, staff training and confidence, reasonable adjustments, care pathways, specialist services and staff, medication use, equitable access to services, joint care planning, and information sharing.

Five data collection activities were used:

1. a scoping review of existing literature (reported elsewhere – Rogers et al., 2022);
2. collation of prevalence data held by healthcare providers;
3. Staff questionnaires capturing all departments working within the prisons;
4. focus groups and interviews with self-reported autistic people or people with learning disabilities in prison;
5. staff questionnaires for teams in pre- and post-prison services.

The evaluation covered the Midlands area of England, and at the time of the review (April 2022–March 2023) included 26 prisons. Of these, 24 engaged in at least one data collection activity: 18 male prisons, three male and young offenders' institutions (YOI), one exclusively YOI, and two women's prisons. The prisons spanned the range of male prison security categories (A-D) and functions (local, training, resettlement, women's). Fifteen focus prisons were selected to ensure a range of categories and types. Focus prisons were the location of focus groups and interviews with autistic people and people with learning disabilities in prison.

An advisory board oversaw the project. The board included people with lived experience of the justice system and neurodivergent people. The board focused on reviewing the engagement strategy, designing materials, supporting analysis, and developing recommendations. For the remainder of this method section, only the elements utilised in this chapter (qualitative data collected within prisons from staff and people detained in prison – activities 3 and 4) will be described.

5.3.2 *Sample*

Ninety-three autistic people and people with learning disabilities took part in focus groups or interviews, with 81 identifying as male or transgender male and 12 identifying as female or transgender female. The age of participants ranged from 19 to 62, and the majority (73% for focus groups and 76% for interviews) described their ethnicity as White British. In terms of neurodivergence, 66% of the participants in focus groups and 71% in the interviews had confirmed diagnosed or self-reported autism, and 41% in the focus groups and 71% in the interviews reported learning disabilities (many declared both). Many participants also declared other neurodivergent variations such as ADHD, but this was not formally recorded due to being outside the scope of the evaluation. For the prison staff questionnaire, 175 people responded with sufficient information from 23 prisons.

5.3.3 Evaluation Tools

Focus groups and interviews followed a semi-structured interview schedule. This asked people to describe their demographic information, followed by experiences of being autistic or having a learning disability in prison. The inquiry explored suggestions for future support delivery. A 33-item questionnaire was developed for prison staff, aligning to the overarching service evaluation questions.

5.3.4 Procedure

Focus groups were conducted by two researchers. Before each group or interview, the information sheet was discussed, and informed consent was secured. Focus groups and interviews were either audio recorded for later transcription, or in a few cases where security clearance had not been granted for using a Dictaphone, detailed notes with verbatim quotes were captured. It is acknowledged this may have presented gaps in the data captured, but this was facilitated by having two researchers present. Questionnaires were administered using the online survey platform, Qualtrics. The link to the questionnaire was circulated via e-mail to all staff within each prison. This captured staff employed by the prison alongside partner agencies including healthcare and education.

5.3.5 Analysis

Qualitative data were organised using NVivo software and analysed through the person-centred lens.

5.3.6 Ethics

Ethical approval was sought from both HMPPS National Research Committee (Reference 2022_193) and the University of Lincoln Ethics Application Service (Reference 2022_10018). Information sheets informed participants of the voluntary nature of their involvement, their ability to withdraw, and the confidential nature of participation. This was caveated with the acknowledgement that disclosures which suggested a risk to self or others would be escalated. Sources of support were included on the information sheet and consent was gained from each participant.

5.4 Results and Discussion

The results of the service evaluation in answering the 15 questions set by NHS England are reported elsewhere (Kargas et al., 2023). In summary, the evaluation made four key recommendations to help improve the support for neurodivergent people in prison. These were:

1. Creating a universal care pathway.
2. Developing staff training.
3. Facilitating reasonable adjustments.
4. Improving information sharing.

For the purpose of this chapter, the qualitative data from the staff questionnaires alongside the focus groups and interviews with autistic people and people with learning disabilities were re-analysed to explore the application of person-centred care and the three core conditions of unconditional positive regard, empathy, and congruence (Rogers, 1942, 1967).

5.4.1 Unconditional Positive Regard

There appeared to be two core barriers to staff displaying an unconditional positive regard towards people in prison. The first was that some prison staff appeared to deny the existence of autism or additional needs, meaning that people in prison felt unheard and unsupported:

> I know certain officers have searched my condition out, and then they go, 'well, there's nothing really wrong, you know', and I went, 'well if you don't believe me, contact [healthcare]'.
>
> (man in prison)

> Prison staff do not understand with many actively either denying autism or making fun.
>
> (staff)

Denial and suspicion among some staff appeared to have led them to conclude that some people were being manipulative, and this negatively impacted their interactions with people in prison, leading to confusion:

> I've tried to tell the truth about something, they've turned back around and said, 'you're trying to manipulate us'. And they're claiming I've lied, but when I told the truth, they're saying that I'm trying to manipulate, and that makes me think, shall I try and tell the truth, or should I just lie? Because when I do tell the truth they're saying I'm manipulating.
>
> (young person in prison)

Such misunderstanding aligns with historical literature (Martin, 1927) and more recent reporting (User Voice, 2021) which highlighted that neurodivergent prisoners are frequently misunderstood and misinterpreted, leading to the second barrier we saw. There were many accounts of where misinterpretation led to negative consequences for the individual and was akin to what Martin reported in 1927 with the use of seclusion:

> I believe that all too often autistic prisoners who are in meltdown/shutdown are seen as difficult, troublesome and somehow trying to fight the system.
>
> (staff)

> Many of the autistic prisoners end up in segregation because of their behaviour while they are in distress.
>
> (staff)

A common misinterpretation was that people were being rude or disruptive when this was not their intention. For some, the behaviour was a result of trying to cope with their environment, echoing observations from staff that distress could end in a punishment for people. This could result in poorer outcomes within the system, reminiscent of the challenges in accessing equitable justice raised by Gormley and Watson (2021):

> I get told I am disruptive because I am interrupting or making excessive noise to get attention, or fidgeting, known as stemming, or using bad language. I am not disruptive, it is a cry for help, but it doesn't get recognised.
>
> (man in prison)

> [In an adjudication] I became so disruptive as I wasn't given the support I needed. I was removed from the room. I was struggling to understand the questions that were being asked of me in a way I could understand, I ended up getting a loss of canteen for 14 days.
>
> (man in prison)

> Go through it slowly with me instead of ploughing straight into it, I can't digest it properly, can't focus on it properly, it gets you irritated and then you just leave the room, this happened in the parole board. They were rushing through everything and I couldn't understand. It affected my parole hearing by a year.
>
> (transgender woman in prison)

Overall, the inability to develop relationships based on unconditional positive regard reduced opportunities for people in prison:

> It feels like a game of snakes and ladders to be fair, if you think you're making progression, and suddenly, it's like two steps forward, and then you hit a snake, you've got to go back to the start.
>
> (man in prison)

The judgement and behaviours described above show a contradiction to the guidance on person-centred care (NHSE, 2021). Conversely, when staff were able to suspend judgement and hold people in unconditional positive regard, this contributed to reduced incidents and improved outcomes for people in prison. This was achieved through taking time to get to know and understand the person, and through exploring behaviours rather than punishing them:

> I'd say that understanding with a prisoner's point of view, it stops the violence for one…their understanding of the person, or understand that they're not doing it because they wanna do it, they're doing it because their brain works in a different way.
>
> (young person in prison)

> Staff here take the time to get to know you. Since being on the wing, I'm enhanced, I'm a cleaner, I have structure, regime, and staff get to know you a bit more, they have one to one sessions with you and they ask, 'can we help you?'
>
> (man in prison)

> [Healthcare staff] has a lot more understanding because she will sit there and she'll talk to you and plus, she listens. And she goes, 'you need to do it that way'...she'll try and guide you in the right direction. If it wasn't for [staff], I would be getting nicked every week.
>
> (man in prison)

However, even when there were no practical solutions, feeling unjudged, heard and supported was received positively:

> When it is someone that is willing to help, because they want to help, I don't care if my problems never get fixed but if there is somebody that is willing to, it is great... if you have genuine people around you can see the light, just knowing you have support no matter what, even when you are having bad days.
>
> (man in prison)

One place participants frequently reported unconditional positive regard was within prisoner-led initiatives such as groups run by autistic people or peer mentoring schemes. These provided opportunities for people to be their authentic selves while connecting with others:

> I don't mind speaking to listeners. I mean, I've told them my mental health problems in the past. And, obviously, I'm just telling him that I feel uncomfortable sometimes and they just listen.
>
> (man in prison)

> I found out other people had similar issues, learning difficulties as I did, and then just started talking...it became more relaxed, and more people started communicating. Because to start with, I didn't communicate with anyone.
>
> (man in prison)

Peer support provided the unconditional positive regard people wanted, to not be judged for being themselves. As well as providing a direct benefit to neurodivergent people in prison, peer supporters benefited through a sense of purpose and satisfaction when helping others:

> As peer reps, we're role models and if I'm concentrating on others, I'm not worrying about myself so it helps us both.
>
> (man in prison)

> I love helping people but it also gives me the opportunity to learn everyday about different prisoners and cultures and experiences and different challenges people face...being a mentor is helping me cope.
>
> (man in prison)

Such peer-led initiatives are reflective of existing literature that has highlighted the value of peer support and relatable interactions, often more effective than formal authoritative interactions (CJJI, 2021; Slokan and Ioannou, 2021; Walker, 1978).

5.4.2 Empathy

A core part of showing empathy, being able to see things from another person's perspective, requires the person to have an awareness of difference and to be able to perspective-take. However, many of the people we spoke to in prison felt that staff did not understand neurodivergence. They suggested further training would be advantageous for effective relationships, supporting findings by Vinter et al. (2024):

> There's a misconception that it's like a kid's disease. Something you should have grown out of when you were 12. And I am a 36-year-old man and I'll be honest with you, I think my symptoms got worse as I got older...the lack of awareness really, really shouts out, especially the staff.
>
> (man in prison)

> Any other profession that says we're a human being, has professional training on how to look after a human being. These [officers] learn how to double lock a door.
>
> (man in prison)

In staff responses, they noted this lack of understanding of neurodivergence and wanted further training. Responses demonstrated limited awareness of processes relating to support and integration within the broader prison system:

> There is an NHS specialist in Neurodiversity. Once a prisoner is referred to her, I am not aware of the exact process.
>
> (staff)

> We have a department who will screen, not diagnose, anyone that comes into the Education department who either self-declare or are referred by the tutor during the course. This is recorded on our education data but is not recorded anywhere on the prison system.
>
> (staff)

Lack of understanding for some was due to cultural differences. This raises the importance of considering the intersectionality of autism and learning disabilities with other protected characteristics such as ethnicity and gender. There is a need for cultural competence in developing person-centred care:

> I come from an African background. Mental health and disabilities are unspoken, it's such a very traditional way of thinking that they believe if you have any of those issues, then you need church and God. You know, you say you can't concentrate, it must be the devil. It's a very religious way of thinking (man in prison).
>
> People think you play on it. I've actually heard officers say something about, 'oh, you only play it on it'...little digs. And racism...the two things are linked. They think your cultural background means you're more likely to lie about certain medications or having an issue or having a problem...it's degrading...it makes me feel like an animal. They don't trust you.
>
> (man in prison)

For some people in prison, they believed that without being neurodivergent, it would be hard to truly understand someone who is, resulting in difficulty in showing empathy. The responses we heard from people clearly reflected the dynamics of the double empathy problem (Milton, 2012):

> Someone that isn't autistic, against the person that's autistic, they clash. It doesn't work, because they're not in the same boat and they won't understand. Doesn't matter how much time you spend with them; they're not in your shoes.
>
> (man in prison)

Finke and Dunn (2023) argued that a potential solution to the double empathy problem was exposure, patience, and continuous engagement between neurotypical and neurodivergent people. However, the quote above highlights that for some people, they are dubious about that possibility.

A reason for a lack of empathy sometimes shown by staff or felt by people in prison was due to compassion fatigue; a form of professional distress, emotional exhaustion and reduced empathy arising from prolonged exposure to others' suffering, culminating in diminished capacity to provide compassionate care. In high-stress environments such as prisons, this fatigue can impair decision-making, reduce professional boundaries, and compromise quality of care and safety for staff and those in custody (Cavanagh et al., 2020; Ondrejkova and Halmova, 2022). Some staff reported compassion fatigue due to working conditions and a lack of resources. People in prison told us similarly; that staff have no time to support them, resulting in a lack of empathy:

> Staff need to be more aware of how this influences behaviour. However, I'm concerned compassion fatigue, due to issues with resourcing, may hinder empathic approaches. I'm also concerned that staff may not understand. Therefore, supervision for officers would be beneficial.
>
> (staff)

> Staff have not got time for people with autism. For example, I might be anxious and repeating myself and the peer mentor is the only one who helps me. The staff have no time.
>
> (woman in prison)

Despite this, some staff did show empathy. For some, this was due to their own experiences of neurodivergence, or those of family and friends. Some reported having completed previous training or work with neurodivergent people, or undertaking courses for their own development outside of work, and this helped in their prison roles:

> I have Asperger's Syndrome so despite having some training, I have lived experience so I know what I would want from prison if I was ever in custody.
>
> (staff)

> I spoke to an officer with ADHD and I thought 'she gets me'. Sometimes I wish I wouldn't wake up and then I'd be out of my misery, but she's listened to me. Some staff just don't know what I'm getting at, it's like talking to a brick wall but she understands because she goes through the same stuff as I go through.
>
> (man in prison)

> I've taken my own Supporting Young People with Autism training outside of work.
>
> (staff)

People in prison felt supported when staff had a better understanding of neurodivergence and of treating people as humans:

> One of the members of staff is training in it and he's been quite understanding throughout. The others...seem to almost understand it, they don't always get it right but they're better on here than on the other wings.
>
> (man in prison)

This quote indicates the importance of trying to understand and help. Having training or knowing the 'right' thing to do is good, but the ability to show compassion and try to understand can be significant for helping people to connect. The training toolkit in person-centred care from Health Education England, Skills for Health, and Skills for Care (2017) alludes to this being the first step; being able to engage and have conversations with people is the starting point and communication skills are the foundation of showing empathy. In addition, as Slokan and Ioannou (2021) suggested, instead of trying to equip people with knowledge about neurodivergent variations, training should focus on developing skills that help to identify when people need support which includes relational and communication skills.

5.4.3 Congruence

An authentic approach using patience, understanding, warmth, compassion, adaptability, calmness, reassurance, and being open to feedback was reported by staff to be fundamentally important in building positive congruent relationships. This has been supported by existing literature for a long time, with authentic and reassuring relationships being critical to successful outcomes (Coons, 1982). The feedback from staff was echoed by people in prison:

> The staff who are good take time to ask how are you feeling? They give reassurances, tissues, water, just little things and then they check if you're feeling better.
>
> (woman in prison)

Giving people time and enabling them to feel heard was an important element of positive relationships, helping people to enjoy time spent together. This needs to be managed within professional boundaries, recognised by staff in their comments in the questionnaires and from people in prison who said they need to know where they stand in relationships, with consistency being key:

> I was being listened to and it makes a big difference. If I say I feel down, they care and they [officers] talk to me. I've not had that before. When I put my bell on, they come straight away.
>
> (man in prison)

> That have a laugh, we can like have a joke with staff and, like, swearing they don't care they'll swear at us back, they'll have a joke.
>
> (man in prison)

Whilst consistency can be difficult due to the variability in emotions faced, acknowledgement of this is aligned with being congruent. Consistency in interactions supports Finke and Dunn's (2023) position on the importance of repeated authentic engagements, and that over time, this can help people feel safe and settled. Showing kindness was positively received by people in prison, with such approaches underpinning the relational care promoted by trauma-responsive approaches (Day, 2025):

> At night time when they say goodnight it's pretty weird. When I first came in I was like, 'ok why you saying goodnight?' cos I've not been in prison where officers say good night. All they've done is just slammed door and they just leave you...But I've now got into the gist that it's kindness and at least they're treating us like a normal human being. That's how you want people to talk to you.
>
> (man in prison)

5.4.4 Awareness of the Impact of the Environment

There was clear evidence of Roger's (1942, 1967) three core conditions of unconditional positive regard, empathy, and congruence being prevalent in the data. However, our reanalysis showed that the interplay between relationships and the prison environment cannot be ignored during the application of a humanised approach to effective support. Martin (1927) discussed the importance of the prison environment in exacerbating what now may be considered neurodivergence, supporting the findings from our review on the significance of this interaction. Understanding the need for routines, structure, purposeful activity, and preparation for change was raised. Without these considerations, a humanised approach would be undermined, supported by Pellicano and den Houting (2022) who highlighted the need to understand the barriers that may be presented by the environment people are interacting with:

> Jail likes to throw little spanners in the works to mess it up like. If you're meant to be out at a certain time or appointments get set, then they take the appointment away, like. To people like me, that can make a big whirlpool.
>
> (man in prison)

> I just hope I stay on there, cos like, through my life, I don't like to be unsettled, I've moved a lot around in my life.
>
> (man in prison)

Aside from these issues, echoing previous research (Vinter et al., 2024), a need to understand and respond to sensory issues was also prevalent in the feedback from people in prison. Again, without this, achieving a truly humanised approach would be challenging:

> I used to get a lot of stick when it first came in, because certain smells used to trigger me off and make me feel uncomfortable. I know it sounds weird, but like when people were frying bacon or something like that, it just didn't feel right for

> me...if people just understood a bit more, I'm not saying they're going to have to be fully qualified in it, but a general understanding, perhaps there'd be less aggravation, less frustration, and potentially less harming people.
>
> (man in prison)
>
> It's been a couple of times where it's gotten too much and I just wanted to, like explode. There was nowhere that I could go to just sit down and be chilled.
>
> (man in prison)
>
> I was thrusted into a class where there's 20 people and we are all crammed in like sardines close to each other. I struggle with background noise more than anything else, if the teacher is talking to me, I will listen to the people behind me instead... there's like all those people, I will be listening to them and I don't have a clue what the person at the front is saying.
>
> (man in prison)

5.4.5 Humanised Approach

Application of person-centred care with awareness of the impact of the environment results in a humanised response, which staff and people in prison both acknowledged was essential for delivering effective support. This reinforces that the person should be central in discussions of support (Porter, 1988; Knopes, 2025). Whilst services and different prisons may have a varied offer of support for neurodivergent people, effective relationships can be a bridge to overcoming inconsistencies:

> Good positive relationships allow the prisoner to have trust that they have staff support and staff are knowledgeable of their individual needs and will support.
>
> (staff)
>
> I just want people to make sure I'm alright. It makes me feel better.
>
> (man in prison)

The NHSE (2021) guidance on delivering healthcare to autistic people and people with learning disabilities in prison emphasises the need for respect and upholding the wishes of individuals. People in prison reported their need to be respected, treated as a human, and to feel safe:

> A bit of human kindness. It can't just be me against the system... The staff talking to me makes me feel good because in YOIs previously, people treat me like I'm just a violent bastard and the officers didn't speak to me because they were just locking me up.
>
> (man in prison)
>
> If someone asks me to do a job, I'll do it, because you asked me nicely, but if you're telling me to do something, I won't do that. Even if I get a nicking for it. I

> won't care because you're basically not treating me like a normal human being. And if you want respect, you give me respect.
>
> (man in prison)

> To help someone that's got autism, or learning difficulties, they also need to understand the history of how they grew up, and everything, what they're about. So then, you can go hand in hand because if there's no trust on the things like the abuse and how you grew up or whatever, they can't get through to the autism, or the learning.
>
> (man in prison)

> I'm safe here... Everyone accepts you for who you are.
>
> (transgender man in prison)

Working collaboratively helps people to develop an understanding of each other, encouraging advocacy and empowerment. This aligns with Pellicano and den Houting (2022) and the guidance from NHSE (2021) who argued that collaboration with neurodivergent people was fundamental for providing support and achieving change:

> Depends on the individual and to how we can and would support them. If I suspected an individual to be autistic or have learning disability, I would book an appointment to explore this and what it means for them from their point of view, I would also review previous medical records and contact any other service providers they have had contact with in the community so that we could replicate and ensure a continuity of those care needs as closely as possible in the prison. I would also do all of this with patient (staff).
>
> [Healthcare staff] speaks to me and helps me with things. She understands what I need and helps get it like reading lessons and courses like maths and English, health and safety, and waiting for courses on drugs and alcohol. It will give me something to do and makes me feel good.
>
> (man in prison)

In addition to staff and people in prison working collaboratively, participants also noted the need for different professionals across the justice system to work together. Preventing a siloed approach to care can help avoid people repeating traumatic information and ensure continuous support when people move through the system. As Gormley and Watson (2021) stated, there is a need for a system that supports people end-to-end, without relying on individuals chasing this for themselves. To facilitate this, information sharing needs to be facilitated:

> Education, Programmes, POM, Mental Health Team – anybody who works with somebody's learning or information processing. If you were to establish

a singular route the information could be obtained by one specific agency and their tool and shared between organisations during an induction and recorded somewhere such as [prison IT system], different departments could have it mandated into their assessments.

(staff)

I had contact with different organisations but [they're] all disconnected, no-ones quite got the full picture. I needed a key worker, someone to join those dots.

(transgender woman in prison)

Humanised responses require recognition of limitations in service offers, and a need to have specialist services or roles in place:

You don't need to shove us in hospital, you don't just need to shove us into specialist units, you need the specialist people to be in the mainstream system.

(man in prison)

I do speak to the Listeners but their trained by the Samaritans, they're not trained in mental health, ADHD and everything else. There needs to be extra courses for Listeners of how to help us.

(man in prison)

Responsive care that is developed over time is key. Staff and people in prison noted that there needed to be reviews of the support in place as people get to know each other and as people settle into the environment, supported by Walker et al. (2025) when discussing a 'neurodiverse model of care'.

It's like a lasagne, you've got one where you pour the lasagne leaves at the bottom then you pour the sauce on then you do it again and then you get the sauce on the top where you put the cheese on the top, so it's like in order for you to work with someone, you've got to try break through them layers, but in order to break through them layers you've got to work with the person regularly, in order to do that you have to gain the persons trust.

(man in prison)

There are a variety of tools in place to support those with autism, regular meetings to review progress and update strategy plans, reviewing of resources that are successful or not and amending different resources, wing support, staff support, buddy system.

(staff)

Finally, effective approaches should be based on individual strengths and needs, as identified by both staff and people in prison. This should avoid treating neurodivergent people as a homogeneous group and support the recognition of cultural and gender differences, alongside intersectionality, which needs to be considered (Simmonds and Sukhareva, 2020):

> For people to actually know how your autism works, as yourself, not as a group of people. There might be one, two, or three people I've seen that have the same autism, but a lot of people have different, like me, and you and all three of us have different autism. They need to realise that you need to be treated for how you are.
>
> (young person in prison)

> I treat everyone as an individual and adjust to meet their needs. Otherwise, we could be in danger of saying we also need to have mental health training, and training on other subjects which is not practical for anyone.
>
> (staff)

Day (2025) reported the effectiveness of creating collaborative spaces that build trust and focus on strengths and individual needs. The same points came through clearly in our research; neurodivergent people in prison want to be treated in a person-centred way, and staff want to be equipped with the skills and knowledge to do this.

5.5 Conclusion

This chapter has re-evaluated the effectiveness of prisons in meeting the needs of autistic adults and adults with learning disabilities through a person-centred lens, as defined by Rogers (1942, 1967). Drawing on qualitative data from autistic people and people with learning disabilities in prison and staff working in them, the data highlighted the continuation of issues which were first identified in the literature almost a century ago. These include a lack of awareness among staff, leading to misunderstanding and misinterpretation of neurodivergent people, resulting in poorer outcomes for people in prison. A neuroaffirmative, strengths-based model of care would focus on using the core conditions whilst considering the environment. Unconditional positive regard can be strengthened through the proactive use of peer-led initiatives, which foster non-judgemental listening and build mutual respect between staff and people in prison. Staff training would play a pivotal role in developing empathy and would include neurodivergent-specific training alongside how to recognise distress, cultural competence, and supportive communication skills. Embedding the principles of the Double Empathy Theory within training frameworks would encourage mutual understanding of communication differences across neurotypes, helping staff to respond more empathetically to neurodivergent individuals. In addition, initiatives to raise awareness and support for compassion fatigue would help to mitigate the negative impact this can have on empathetic responding. Finally, congruence could be developed through consistency in relationships, for example by maintaining consistent key workers, and through consistency in staff responses to people. This could be facilitated through reflective support approaches, such as supervision, which helps people to recognise how their own thoughts and feelings may present a barrier to consistency. Congruence may also be supported through timely screening and appropriate environmental adaptations, which signal a proactive and authentic effort to respond to individual needs. This humanised response is founded on relational support with kindness, respect, collaboration, and responsivity, providing a place of safety.

Despite longstanding recognition of the need for person-centred care in prisons, neurodivergent people continue to face systemic barriers to receiving this. Many professionals discuss "person-centred care" in their practice, but the operational reality of delivering this seems to be somewhat lost, with additional challenges faced within a prison. However, the data underpinning this chapter also showed that returning to the basics of delivery within the three core conditions of this approach, alongside consideration of the environmental context, is useful. Such an approach does not require a focus on diagnosis but advocates a focus on a holistic and humanised approach to supporting neurodivergent people, underpinned by consistent and compassionate approaches, collaborative, strength-based support, continuity of care and information sharing, and recognition of the impact of the prison environment. A renewed commitment to the principles of person-centred care, applied universally, not just to neurodivergent people, could transform prison care into a more inclusive, effective, and humane system.

5.5.1 Strengths and Limitations

The service evaluation conducted was extensive and included a wealth of perspectives and experiences from 93 autistic people and people with learning disabilities across 15 different prisons. However, it is important to note the limitations. Not all prisons across the Midlands engaged in this evaluation and this may mean that good practice was missed from these sites. Although 175 prison-based staff responded to the questionnaire, this is a low response rate given the number of people who would be working across the 26 prisons in scope. The low response rate may be due to ongoing staff shortages in prisons.

Notes

1 A note on language: throughout this chapter we use identity-first when referring to autistic people and person first when referring to people with learning disabilities. We acknowledge that these are two variations when considering neurodivergence, and for clarity, the focus of our evaluation was on autism and learning disabilities although we found many comorbidities with other variations of neurodivergence.

2 (neurodivers* or autis* or adhd or neurodiverge* or "acquired brain injury" or "learning disabilit*" or "learning difference") AND (prison* or jail or incarcerat* or imprisonment or "correction facilities" or inmates or criminals or offenders).

References

Bahri, G., Turnbull, L. and Fish. R. (2024) *LVRN – Violence reduction intervention: HMP Wymott sensory room evaluation.* Available at: https://clok.uclan.ac.uk/id/eprint/55418/1/55418%20Bahri%20et%20al.%20VOR.pdf.

Browning, H. and Veit, W. (2025) The neurodiversity model and medical model: Competitors or alternative perspectives?. *AJOB Neuroscience*, *16*(1), 32–34. https://doi.org/10.1080/21507740.2024.2437994.

Camm-Crosbie, L., Bradley, L., Shaw, R., Baron-Cohen, S. and Cassidy, S. (2018) 'People like me don't get support': Autistic adults' experiences of support and treatment for mental health difficulties, self-injury and suicidality. *Autism*, *23*(6), 1431–1441. https://doi.org/10.1177/1362361318816053.

Cavanagh, N., Cockett, G., Heinrich, C., Doig, L., Fiest, K., Guichon, J. R., Page, S., Mitchell, I. and Doig, C. J. (2020) Compassion fatigue in healthcare providers: A systematic review and meta-analysis. *Nursing Ethics*, *27*(3), 639–665. https://doi.org/10.1177/0969733019889400

Cleland, J. and Cotton, P. eds. (2011) *Health, behaviour and society: Clinical medicine in context*. SAGE.

Coons, W. H. (1982) Learning disabilities and criminality. *Canadian Journal of Criminology*, *24*(3), 251–265. Available at: https://research.ebsco.com/linkprocessor/plink?id=81167a44-5689-39bb-b519-77ae6c1e19f5.

Criminal Justice Joint Inspectorate (2021) *Neurodiversity in the criminal justice system: A review of evidence*. Available at: https://hmicfrs.justiceinspectorates.gov.uk/publications/neurodiversity-in-the-criminal-justice-system/.

Day, A.-M. (2025) Kids "at risk" of school exclusion and youth justice involvement? Or neurodivergent children and families in need of trauma-informed support? *Emotional & Behavioural Difficulties* [Preprint]. https://doi.org/10.1080/13632752.2025.2499788.

Finke, E. H. and Dunn, D. H. (2023) Neurodiversity and double empathy: Can empathy disconnects be mitigated to support autistic belonging? *Disability & Society*, *40*(3), 727–750. https://doi.org/10.1080/09687599.2023.2295802.

Gormley, C. and Watson, N. (2021) Inaccessible Justice: Exploring the barriers to justice and fairness for disabled people accused of a crime. *Howard Journal of Crime & Justice*, *60*(4), 493–510. https://doi.org/10.1111/hojo.12433.

Health Education England, Skills for Health, and Skills for Care (2017) *Person-centred approaches: Empowering people in their lives and communities to enable an upgrade in prevention, wellbeing, health, care, and support*. Available at: https://www.skillsforhealth.org.uk/wp-content/uploads/2021/01/Person-Centred-Approaches-Framework.pdf.

Hirvikoski, T., Mittendorfer-Rutz, E., Boman, M., Larsson, H., Lichtenstein, P. and Bölte, S. (2018) Premature mortality in autism spectrum disorder. *The British journal of psychiatry*, *208*(3), 232–238. https://doi.org/10.1192/bjp.bp.114.160192.

Independent Monitoring Boards (IMB) (2024) *Mental health crisis forces prisoners into inhumane isolation.* Available at: https://imb.org.uk/news/mental-health-crisis-forces-prisoners-into-inhumane-isolation/.

Jokiranta-Olkoniemi, E., Gyllenberg, D., Sucksdorff, D., Suominen, A., Kronström, K., Chudal, R. and Sourander, A. (2020) Risk for premature mortality and intentional self-harm in autism spectrum disorders. *Journal of Autism and Developmental Disorders*, *51*(9), 3098–3108. https://doi.org/10.1007/s10803-020-04768-x.

Kargas, N., Mason, R., Smith, L., Rogers, J. and Hogue, T. (2023) *Independent review of services for adults with a learning disability and autistic adults in Midlands prisons: Report of findings for NHS England.* University of Lincoln. https://hdl.handle.net/10779/lincoln.24959559.v2.

Knopes, J. (2025) Mental health conditions between neurodiversity and the medical model. *AJOB Neuroscience, 16*(1), 20–31. https://doi.org/10.1080/21507740.2024.2412549.

Lambert, E. G., Barton-Bellessa, S. M. and Hogan, N. L. (2014) The association between correctional orientation and organizational citizenship behaviors among correctional staff. *International Journal of Offender Therapy and Comparative Criminology, 58*(8), 953–974. https://doi.org/10.1177/0306624X13489510.

London, A. S. and Landes, S. D. (2016) Attention deficit hyperactivity disorder and adult mortality. *Preventive medicine, 90*, 8–10. https://doi.org/10.1016/j.ypmed.2016.06.021.

Loucks, N. (2007) *No one knows: Offenders with learning difficulties and learning disabilities – Review of prevalence and associated needs.* Available at: https://prisonreformtrust.org.uk/wp-content/uploads/old_files/Documents/No%20One%20Knows%20Prevalence%2C%20full%20report.pdf.

Martin, W. B. (1927) The development of psychoses in prison. *Journal of the American Institute of Criminal Law & Criminology, 18*(3), 404–415. Available at: https://scholarlycommons.law.northwestern.edu/cgi/viewcontent.cgi?article=2069&context=jclc.

Milton, D. E. M. (2012) On the ontological status of autism: The 'double empathy problem. *Disability & Society, 27*(6), 883–887. https://doi.org/10.1080/09687599.2012.710008.

Newell, V., Phillips, L., Jones, C., Townsend, E., Richards, C. and Cassidy, S. (2023) A systematic review and meta-analysis of suicidality in autistic and possibly autistic people without co-occurring intellectual disability. *Molecular Autism, 14*, 12. https://doi.org/10.1186/s13229-023-00544-7.

NHS England and NHS improvement (2021) *Meeting the healthcare needs of adults with a learning disability and autistic adults in prison Guidance on the design and delivery of prison healthcare for adults with a learning disability and autistic adults accessing healthcare services whilst in prison.* Available at: https://www.england.nhs.uk/publication/meeting-the-healthcare-needs-of-adults-with-a-learning-disability-and-autistic-adults-in-prison/.

Nikolić, N., Sculthorpe, C., Stock, J., Stevens, D. and Eccles, J. (2024) Determining unmet need: Clinical relevance of suspected neurodivergence in first-episode psychosis. *BJPsych Bulletin*, 1–6. https://doi.org/10.1192/bjb.2024.64.

Oliphant, R., Smith, E. and Grahame, V. (2020) What is the prevalence of self-harming and suicidal behaviour in under 18s with ASD, with or without an intellectual disability?. *Journal of Autism and Developmental Disorders, 50*(10), 3510–3524. https://doi.org/10.1007/s10803-020-04422-6.

Ondrejková, N. and Halamová, J. (2022) Stressful factors, experiences of compassion fatigue and self-care strategies in police officers. *Journal of Police and Criminal Psychology, 37*(4), 892–903. https://doi.org/10.1007/s11896-022-09538-2.

Pellicano, E. and den Houting, J. (2022) Annual research review: Shifting from 'normal science' to neurodiversity in autism science. *Journal of Child Psychology and Psychiatry, 63*(4), 381–396. https://doi.org/10.1111/jcpp.13534.

Porter, L. S. (1988) The what, why and how of hyperkinesis: Implications for nursing. *Journal of Advanced Nursing, 13*, 229–236. https://doi.org/10.1111/j.1365-2648.1988.tb01412.x.

Quinn, A., Wood, A., Lodge, K. M. and Hollins, S. (2023) Listening to the experts: Person-centred approaches to supporting autistic people and people with an intellectual disability in the mental health system. *BJPsych Advances*, *29*(5), 308–317. https://doi.org/10.1192/bja.2023.31.

Rogers, C. R. (1942) *Counseling and psychotherapy: Newer concepts in practice.* Houghton Mifflin Company.

Rogers, C. R. (1967) *On becoming a person: A therapist's view of psychotherapy.* Constable.

Rogers, J., Kargas, N., Smith, L., Mason, R., Kusyk, I. and Hogue, T. (2022) *Services for autistic adults and adults with a learning disability in prisons: A rapid evidence review.* University of Lincoln. https://hdl.handle.net/10779/lincoln.24959550.v2.

Santorso, S. (2021) Rehabilitation and dynamic security in the Italian prison: Challenges in transforming prison officers' roles. *The British Journal of Criminology*, *61*(6), 1557–1574. https://doi.org/10.1093/bjc/azab015.

Simmonds, C. and Sukhareva, G. E. (2020) The first account of the syndrome Asperger described? Part 2: The girls. *European Child & Adolescent Psychiatry*, *29*(4), 549–564. https://doi.org/10.1007/s00787-019-01371-z.

Slokan, F. and Ioannou, M. (2021) "I'm not even bothered if they think, is that autism?": An exploratory study assessing autism training needs for prison officers in the Scottish prison service. *Howard Journal of Crime & Justice*, *60*(4), 546–563. https://doi.org/10.1111/hojo.12432.

Solell, P. and Smith, K. (2019) If we truly cared': Understanding barriers to person-centred nursing in correctional facilities. *International Practice Development Journal*, *9*(2). https://doi.org/10.19043/ipdj.92.007.

Tulchinsky, T. H. and Varavikova, E. A. (2014) Chapter 7 - Special Community Health Needs, Editor(s): Theodore H. Tulchinsky, Elena A. Varavikova, The New Public Health (Third Edition), Academic Press, 2014, Pages 381–418, https://doi.org/10.1016/B978-0-12-415766-8.00007-0.

UserVoice (2021) *Neuro... what? Neurodiversity in the criminal justice system.* Available at: https://www.uservoice.org/wp-content/uploads/2021/07/Neurodiversity-in-the-Criminal-Justice-System.pdf.

van Ginneken, E. F., Bosma, A. Q., Pasma, A. and Palmen, H. (2020) Unzufriedenes Personal, unzufriedene Gefangene? Die Beziehung zwischen Arbeitsklima und Gefängnisklima in niederländischen Gefängnissen. *Kriminologie-Das Online-Journal| Criminology-The Online Journal*, *2(2)*, 182–200. https://doi.org/10.18716/ojs/krimoj/2020.2.5.

Vinter, L. P., Dillon, G. and Winder, B. (2023) 'People don't like you when you're different': Exploring the prison experiences of autistic individuals. *Psychology, Crime & Law*, *29*(3), 243–262. https://doi.org/10.1080/1068316x.2020.1781119.

Vinter, L. P., Harper, C. A., Dillon, G. and Winder, B. (2024) Mental wellbeing, but not prison climate, mediates the association between autistic traits and treatment readiness among men with sexual convictions. *Journal of Sexual Aggression*, 1–7. https://doi.org/10.1080/13552600.2024.2378022.

Walker, B. A. (1978) Milieu therapy with the adolescent sociopath. *Adolescence*, *13*(52), 531–536. Available at: https://research.ebsco.com/linkprocessor/plink?id=dac5541d-2904-31fb-a608-6bda1ccbd3fc.

Walker, F., Murphy, D., Groger, L. and Moore, E. (2025) Prevalence of neurodiversity in a UK high secure psychiatric hospital cohort: A records study. *Criminal Behaviour & Mental Health*, *35*(3), 170–178. https://doi.org/10.1002/cbm.2363.

Wilson, C., Butler, N., Quigg, Z., Moore, D. and Bellis, M. (2024) Relationships between neurodivergence status and adverse childhood experiences, and impacts on health, wellbeing, and criminal justice outcomes: Findings from a regional household survey study in England. *BMC Medicine*, *22*(1). https://doi.org/10.1186/s12916-024-03821-1.
World Health Organisation (2016) *International statistical classification of diseases and related health problems (ICD) 10th revision.* Available at: https://icd.who.int/browse10/2019/en.

Chapter 6

Supporting Autistic Individuals in the English Prison System

Kim Turner, Alexandra Lewis, and Mo Foster

6.1 Introduction

There has been growing awareness over the last 20 years of the over representation of neurodivergent children and adults in prison settings (Loucks, 2007) and the additional difficulties they may experience in this environment (Paterson, 2008; Helverschou et al., 2018). Alongside this, the underdiagnosis of these individuals prior to contact with the criminal justice system poses issues with identification and provision of support (French et al., 2023).

There is no conclusive figure for autistic individuals in contact with the criminal justice system (whether as victims, witnesses, or perpetrators); however, the evidence base strongly indicates high rates of vulnerable individuals (Hughes et al., 2012) and emerging evidence appears to suggest a specific over-representation of autistic individuals (Cooper et al., 2022). A recent study by Payne and Gooding (2025) found a prevalence rate of 4.78% across the English, female custodial estate, 13.7 times higher than in the general population. Rates of autism diagnosis continue to increase in the general population, with a 787% rise in autism diagnoses occurring in the UK between 1998 and 2018 and the greatest rise occurring in females and adults (Russell et al., 2022). However, some populations are less likely to receive a diagnosis (Ames et al., 2022), this includes black males who are disproportionately represented in the prison population. There has also been an increase in the median age of the prison population, and these older adults are likely to include individuals with undiagnosed neurodivergent conditions. Identification of autism before, or early in, an individual's criminal justice journey could allow for more effective support, minimise the risk of additional mental ill health developing, highlight the need for specialist support, enable diversion, and reduce the risk of reoffending.

Whilst literature shows that neurodivergent individuals and those with mental health difficulties and cognitive impairments are more likely to be victims and witnesses (Beadle-Brown et al., 2014), a number are also defendants. It has been hypothesised that characteristics associated with autism, for example, social naivety, sensory sensitivities, hyper-focus, special interests, and difficulties managing change may influence contact with the criminal justice system (Gunasekaran and Chaplin, 2012). These characteristics could make it more difficult for someone to manage

DOI: 10.4324/9781003638742-7

in a prison setting. Noise is persistent and loud within prison environments and has been shown to have negative psychological effects on residents (Fairweather, 2013). This is sadly highlighted by the death in custody of Kay Melhuish, where the noisy environment was explicitly referenced as a key factor in her taking her own life (Voisin, 2024).

More recently, the focus has turned to neuroinclusivity[1] and practical ways of supporting autistic individuals in prison settings, with a number of significant developments in England: the creation of autism standards (Lewis et al., 2016), the appointment of neurodiversity support managers within prisons, a governmental review (Ministry of Justice, 2021), and the opening of prison wings specifically created for neurodivergent individuals. The importance of high-quality care at times of transition – entering and leaving custody – has been recognised as important for all individuals and autistic individuals in particular (Dein and Woodbury-Smith, 2010; Reyes et al., 2021). This chapter explores these practical supports, transition points, and life within prison more broadly, focusing on how these may be experienced by autistic individuals. It takes an interdisciplinary approach to explore these advances, supports currently provided, and potential for future developments, with each section concluding with a specific recommendation for change.

6.2 The History of Neurodivergence in the Prison Estate

Autism support in prisons has, historically, been seen as a health and social care matter (Lewis and Turner, 2014). Whilst it is our contention that autism is a matter for all criminal justice partners, it is helpful to provide some background to the health services on offer to neurodivergent individuals.

In 1996, Lord Ramsbotham, HM Chief Inspector of Prisons, published a report identifying that, although there were high levels of health need among individuals in custody, there was not equity of care with those in the community. This prompted the transfer of budgetary responsibility for health from the Home Office to the Department of Health with the effect that, since 2006, all healthcare within prisons in England and Wales has been provided by the National Health Service (NHS). Whilst this change has driven increased standards in overall healthcare provision within prisons and access to services, there remain difficulties because the primary focus of prison mental health tends to be on acute episodic illness and transfer to hospital of those whose needs cannot be adequately managed in custody, rather than the identification and support of those with less acute or more subtle presentations such as autism (Durcan et al., 2014). Within prison populations, the rates of mental health and neurodivergent needs are higher than in the general population (Hughes et al., 2012). Whilst the Ramsbotham review required prison health to provide parity with community services, the higher levels of neurodivergence within the prison system are likely to result in challenges accessing diagnosis and support.

Prison healthcare services are commissioned regionally based on local need. The underdiagnosis of autism and other neurodivergent conditions in this population prior to contact with the criminal justice service (Loucks, 2007) means the level of need is not accurately recognised, making it hard to advocate for services. Not all healthcare teams within prison settings have specialist neurodivergence trained staff and fewer still provide autism diagnostic services within a custodial setting.

Recommendation 1: All prison healthcare teams to provide access to diagnostic services, to support individuals in their self-identity (de Broize et al., 2022) and access to services.

6.3 Reducing the Number of Autistic Individuals Entering Prison

Autistic individuals should be entering prison solely as a last resort. Over the last decade, there has been an increasing push to divert those with significant health needs, including autistic individuals, away from the criminal justice system. This has been supported by the development of several new services.

Since March 2020, Liaison and Diversion Teams (L&D) have been embedded within police services in England. L&D services are designed to support vulnerable people through the early stages of the criminal justice pathway, refer them for appropriate health or social care, or enable them to be diverted away from the criminal justice system into a more appropriate setting, such as a mental health unit or a care package in the community, if required. Individuals supported by L&D are those with mental health needs, a learning disability, substance misuse issues or other vulnerabilities, including those with neurodivergent conditions. It is hoped that these services will reduce the number of autistic individuals entering prison settings and instead receiving community support.

Another diversionary development is Community Sentence Treatment Requirements (CSTRs),[2] the collective name for three treatment orders – mental health treatment requirement (MHTR), drug rehabilitation requirement (DRR) and alcohol treatment requirement (ATR) – that can be handed down at sentencing. These orders may be used as alternatives to custodial disposals. They are designed to reduce the individual's offending by addressing the underlying wellbeing issue that is thought to be contributing to their offending and are commissioned by NHS England. Reasonable adjustments can be provided to ensure that CSTR interventions are accessible to autistic and neurodivergent individuals. This is important as perceived failure to engage with a CSTR intervention could result in an individual being regarded as having wilfully breached their conditions with the consequence of being returned to court, where they may be at risk of being re-sentenced to custody.

Recommendation 2: Diversion should be considered for all autistic individuals at risk of contact with the criminal justice system.

6.4 Entering Custody

Healthcare evidently has a central role in supporting neurodivergent individuals in prison (HM Government, 2018) and in programmes that keep them out of prison.

There is, however, an important interplay between health and custodial services when supporting neurodivergent people. This includes 'interactions between prison and health improving overall health and wellbeing may be as much about changes to the regime, custodial staffing levels, food, accommodation, access to exercise, training, employment etc. as delivering specific health services. There is an interdependency of health and custodial services' and it begins on arrival at prison. Arriving in prison can be an overwhelming experience for anyone as illustrated by the quote below:

> Jail can be scary, the unfamiliar surroundings, the loud noises, a routine that revolves around time...
>
> (Prisoner, HMP Parc, Mental Health Foundation, 2022)

This can be further exacerbated for autistic individuals who may be particularly sensitive to loud noises or struggle with changes in environment and establishing new routines. If an individual has a pre-existing diagnosis, this can be disclosed on admission and early support, where available, can be put in place. However, for most individuals who do not have a formal diagnosis in place before arriving in prison, they cannot disclose and are unlikely to receive any support. As discussed earlier, there are long waits for autism diagnosis in the general population, and if an individual presents with 'challenging' behaviour or has had limited engagement with statutory services, this may further impact the likelihood of receiving an early autism diagnosis. Kojo's case study demonstrates how early opportunities for diagnosis can be missed but also how prison may provide an opportunity to identify need and provide support.

Case Study – Kojo

Kojo was a 19-year-old male who had just arrived at prison reception. He had moved to the UK aged nine with his mother. His mother had a history of significant mental health difficulties and had moved to be closer to family. He started at primary school in the UK aged nine, where his difficulties were attributed to moving to an unfamiliar country and learning English as an additional language. At secondary school, his mother's mental health meant that he divided his time between his mother and aunt when his mother was unable to care for him. This involved attending two different secondary schools. His difficulties here were attributed to the changes in schools, his routine, and difficulties at home. One time when his mother was seen at home by her mental health nurse, they suggested that she take her son to the GP as they thought he might be autistic. This was not followed up. Kojo, now aged 19, arrived at prison reception and was rocking back and forth, visibly distressed. Within two minutes of arriving in prison, the officer on reception recognised his needs and made a referral to healthcare for an assessment.

On admission to prison, each individual will be seen by prison and healthcare staff in the first few hours. They are asked about their physical and mental health, as well as any vulnerabilities they have. There are no explicit questions asking if the individual is, or suspects they may be, autistic. It is reliant on the individual to disclose their needs. If the individual has had negative experiences of previous disclosure or does not recognise why it might be helpful to disclose their condition, they may not share this information (Huang et al., 2022). Current admission processes and the high numbers of individuals undiagnosed mean there will be significant numbers of individuals who would benefit from additional early support not receiving this.

Recommendation 3: Systematic screening of neurodivergent needs for all on admission.

6.5 Developing a Neuro-Inclusive Environment

As demonstrated above, a large number of autistic individuals may not be identified on admission. In addition, information sharing and record keeping in the prison estate is complex, with health, prison, education and third sector organisations all collecting information on individuals but recording it in different ways on different systems. If the individual discloses that they are autistic to the prison staff, this may not be shared with healthcare and vice versa (Health Services Safety Investigation Body, 2025). This can be another obstacle to individuals receiving the required support.

One potential way of addressing these barriers is to provide universal support, so the onus is not on the individual to disclose or reliant on information being shared. There are examples of good practice in universal support from both prison and police custody. Dr Chloe Holloway-George has worked with autistic individuals to help understand their experience of being in police custody and what changes could be made; this work is now being adapted for use in prison settings (Holloway *et al.*, 2020). Key findings from the police custody walkthrough were:

1. Autistic individuals were prevented from effectively participating in custody processes.
2. There exist barriers to communication affecting interactions between officers and autistic detainees.
3. The custody environment creates sensory difficulties for autistic detainees.
4. Officers are prevented from providing effective support due to the demands of custody.
5. Changes to practice, the custody environment and policy will help improve support.

From this initial work, the team developed a Custody Toolkit (University of Nottingham, undated) which supports police forces to implement simple changes that make the environment more supportive for autistic individuals. This includes providing accessible information about their detention, visual aids to support communication, and a prompt for staff around potential adaptations. Adaptations may include alternative lighting (strip lights typically used in prison settings can be too intense and cause sensory overwhelm), a tactile wall, a chalk board, and in-cell activities. These adaptations could be easily tailored to a prison setting.

HM YOI Feltham and the National Autistic Society worked together to develop standards for supporting autistic individuals in a prison setting (Lewis *et al.*, 2015). The standards led to practical changes in the admission process for all. The reception suite, for example, was painted pastel colours which have a calming effect. Colour-blocking was also used to clearly designate each area – healthcare, education, residential. The admissions process was then explained using accessible visual aids and supported by the colour-coding to enable individuals to understand the process ahead. Autistic individuals were also offered a first night pack – comprising a sleep mask, ear plugs and an activity pack to support them to manage sensory issues and provide a focus. Whilst these changes were designed to support autistic individuals, informal feedback from young people and officers indicated that they were supportive for individuals with a range of neurodivergent conditions and even more broadly – for example, those with low literacy skills found the accessible information about the admissions process helpful.

Recommendation 4: Each prison should have a systematic approach to supporting autistic individuals including environmental adaptations and easy read materials.

6.6 Screening and Assessment

Whilst universal support can be broadly helpful, each individual is different and will have specific requirements. Screening, identification and diagnosis are therefore important steps in identifying the specific support needed. Receiving a diagnosis can indeed be transformative:

> It opened my eyes to why I was doing things...I was aware of it a bit more after that and I could see 'yes I'm doing this, I'm doing that'...and then I connect that with what I've read about it...possibly it gave me a reason for why I pushed it and pushed it.
>
> (sexual offences) (Allen et al., 2008)

There has been systematic screening for neurodivergence, including autism, in the Children and Young Person's Secure Estate since 2016 through the Comprehensive Health Assessment Tool (CHAT, Shaw *et al.*, 2014a). This screening assessment is completed by healthcare staff within the first 10 days of admission; the guidance indicates it should be carried out by a mental health or learning disability nurse (Shaw et al., 2014b). The screen includes a review of that individual's records and a conversation with the young person. The nurse is then asked to reflect on specific areas of that interaction and decide whether the individual has needs in this area. If needs are identified, a risk review should be completed, a care plan developed and consideration of onward referral. The pilot study – conducted with 93 young people in the custodial estate – found that the diagnostic accuracy for mental health and substance use was over 75% whilst it was only 53% for neurodisability, the section in which autism is included (Lennox et al., 2013). However, none of the 93 young people involved in the study were autistic. Whilst there is limited evidence to demonstrate how effective the tool is in identifying autistic individuals, it is a step forward that each young person is systematically being screened.

From October 2025, all adults in prison in England will have access to screening via prison education providers. The Do-It-Profiler (Kirby, 2016) will be used to identify individuals with neurodevelopmental and neurodivergent learning needs and provide them with support strategies (both for themselves and those they interact with). It is a self-administered tool, either paper-based or electronic. The screening tool is divided into modules that can be completed at once or at different time points, to support accessibility. If accessed electronically there is the ability to alter text and background colour, and a read-aloud function available in different languages. The modules were developed collaboratively with health and education staff working in a prison setting to establish their practical efficacy in this population. It has yet to be independently evaluated.

Both the CHAT and Do-It-Profiler are screening tools, but not diagnostic. They provide a helpful starting point but cannot and should not replace a formal diagnostic assessment. However, it is beneficial for recognising those who may benefit from additional support at an early stage of their journey and provides a structured facility for onward referral.

As described earlier, diagnostic services are patchy. Where diagnostic services are provided, these can be transformatory for the individual and also support those around the individual (Lewis et al., 2015). The Children and Young Person's Secure Estate in England (CYPSE) has led the way in improving support for mental health and neurodevelopmental needs for the children in its care. It recognised that many detained young people appeared to have unmet neurodevelopmental needs, but access to support depended on them being formally assessed and diagnosed. Bottlenecks in neurodevelopmental diagnostic pathways meant that young people could wait many months or even be released from custody before the diagnostic assessment was completed, and so they spent their time in custody unsupported.

A decision was made to make provision of support contingent only on identified need without a requirement of a formal diagnostic label. A new approach called the Framework for Integrated Care, sometimes referred to as SECURE STAIRS, was introduced (see Anna Freud National Centre for Children and Families, 2022). This is a comprehensive, trauma-informed, developmentally sensitive framework. The framework's goals are to co-develop a psychological formulation for every child who is in the system, identify any unmet needs and use this to inform interventions and support. It therefore does not produce diagnoses but will identify if a person in custody appears to be neurodivergent and subsequent care plans will be informed by this impression. This means the young person will get immediate support whilst they wait for any formal diagnostic assessments. Independent evaluation has been so encouraging that the framework is now being piloted in the community (Taylor et al., 2018).

Although this increase in needs-based neurodevelopmental support in CYPSE is welcome, the adult estate has been slower to develop in this area, and there remains a lack of access to neurodevelopmental diagnostic services across all prison settings. Where diagnostic teams are provided, the impact can be transformational, both for life in custody and beyond, as demonstrated in John's Case Study.

Case Study – John

John was admitted to prison and was immediately identified by officers as vulnerable, with an Assessment, Care in Custody and Teamwork (ACCT) document[3] being opened to protect his safety. He was shortly transferred to the healthcare wing due to high levels of anxiety, isolation and concerns about the risk of harm to self. On transfer to healthcare, he was identified as having autistic traits and a diagnostic assessment was completed with John and his family. He was diagnosed as autistic, engaged in sessions to understand his diagnosis, and commenced anxiety medication. With the support of the medication and increased understanding of his needs (both self-awareness and staff awareness), John was able to begin work within prison. Initially, it was suggested that gardening may be a good fit due to the quieter environment and limited interaction with others. However, John found the lack of routine and structure in gardens difficult. He transferred to the library and worked as a librarian support where his interest in books and eye for detail proved very beneficial. He was no longer deemed a risk to self and the ACCT document was closed. Through the diagnosis, John was able to access supported living in the community on release.

NHS England and justice services are now recognising the need for more systematic identification and support. They have published guidance on improving lives for those in prison (NHS England, 2025). The document sets out a strategic vision for the delivery of health and justice services and provides a framework for NHS commissioners, service providers, those with lived experience, and cross-departmental partners to work collaboratively to improve health and wellbeing outcomes for those in contact with the youth justice and criminal justice systems. NHS England states that collaborative work is fundamental in effectively tackling the health inequalities that autistic individuals face, along with improving their life chances as individuals move through the criminal justice system. One of the 12 commitments within this framework is 'supporting people with neurodiversity and complex health needs'. The programme of work within this commitment includes 'establishing a nationally agreed screening process and communication protocol with Integrated Care Systems (including shared IT) to ensure people with neurodiversity are identified and properly supported across all services'.

Recommendation 5: Information regarding needs to be effectively communicated between individuals and services.

6.7 The Prison Regime

We know that autistic individuals can be particularly vulnerable in prison due to differences in their social interactions and communication. These differences may increase the risk of not coping in a prison setting, being bullied, exploited, or manipulated by fellow prisoners. Many autistic individuals will find prison a difficult place to be; however, this is not universally true. Allen et al. (2008) found that some autistic individuals described positive elements of prison life. One participant commented that having more structure and less free time was a clear positive about a prison environment. The routine of the regime in prison can create structure that the outside world lacks.

Part of the prison regime includes attending work and/or education and engaging with rehabilitation programmes. For some autistic individuals, maintaining employment or building relationships with others in prison can be difficult. An autistic person's ability to effectively access and engage with rehabilitation interventions may be impacted. These programmes may also not meet the needs of the individual, as illustrated in Asif's case study.

Case Study – Asif

Asif was being assessed for inclusion in a Sex Offenders Treatment Programme (SOTP) as he had been convicted of sexual assault. He had a mild learning disability and autism. The Mental Healthcare Team (MHT) was asked for input around his ability to engage with the language demands of the programme. MHT raised that they believed there was no sexual intent in his offending but that this was driven by his sensory sensitivities, a particular desire to touch certain materials, and a lack of understanding about appropriate touch. It was agreed that rather than engage in the SOTP he would receive psychoeducation around consent and appropriate touch. Asif was also given a piece of fabric to carry that he could touch, instead of inappropriately touching a stranger. This approach kept Asif and the wider community safer than him engaging in the SOTP, which would not have addressed the underlying reasons for the offence.

Autistic individuals require support throughout the day and across all environments, and this cannot be supported by one service alone. There can be additional benefits of changing the wider environment in that it can support all – diagnosed/undiagnosed, neurodivergent/neurotypical (Sun et al., 2021). The work that was undertaken at HMP/YOI Feltham in conjunction with the National

Autistic Society clearly demonstrated the benefits of a whole prison approach to supporting autistic prisoners (Lewis et al., 2016). The standards included changes to processes, policy, training, and adaptations to the prison environment and materials used. The work was described as leading to a 'culture change' in the wider prison. The project was seen to enhance multi-agency working, bringing together the different departments of the prison to improve working life and understanding between teams.

The Ministry of Justice in England and Wales has recognised the need for broader support for neurodivergent individuals, creating the role of Neurodiversity Support Manager (NSM) in 2021. These are now in place in each prison and YOI. The role of the NSM is to raise awareness of neurodiversity in prison and help strengthen approaches for identifying and supporting those with neurodivergent needs. This includes supporting prisoners in accessing and engaging in education, skills, and work programmes in the prison. As a lone individual supporting all neurodivergent individuals within the environment, the NSM is reliant on buy-in and support from management and colleagues to have the greatest impact.

The role embraces important responsibilities, activities and duties including quality assurance; strategy; maintaining systems for education, skills and work activity; data management; tracking progress of prisoners; prison case management; consideration of activities, adaptations and reasonable adjustments for prisoners; and awareness raising. Discharging all the above would be a laudable achievement and very likely to lead to improved outcomes and experiences for neurodivergent individuals; however, they are very challenging to achieve as a lone individual (though case studies detailed by Chadwick et al. (2025) suggest significant progress has been achieved by NSMs). As NSMs are employed directly by the prison, an integrated approach from all services within the prison – health, education and third sector partners, and accountability for all, is required for meaningful change.

Recommendation 6: Identified individuals across all services working in each prison to take a lead role in ensuring autistic individuals are supported throughout their journey.

6.8 Enhanced Support

Prisons house individuals with multiple and complex needs; some of these autistic individuals may find it difficult within the broader prison population, even with support in place. There have been a range of approaches explored to support these high-need individuals.

Some young people detained in Young Offender Institutions require more intensive support than can be provided via standard procedures. For this cohort, NHS England has introduced Enhanced Support Teams (EST) which are staffed by highly experienced staff and often work on Enhanced Support Units (ESUs) that have been adapted to be more neuro-inclusive. The young people receiving care from ESTs/ESUs typically have complex needs related to autism, ADHD, a learning disability, or another neurodevelopmental condition, although many do not have a formal diagnosis.

Other prisons have developed specific neurodivergent units. The Pentonville Neurodivergent Unit is described below, illustrating how these units function.

Case Study – HMP Pentonville Neurodivergent Unit (NDU)

The development of the new unit took approximately 18 months before it was opened to the first residents. Previous interdisciplinary working between healthcare (Speech and Language Therapy), prison and chaplaincy to support a neurodivergent individual had raised everyone's awareness of 'hidden' disabilities and made them committed to making a change. This neurodivergent individual had extremely limited expressive language and kept throwing himself on the netting. Prison policies meant that this behaviour led to the individual being cuffed for everyone's safety; however, this approach was not successful. The Speech and Language Therapist argued for a different approach, which led to discussion about the potential for a neurodivergent unit. Key stakeholders began meeting together for a weekly meeting for over a year to discuss how the unit could work in practice. This required understanding and compromise from all parties for it to work for the individuals' needs but also with the prison regime. There was also an element of pure luck.[4] In the success of the project, when a decommissioned wing became available.

Key elements of the neurodivergent unit include

- Smaller number of cells
- A smaller landing
- Designated prison staff group (electing to work there)
- Regular continuing professional development for all staff groups – to cover reasonable adjustments, sensory equipment, communication supports etc...
- Weekly 'ward round' type meeting. Four weekly rota for discussing everyone; high-risk individuals discussed weekly
- Joint referrals meeting – healthcare and prison jointly agreed on people to be admitted. Admission criteria: suspected or confirmed neurodivergence and difficulty coping in the wider prison
- Weekly reflective space for staff
- Group timetable – education put on specific 'smaller' sessions for NDU residents
- Screening of needs and basic formulation for each person
- Accessible information

Although the unit is a neurodivergent one, autism is the particular focus since these men were identified as the most vulnerable in the general prison. The unit provides greater support and understanding for autistic men including how they are approached (no sudden door knocking), access to sensory equipment, visual agendas for ACCT reviews, more supervision during association time, 'leeway' in rule non-adherence and much more.

The unit has capacity for 45 prisoners in single cells. Access to single cells has been described as the biggest single improvement to quality of life in prison by other neurodivergent individuals (User Voice, 2023). They share a common area for eating and other activities. Staff spend 10 weeks assessing the prisoners who can then benefit from up to 12 weeks of additional support.

Robbie, a unit resident said: 'It relaxes you. It's wicked. The difference is the support.'

The unit opened in October 2022 with the Unit governor reflecting on how it benefited both the neurodivergent individuals resident on the unit but also the staff.

Recommendation 7: All autistic individuals to have access to staff with specialist training and enhanced support where required.

6.9 Training

Systematic training in autism is not currently provided for all staff across the prison estate. A review of evidence undertaken by the Criminal Justice Joint Inspection surrounding neurodiversity (2021) established that provision of support for neurodivergent individuals in the criminal justice system was 'patchy, inconsistent and uncoordinated' whereby 'too little is being done to understand and meet the needs of individuals'. One of the recommendations highlighted the need for specialist training for staff around neurodivergence. Training is not one thing and has different functions and methods. Training functions may involve raising awareness of a topic or can include teaching on underlying philosophies, and/or practical strategies. Training methods include simulation, lectures, team training, shadowing (Martin *et al.*, 2014). The ultimate goal for training in this situation should be for all staff working in this setting to be aware of how autistic individuals might experience prison. Staff groups with different levels of contact with autistic individuals would then require different levels of skills and knowledge to support. Neurodivergent individuals have spoken of the need for specially trained staff to be readily available within prison settings (User Voice, 2023). Where possible training should also be tailored to the specific environment; for example, females may present differently to males (Payne and Gooding, 2025).

Whilst there are currently no systematic training requirements relating to autism, there are pockets of good practice. For example, all healthcare staff are required to complete the Oliver McGowan Mandatory Training, a standardised programme developed to upskill the wider health and care workforce to provide appropriately adjusted care for people with a learning disability and autistic people (NHS England, 2025). In the context of prisons, prison officers undertaking the 'Unlocked Graduates' Masters programme receive two one-hour training sessions on autism awareness and supporting speech, language and communication needs developed in conjunction with individuals with lived experience (Unlocked, undated). Differences in language and communication styles are frequently referenced as a key element in communication breakdown between neurotypical and neurodivergent individuals (Heasman and Gillespie, 2019). As such, understanding of these styles is essential to avoid miscommunication; for example, in a restraint situation the officer leading the incident may ask another officer to 'jump on his head'. If the individual believes this is a literal request, it would be very distressing.

Another training method that has seen positive outcomes is from the use of the 'Autism Bus' (or Autism Reality Experience (Training2Care, undated)), which provides participants with the experience of coming into prison from the perspective of an autistic person. The training is immersive and hand-developed to give neurotypical people an opportunity to experience the sensory processing difficulties. Importantly, this has been tailored for different environments, including prisons. It is intended to replicate how it could feel to be in an unfamiliar, noisy, and unpredictable environment and situation, with the added confusion likely to be felt going through the 'first night' processes, which involve several interviews and the issuing of prison kit and information notices. It can be overwhelming for anyone new to custody, and this may be amplified for someone with autism. Staff feedback from training has been powerful; they have described how effective it was in helping them to understand an autistic person's perspective. Based on the testimonials below, it could be argued that the Autism Reality Experience should be introduced as mandatory training for all prison staff in their induction training.

> Going through the autism bus for prisoners arriving into prison showed me how easily neurodiversity can be mistaken for non-compliance, and how even simple tasks can become overwhelming when you're experiencing the world through different sensory realities.
>
> Quote from staff member in London Prison Group

> Prior to taking part in the ''Autism Bus'' experience I thought I had a good understanding of the needs of those with neurodiversity who come into custody. However, I did not grasp the considerable impact of just how much the normal prison environment we are used to actually has on individuals with neurodiversity; the constant noise, the lights, the banging, the multiple instructions and requests. The experience showed me how overwhelming and difficult the environment can be. It gave me a greater sense of empathy and understanding on how we could improve certain aspects to account for everyone's needs.
>
> Quote from staff member in London Prison Group.

In order to embed awareness and consideration of autistic individuals' needs across the prison setting, training should be ongoing, and all areas of practice need to be considered. The case study below shows how autism awareness can be incorporated within current training requirements.

Case Study – Use of Force Training

A pilot is currently being run at HMP Brixton and HMP Hull to consider the approach to the use of force (UoF) in a prison setting. This pilot is currently being evaluated. UoF is defined as 'any type of physical intervention used on another person'. Within custody, trained operational staff can be required to implement UoF as a last available option to ensure that security and control are maintained. The National UoF team identified that UoF was used more often with neurodivergent individuals. Therefore, a request was made to psychology services for a training package to be developed. The training package's key objectives are to: increase understanding of neurodivergence specifically related to UoF, understand the emotional impact on individuals and staff, and develop skills in communication and de-escalation for neurodivergent individuals. The training is delivered face to face as part of the mandatory annual UoF refresher training. If the pilot proves successful in addressing its aims, it is possible that this will be rolled out more widely.

Recommendation 8: Autism awareness is to be included as a mandatory element of foundation training for all those who work in a prison setting. Further training to be provided as needed in line with job role.

Recommendation 9: Individuals with lived experience to be consulted regarding the development of training packages.

6.10 Transition(s)

Managing change and transitions can be difficult for everyone but especially so for autistic individuals (Davies and Bagnall, 2025). Careful planning and preparation are key to supporting transition (Cooper *et al.*, 2022), ensuring the plans are clear, the individual can self-advocate for their specific needs, those involved in supporting the individual moving forward are equipped with the required knowledge and skills, and onward referrals are in place to support continuity of care. Recent changes in legislation to increase early release are likely to hinder the ability to thoroughly plan and manage these transition points. Alongside this, due to security issues, system pressures, and legal language, not all elements of the transition may be known or be able to be communicated explicitly. A very basic example of this is that anyone who is sentenced has an eligible date for release; this does not mean you will be released on that date, but you could be. This creates uncertainty for all and hampers the ability to create a clear, structured, detailed plan.

An additional issue for autistic adults who have had a late diagnosis is that there is limited availability of adult community health care services, especially for those without a coexisting learning disability. Community support is crucial in managing successful transitions. RECONNECT is an example of a care after custody service that seeks to improve the continuity of care of individuals leaving prison with an identified health need, including autistic individuals (NHS England, undated).

RECONNECT works with individuals before they leave prison to support their transition to community-based services with the aims of improving the wellbeing of people leaving prison, reducing inequalities and addressing health-related drivers of offending behaviours. RECONNECT offers liaison, advocacy, signposting, and support to facilitate engagement with community-based health and support services.

Understanding one's own diagnosis can support self-advocacy and enable the individual to manage their transition needs in the most effective way for them. Simon's case study below, taken from the Chief Medical Officer's annual report (2012), shows how staff working together to support Simon to understand his needs helped him advocate for his specific needs to increase his chances of a successful transition out of custody.

Case Study – Simon

Simon was referred to the speech and language therapist. He appeared to be isolating himself from others on the unit. He was also prone to violent outbursts, and staff generally struggled to manage his behaviour. An initial speech, language, and communication assessment identified some deficits in social communication and recommended a more detailed assessment. This identified a diagnosis of Asperger syndrome.

The speech and language therapist and the psychologist within HMP YOI Feltham worked jointly with Simon to address both speech, language and communication needs and emotional/behavioural needs. They also provided support to the wider staff team. During this work, Simon was able to improve his understanding of his behaviour and why he felt the way he did. As a result, he became 'easier to manage' and was able to develop more appropriate coping strategies. There were no further episodes of violence and destructive behaviour in custody and, as a result, Simon was considered for early release. At the release meeting, in recognition of this progress, he was initially offered a reduced period on Home Detention Curfew (or 'tag'). However, to his credit, he was able to recognise that he needed an additional period of monitoring to help him embed and maintain a more socially acceptable and productive routine and avoid going back to his old ways. Simon therefore argued, in front of a group of professionals, for an extended period of curfew to support his progress (CMO, 2012).

Recommendation 10: Considered planning of transitions within the prison estate and into the community, with involvement of the autistic individual.

6.11 Other Promising Interventions

'No Wrong Door' (Lushey et al., 2017) is a community intervention to support adolescents in, or on the edge of care. These individuals tend to have quite complex lives and have contact with a huge range of services – education, health, social services, and criminal justice. This has parallels with many autistic individuals in prison. The No Wrong Door approach supports an integrated wraparound service.

The adolescent is supported by one key member of staff; other services are then accessed through that member of staff who acts as a conduit. This facilitates access to services and removes a level of complexity for the adolescent. We understand that most autistic individuals are supported by consistency in their day-to-day life and may benefit from a similar approach. However, it must be acknowledged that there would be significant complexities to overcome to implement this approach in a prison setting.

The HOPES Model is a programme to end long-term segregation for children and young people, autistic adults and/or adults with a learning disability in inpatient hospital settings. The programme has been evaluated and has been found to be hugely effective for changing the life course for several individuals in long-term segregation, with several now integrated into community settings. This approach shows promise and may potentially be successfully extended to vulnerable individuals in long-term segregation in prison settings (Fradley et al., 2025).

Research has found that staff do not have sufficient awareness of neurodivergence and this impacts how individuals experience life in prison (Loucks, 2007; User Voice, 2023). As part of the implementation of Autism Standards at HMP/YOI Feltham, staff members volunteered to become Autism 'Champions'. These Champions received additional training from healthcare staff and individuals with lived experience. They could also attend monthly breakfast or lunch drop-ins to discuss anything they wished with experts. At least one Champion was identified from each prison wing. The member of staff then wore a Champion pin on their lanyard to identify them. Individuals arriving in prison were made aware of this scheme and they could speak to these individuals for advice and support. Where possible, these Autism Champions were also assigned as Personal Officers to autistic individuals to facilitate understanding and support. In addition, 'listeners' – who provide peer support within prisons – also received similar training from the Samaritans, so that individuals who preferred to speak to their peers were able to do so and receive advice and signposting.

A promising indirect support for autistic individuals has been explored at HMP Berwyn. Violent and challenging incidents occur in all prisons; as such, it is important to understand and learn from these when they occur. At HMP Berwyn, the Speech and Language Therapist joined the prison staff when debriefing and looking at incidents to provide a different viewpoint, explain communication breakdowns and offer ideas and strategies for approaching future incidents. The inclusion of a member of staff with specialist knowledge of autism in debriefs saw a positive change in how incidents were viewed and managed (Learoyd and Bryan, Forthcoming).

6.12 Conclusion

There has been a marked increase in support available for autistic individuals in prison settings in England over the last decade. There have been many positive initiatives, and awareness of the additional difficulties experienced by neurodivergent individuals is broadly accepted. It has also been recognised that to make significant progress, all partners working in prison settings must be involved. However, there remain many further improvements that could be implemented with low or no cost implications to further improve the individual's lived experience. Allen and colleagues (2008) asked autistic individuals in contact with the criminal justice system what would make the biggest improvement to their experience. Their primary wish was for greater understanding of autism so that their behavioural and support needs could be better recognised and met. This could be, in part, accomplished by working towards the recommendations threaded through this chapter:

- All prison healthcare teams to provide access to diagnostic services, to support individuals in their self-identity (de Broize et al., 2022) and access to services.
- Diversion should be considered for all autistic individuals at risk of contact with the criminal justice system.
- Systematic screening of neurodivergent needs for all on admission.
- Each prison should have a systematic approach to supporting autistic individuals including environmental adaptations and easy read materials.
- Information regarding needs to be effectively communicated between individuals and services.
- Identified individuals across all services working in each prison to take a lead role in ensuring autistic individuals are supported throughout their journey.
- All autistic individuals to have access to staff with specialist training and enhanced support where required.
- Autism awareness to be included as a mandatory element of foundation training for all those who work in a prison setting. Further training to be provided as needed in line with job role.
- Individuals with lived experience to be consulted regarding the development of training packages.
- Considered planning of transitions within the prison estate and into the community, with involvement of the autistic individual.

Once systematic screening is in place, this will allow for better measurement of future advances, ensuring that in the future all autistic individuals are effectively supported within the prison setting and do not experience inequalities.

Notes

1 There is a broad range of terms used in this sphere, somewhat interchangeably – neurodiversity, neurodivergent, neuroaffirming, neuroinclusivity. In this chapter, we will primarily use autistic or neurodivergent. Autistic relates to those with a (self) diagnosis of this condition. Neurodivergent relates to those with a range of conditions including autism. Other terms are used where those are specifically used in the literature or job title e.g. Neurodiversity Support Manager.

2 For more information about Community Sentence Treatment Orders https://www.england.nhs.uk/commissioning/health-just/
3 ACCT documents are designed to identify and support individuals who may pose a risk of harm to themselves.
4 Described as 'pure luck' by one of the key stakeholders!

References

Allen, D., Evans, C., Hider, A., Hawkins, S., Peckett, H. and Morgan, H. (2008) 'Offending behaviour in adults with Asperger syndrome', *Journal of Autism and Developmental Disorders*, 38(4), pp. 748–758.

Ames, J. L., Morgan, E. H., Giwa Onaiwu, M., Qian, Y., Massolo, M. L. and Croen, L. A. (2022) 'Racial/ethnic differences in psychiatric and medical diagnoses among autistic adults', *Autism in Adulthood*, 4(4), pp. 290–305.

Anna Freud National Centre for Children and Families (2022) 'Independent evaluation of the Framework for Integrated Care (SECURE STAIRS)'. [Online]. Available at https://d1uw1dikibnh8j.cloudfront.net/media/15924/secure-stairs-independent-evaluation-full-report.pdf (Accessed: 25/11/25).

Beadle-Brown, J., Richardson, L., Guest, C., Malovic, A., Bradshaw, J. and Himmerich, J. (2014) 'Living in fear: Better outcomes for people with learning disabilities and autism'. [Online]. Available at https://www.inclusionlondon.org.uk/wp-content/uploads/2015/08/Living-in-Fear-Main-Research-Report.pdf (Accessed: 25/11/25).

Chadwick, L., Smith-Emes, D., Owen, H., Collier, R., Duffy-Griffith, L., Pinnock, D., Henson, L. and Stokes, R. (2025) 'Neurodiversity support managers:improving support for neurodivergentpeople in prison'. *Prison Service Journal*, 280, pp. 31–38.

Chief Medical Officer (2012) *Annual report. Our children deserve better: Prevention pays.* London: Department of Health, UK.

Cooper, D. S., Uppal, D., Railey, K. S., Blank Wilson, A., Maras, K., Zimmerman, E., Bornman, J. and Shea, L. L. (2022) 'Policy gaps and opportunities: A systematic review of autism spectrum disorder and criminal justice intersections', *Autism*, 26(5), pp. 1014–1031.

Davies, J. and Bagnall, C. (2025) '"A good transition is just key": The views and experiences of disability support staff in supporting autistic students transition to university', *Autism in Adulthood*, 7(2), pp. 155–170.

de Broize, M., Evans, K., Whitehouse, A. J., Wray, J., Eapen, V. and Urbanowicz, A. (2022) 'Exploring the experience of seeking an autism diagnosis as an adult', *Autism in Adulthood*, 4(2), pp. 130–140.

Dein, K. and Woodbury-Smith, M. (2010) 'Asperger syndrome and criminal behaviour', *Advances in Psychiatric Treatment*, 16(1), pp. 37–43.

Durcan, G., Saunders, S., Gadsby, B. and Hazard, A. (2014) *The Bradley Report five years on: An independent review of progress to date and priorities for further development.* London: Centre for Mental Health.

Fairweather, L. (2013) 'Psychological effects of the prison environment', in Fairweather, L. and McConville, S. (eds.) *Prison architecture*. London: Routledge, pp. 31–48.

Fradley, K., Rajan, D. G. and Haines-Delmont, A. (2025) *Evaluation of the National HOPE(S) Programme to end long-term segregation (LTS) for* final report. Research Report. Manchester Metropolitan University, Manchester [Online]. Available at: https://e-space.mmu.ac.uk/640963/

French, B., Daley, D., Groom, M. and Cassidy, S. (2023) 'Risks associated with undiagnosed ADHD and/or autism: A mixed-method systematic review', *Journal of Attention Disorders*, 27(12), pp. 1393–1410.

Gunasekaran, S. and Chaplin, E. (2012) 'Autism spectrum disorders and offending', *Advances in Mental Health and Intellectual Disabilities*, 6(6), pp. 308–313.

Health Services Safety Investigation Body (2025) 'Healthcare provision in prisons: Data sharing and IT' [Online]. Available at: https://www.hssib.org.uk/patient-safety-investigations/healthcare-provision-in-prisons/third-investigation-report/pdf/.

Heasman, B. and Gillespie, A. (2019) 'Neurodivergent intersubjectivity: Distinctive features of how autistic people create shared understanding', *Autism*, 23(4), pp. 910–921.

Helverschou, S. B., Steindal, K., Nøttestad, J. A. and Howlin, P. (2018) 'Personal experiences of the criminal justice system by individuals with autism spectrum disorders', *Autism*, 22(4), pp. 460–468.

HM Government. (2018) 'National Partnership Agreement for Prison Healthcare in England 2018–2021', England: Department of Health and Social Care; Ministry of Justice; NHS England; Public Health England. [Online]. Available at:https://assets.publishing.service.gov.uk/government/uploads/system/uploads/attachment_data/file/767832/6.4289_MoJ_National_health_partnership_A4-L_v10_web.pdf

Holloway, C. A., Munro, N., Jackson, J., Phillips, S. and Ropar, D. (2020) 'Exploring the autistic and police perspectives of the custody process through a participative walkthrough', *Research in Developmental Disabilities*, 97, p. 103545.

Huang, Y., Hwang, Y. I., Arnold, S. R. C., Lawson, L. P., Richdale, A. L. and Trollor, J. N. (2022) 'Autistic adults' experiences of diagnosis disclosure', *Journal of Autism and Developmental Disorders*, 52(12), pp. 5301–5307.

Hughes, N., Williams, H., Chitsabesan, P., Davies, R. and Mounce, L. (2012) *Nobody made the connection: The prevalence of neurodisability in young people who offend*. London. [Online]. Available at: https://www.childrenscommissioner.gov.uk/publication/nobody-made-the-connection/.

Kirby, A. (2016) *Using data driven decision systems to deliver person-centred approaches in developmental disorders: One example of complexity - The criminal justice system*, 3rd. Leeds: University of Leeds.

Learoyd, J. and Bryan, K. (Forthcoming) 'Communication difficulties and violence in prisons', in Morken, F., Helland, W. A. and Jones, L. (eds.) *Language and communication difficulties in the prison population*. Routledge.

Lennox, C., King, C., Chitsabesan, P., Theodosiou, L. and Shaw, J. (2013) *The development and pilot of the Comprehensive Health Assessment Tool (CHAT): Young people in the secure estate*. Manchester. [Online]. Available at: https://www.click2go.umip.com/i/coa/chat.html.

Lewis, A., Pritchett, R., Hughes, C. and Turner, K. (2015) 'Development and implementation of autism standards for prisons', *Journal of Intellectual Disabilities and Offending Behaviour*, pp. 68–80. ISSN 2050-8824.

Lewis, A. and Turner, K. (2014) 'Developing a "better" Autistic Spectrum Disorder service in a young offenders' institution', in *Youth, risk and mental health: Multiple roads to recovery*. 4th European Congress for Forensic Adolescent Psychiatry, Psychology and other involved Professions. Manchester [Online]. Available at: https://www.efcap.eu/wp-content/uploads/2015/06/EFCAP-Programme-Final-12-June-2014.pdf.

Lewis, A. H., Hughes, C., Foster, M. and Turner, K. (2016) 'Improving the management of prisoners with autistic spectrum disorders (ASD)', *Prison Service Journal*, 226, pp. 22–26.

Loucks, N. (2007) *No one knows - offenders with learning difficulties and learning disabilities - review of prevalence and associated needs*. London. [Online]. Available at: http://www.prisonreformtrust.org.uk/WhatWeDo/ProjectsResearch/Learningdisabilitiesanddifficulties/NoOneKnowspublications.

Lushey, C., Hyde-Dryden, G., Holmes, L. and Blackmore, J. (2017) *Evaluation of the no wrong door innovation programme research report*. Loughborough.

Martin, B. O., Kolomitro, K. and Lam, T. C. M. (2014) 'Training methods: A review and analysis', *Human Resource Development Review*, 13(1), pp. 11–35.

Mental Health Foundation (2022) 'Looking after your mental health in prison: A guide for male prisoners'. https://www.mentalhealth.org.uk/explore-mental-health/publications/looking-after-your-mental-health-prison-guide-male-prisoners (Accessed: 25/11/25).

Ministry of Justice (2021) *Evidence review on neurodiversity in the criminal justice system*. Available at: https://www.justiceinspectorates.gov.uk/hmiprisons/about-hmi-prisons/current-consultations/evidence-review-on-neurodiversity-in-the-criminal-justice-system/ (Accessed: 13/03/2021).

NHS England (2025) 'Health and justice framework for integration 2022-2025: Improving lives – reducing inequality'. [Online]. Available at: https://www.england.nhs.uk/long-read/health-and-justice-framework-for-integration-2022-2025-improving-lives-reducing-inequality/ (Accessed: 25/11/25).

NHS England (2025) 'The Oliver McGowan mandatory training on learning disability and autism'. [Online]. Available at https://www.hee.nhs.uk/our-work/learning-disability/current-projects/oliver-mcgowan-mandatory-training-learning-disability-autism (Accessed: 25/11/25).

NHS England (Undated) 'RECONNECT'. [Online]. Available at https://www.england.nhs.uk/commissioning/health-just/reconnect/ (Accessed 25/11/25).

Paterson, P. (2008) 'How well do young offenders with Asperger syndrome cope in custody?', *British Journal of Learning Disabilities*, 36(1), pp. 54–58.

Payne, K.-L. and Gooding, E. (2025) 'Prison-reported rates of autism in female prisons in England', *Autism*, 29(1), pp. 265–270.

Reyes, C., Perzynski, A., Kralovic, S., Taylor, H. G., Wexberg, S., Zhu, S., Frazier, T. W. and Roizen, N. (2021) 'Factors associated with transition planning in autism and other developmental disabilities', *Journal of Developmental and Physical Disabilities*, 34, pp. 1–14.

Russell, G., Stapley, S., Newlove-Delgado, T., Salmon, A., White, R., Warren, F., Pearson, A. and Ford, T. (2022) 'Time trends in autism diagnosis over 20 years: A UK population-based cohort study', *Journal of Child Psychology and Psychiatry*, 63(6), pp. 674–682.

Shaw, J., Bailey, S., Tarbuck, P., Chitsabean, P., Theodosiou, L. and Lennox, C. (2014a) *The Comprehensive Health Assessment Tool (CHAT)*. Manchester: The Offender Health Research Network. Available at: https://www.click2go.umip.com/i/coa/chat.html.

Shaw, J., Bailey, S., Tarbuck, P., Chitsabean, P., Theodosiou, L., Lennox, C., King, C., O'Connor, M., Law, H., Calame, S., Turner, O., Alam, F., McCartan, F., Seethapathy, V., Thomas, R. and Verstreken, P. (2014b) *CHAT manual: Young people in the secure estate*. Manchester. [Online]. Available at: https://www.click2go.umip.com/i/coa/chat.html.

Sun, K.-T., Shieh, T.-M., Hsia, S.-M., Ningrum, V., Lin, X.-Y. and Shih, Y.-H. (2021) 'Easy to read health education material improves oral health literacy of older adults in rural community-based care centers: A quasi-experimental study', *Healthcare*, 9(11), p. 1465.

Taylor, J., Shostak, L., Rogers, A. and Mitchell, P. (2018) 'Rethinking mental health provision in the secure estate for children and young people: A framework for integrated care (SECURE STAIRS)', *Safer Communities*, 17(4), pp. 193–201.

Training2Care (Undated) 'Autism reality experience'. [Online]. Available at https://www.training2care.com/autism-reality-experience.htm (Accessed: 25/11/25).

University of Nottingham (Undated) 'Nottinghamshire autism police partnership'. [Online]. Available at https://www.nottingham.ac.uk/research/groups/autismandpolicing/resources/index.aspx (Accessed: 25/11/25).

Unlocked (Undated) 'Unlocked graduates'. [Online]. Available at https://unlockedgrads.org.uk/ (Accessed: 25/11/25).

User Voice (2023) *"Not naughty, stupid, or bad" the voices of neurodiverse service users in the criminal justice system*. [Online]. Available at: https://www.uservoice.org/wp-content/uploads/2023/12/User_Voice_Neurodiversity_Dec_2023-1.pdf.

Voisin, M. E. (2024) *Kayleigh Melhuish: Prevention of future deaths report*. Avon, England: Ministry of Justice. [Online]. Available at: https://www.judiciary.uk/prevention-of-future-death-reports/kayleigh-melhuish-prevention-of-future-deaths-report/.

Chapter 7

Being a Safe Harbour in the Storm

Mitigating the Double Vulnerability of Neurodivergence in Youth Justice through an Experience-Sensitive Approach

Claire Westwood and Victoria Turley

7.1 Introduction

The 'Child First' framework guides the youth justice system (YJS) in England and Wales (E&W), prioritising children's needs over punitive measures (Youth Justice Board, 2022). It advocates an individualised, strengths-based approach to divert children from criminality without stigma. This philosophy mirrors broader societal shifts across multiple sectors, including in neurodevelopmental healthcare services that are moving from a medical model of individual disorder, impairment and treatment towards a social model of environmental adaptation, neuro-affirmative allyship and equity of access (Singer, 1998).[1] This is relevant to the YJS as at least one in three people in the criminal justice system (CJS) in E&W are neurodivergent (Cruise et al., 2011) and neurodivergent children are significantly over-represented in the YJS nationally and internationally (Day et al., 2024). Neurodivergent children in the YJS uniquely experience a double vulnerability. Not only are they categorised as vulnerable in the CJS purely due to being under the age of 18 years old (Police and Criminal Evidence Act, 1984), but an additional layer of vulnerability exists due to the inherent nature of being neurodivergent and justice-involved.

Neuro-majority biases from an overwhelmingly neurotypical CJS workforce can affect legal treatment, from misinterpreted non-verbal cues to courtroom sensory overwhelm, impacting fair trial access. This includes understanding how charges, cautions, bail conditions and court orders are understood (Kirby, 2021) and aligns with the findings from the Equality and Human Rights Commission that the CJS is failing autistic people and those with learning disabilities, with reform needed to ensure a fair trial for all (EHRC, 2020). Specifically for neurodivergent justice-involved children, Gormley (2022) found that there can be a range of 'hidden harms' where adults fail to recognise, assess, understand and respond effectively to these children's needs. Similarly, Slavny-Cross et al. (2022) found that at both an individual and systemic level of the CJS there is a lack of awareness of neurodivergent experiences and access needs. This can perpetuate a labelling and disabling cycle, with isolation of and segregation for these children (Day, 2022), leading to repetitive recidivism.

DOI: 10.4324/9781003638742-8

This chapter asks: how can the 'Child First' approach be tailored specifically for neurodivergent justice-involved children to mitigate these double vulnerabilities? We make the case for the integration of an experience-sensitive approach in the YJS (McGreevy et al., 2024), to ensure neurodivergent children receive the individualised and supportive approach required. This approach has been chosen as it encompasses a holistic conceptualisation of how professionals can affirm neurodivergent identities and uniquely prioritises wellbeing over behavioural conformity, whilst still working towards the same goals of cessation of offending and pro-social integration into society. The approach honours lived experience and enables environments where neurodivergent young people can feel seen, heard and valued. It aligns seamlessly with Child First principles by fostering dignity, agency, and emotional safety, and by recognising that meaningful engagement and positive outcomes arise when care is responsive to the unique sensory, cognitive, and relational needs of each young person. In doing so, it not only reduces the risk of re-traumatisation and exclusion but also promotes authentic participation and long-term flourishing for the children involved. This chapter discusses the eight dimensions of an experience-sensitive approach using academic theory, real-life implications and starts and ends each section with commentary from one of the authors (Victoria Turley), who has lived experience as a neurodivergent adolescent in the YJS. Please note that this chapter contains discussions and reference to self-harm and suicide, which some readers may find distressing.

7.2 What Is an Experience-Sensitive Approach?

An experience-sensitive approach is an alternative humanistic framework of neuro-affirming care that promotes a dignified, respectful and personalised approach when working alongside neurodivergent communities (McGreevy et al., 2024). It is adapted from Galvin and Todres' 'Caring and Wellbeing: A Lifeworld Approach' (2013) and has eight key dimensions: insiderness, agency, uniqueness, togetherness, sense-making, personal journey, sense of place, and embodiment. Each will be considered in turn. At the core of neurodivergent-affirming care are three key themes: acceptance, belonging, and connection (McGreevy et al., 2024). This is important for the YJS as feelings of safety, security and belonging have been found to be vital factors for positive outcomes (Paterson-Young et al., 2021); in contrast, many justice-involved young people report feeling a sense of being othered.

A key component of a neurodivergent-affirming approach is '#FlipTheNarrative' thinking (Chapple, 2023). This is a movement aimed at reframing conceptualisations of neurodiversity away from a focus on deficits and towards neuroinclusive practice that values human diversity as a natural form of human variation. This chapter will now discuss the eight dimensions of an experience-sensitive approach in the context of being neurodivergent in the YJS.

7.3 'Insiderness'

> Regardless of which side of the system I was on at the time, it felt that both times I was the one being interrogated, distrusted and othered.
>
> *Victoria Turley*

The first key dimension of an experience-sensitive approach is 'insiderness': the concept that everyone has their own personal world and authority on their inward self (McGreevy et al., 2024). Each neurodivergent child in the YJS has developed their own understanding of the world and who they are, and the same applies for a neurotypical-majority CJS workforce. This mismatch in worldview and perception can often lead to the Double Empathy Problem (Milton, 2012) – that is, the concept that there can be a mutual misunderstanding between people with different cognitive styles. Neurotypical people can struggle to understand neurodivergent people during interactions, and vice versa. Common examples include neurotypical people's use of figurative and non-literal language which neurodivergent people can interpret literally, or neurodivergent people's interests in favoured topics can be seen as 'too much' by neurotypical people who have a wider and shallower set of preferences.

However, as the neuro-minority in current society, neurodivergent people regularly carry the burden of adaptation, meaning they often 'mask' or 'suppress' their true self or identity to blend in with or survive in the neurotypical norm (Miller et al., 2021). This concept can be extended further in professional dynamics to the Triple Empathy Problem (Shaw et al., 2023); that is, an additional layer of bi-directional misunderstanding where neurodivergent people are additionally vulnerable due to the power differential held by those in authority, the majority of whom are, again, neurotypical.

In the CJS context, both the Double and Triple Empathy gaps manifest in the attempts of majority neurotypical police officers, judges, and probation officers to reduce recidivism with neurodivergent cohorts. This immediately puts the neurodivergent justice-involved at a disadvantage. For example, neurotypical professionals may interpret neurodivergent children's behaviour through a neurotypical lens. This could look like a police officer inferring that a lack of eye contact from an autistic young person during an interview indicates a lack of compliance in the process and not a sensory shutdown; or a teenager being deemed not to be showing remorse by a YJS officer because of a neutrality of facial expression in conversation. Ultimately, it can mean that neurodivergent justice-involved people can face institutional ableism from arrest to sentencing. The effects of these ineffective interactions can be seen later through the high proportion of neurodivergent adults 'trapped' in repeat contact with the CJS for low-level offences (Revolving Doors, 2022). This begs the questions: if the access needs of neurodivergent children are not met at the first police contact, how do they successfully pivot away from the justice system back to society? And how do we mitigate this double vulnerability?

It is widely recommended in the literature that as a starting point CJS professionals receive training on neurodivergence (Day, 2022; Slavny-Cross et al., 2022 and Shaw et al., 2023). This training would enable staff to check their neurotypical privilege, that is, the special and unearned advantage afforded by those who happen to have the most common cognitive expression (Milton, 2022). This will enable professionals to examine their own biases around neurodivergence and reduce the likelihood of objectification (reducing someone to their diagnostic profile and/or offence). McGreevy et al. (2024) advocate for 'compassion, connection and curiosity' in understanding the viewpoints and experiences of neurodivergent children. It is important to authentically hear the young person's voice when they are telling their stories:

- Embrace neurodivergent communication styles – these children may find it easier to express themselves in the context of a hyper-focused interest or may require a setting where eye contact is not required.
- Practice active listening – this may include accepting different conversational turn lengths or narratives given in a non-chronological order.
- Respect boundaries – some days may be easier to communicate than others for neurodivergent people, for reasons not able to be perceived by neurotypical individuals (for example, related to sensory differences).

7.3.1 Victoria's Commentary

Understanding why a crime occurs is central to the YJS, but when neurodivergent people are involved, justice isn't as clear-cut as many believe. As a neurodivergent woman, I've experienced both sides – first as a victim, then as an offender (both times as a youth). Both experiences highlighted the extreme lack of understanding from the system and workers; the stereotyping neurodivergent people are subject to in the system; and how the system is failing the neurodivergent people it encounters. My first interaction with the CJS was as a victim of abuse at 13. I was made to endure long, uncomfortable and traumatic interviews which later shaped my relationship with authority. In these interviews, I was often placed in brightly lit rooms, with uncomfortable seating, cameras in my face and a stranger pressuring me to answer questions 'directly'. They often asked me the same questions which came across as them not believing my answers because I couldn't give them in the manner they thought was correct or believable. I rarely met the same officer twice, and the only consistency I had in this was my mother. For a year I endured this and more, and eventually the case was dismissed as not having enough evidence because my testimony was not 'reliable enough'. This came down to the fact that every worker I saw had no understanding of neurodivergence, what it looks like in victims and how to actually communicate and help appropriately.

In fact, they were so unsure that my neurodivergence was not discovered until after I was involved as an offender. As an offender, I found it interesting that reliability was not something that seemed as important to the police, compared to when I was the victim. I shut down during the whole process and gave minimal engagement. I was given community service and required to have speech and language therapy. It was during this therapy that I felt I was heard, because I was speaking to someone who understood and made the right time and space for me as a neurodivergent person. I was able to get a diagnosis and understand myself, my needs and how to help myself so much better and since then I have not been involved with the CJS as an offender. I am the proof that with diagnosis, compassion, understanding and actual empathy that neurodivergent people can stay out of the system, as offenders and even potentially as victims, since the more we understand ourselves, the easier it becomes to recognise when we are unsafe, being abused or manipulated. I do believe the CJS has a responsibility and duty to do their best to see, hear and truly protect our neurodivergent youths. This includes the duty to identify and recognise double vulnerability and adapt plans of action to fit the needs of the person.

7.4 'Agency'

The second dimension of an experience-sensitive approach outlines the importance for neurodivergent people to experience autonomy and choice, to facilitate a sense of dignity and control (McGreevy et al., 2024). Neurodivergent adults report that in the context of a pervasive lack of control, emotional dysregulation occurs, and they may have limited awareness of their internal state until it is 'too late' (Beck et al., 2024). In a CJS context, this may look like an autistic young person shouting and crying in the police station due to sensory overload but lacking awareness that this is what is happening and being perceived again as 'defiant' or 'aggressive'. Triggers for this can be vast and varied. Neurodivergent people report that unmet sensory sensitivities may contribute to emotional dysregulation, as well as sudden changes in routine or being misunderstood by a neurotypical person. Escalations can also occur when serious consequences are threatened as a response to this emotional dysregulation (Beck et al., 2024), such as being arrested. When receiving professional services, a lack of agency can result in passivity. For a neurodivergent child in the YJS, this can look like imposed attitudes and practices being 'done to' rather than 'with' the child, making them a powerless recipient. This can be seen in YJS through generic and didactically delivered rehabilitative sessions on 'knife crime' or 'weapons awareness' as outlined on court orders and is in opposition to the 'Child First' values that require practice to be meaningful and person-centred.

How do we facilitate autonomy and advocacy for neurodivergent children in the YJS? Utilising the 'Child First' principle of an individualised approach, we can find what creates a sense of safety for young people. McGreevy et al. (2024) emphasise that 'engagement itself is the priority'. Examples of this include:

- Making the purpose and format of sessions clear from the outset using task plans or visual timetables.
- Accepting asynchronous forms of communication (e.g. emails or texts rather than phone calls when organising meetings).

- Providing multiple activity options that all address the objective of the session.
- Incorporating hyper-focus topics or interests into required activities.
- Integrating breaks and making it clear when and for how long they will occur.
- Allowing a young person to bring in anchoring objects to provide comfort and reassurance.

To facilitate this, young people need access to safe places, safe people and safe responses (see more on this in Section 7.9– 'Sense of Place'). By accepting and advocating for neurodivergent ways of being, this enables young people to feel safe and be engaged in what is happening. Without this, these same young people can experience increased distress, a loss of hope and diminished personhood (McGreevy et al., 2024) increasing their vulnerability to further criminalisation and negative life chances.

7.4.1 Victoria's Commentary

As an autistic person, I find that agency over myself is one of the most important things I value. When I find I cannot make my own decisions and choices in matters that relate to me, it leads to meltdowns and shutdowns. Growing up not knowing I was autistic meant I spent most of my mental energy learning how to act 'normal.' I always sensed I was different and felt out of place, which fuelled immense anxiety at a young age. During this period, I catered to others' expectations – sitting where the cool kids in primary school told me and doing everything in high school to gain the impression of being 'normal.' I was unaware that my anxiety stemmed from never having a choice; I felt there was no way to survive without forfeiting my agency, and it was suffocating. During that time, my meltdowns were more frequent. I often absconded and put myself in increasingly dangerous situations, leaving the house late at night and never telling anyone where I was. I spent a lot of time in hospitals under watch for self-harm, including suicide attempts, because I felt fundamentally wrong in my own body and mind.

In school, the idea of authority never fully clicked for me – a struggle that continues today. I was often put in isolation for wearing the 'wrong' shoes or trousers because I needed clothing that wouldn't distract my brain with sensory discomfort during lessons. Now that I understand my own needs, I question why certain mandates strip me of agency. For instance, strict work uniforms are a challenge. As someone who is expressive and autistic, I have issues with certain materials. I experience heightened anxiety with my hair tied back – it's a sensory nightmare – and I prefer keeping my piercings as they provide a sense of safety. These requirements don't affect my work performance, so I struggle to see the basis for them. Instead, I was often labelled 'defiant' and said to have an 'attitude' for questioning rules, accused of disrespect when I was simply trying to avoid discomfort. This links so heavily into why the CJS absolutely must increase their ability and willingness to adapt for neurodivergent people. For me, while being interviewed as a victim at the police station, none of my sensory needs were met or even questioned.

The room alone was a personal nightmare to be in, let alone discuss in detail trauma that had happened. I completely shut down and gave minimal, simple answers. This would affect my entire case in terms of sufficient evidence and because of my 'defiance' I was not given any trust or belief from the CJS.

Simple adjustments – like offering at-home interviews, rooms with softer lighting, or various seating options – can give neurodivergent individuals a greater sense of agency. These changes not only help them engage fully in the process but also promote cooperation, leading to more effective investigations. It's the responsibility of the CJS to educate and equip themselves to adapt processes for neurodivergent people. Without this, access to police and related services is inherently unfair to those who think and experience differently from the majority – this isn't a valid reason to deny truly fair access. True fairness and agency will only be achieved when neurodivergent individuals aren't penalised for their natural responses to system-imposed stimuli. Imagine a police station where a neurodivergent person can ask for help without fear of pressure, discomfort, or disbelief due to not acting 'the right way.' I no longer feel comfortable reaching out for help because I feel forced to surrender my agency, worsening my situation. Many neurodivergent people share this experience, which puts us at greater risk of victimisation, especially when our genuine needs are dismissed.

7.5 'Uniqueness'

> No one could 'see' my autism because they hadn't been taught what autism looks like in women.
>
> – Victoria Turley

The third facet of an experience-sensitive approach is to move away from a 'one-size-fits-all' approach via the recognition of neurodivergent uniqueness (McGreevy et al., 2024). Neurodivergent children may have specific needs unrelated to other disabled children (such as sensory differences), and these needs may go unidentified and unmet, particularly if they have no co-occurring learning disabilities (Slavny-Cross et al., 2022). This happens as these young people are likely able to engage in surface-level conversation whilst 'masking' (hiding) any underlying difficulties they are experiencing. An experience-sensitive approach advocates for unconditional positive regard, acceptance, and genuine empathy in interactions with justice-involved neurodivergent children (McGreevy et al., 2024). In the YJS, this might look like meeting sensory-seeking needs during sessions, trying to understand the true reason behind a person's dysregulation that could neurotypically be perceived as 'defiant', or even openly acknowledging the ableist trauma that a neurodivergent child may have historically experienced that has led to a lack of trust within police and justice services. This creates a solid foundation of trust that is required before a depth for sharing of information can be established (for example, life histories or context of offending behaviour).

Another way of embracing this uniqueness is to acknowledge and accept young people's individual characteristics and contexts. This includes the overlapping intersectionalities some neurodivergent children may have related to gender, sexuality, race/ethnicity, religion and/or other disabilities. Acknowledging and embracing cultural identities is particularly important for Black and racialised children due to the narrow societal understanding of neurodivergence still framed in accordance with a White majority (Davis et al., 2022). Furthermore, racially minoritised children are up to five times more likely to receive an incorrect pathologising diagnosis (e.g. conduct disorder or oppositional defiance disorder) instead of being identified as neurodivergent, as compared to their White peers (Fadus et al., 2020). This is important in YJS practice when considering the school-to-prison pipeline and how racially minoritised neurodivergent children may present at the YJS with these behaviour-focused diagnoses rather than having their neurodivergence recognised and supported.

This intersectional approach is also important for neurodivergent girls and trans/non-binary children due to the historically male bias in diagnostic criteria across multiple neurodivergent diagnoses, differences in gendered presentations (Craddock, 2024; Vincenti et al., 2023; Driver and Chester, 2021) and higher prevalence of neurodivergence for gender-diverse people (Warrier et al., 2020). Again, training for YJS professionals on these different neurodivergent presentations is imperative. It is also important for YJS staff to acknowledge and challenge the double, and even triple, discrimination that racially marginalised and/or gender-diverse neurodivergent children can experience in relation to their intersectionalities. By avoiding generalisation of process and interaction, YJS professionals can recognise the intersectionalities within neurodivergent children's lives, and support them to build self-knowledge, understanding and advocacy (McGreevy et al., 2024), as well as embody the Child First values of personalisation and individuality.

7.5.1 Victoria's Commentary

Before anything else, in the CJS I've always been seen as a woman – a status that makes me inherently vulnerable in the system, whether as a victim or an offender. Although recent events, like the Sarah Everard case, have spurred some improvements, there seems to be little to no appreciation of intersectionality or inclusion for other groups of vulnerable people.

Now imagine being disadvantaged on more than one side. This was me. I was not diagnosed until after my time being involved as an offender, which meant that both times I had come into the system, not one person could look further into my behaviour, into why I was in these positions, and I had no way of knowing how to ask for my needs to be met. However, these interactions that I had with the system, looking back, were some of the biggest signs that I was neurodivergent and vulnerable, and that there was more to my story. But not a single person working in the system had the knowledge or training to help me. All these things about my identity affect how my neurodivergence is perceived. This is not an individual's failure; it's a systemic one. Every CJS worker must be trained at an intersectional level to ensure that no one receives less than they need because of their race, gender, religion, disability, or sexuality. Knowing how to respectfully approach any background is essential to making the system truly functional for everyone.

7.6 'Togetherness'

> People expect those who are neurodivergent to be able to cope with trauma or grasp the consequences of their actions without an informed social support group.
>
> – Victoria Turley

In the section above we have discussed how to support neurodivergent justice-involved children's uniqueness. This will now be taken one step further when considering that uniqueness in the context of community networks and a majority neurotypical YJS workforce. McGreevy et al. (2024) discuss that an experience-sensitive approach cannot take place in isolation. They state that through relationships, children (and adults) learn more about themselves via shared commonalities and differences. Specifically in relation to the YJS, it has been established in the literature that for restorative justice practices to succeed, a relational approach must be paramount (Seymour, 2023). This cannot be tokenistic or superficial, but come from a place of genuine connection and acceptance. This approach forms part of key trauma-informed approaches, imperative for neurodivergent people as trauma can happen interpersonally through the aforementioned Double Empathy Problem (Milton, 2012).

Again, this returns to the key action for the YJS: to establish emotional safety through consistency, transparency and empowerment for true collaboration (McGreevy et al., 2024). Practically, in the YJS space, this means professionals doing what they say they're going to do, establishing clear and regular contact where required and accepting neurodivergent ways of communicating within that relationship. A key role of the YJS is to advocate for neurodivergent children's access needs across networks – whether this is within families, at school, or in court. For example, explaining in Post-Sentence Reports how neurodivergence intersects with the context of an offence, or supporting a neurodivergent child at Referral Order Panel to communicate accessibly. By acting as a conduit to strengthen a child's networks through shared understanding of that child's access needs, YJS professionals can be the key to building community and reducing isolation.

7.6.1 Victoria's Commentary

Neurodivergent people have always needed support systems, so the fact that during both of my experiences with the system I felt absolutely no sense of community, support or socialisation is not only harmful but it's borderline diabolical. There is often an assumption that in this world it is the neurodivergent individual's responsibility to adapt to the neurotypical world around them. This assumption is incredibly harmful. The idea that I have to not only navigate trauma I have experienced and go through it detail by detail to a stranger, but I must do it in what seems like a secret coded language for any chance of being understood and believed is extremely distressing. It is like having to call for emergency services in a different country where you cannot understand or speak more than a few words in that language. How do you tell anyone what's wrong? How do you communicate the help you need? The double empathy problem is exactly that: a problem.

A large majority of my trauma comes from the aspects of being isolated at school, work, etc. The only real support system I had was my family (mother and sister) and even then, it wasn't until I was 15/16 years old that they were able to fully understand and support me consistently in a way that benefited me and improved my vulnerability. CJS professionals need to ensure that the community surrounding the neurodivergent person is just as inclusive and supportive of the individual's needs. If support is not consistent, the support is essentially useless to them. If I had experienced a more trustworthy and consistent system, one that didn't make me feel small for not communicating or behaving in a way they expected, I may have a different opinion and outlook now as an adult. Building trust and eliminating the double empathy problem will quite literally and directly help rebuild the trust and relationship between the neurodivergent community and the system.

7.7 'Sense Making'

> Neurodivergent individuals should not have the burden of changing everything about them just to get help or justice.
>
> – Victoria Turley

As outlined at the start of this chapter, neurodivergent justice-involved children can experience a double vulnerability because of their age and disability. Part of this vulnerability can be related to establishing meaning and significance in things, places, events and experiences around them. An experience-sensitive approach accepts and values neurodivergent ways of being and perceiving, seeing them as intrinsically meaningful aspects of society (McGreevy et al., 2024). This can often jar with the CJS, which values neurotypical ways of listening, communicating, showing empathy and remorse. For example, autistic individuals receive longer sentences due to being perceived as less remorseful (Foster and Young, 2022), and because of a perceived difficulty that they struggle to understand how their actions have affected others (Fitzpatrick et al., 2018).

However, if professionals can be an unbiased listening ear and encourage the person to express their inner reflections, this phenomenon could be reframed. An example of this could be during restorative justice sessions with neurodivergent young people where empathy is explored. Professionals can acknowledge neurodivergent ways of demonstrating empathy to bridge the Double Empathy gap

(Milton, 2012). This may look like an autistic young person being very direct, straightforward and unemotional in their description of a victim's response to their behaviour or not being able to name the emotion that was provoked in the victim at that time (alexithymia). By neutrally acknowledging this communication style and not attributing a lack of remorse to a difference in expression, this shows that neurodivergent communication is valued and understood but also avoids ableist prejudice and discrimination.

If inaccurate or misleading stories are constructed and shared about neurodivergent people by professionals (for example, that they aren't sorry because they haven't shown remorse in the expected way), this can lead to disconnection, disengagement and a lack of trust (McGreevy et al., 2024). Professionals can engage in genuine professional curiosity to ask how young people want to share their views and be creative in modifying sessions to enable this – for example, utilising the creative arts as a method of expression. Similarly, young people may wish to express the vocabulary they wish professionals to use in verbal and written communications, e.g. the language used in reporting about their neurodivergence.

7.7.1 Victoria's Commentary

In my opinion, the CJS has an 'ideal' or 'expected' emotional reaction in mind for different offences and sentences. However, this is based on neurotypical perceptions and stereotyping. I know first-hand how much emotional responses can impact the outcome of a case. When I first encountered the CJS as a victim, I was going through some of the biggest trauma of my life... undiagnosed. So not only did I have to process what happened to me, it felt like I had to do it completely alone, as the 'support system' around me didn't understand why I wasn't processing the trauma the way they expected. For me, being in the presence of police was incredibly intimidating. Despite being the victim, I interpreted that this was a serious environment and not the place for a meltdown or emotional outburst. In fact, I was so worried that my meltdown would lead to my own arrest, I did the exact opposite. I shut down emotionally. Completely. Before interviews, I would often lash out or meltdown in front of my Mum to make sure it didn't happen in there. I answered all questions as methodically, logically and clearly as I could, but instead of seeing this as a survivor analysing her traumatic experience, they interpreted it as someone making up facts as they perceived there was no 'emotional response' behind them. No one said it to my face, but it seemed everyone involved (except my mother) thought I was a liar. I was often questioned about how I knew specific details but not others. I was grilled about remembering more things as time went on. Essentially, I wasn't acting 'traumatised enough'.

I never got justice in this case. When I was involved as an offender a couple of years later, I knew I had to 'play their game' and respond in the ways they expected. So, I did. Instead of going into depth about the help I actually needed, I admitted I was wrong, showed them remorse, said I was sorry, painted some bird boxes for community service and that was it. Even though I didn't necessarily feel that way at the time because of the help I actually needed. Emotions are such a complex thing, and they cannot be boiled down to a 'one size fits all' approach. Space needs to be made for neurodivergent people to react in the way their body and mind need, without fear of being discriminated against. As an autistic person, it often takes me a few days to emotionally process how I feel about anything that's happened. For example, if someone was passively or even openly disrespectful it may take me until a couple of days later to process that I feel upset and disrespected. This also applies to most emotions. I'm never really 100% sure if something has made me sad/happy/angry until a period after. At the end of the day, we are human too, we have emotions, we experience them and often in extremes. A little patience, empathy and education make the difference. Even though the neurodivergence spectrum varies, we can interpret in our own ways how you feel about us, how you view and talk about us. Be mindful always.

7.8 'Personal Journey'

> To help people you have to understand that not everyone is what you expect of them.
>
> Victoria Turley

An additional element of an experience-sensitive approach is in relation to how neurodivergent young people are supported to contextualise their past, present, and future context (McGreevy et al., 2024). This is particularly relevant as the YJS undertakes comprehensive assessments, often from the first contact, to understand the circumstances surrounding an offence as well as familial, educational, and health contexts. By exploring this personal narrative, teams can formulate underlying causes and design a plan to move forward towards rehabilitation. Constructing spoken narratives in the neurotypical style can be challenging for some autistic young people (Harvey et al., 2025), particularly in terms of how easy-to-follow and meaningful these stories are perceived to be by neurotypical listeners (Maras et al., 2020; Hilvert et al., 2016). Harvey et al. (2025) found that autistic adolescents produced shorter narratives, with fewer details and less elaboration than non-autistic peers. In a youth justice context, this could look like shorter answers to questions posed about offending behaviours, or about family, peer networks or educational experiences. This relates to the aforementioned negative perceptions that can be held by professionals when met with this 'surly teenage behaviour', mistakenly attributed to some neurodivergent adolescents.

As in the previous section, McGreevy et al. (2024)'s experience-sensitive approach advocates for unconditional acceptance of neurodivergent ways of being and communicating when listening to young people sharing their stories and life experiences. Training for youth justice professionals in neuro-affirmative approaches would enable more authentic interactions and outcomes for these neurodivergent young people involved in the justice system. Practitioners can support young people by scaffolding the structure of their stories using visual templates

Table 7.1 A narrative grid to elicit a story

WHO	WHERE	WHEN
FIRST	NEXT	LAST

(e.g. narrative or story grids, see Table 7.1), providing emotional and contextual anchors (e.g. asking prompting questions about time, place, emotions, or relationships), and advocating for the use of creative outlets (e.g. painting, photography, comic strips, or songwriting).

The consideration of personal journeys does not apply only to explorations of the past. By supporting where a person has been, it can support with the unfamiliar and uncertain conceptualisation of the future. Future planning is a key part of supporting young people to move from criminality into pro-social spaces to reduce the risk of recidivism. McGreevy et al. (2024) discuss the importance of co-constructing and facilitating future planning. Youth justice workers will often facilitate future contexts with young people through the creation of networks with further education, training providers and employers as part of a court order's requirements. They state that the key is for adults to pay attention to both a young person's history and their future hopes and goals, rather than making assumptions based on a snapshot of their life at present gained during interview. One way of moving forward with this might look like true co-production during Referral Order Panels where contracts are made with the young person and their family, rather than 'done to' them.

Finally, for this section, it is important to consider how the young person inevitably transitions out of the YJS. McGreevy et al. (2024) advocate for giving extended timeframes to navigate transitions to accommodate for processing time required and the emotional impact of the end of this chapter and the start of the next. A transition map out of the service can be created with the young person to clearly establish what is happening next and when, with concrete timelines and meaningful goals used as a staircase either into adult probation services or back into the community.

7.8.1 Victoria's Commentary

If the goal for the CJS is for authentic and true justice, then individual adaptive processes are the way forward. Understanding, empathy, and flexibility in these approaches are essential. When you come across these people, they are going to be in some of the worst spots in their life and they need help – real, unbiased help. They need help in that moment and for the future; planning and following through on these plans can be the key difference for some neurodivergent people who may spend the rest of their lives involved with the CJS. They cannot do this without understanding, empathy, and care from the people around them and those involved.

CJS professionals need to find ways to adapt their processes to allow neurodivergent individuals to communicate as they need and be accepted. For example, using picture cards to help identify areas of the body may take the pressure off neurodivergent people having to find the correct word for the situation. I often struggle to identify what is the best language to use when referring to private areas depending on the environment, so in important settings I often opt not to use the words at all. But for a neurodivergent victim that has experienced sexual abuse, it will be vital that they can communicate, in their own clear way, what happened. Professionals can also adapt interview locations. Maybe they can be mobile interviews for neurodivergent people who feel more comfortable outside; interviews and statements taken at home, school, community centres are all possible adaptations that can change so much for neurodivergent people. Becoming aware of new ways to communicate, approach, and support neurodivergent people can only make you better at what you do. It can only make you a better professional, who is more capable of understanding and obtaining the whole truth, because trust and understanding are everything to us as neurodivergent people and it makes all the difference.

7.9 'Sense of Place'

> Are we 'hard to engage' or are services 'hard to approach'?
>
> Victoria Turley

For the seventh element of an experience-sensitive approach, McGreevy et al. (2024) outline how neurodivergent people can feel a sense of 'dislocation' rooted in the experience of being a neurominority within society. Daily navigation of a neurotypical culture at home, at school and in the community, that is so different from neurodivergent experiences, can be physically draining and emotionally isolating. For some neurodivergent young people, an additional key space in which this dislocation can occur is the YJS, particularly for those on remand or in custody, where the environment, interactions and expectations do not align or reflect their needs or what is familiar. This is important for practitioners to consider as isolation, confinement and a lack of support for those who are both neurodivergent and justice-involved can lead to long-term negative mental health impacts (Finer, 2024). For example, changes in routine, whether that is a move into custody or adaptation to the requirements of a community court order, can lead to distress and/or dysregulation.

To mitigate this, again we revisit the principles of building neuro-affirmative psychological safety in interactions with young people. Professional curiosity allows us to ask the question of what creates a sense of home and place for that individual (McGreevy et al., 2024). This may be through a conversation on what their access needs are and how they can be met, or you may ask what can support them in feeling calmer or more regulated in that environment.

This relates back to the Child First principles of an individualised approach but making sure to do this via a neuro-affirmative lens. These questions will need to be expressed in a way that is accessible to the young person both in terms of being age-appropriate and communication style.

Moreover, practitioners can explore the principles of 'SPACE' (Doherty, 2023) to extend this approach. This is a framework for ensuring accessible physical, processing and emotional spaces and is beyond the scope of this chapter to discuss fully. However, key components relating to youth justice are:

- SPACE: managing sensory needs via the adjustment of physical environments (quiet rooms, dimmed lighting etc.) and the addition of sensory tools.
- PREDICTABILITY: clear communication of legal processes and what will happen, visual schedules or written step-by-step guidance.
- ACCEPTANCE: showing understanding of autistic ways of being and communicating.
- COMMUNICATION: incorporating alternative communication methods (e.g. written, pictorial or technological) and providing additional processing time.
- EMPATHY: recognising the unique and heightened needs of neurodivergent people who are justice-involved and ensuring compassion is central to all interactions.

The overall aim of this part of an experience-sensitive approach is to support neurodivergent justice-involved young people to find meaning, safety and connection, to feel welcome, and be empowered in their identity (McGreevy et al., 2024).

7.9.1 Victoria's Commentary

This is going to be one of the first steps you take towards being more inclusive as a practitioner. This will be where you learn from all kinds of different people and start learning and improving for every person you meet from that point. Being able to create a sense of place and a sense of belonging, you'll see how much neurodivergent people can open up. We're often labelled as 'hard to engage' or 'unwilling to engage' when in reality, we're processing something big, in a space in which we do not feel safe to do so. So for our own safety and protection, we mask it until it becomes something we can no longer contain. This pattern tends to lead to a meltdown or shutdown of some sort. A great starting point is to offer a physical safe space for neurodivergent people; don't guess what their needs are, don't try to predict what they might need or just ask them, find a way to open a basic level of communication so that they can tell you what they need from you in this time. These things can vary from different lighting to different seating, different background noise or stimming toys. Allowing people to process things in a space they want and need is the safest thing for them. I often find I need a lot of stimulation but only in specific ways. For example, I like a room with a lot of lights but never the main light. I prefer colourful lamps and a dimmer setting but that is lit enough for me to see what I need to do. I also always require background noise e.g. a TV show I like or music but never background noises of electricity or fans. I also prefer floor-based seating compared to chairs. Having these things accessible to me makes all the difference in how I react to things.

7.10 'Embodiment'

> I've had adult professionals both in the CJS and school, tell me if I wanted to be believed I'd have to 'buck up' and 'get my words out'.
>
> Victoria Turley

The final aspect of an experience-sensitive approach is that of embodiment, or how we experience the world and our perception of its context, possibilities and limits (McGreevy et al., 2024). For neurodivergent young people growing up in a majority neurotypical society, this feeling of being different or 'other' may place limits on how they feel able to have their emotional needs met. Historically, disabled and neurodivergent people have been medicalised, institutionalised and othered. This still manifests today in deficit-based systems and processes. If we think of how neurodivergent justice-involved young people are treated in schools, police stations and prisons, we see how negative interactions can shape their world viewpoints. To counteract this, McGreevy et al. (2024) outline how practitioners can cultivate positive identities through a strengths-based approach. YJS spaces can adapt this approach by centring interactions around what a young person is good at or enjoys. For example, if a complex concept such as 'joint enterprise' has to be explained and the young person enjoys Lego, the Lego figures can be used to model the concept.

By focusing on each young person's inherent strengths and co-creating pathways that resonate with their interests and assets, practitioners lay the groundwork for lasting self-efficacy and resilience. This paves the way not just for a reduction in negative self-perception, but also for the development of coping strategies that empower individuals to overcome future challenges. Moreover, neurodivergent young people who also belong to racial, gender, or socioeconomically minoritised communities often face layered exclusions. This intersectionality intensifies the feeling of not fitting in and reinforces societal barriers that prevent them from fully accessing emotional and social support. Integrating mentors or peer supporters who share similar neurodivergent experiences can provide invaluable role models. When neurodivergent youth witness others who have not only navigated similar challenges but have also forged positive, resilient identities, it challenges the prevailing deficit narratives and provides authentic, life-affirming perspectives. By avoiding making assumptions or value judgements, by assuming competence, and by seeing these young people as people first, we aim to mitigate these feelings of shame and loss (McGreevy et al., 2024). Neurodivergent justice-involved young people hear enough negative stories told about themselves – professionals don't need to add to this. Compassion in these times of intensity and stress can be the safe hands that a young person needs to start to understand themselves and move forward with their lives.

7.10.1 Victoria's Commentary

I have always been autistic. My entire life has been spent living autistically even if no one was aware of that. However, the world has always placed its limits on me. As early as year 2, I was reading at a high level for my age, but I also had no friends and was often picked on. I felt a lot of pressure develop around my academia and navigating people was my worst nightmare. This pressure developed into holding my academic ability higher than anything else in life, including my own physical health and relationships. As I got older, I found it interesting that while doctors debated what was 'wrong' with me, people at school were already bullying me for being 'weird' and 'different'. I've always known that compared to the majority expectation, I have had limits put on my life. For example, people expect me to work in one job for 40 hours a week as opposed to multiple jobs that I enjoy and help me prevent burnout. People assumed that university would be easy for me because of the academic aspect, but they also didn't expect me to choose a BA in Acting because of the creative aspects. For neurodivergent people in the minority, I often find limits are placed on them without full awareness. These limits placed on us range from academic expectations to emotional ones too.

I have spent a lot of my time alive asking questions like 'what could life have been if I wasn't this way?' 'how do I become someone else?' and 'would life be easier without me?' I have spent countless summer holidays trying to 're-invent' myself with new personalities in the hope that, one day, I'd be considered 'normal' enough to not feel the way I did. I have battled so hard with accepting who I am, even after my diagnosis, to some degree even more so now I'm sure I'm autistic. I have still had moments of 'what could my life have been if I wasn't autistic?' I still grieve a life I cannot have because the world is not a truly accepting place. CJS professionals have the potential to reshape these thoughts in young neurodivergent people by wholly accepting them and their experiences, creating safe spaces and leading in an adaptive way.

7.11 Conclusion

This chapter has examined how an experience-sensitive approach (McGreevy et al., 2024) can create safe, equitable spaces for neurodivergent young people in the YJS, outlining eight key dimensions that – implemented appropriately – can foster acceptance, belonging, and connection through authentic engagement and emotional safety. Aligned with the Child First framework (Youth Justice Board, 2022), this approach promotes pro-social identities to divert children from criminalisation and stigma. To achieve this, YJS practitioners must be trained not just in neurodiversity awareness, but in neuro-affirmative, strengths-based practices, ensuring fair treatment through proactive reasonable adjustments. Crucially, reasonable adjustments should not rely on formal diagnoses, as systemic barriers and biases may prevent access for neurodivergent justice-involved children. Ending the school-to-prison pipeline for neurodivergent children is a collective responsibility. McGreevy et al. (2024) argue that professionals can be the oasis a neurodivergent person needs to flourish in a desert of adversity. Ultimately, justice means ensuring fair access and opportunities for all. Victoria's concluding commentary is as follows:

> Going forward, please remember we are people too. We are more than what we can or cannot do, we are more than the limits you perceive us to have, and we have so much to contribute to the world, the system and (in the YJS) the case. You just have to truly see us as the people we are.

Note

1 This chapter adopts identity-affirming and inclusive terminology when referring to neurodivergent individuals. It recognises neurodivergence as a natural variation in human cognition rather than a deficit or disorder. Terms such as 'neurodivergent', 'neuroaffirmative', and 'neurotypical' are used intentionally to centre the voices and perspectives of those with lived experience, challenge pathologising narratives, and promote dignity and respect. Where diagnostic labels are referenced (e.g., autism, ADHD), they are used contextually and with sensitivity to individual preference and social implications.

References

Beck, K. B., MacKenzie, K. T., Kumar, T., Breitenfeldt, K. E., Chang, J. C., Conner, C. M., Mandell, D. L., White, S. W., and Mazefsky, C. A. (2024) 'The world's really not set up for the neurodivergent person: Understanding emotion dysregulation from the perspective of autistic adults', *Autism in Adulthood,* https://doi.org/10.1089/aut.2023.0214.

Chapple, E. (2023) *Diversity is the key to our survival: The shoeness of a shoe*, TEDxNorwichED, Available at: https://www.youtube.com/watch?v=DXBdiGUQ8Lw [Accessed: 07.06.2025].

Craddock, E. (2024) 'Being a woman is 100% significant to my experiences of attention deficit hyperactivity disorder and autism: Exploring the gendered implications of an adulthood combined autism and attention deficit hyperactivity disorder diagnosis', *Qualitative Health Research*, 34(14), p.g.1442–1455, https://doi.org/10.1177/10497323241253412.

Cruise, K., Evans., L., and Pickens, I. (2011) 'Integrating mental health and special education needs into comprehensive service planning for juvenile offenders in long-term custody settings', *Learning and Individual Differences*, 21, p.g.30–40.

Davis, A., Soloman, M., and Belcher, H. (2022) 'Examination of race and autism intersectionality among African American/Black young adults', *Autism in Adulthood*, https://doi.org/10.1089/aut.2021.0091.

Day, A.-M. (2022) 'Disabling and criminalising systems? Understanding the experiences and challenges facing incarcerated, neurodivergent children in the education and youth justice systems in England', *Forensic Science International: Mind and Law*, 3, p.g.100102, https://doi.org/10.1016/j.fsiml.2022.100102

Day, A.M., Allely, C., Robinson, L., Turner, K., Gerry, K. C. F., and Forrester, A. (2024) 'The over-representation of neurodivergent children in youth justice systems and the youth court', *Medicine, Science and the Law*, 64(4), p.g.255–258, https://doi.org/10.1177/00258024241274073.

Doherty, M., McCowan, S., and Shaw, S. C. K. (2023) 'Autistic SPACE: A novel framework for meeting the needs of autistic people in healthcare settings', *British Journal of Hospital Medicine*, 84, p.g.1–7, https://doi.org/10.12968/hmed.2023.0006.

Driver B., and Chester, V. (2021) 'The presentation, recognition and diagnosis of autism in women and girls', *Advances in Autism*, 7(3), p.g.194–207.

Equality and Human Rights Commission (2020) *Inclusive justice: A system designed for all*, London: equalityhumanrights.com, Available at: https://www.equalityhumanrights.com/inclusive-justice-system-designed-all [Accessed: 15.06.2025].

Fadus, M. C., Ginsburg, K. R., Sobowale, K., Halliday-Boykins, C. A., Bryant, B. E., Gray, K. M., and Squeglia, L. M. (2020) 'Unconscious bias and the diagnosis of disruptive behavior disorders and ADHD in African American and Hispanic youth', *Academic Psychiatry*, 44(1), p.g.95–102, https://doi.org/10.1007/s40596-019-01127-6.

Finer, L. (2024) *Understanding and supporting the needs of neurodivergent people in prisons is a human rights issue*, Penal Reform International, 30 July. Available at: https://www.penalreform.org/blog/understanding-and-supporting-the-needs-of-neurodivergent-people/ [Accessed: 22.03.2026].

Fitzpatrick, P., Frazier J. A., Cochran, D., Mitchell, T., Coleman, C., and Schmidt R.C. (2018) 'Relationship between theory of mind, emotion recognition, and social synchrony in adolescents with and without Autism', *Frontiers in Psychology*, 9(1337), https://doi.org/10.3389/fpsyg.2018.01337.

Foster, T. and Young, R. (2022) 'Brief report: Sentencing outcomes for offenders on the autism spectrum', *Journal of Autism and Developmental Disorders*, 52(7), p.g.3314–3320, https://doi.org/10.1007/s10803-021-05212-4.

Gormley, C. (2022) 'The hidden harms of prison life for people with learning disabilities', *The British Journal of Criminology*, 62(2), p.g.261–278, https://doi.org/10.1093/bjc/azab061.

Harvey, A., Spicer-Cain, H., Botting, N., and Henry, L. (2025) 'Everyday narrative skills in autistic adolescents', *First Language*, 45(2), p.g.196–227, https://doi.org/10.1177/01427237251315253.

Hilvert, E., Davidson, D., and Gámez, P. B. (2016) 'Examination of script and non-script based narrative retellings in children with autism spectrum disorders', *Research in Autism Spectrum Disorders*, 29, p.g.79–92, https://doi.org/10.1016/j.rasd.2016.06.002.

Kirby, A. (2021) *Neurodiversity – A whole child approach for youth justice*, London: HMIP Academic Insights Paper 8. Available at: https://justiceinspectorates.gov.uk/

hmiprobation/wp-content/uploads/sites/5/2021/07/Neurodiversity-AI.pdf [Accessed: 15.06.2025].

Maras, K., Dando, C., Stephenson, H., Lambrechts, A., Anns, S., and Gaigg, S. (2020) 'The witness aimed first account (WAFA): A new technique for interviewing autistic witnesses and victims', *Autism: The International Journal of Research and Practice*, 24(6), p.g.1449–1467, https:// doi.org/10.1177/1362361320908986.

McGreevy, E., Quinn, A., Law, R., Botha, M., Evans, M., Rose, K., Moyse, R., Boyens, T., Matejko, M., and Pavlopoulou, G. (2024) 'An experience sensitive approach to care with and for Autistic children and young people in clinical services', *Journal of Humanistic Psychology*, https://doi.org/10.1177/00221678241232442.

Miller, D., Rees, J., and Pearson, A. (2021) '"Masking is life": Experiences of masking in autistic and nonautistic adults', *Autism Adulthood*, 3(4), p.g.330–338. https://doi.org/10.1089/aut.2020.0083

Milton, D. E. M., Gurbuz, E., and López B. (2022) 'The "double empathy problem": Ten years on', *Autism*, 26(8), p.g.1901–1903.

Milton D. E. M. (2012) 'On the ontological status of autism: The "double empathy problem', *Disability and Society*, 27(6), p.g.883–887.

Paterson-Young, C., Bajwa-Patel, M., and Hazenberg, R. (2021) '"I ain't stupid, I just don't like school": A "needs" based argument for children's educational provision in custody', *Journal of Youth Studies*, 25(4), p.g.452–469, https://doi.org/10.1080/13676261.2021.1900553.

Police and Criminal Evidence Act (1984) c. 60, Available at: https://www.legislation.gov.uk/ukpga/1984/60/contents [Accessed: 15.06.2025].

Revolving Doors (2022) *Exploring the links between neurodiversity and the revolving door of crisis and crime*, Available at: https://revolving-doors.org.uk/wp-content/uploads/2022/09/Revolving-Doors-neurodiversity-policy-position.pdf [Accessed: 15.06.2025].

Seymour, G. F. (2023) *How can we support a sense of belonging in the school community for children and young people with youth justice involvement?*, Doctorate in Applied Educational Psychology thesis, Newcastle University.

Shaw, S. C., Carravallah, L., Johnson, M., O'Sullivan, J., Chown, N., Neilson, S., and Doherty, M. (2023) 'Barriers to healthcare and a "triple empathy problem" may lead to adverse outcomes for autistic adults: A qualitative study', *Autism*, 28(7), p.g.1746–1757, https://doi.org/10.1177/13623613231205629.

Singer, J. (1998) *Odd people in: The birth of community amongst people on the "autistic spectrum": A personal exploration of a new social movement based on neurological diversity* (Bachelor of Arts Social Science [Honours] thesis). Faculty of Humanities and Social Sciences, University of Technology, Sydney.

Slavny-Cross, R., Allison, C., Griffiths, S., and Baron-Cohen, S. (2022) 'Autism and the criminal justice system: An analysis of 93 cases', *Autism Research*, 15(5), p.g.904–914, https://doi.org/10.1002/aur.2690.

Vincenti, S. C., Galea, M., and Briffa, V. (2023) 'Issues which marginalize females with ADHD - A mixed methods systematic review', *Humanities and Social Science Research*, 6(2), 30, https://doi.org/10.30560/hssr.v6n2p30.

Warrier, V., Greenberg, D. M., Weir, E., Buckingham, C., Smith, P., Lai, M. C., Allison, C., and Baron-Cohen, S. (2020) 'Elevated rates of autism, other neurodevelopmental and psychiatric diagnoses, and autistic traits in transgender and gender-diverse individuals', *Nature Communications,* 11, p.g.1–12, https://doi.org/10.1038/s41467-020-17794-1.

Youth Justice Board (2022) *A guide to child first,* Available at: https://yjresourcehub.uk/wp-content/uploads/media/Child_First_Overview_and_Guide_April_2022_YJB.pdf [Accessed: 15.06.2025].

Chapter 8

Don't Ask Him – Ask Me!

David Wilkin

8.1 Introduction

Neurodivergent people can face challenges when reporting victimisation and being otherwise involved with the CJS. These can include difficulties with communication, misinterpretation of their behaviours and a reticence to disclose information (Trickett and Hamilton 2014). These all act as barriers when making an initial report and, latterly, when being questioned and statements are constructed (in ibid). These experiences are not unusual. Williams and Jobe (2024) argue that misunderstandings, misinterpretations, and assumptions about neurodivergent people lead to discrimination. Evidence shows that neurodivergent people, for example, face the same or similar challenges when needing to discuss anything from welfare issues to the reporting of a crime, whereby they are often not adequately understood or believed (Cooper et al., 2024). On occasion, communication between the neurodivergent person and the reporting authority may rely upon an intermediary, a factor which can further complicate and confuse important conversations, and examples of this can be seen in the case studies below. These are important factors to bear in mind when referring to the reporting of a crime as the initial report can be crucial to decision-making by the receiving authority at a later date. For example, such a report may determine whether an investigation is made, how seriously the complaint is taken, and any evidence gathered at this stage might be used in court should the pathway to justice take the victim there.

The aim of this chapter is to explore the above issues more deeply by putting forward lived experience case studies and by placing the researcher – a neurodivergent person – and their life experiences at the centre of the phenomenon under discussion. It is felt that this is a unique and important contribution to this book as we, as researchers, must not be distanced from any claims of discrimination and indeed must be cognisant of establishing why neurodivergent people have additional difficulties in using the CJS. Moreover, as researchers we must address neurodivergent persons as victims but also as offenders and importantly be aware of the perhaps more compounded impact of the victim/offender overlap in relation to neurodivergent people.

DOI: 10.4324/9781003638742-9

The methodological approach to this chapter is grounded in qualitative lived experience data, which uniquely includes the positioning of the researcher and their life experience within the research space. Therefore, the chapter will commence by providing some of my early life experiences of being diagnosed with autism, the impact on my early adult life, and then my later life, where I moved into the academic space and began to dedicate a portion of my life to helping others with neurodivergence differences.[1] The chapter then moves on to discuss several case studies. The case studies used in this chapter are personal and impactful accounts from participants. No academic theorisation or professionally controlled debate can reflect or reveal the reality of actually being a victim. No 'catch up' over sparkling spring water with a flipchart can recount the distress of the victim. The case studies are personal accounts which relate to the failings or opaqueness of the CJS or associated agencies. For the systems that deal with criminality and justice to change and evolve, there needs to be a better understanding of these impacts. This chapter is therefore an appreciation of the personal impacts of neurodivergent people who have endured the unfairness of criminal justice in E&W.

Whilst it is accepted that not all neurodivergent people will experience unfairness within the system, these case studies represent those when negative experiences were documented; the aim of this chapter is to give a voice to these concerns for consideration in future research, practice and policy. It is important to recognise that a common thread through my life – and the case studies detailed – was that no matter what decision needed to be made or action to be taken, I was not part of that process. Similarly, the data below highlights that the common thread running through this chapter is that the neurodivergent person is often excluded from conversations and from actions which directly concern that individual. I start the chapter with a personal reflective account. The chapter is written cumulatively, starting in the mid-1960s and building on personal experiences when young and developing into adulthood, before detailing the plight of others in being victims of state disregard. Please note, readers should be aware that some of the experiences described contain disturbing themes, including bullying and physical abuse.[2]

8.2 Personal Reflection

8.2.1 *Voices Down Corridors*

It can seemingly be difficult to recall experiences from childhood, but several remain in my mind as uncomfortable memories. For example, I remember sitting in a treatment room in a health clinic and my mother being ushered down the corridor to be told something by a clinician. But they did not go far enough down that corridor for me not to hear the conversation. The clinician said that 'he (that is, me) is different and may need special help' and that my parents should be 'strong' and to 'expect the unusual.' At no point did anyone tell me any of these things directly. Although I was around six or seven years of age, it seemed important for them that

I knew nothing of what other people judged to be 'wrong with me.' In fact, and on reflection, it was a diagnosis of autism. The initial approach to the clinic was made because of my strange behaviours and mannerisms; and that these were causing concern to my parents. Moreover, it was merely noted on my medical records. No follow-up, treatment plan or further consultations were initiated. But from that point in time forward, people knew why I was different. This was a fundamental decision which wholly concerned me and the trajectory of the remainder of my life, but I was excluded from it and from any further discussion. I was the person at the centre of all of this, yet I was the only person not consulted. I recall the female clinician referring my case to a male colleague and asking him what he thought was the best course of action regarding provision of my education. I didn't hear that conversation further and no further actions were taken. I was not involved directly. My profound thought at that time was 'don't ask him – ask me'!

8.2.2 Some Sense Knocked into Me

As I moved through my school years, life became increasingly difficult. As I, and the children around me, grew older, my differences became weaponised against me and the bullying started. Spitting in my face was quite normal, kicking and punching were seemingly acceptable approaches, and then I got the occasional special treatment. For example, once I was clubbed around the head with a cricket bat by a fellow pupil who said that he was 'knocking some sense into me.' I was concussed but alas no sense increment was forthcoming. At 12 years of age, I could not cope anymore. But one thing I decided was never to attend school again. This made perfect sense. As school was the place where I was bullied the most, I could avoid those experiences by not going to school – simple. However, it did result in me not being able to write in a grammatically accurate way and having gaps in my knowledge. That said, I could live with those skills deficits because I had escaped an environment which was causing me great upset and trauma. I had alerted my parents to what was happening to me at school and they did try, on more than one occasion, to get proper provision to allow me to continue with my education. However, they did not succeed, and my schooling life remained intolerable. Again, I was not involved in any of these discussions, nor were my concerns ever sought and/or addressed.

8.2.3 Arrested – But not a Suspect

After I left school – not that I had attended very much – I then began to seek jobs that needed no formal qualifications (as I did not have any) and that were easy to apply for. In other words, not involving long forms or tests. I did not have the requisite skills to complete these. I was once asked at an interview, 'how is your grammar?' My response was 'she's dead,' which was my attempt to distract the interviewer. But I was a lost soul. No career path, no planning, and no idea of which way I wanted to travel in life. I worked in short-term roles and developed a problem with alcohol. One evening I was arrested for assaulting a female police officer – something which I did not do. I was thrown into a police car (upside down) and taken to a police station where I was told that I was 'scum' and beaten up by police officers there. I was not offered legal representation, nor was I told what my rights were. I asked for water, but this was denied and I was told that I would 'only piss myself and someone would need to clean it up.'

After a night in a cell and being covered in bruises, I was informed that they had found the female who had assaulted the female officer, and she had been charged with an offence. When I questioned why I was in custody when they had been looking for a female all along, I was told that 'life was too short to complain against the police.' During this horrible process, I was not questioned directly; I was not asked if it was me that perpetrated the assault or, indeed, where I was at the time of the incident. When I was standing in front of the custody sergeant, other officers were answering questions about me, on my behalf. One also said, 'you know what this lot [autistic people] are like; you won't get any sense out of him.' Another had mentioned that I would not feel the bruises as I obviously had 'no sense.' I still feel those bruises, 48 years later. This behaviour opened my eyes to how some police, in an organisation that I had been taught to trust and admire, behave in a manner alien to me. I, sadly, would never again accept that those involved with criminal justice were beyond question.

8.3 From Personal Experience to Practical Support

8.3.1 Later Career and Academia

A change in my life came when I graduated with an undergraduate degree in Geography and Sociology from the UK's Open University (OU). I could study whilst working. I studied with the OU because no other UK university would have accepted me without school-based qualifications. Following a further undergraduate degree, a master's degree, and a PhD, I am now combining my experience of helping others with academic research skills to find justice for disabled people who have been victims of hostility and injustice. I also use ethically sound research, and the publishing of my findings, to raise awareness of the plight of these victims.

8.4 The Case Studies

This chapter is an opportunity to reveal some occasions where other neurodivergent people have been treated unfavourably during involvement with the CJS. As such, this section uses case studies to argue that justice is often more difficult to obtain for neurodivergent people. Participant names are pseudonyms. These cases constitute a broadly representative sample of my work. I chose these examples to represent a wider caseload and are somewhat typical of those routinely experienced by victims of injustice for neurodivergent people with whom I have worked over the years. In this respect, the case studies are exemplary types of cases from which findings can be drawn. The case studies are displayed in a vignette-style format to allow for a lived experience narrative to emerge. The case studies have been reviewed by the participants to ensure that they accurately represent the lived experience represented. Each case study is initially discussed with follow-on analysis.

8.4.1 Ethical Protocol

I am a co-lead of the Disability Hate Crime Network in the UK. It has around 4,000 members and we raise awareness and discuss acts of hostility against disabled people. I also undertake public and academic talks and lectures on this issue and work in partnership with agencies to raise awareness of it and try to reduce incidents of hate against disabled victims. Other work includes support for victims in specific court and tribunal cases to try to achieve justice for those individuals. Whilst not legally qualified to act as an advocate, I am, with my awareness of the CJS in E&W, well placed to provide support and guidance for victims of hate. Having worked with many victims of hostility and their associates, carers, and family members, I have accrued many contacts and much experience working with victims, many of whom are very keen to reveal and discuss their experiences of the CJS. I have helped 116 victims and their associates to the date of writing this chapter (spring 2025). As a supporter of disabled victims and an established researcher, I am more than aware of the influence and power that I may hold in these relationships – therefore the ethical approach that I need to take in any research study involving these victims must be carefully considered and implemented to protect both the participants and me as a researcher.

Whilst I have previously successfully submitted research proposals to university ethical committees, I now, as an independent researcher, cannot submit ethically aligned research proposals to such a committee. But I do follow the same ethical procedures that would be expected of me if I were committing to research through the auspices of a university. Participants in the cases represented in this chapter have given written, informed consent to have their information used and published using pseudonyms. They had all passed a routinely administered mental capacity test consisting of two questions relating to the research study (see Mental Capacity Act 2005 (UK)). This is an enabling Act of law that assures researchers that the informed consent received from participants is taken from somebody with the capacity to deliver it. This Act, and its two-stage test, is used in everyday work by the National Health Service (NHS) in the UK and other agencies as well (Dow, 2008; Social Care Institute for Excellence (SCIE), 2024). The participants cited in these case studies have all been offered support and counselling if required. Follow-up briefings discussed the research outputs and any potential publication as well as the situation of the participants. Participants have been asked to review the written content pertaining to them before submission of this chapter. Therefore, every ethical protection that would be expected has been used or offered to the participants of these case studies and used by the researcher; these will be summarised below.

I was already familiar with the cases cited before the production of this chapter and had worked with these participants in a bid for justice. I then conducted further interviews with the victims, which were conducted with this publication in mind. Some of the detail from the interviews may contain shocking or disturbing facts. The interviews for publication were all conducted in early 2024/5, in a place which was considered safe by all parties where a private conversation could take place – but not isolated from help or public intervention should it be required. These anonymised case studies were chosen to be representative of the cases I worked with in that they are typical examples of the type of engagement which can be suffered by neurodivergent people seeking justice in E&W.

All participants are anonymised; the original identities are known only to me. All records are kept in securely locked areas with only me having access until the end of the project. Participants had already worked with me and were given full information regarding the project; they were then asked if they wished to participate. Written information was provided and written, informed consent gained. Repeatedly, the right to withdraw without repercussion was stated. Collected and edited data were reviewed by each participant, and their authorisation for publication gained. The use of the Mental Capacity Act styled tests protected both the research and the participants. The benefit of lived experience is clear: no theoretical debate by academics who are devoid of any lived experience in these matters can replace the knowledge produced by actual victims and those who have suffered. Therefore, this data gathering and publication are fully justified.

8.4.2 Case Study 1: Clive

Clive, at the time of needing to report a crime, was a 33-year-old male with a diagnosis of autism. On several occasions, Clive had been a victim of disability hate crime. These are incidents of hostility or abuse which occur against disabled people, their family, friends, or carers, because of personal disability. Although, in E&W, there is no actual piece of legislation which proscribes hate and hostility specifically used against disabled people, public order offences can be recorded when disabled victims report this type of crime and latterly, in court, an enhanced sentence can be handed down if it can be proven that the motivation for the crime was based on the victim's disability (CPS, 2025). At the time of reporting, Clive estimated he had been a victim of abuse, hostility, or violence on at least 150 occasions. Several of these incidents were perpetrated by another tenant in the social housing complex within which Clive lived, with abuse ranging from being rebuked for mannerisms associated with Clive's autism and Clive's use of unfamiliar language. Therefore, Clive had sought the advice of the housing team which managed the social housing apartment in which he lived. Yet, they offered no support, guidance, or advice, despite having access to a multitude of sanctions which they could apply to the social housing tenants who were perpetrating the attacks. Clive was classified as a 'vulnerable adult' by the housing team and was known for having regular contact with that team because of a range of concerns associated with living on that particular housing estate.

Clive had wanted this abuse to stop; much courage and effort were used by Clive to report the matter both to the housing team and the police, which included physical attendance at the police station: the online reporting platform was not suitable because Clive was not confident in using it, and the telephone service was unsuitable for Clive due to his speech impediments. On arrival at the police station, he had to queue for approximately 40 minutes, with no access to a toilet. Clive could not easily communicate with the officer at the enquiries desk but did have a card stating that he (Clive) was considered a vulnerable adult. This factor could have triggered the police to consider utilising someone who could represent Clive's interests and assist him whilst discussing matters with the police. However, despite the presentation of the card, no other support was offered.

During the interview, a police officer was responsible for recording Clive's account of the abuse. Clive reported the occurrences of hostility and identified the name and address of the perpetrator and illustrated the nature of the attacks and the impacts that he had suffered over approximately three years of abuse. At first, the police officer considered that Clive's utterances required interpretation and stated that Clive's testimony was unintelligible; he said that it was 'impossible to understand what Clive was trying to say.' After approximately 20 minutes, that officer changed from being unable to understand to offering a descriptive account of Clive's words. However, according to Clive, the officer had not suddenly learned to understand Clive; rather, the officer gave a completely inaccurate representation of what Clive was trying to say, bearing little relation to what Clive was trying to report. For example, when Clive was trying to report the verbal abuse suffered, the officer talked about being 'looked at in a funny way,' and when Clive was describing how his window was broken by the same perpetrator, the interpreting officer stated that Clive had broken it during the accidental use of a screwdriver. In other words, the testimony primarily offered by Clive was significantly changed to the point that it was nothing like what Clive was trying to say. The incidents that had occurred were made to sound like accidents or mishaps, some of which were conducted by Clive himself.

This led to Clive being very frustrated, not only because he was unable to communicate concerns to the police, but also in that nobody was mobilised to help. For Clive, justice was no nearer than before he made the decision to report these matters. Added to these frustrations were the misrepresentations made by the police officer interpreting Clive's words. This may have been due to mere misunderstanding, or more concerningly, deliberate misinterpretation for the police's convenience (which is Clive's belief). Clive was not receiving justice, but Clive also felt like he was made to look foolish, reporting that he was made to look like an unreliable witness. Frustration resulted in Clive banging the table with clenched fists, which caused the police officers to restrain him. They told Clive that his actions were unacceptable, and that further action could be taken to restrain Clive, if necessary.

Clive left the police station on that occasion for the long journey back home. He had not even begun to find a pathway to justice for being a victim of hate and hostility. He had not been listened to and even had testimony changed. Clive felt that the officer compiling his statement paid more attention to the officer interpreting Clive's comments than to Clive himself. Clive was completely sidelined, and it was not until two years later that he finally received justice through a long, hard fight.

This account portrays the need that all of us might have for support in being a witness or victim of a crime. For the police to build a firm picture of what is happening and to accumulate a portfolio of evidence, it is arguably essential that the police have techniques and assistance to extricate as much detail as is possible. Making witnesses and victims feel disengaged, or worse, further victimised, cannot be helpful in building a case or providing support to a victim whom they might hope will later give evidence in court.

8.4.3 Case Study 2: Kannah

Kannah was a 41-year-old autistic transgender person who had previously fled Iran to the relative safety of the UK and lived in a social housing complex. Kannah has an interesting intersectionality in that Kannah is both transgender (M-F) and autistic, with flares of fibromyalgia. Kannah has been targeted for being both transgender and autistic. The abuse has included her windows being broken as well as graffiti sprayed across the windows and doors of her home. Being at the intersection of gender and disability means that Kannah is still susceptible to being discriminated against for both characteristics. On one occasion, Kannah was filmed by local youths and this film appeared on social media with a wrong description that Kannah was a paedophile and was grooming local children for potential abuse. This broadcast led to enhanced vandalism and a burning newspaper being pushed through the letterbox of Kannah's flat.

Kannah was too scared to involve the police as she thought that the perpetrators – who were known to the police – would be arrested and that, consequently, the abuse would escalate further in retaliation. Kannah also feared that criminal justice involvement could span many years and that she would have to wait years for the case to reach the courts, during which time the perpetrators could continue their abuse. Kannah was additionally scared *of* the police in that she did not know what the repercussions of reporting crimes might be. Kannah considered the stories of the Iranian police authorities and their treatment of victims, witnesses and offenders, and so she remained reticent to even call the police.

Instead, Kannah established that the housing association, which was the landlord of the flat Kannah lived in, had a legal duty of care towards all their residents, which included safeguarding vulnerable people and victims of crime, as well as duties to deal with and ultimately remove troublesome tenants. Kannah had an interview with the housing association case worker. In that interview, Kannah outlined personal safety concerns and the ongoing vandalism to which she had been subjected. She further indicated personal vulnerability and diagnoses of autism and fibromyalgia. Kannah was hopeful that the case worker would suggest that the law be enforced and that the housing association would use its powers to at least warn the perpetrators of abuse and potentially remove them as they were in breach of their tenancy agreement. The housing association was also known to work closely with the police, and Kannah hoped that the police would also therefore be informed.

At the end of the interview, the case worker stated that because of the range of conditions that Kannah 'suffered,' the 'best outcome' was to obtain medical help. Kannah was both devastated and surprised at this formal advice. Instead of the autism and fibromyalgia being used to strengthen the case against the perpetrator, Kannah perceived that the conditions were being used to deflect Kannah away from justice and instead, towards finding medical treatments. Thus, rather than Kannah's conditions and vulnerability being key factors in seeking justice, they were actually used as key factors in Kannah's victimhood. It was clear that the case worker had no intention of interviewing or sanctioning the perpetrator of these crimes. It was Kannah who would have to find the solution to a problem that was not of her design. The case worker did say that under E&W law, Kannah could resort to the process of civil law (without requiring the support of the police) and take the perpetrator to court to recover damages – a potentially very expensive solution. The case worker also advised that Kannah could alternatively contact the police. However, this was one that Kannah avoided for personal safety reasons, highlighting the often-complex relationship between disabled victims of crime and the police, and indeed other arms of the CJS. Kannah informed the case worker that the housing association had a legal duty of care, and that this outcome failed to discharge that duty, yet no further help was offered. The housing association was unwilling to coordinate action with the police for a tenant who was scared to directly engage with the police.

It is understandable that Kannah feared direct police involvement as cases are known to take many years to reach the courts, if they get there at all. In early 2025, Kannah was awaiting rehousing on a different housing estate. She represents yet another example of an autistic person not being safeguarded but being labelled as the problem.

8.4.4 Case Study 3: Kayleigh

Kayleigh was in formal social care from ages 12 to 18 and had been sexually abused whilst in care on several occasions by a member of staff of the care home within which she was resident. As an autistic teenager, Kayleigh wanted to spend much of her time alone and did not try to communicate with other children or with staff in the care centre. Kayleigh found it difficult to report the abuse, and it is possible that for this reason she was targeted by the member of staff who abused her. Kayleigh was keen to leave the centre and did so as soon as she could, leaving with an unsettled and at times chaotic lifestyle. She did not have regular or structured employment, no fixed place of residence, and no regular friends or relationships for many years. As an adult, in her early to mid-twenties, Kayleigh used alcohol regularly and, on occasion, used a range of drugs.

By the time Kayleigh was 28, she wanted to find justice for what had happened to her in the care home. The process was not easy – and Kayleigh was not expecting it to be so. But she had secured the help of a social worker, who was Kayleigh's caseworker for other matters, including housing and potential employment. Kayleigh was fortunate in this respect because she had with her on this journey to justice someone whom she trusted and could communicate with confidently. Cheryl, her caseworker, was very experienced, but, like most of her colleagues, had a huge workload, with many cases outstanding at any one time. Kayleigh was also distrustful of the police, her only previous contact being when she was questioned for possession of drugs. With Cheryl by her side, Kayleigh was more confident in reporting the sexual offences. The investigation began; Kayleigh, with Cheryl, made statements and gave interviews under police caution. These were serious matters, and evidence needed to be collected meticulously.

Because of heavy workloads, social support case workers may be replaced without much warning. This happened with Cheryl, who was removed from Kayleigh's case and allocated to other work. Three other case workers were allocated to Kayleigh over the course of the following 18 months, during a period when Kayleigh needed strong and personal support for going through a difficult and emotional association, working with the police investigators. It was not that the police were not professional or empathetic in their work – they were – they were extremely helpful, and on several occasions stated that they wanted what was best for Kayleigh and to see justice done. But Kayleigh, as the primary victim, lost confidence in the process of building a case. Kayleigh found it difficult to communicate with strangers anyway, and Cheryl had helped to overcome these difficulties. Now, with an unfamiliar case worker and numerous police officers involved with her case, communication was much more difficult. At times, Kayleigh did not want to talk to anyone, and appointments with case workers and the police were cancelled at short notice.

What Kayleigh did find, however, was that the social workers representing Kayleigh often misinterpreted what Kayleigh was trying to say to the police. In such an important matter, where a court case was likely to ensue, it was vital to get the facts right, establish who was responsible, and when these incidents happened. Kayleigh found that facts would be stated, but then these were wrongfully interpreted by the social worker who would pass this incorrect information onto the police investigator, who would note these as evidence. This was crucially frustrating for Kayleigh who was not getting vital points across. What was being said was being changed and therefore the evidence being noted by the police was incorrect. Kayleigh felt out of control of the situation, that evidence was being 'hijacked,' and was consequently losing its credibility because it was not what Kayleigh was trying to say. Kayleigh thought that during court cross-examination, defence barristers would easily find out that the supposed facts were not the facts at all. Potentially, Kayleigh could be consequently sanctioned for misleading the court. This was all going horribly wrong for Kayleigh.

Kayleigh's case, however, had a more positive conclusion. The Police Staff Investigator (PSI) leading the interview and evidence collection could see how emotionally distressed that Kayleigh was becoming. In Kayleigh's words, the PSI 'stopped me from walking out the door, made me a cup of tea, and we sat down and we talked.' The PSI 'looked at me straight and knew I was being understood,' he told me that he 'wanted to get this case right.' For Kayleigh, this investigating officer – who was a civilian member of police staff and whose sole purpose was interviewing and evidence collection – saved Kayleigh from withdrawing from giving evidence and kept the case 'alive.' Kayleigh built up a strong rapport with this officer and evidence was collected from Kayleigh on several occasions over the forthcoming months. The professional and empathetic care shown by the member of police staff overcame the problems inflicted by continually changing social workers and other police staff who had difficulty understanding Kayleigh and her predicament. The case was heard in the Crown Court, and the defendant (the care home worker) was convicted and sentenced to a lengthy prison term.[3] Kayleigh now has a flat and has started her own project to help autistic teenagers using art and dance.

This is an account where the building of a relationship is key to the gathering of evidence and the subsequent building of a (successful) case. If criminal justice professionals were to invest the time needed to properly engage with and support neurodivergent people, they could not only learn a great deal more about neurodivergence, but they could also ensure justice is not denied for neurodivergent victims and suspects. For example, the processing of people with a range of neurodivergence could produce both more successful outcomes for the victims or service users and improve the understandings and skills of the police officers. Surely, to dissuade victims and witnesses from giving evidence impedes justice. For agencies in the CJS to work efficiently and effectively, a range of tools is required to engage with a range of people and their individual needs.

8.4.5 Case Study 4: Shannon

Suspected of drug dealing, Shannon was arrested and taken to a police station. For the clarity of this case study, Shannon was in possession of a small amount of cannabis and had stated that this was for 'personal use.' However, the police thought that the amount constituted possession for the purpose of re-selling it and arrested her on suspicion of committing that offence. Shannon was allocated a duty solicitor for her police interview and, as a vulnerable adult with autism, was also allocated an Appropriate Adult (AA) to protect her interests in the police station. The police were acting responsibly, reasonably and in line with procedure. It was not Shannon's first visit to a police station and not her first offence. Shannon had accrued a short history of drug dealing and, during the research interview, did not try to deny that it happened and did not offer any defence for this behaviour.

What Shannon did say was that if you were already a convicted drug dealer, the police would be likely to visit you first as a matter of course if there was an increase in localised drug dealing. In other words, the police had knowledge of local dealers who would be first in line for a visit if any purge on drug use and selling was taking place. Shannon suspected that she would be given much opportunity to account for the drugs because, in her experience, the police did not listen to the accounts of people suspected of drug dealing but instead wanted to progress the matter more quickly to a charging decision by the Crown Prosecution Service (CPS). On one occasion, however, she recalled not being listened to at all. Instead, the police investigator, the AA and the solicitor were discussing the case among themselves during pauses in the interview. Shannon recalled that they were completely ignoring her and any comments that she was trying to raise. She recalled that around ten minutes of conversation must have taken place before the police investigator said 'right, we have come to the decision that you should accept a police caution.' Shannon relayed to me that she thought that a police caution, or a community resolution, might be the outcome of the investigation anyway. But, on this occasion, Shannon was angry and unhappy that the solicitor, police investigator and AA should 'cook up' this deal among themselves without consulting her. She believed that this was a flagrant breach of her personal rights.

Shannon's attitude immediately changed from one where she was prepared to accept what the police decided – to one where she was furious at not being included in her own case. Shannon had experienced times like these before when the officials in the room took over the conversation and worked things through between them. This approach often saved time if Shannon found it difficult to communicate and her autism had prevented full engagement. But this was different. Shannon felt that this *convenient* deal was being concocted without her involvement and that this was wrong. She did not have much knowledge of the law or police procedure, although she had been 'lifted' for dealing before this occasion. But Shannon knew that this should not happen without personal direct involvement.

Shannon insisted on being listened to. The solicitor, the police investigator and the AA all protested that they were doing what they did for Shannon's benefit and that, because of Shannon's autism, it would be a speedier path to (what was) an inevitable conclusion. But even though Shannon knew that they were right in their predictions, Shannon wanted to be 'a part of her own destiny.' She insisted that she be consulted and that her comments be recorded – even if the whole event took much longer. Shannon felt that she was not there for the convenience of others and wanted to play a full part in the case process. Shannon then took part in a formal police interview, and her comments were recorded and included in the charging process. Inevitably, perhaps, Shannon was charged with the offence of drug possession with intent to supply. She then received a police caution and accepted this as a way of avoiding an appearance in the magistrates' court. Although the same outcome was achieved, Shannon was able to assert her right to participate and her agency through involvement in decision-making.

Shannon's case has moved the discussion in this chapter from neurodivergent victims and witnesses to a neurodivergent person accused of a crime. Although suspected of a crime, the suspect remains entitled to be treated fairly and with respect. Respecting an individual's rights may mean taking the time to engage them in decisions that affect them, even if the outcome ultimately ends up the same. If law enforcement and other legal actors were to recognise and respect individual autonomy, justice may be better served.

8.5 Conclusion

Research on neurodivergence and the CJS, from both the perspective of the victim and offender (and indeed related to the victim/offender overlap), requires greater attention. Areas such as offence type and offending motivations require further exploration (King and Murphy, 2014). However, interactions with the system, either as victim and/or offender in terms of communication and case progression, are of equal importance (Cooper et al., 2024; Williams and Jobe, 2024); this is key to equity of access to justice.

If the police are not proficient at managing neurodivergent victims, witnesses, and offenders, then justice is more difficult to achieve, and information is more difficult to obtain. Indeed, in many cases, a record of the presence of neurodivergence and/or vulnerability may not be recognised. Of the little research that has been completed into understanding the experiences of neurodivergent people using the CJS, it is clear that there is little satisfaction with the fairness of the experience. Disabled victims and witnesses have reported feeling dissatisfied with their interactions (see Love et al., 2024). However, even Love et al. acknowledge that their research is stymied by the paucity of many professionals who speak on *behalf* of neurodivergent people. It seems that research studies asking neurodivergent people themselves about their lived experiences with the CJS are rare. Therefore, the case studies above are of great value in recounting these experiences.

In summary, this chapter has established the value of conducting and collecting lived experience in criminology and associated disciplines. But how can we move forward to be more inclusive of neurodivergent people and other disabled people seeking justice? Part of the problem is the poor ability, in many cases, that the police have in communicating with people holding a range of disabilities (Trickett and Hamilton, 2014). Moreover, as Trickett and Hamilton argue, many disabled people live in a 'friendship vacuum' (2014:208), where disabled people tend to have fewer friends and informal support networks to call upon for advice, support, and guidance. Consequently, they find it difficult to compare experiences with the police and therefore to discover ways to remedy that difficulty. This could lead us immediately to suggest that the police and similar authorities should receive more training in sessions which are co-produced between the police and disabled people. But that solution itself is problematic; there are many disabilities, each with their own characteristics to become aware of. It may be, therefore, that a comprehensive suite of training is impossible to deliver. Moreover, police forces, certainly in E&W, are facing funding problems and resourcing issues along with time restraints in terms of training officers and staff (National Police Chief's Council, 2017; Police Federation, 2023).

This chapter has provided a rare, but important, contribution to the discussion regarding neurodivergent people and their involvement with the CJS in E&W – much of which might translate to the international stage. The chapter has exemplified that, for neurodivergent people, paying more attention to the approaches and tools that are used within evidence collection is key to ensuring equal justice for all. By citing the lived experience of victims and others, we can establish that, by making sometimes simple adjustments, working with neurodivergent people can be more productive for those agencies established to protect all of us. We have learned that some people are scared to contact the police, and others have been subjected to procedural shortcuts. Yet, when people are listened to and respected, and the approach is constructive and informed, justice can be served. By listening to people who have been directly affected, we can learn so much. Nothing about us – without us!

Notes

1 This chapter makes no apology for writing in the first person; in parts, it is a very personal account.
2 The chapter adopts an identity-first construction when discussing autistic and neurodivergent people. Some of the language used in this chapter might be contentious in terms of newly enlightened writing about disability. But there are occasions when language needs to be a little raw to bring to light negative occurrences of being a victim. I do apologise for this.
3 The dates of the trial and the exact sentence are not stated to protect the participant in this study.

References

Cooper, D. *et al.* (2024) 'What do we know about autism and policing globally? Preliminary findings from an international effort to examine autism and the criminal justice system,' *Autism research* [Preprint]. Available at: https://doi.org/10.1002/aur.3203 (Accessed: 02/03/25).

Crown Prosecution Service (CPS) (2025) *Disability hate crime and other crimes against disabled people - Prosecution guidance*. Online at: https://www.cps.gov.uk/legal-guidance/disability-hate-crime-and-other-crimes-against-disabled-people-prosecution-guidance (Accessed: 15/10/2025).

Dow, J. (2008) 'Mental Capacity Act, *Journal of Integrated Care (Brighton, England)*, 16(1), pp. 18–21. Available at: https://doi.org/10.1108/14769018200800004 (Accessed 02/03/25).

King, C. and Murphy, G.H. (2014) 'A systematic review of people with autism spectrum disorder and the criminal justice system', *Journal of Autism and Developmental Disorders*, 44(11), pp. 2717–2733. Available at: https://doi.org/10.1007/s10803-014-2046-5 (Accessed: 15/03/25).

Love, A.M.A. *et al.* (2024) 'Creating the global criminal justice survey: A questionnaire designed to gather perspectives from the autism community and criminal justice professionals', *Journal of Autism and Developmental Disorders*, 54(4), pp. 1425–1437. Available at: https://doi.org/10.1007/s10803-022-05835-1 (Accessed: 15/03/25).

National Police Chief's Council (UK) (2017) Police funding: Do we have the resources we need? Online at: https://news.npcc.police.uk/releases/police-funding-do-we-have-the-resources-we-need (Accessed: 17/03/25).

Police Federation (UK) (2023) *Recruitment and retention crisis will worsen without fair pay and conditions*. Online at: https://www.polfed.org/news/latest-news/2023/recruitment-and-retention-crisis-will-worsen-without-fair-pay-and-conditions/ (Accessed: 17/03/25).

Social Care Institute for Excellence (SCIE) (2024) *MCA: Assessing mental capacity*. Online at: https://www.scie.org.uk/mca/practice/assessing-capacity/ (Accessed: 26/11/25).

Trickett, L. and Hamilton, P. (2014) *The policing of hate crime in Nottinghamshire*. Nottingham: Nottingham Law School. Available at https://www.report-it.org.uk/files/nottinghamshire_police_final_draft.pdf (Accessed: 26/11/25).

Williams, H. and Jobe, A. (2024) 'Testimonial injustice: Exploring "credibility" as a barrier to justice for people with learning disabilities/autism who report sexual violence', *Disability & Society*, pp. 1–23. Available at: https://doi.org/10.1080/09687599.2024.2323455 (Accessed: 02/03/25).

Chapter 9

The Challenge and Promise of Understanding the Criminal Justice Response to Neurodivergent Children and Violent Extremism

Gina Vale and Craig Webber

9.1 Introduction

Speaking at a Commons Home Affairs Committee meeting, Home Secretary Yvette Cooper (2025) expressed concern that the counter-terrorism caseload involving teenagers has trebled in the last three years. Concurrently, an investigation by the *Financial Times* revealed that persons with autism spectrum disorder (ASD) account for approximately 13 per cent of counter-terrorism policing casework, compared with a population base rate of 1 per cent (Warrell, 2024). Carried forward to conviction, according to open-source data, almost one-third of juvenile terrorism offenders in England and Wales since 2016 had been clinically diagnosed as neurodivergent.[1] When isolated to extreme right-wing offenders, the proportion rises to 12 of 30, or 40 per cent (Vale and Rose, 2025). Neurodivergence can manifest in differences such as hyperfixation and circumscribed interests, need for rigidity and predictability, and communication and socialisation difficulties (Gray *et al.*, 2024). When combined with the absolutism of ideological narratives, and the accessibility and asynchronous communication of online platforms, these facets work to contextualise a heightened risk of radicalisation (Salman and Al-Attar, 2023a). Maria Lovegrove, Head of Interventions at the UK Counter-Terrorism Police, reflects that these cases represent "a real shift to the fact that people can present as being vulnerable and dangerous simultaneously" (cited in Warrell 2024).

Responsive efforts should alleviate, rather than exacerbate, harm. Our analysis does not suggest or investigate a causal link between neurodivergence and violent extremism. To do so would only amplify stigmatisation (Skinns, 2011; Walter *et al.*, 2021). However, the growing number of neurodivergent children entering the criminal justice system in connection with violent extremism highlights the urgent need to (re)consider the response to these cases.

While neurodivergence and youth shape an individual's experience of criminal justice writ large, our focus is on police custody as a critical gateway: to multi-agency welfare or pursuance of prosecution. Custody is the first time that detainees are faced with the weight of criminal law, as they are stripped of personal

DOI: 10.4324/9781003638742-10

possessions, must navigate the complexities of their rights and obligations, are interviewed under carefully controlled conditions, and meet a variety of different professionals representing the law, health, and justice (Bevan, 2022; Kemp and Watkins, 2022; Skinns *et al.*, 2017; Skinns and Wooff, 2021). The average time that a child is in police custody before being released or processed further is 11 hours and 36 minutes, with 54 per cent detained overnight (Kemp *et al.*, 2023, p. 10). Section 41 of the Terrorism Act 2000 permits extended pre-charge detention up to a maximum of 14 days, with no specific or separate timeframe for children. The latest annual Home Office (2025) statistics indicate that the most common pre-charge detention period for terrorism-related offences is 6–7 days, but again without age disaggregation. This extended period in an unfamiliar environment can be especially distressing for neurodivergent children (Dehaghani and Smith, 2024). The sensory overload of the custody suite with its harsh, unrelenting fluorescent lighting, and the complex information from different people whose roles might be barely comprehensible, all create a particularly challenging experience for those who struggle with sensory processing, changes to routine, and communication difficulties (Holloway *et al.*, 2020; Kemp *et al.*, 2023; Parsons and Sherwood, 2016b). Add to that any other challenges such as learning difficulties or English as a second language, and the experience is one that can heighten anxiety and trigger behaviours—such as shutting down or not engaging with staff "properly"—that can be misread as non-compliant, deceitful, or even threatening (Murphy, 2018; Al-Attar, 2018).

This chapter explores whether and how the criminal justice system (CJS) in England and Wales adopts a Child First approach to neurodivergent children suspected of involvement in violent extremism. The "Child First" strategy is intended to encourage, if not compel, criminal justice professionals to regard minors as children first, and suspects second. In practice, this means taking a more welfarist, rather than punitive, stance on juvenile offending that encapsulates the duality of vulnerability and risk.[2] However, while this may hold promise in theory, there are challenges in practice. With a primary focus on police custody, we identify governance-borne inconsistencies and lack of police training on neurodivergence and youth-specific needs that can embed misunderstandings concerning criminal intentionality and violent extremist ideation. Yet, new developments offer an opportunity to improve the experiences of neurodivergent children in police custody and provide technological assistance to detention and interviewing for frontline policing staff. We critically analyse the example of video-books and symbols-based information systems, and consider how these tools can best support both child detainees and custody staff to navigate the complex nexus of neurodivergence, youth, and violent extremism. Finally, we consider how the broader CJS might move beyond piecemeal innovations towards more fundamental changes in culture, training, and procedures that genuinely embed Child First principles in responses to neurodivergent children suspected of violent extremism.

9.2 Neurodivergent Children and Violent Extremism

Scholarship on the nexus of neurodivergence and violent extremism is relatively nascent. It is important to reinforce at the outset that the extant literature does not definitively conclude, nor does it suggest, an empirical link between neurodivergence and violent extremism in the general population. In other words, neurodivergent individuals do not pose a greater risk of engagement than their neurotypical counterparts (Druitt *et al.*, 2023). Rather, where neurodivergence is identified in cases of planned or perpetrated terrorist or violent extremist acts, scholarship has sought to conceptualise and unpick associated differences as *contextual* to—not causative of—the individual's radicalisation pathway (Al-Attar, 2020; Al-Attar and Worthington, 2025).

While careful to avoid conflation, the burgeoning literature on violent extremism and neurodivergence appears to focus primarily on ASD and autistic individuals. Differences associated with ASD have been found to shape experience, functioning, and behaviour that may in some instances exacerbate a young person's vulnerability to radicalisation (Walter *et al.*, 2021). A key example is restricted repetitive behaviours and circumscribed interests—a narrow, preoccupying, and particularly intense focus often directed towards particular items, objects, or factual information (Anthony *et al.*, 2013, p. 648), through which the individual may acquire expert knowledge. A heightened sense of social justice and equality is also common and can manifest in activism and political engagement (Kapp, 2016). While these interests most often pertain to everyday topics such as gaming, music, and film, it is also recognised that there may be an association with violent content (Woodbury-Smith *et al.*, 2010). In the context of violent extremism, the intensity of the interest may manifest in the accumulation and engagement with substantial amounts of harmful content, such as repeated viewing of propaganda videos or engagement in manufacturing weapons guided by instructional manuals and manifestos circulated online (Vale and Rose, 2025, p. 11). However, Allely *et al.* (2024, p. 184) caution against misinterpretation of such pre-occupational interests as an indicator of an intense commitment to extremism. Rather, scholars question whether this behaviour may be attributed to the obsessionality, rigidity, and firm beliefs associated with ASD, thereby prompting reconsideration of the default securitisation approach to ideas and behaviours that do not have clear ideological objectives or operational involvement (Al-Attar, 2020, p. 937; Woodbury-Smith *et al.*, 2022, p. 3).

The hyper-focus of such interests often comes at the expense of other attachments such as social connections and relationships. Diagnosis for neurodivergent conditions hinges on a range of social and communication differences that could contextualise push/pull factors for violent extremism (Al-Attar, 2020, pp. 939–941). For example, difficulties in determining acceptable social behaviours, reading implicit and non-verbal cues, and discerning another's agenda or nefarious intent all create difficulties in forming relationships and differentiating between positive social contacts and those who might pose a risk (Walter *et al.*, 2021, p. 418;

Inderberg *et al.*, 2019). Navigating the social world—reliant on neurotypical strengths in social and emotional processing—can therefore be daunting and anxiety-provoking for neurodivergent individuals, who, as a result, may withdraw into solitude or miss out on meaningful social connection (Al-Attar, 2020, p. 939). Social exclusion and bullying are common among neurodivergent children and adolescents (Forrest, Kroeger and Stroope, 2020), which can fuel feelings of hopelessness as well as anger and resentment towards peers and victimisers. The relationship between bullying, social exclusion, and mass violence is unclear, with mixed results found in school shooter cohorts (see Langman and Straub, 2019; Paolini, 2015). However, there is some evidence to suggest a higher prevalence of ASD among lone-actor terrorists (Corner, Gill and Mason, 2016, p. 564), with "social problems" identified as a driver of isolationist attitudes (Spaaij, 2012).

In the face of offline challenges, online platforms can enable neurodivergent youth to pursue effective information gathering for circumscribed interests (Shane-Simpson *et al.*, 2016), and expand opportunities for social engagement via more structured, visualised, and asynchronous communication (van Schalkwyk *et al.*, 2017, p. 2805). However, for neurotypical youth, the turn to online communities to receive validation and social currency has also been found to heighten the risk of being drawn into violent extremist ecosystems (Browne, 2018, p. 141). This was particularly pronounced during the Covid-19 pandemic (Lowe, 2021), which—concurrent with the expansion of right-wing and incel content (Davies, Wu and Frank, 2021)—correlated with a significant spike in juvenile right-wing terrorism offending in England and Wales (Rose and Vale, 2023, p. 20). Indeed, interruption of teenagers' offline processes of identity development has been linked to increased vulnerability to violent anti-system, grievance-based, and conspiratorial ideals (Borum and Patterson, 2019, p. 1143). This risk is heightened for neurodivergent youth with differences in ability to critically analyse the philosophy and beliefs of radical groups and ideologies (Allely and Faccini, 2017; Palermo, 2013). In a recent study using a simulated social media environment, individuals with ASD were found to be more likely to engage with misinformation and endorse conspiracy theories that align with a more internally consistent worldview (Georgiou *et al.*, 2024, p. 296). Moreover, of particular concern for adolescent boys and young men, the algorithmic push of violent content on social media platforms has been associated with heightened risk of being drawn into hateful and misogynistic online communities (Regehr *et al.*, 2024, p. 29), where self-reports highlight the prevalence of neurodivergence among members (Moskalenko *et al.*, 2022; Speckhard and Ellenberg, 2022).

When combined with the allure of absolutist and rules-based ideological narratives, and the accessibility, connectivity, and anonymity of online platforms, manifestations of neurodivergence can thus become significant contextual factors for juvenile violent extremist engagement. This duality of heightened vulnerability and risk prompted Jonathan Hall KC, the UK Independent Reviewer of Terrorism Legislation, to state that it is "necessary to speak about autism" in the context of the current terrorist threat. Though he qualified that by saying "there is a very real and respectable fear that making any sort of link will lead to stigma" (2021, p. 3; see Bronner, 2014).

9.3 The Securitisation of Neurodivergent Children in Counter-Terrorism Practice

Woodhouse *et al.* (2024, p. 1) emphasise that neurodivergence has implications for an individual's journey throughout the CJS, "from police questioning and engagement in court proceedings through to risk assessment, formulation, therapeutic approaches, engagement with support services, and long-term social and legal outcomes". When the context of violent extremism is added, compounding vulnerabilities are evident even earlier, to include experiences of Prevent—the UK's counter-terrorism strategy. The referral mechanism is designed to identify individuals at risk of radicalisation and provide tailored safeguarding and multi-agency support via the Channel programme. Following decades of controversy surrounding Prevent's predominant focus on Islamist extremism and the construction of Muslims as a "suspect community" (Awan, 2012), Pawlowski (2023, p. 319) observes a "recent shift to promote the problematisation of suspicious behaviours instead of focusing on suspicious people". However, she cautions that this shift has merely addressed issues of exclusion and discrimination on a "superficial level" and that "the persistent stereotypical stigmatisations of who and what counts as potentially dangerous are still reproduced but can be hidden more easily under the disclaimer of a non-discriminatory approach" (Ibid). Dresser *et al.* (2025) build on this to question an extension to the suspect community thesis to include neurodiversity. Their analysis of public-facing counter-terrorism training finds that "perception of threat is consolidated through 'seeing' (i.e. judging) normative (yet highly subjective) baseline behaviour(s)" (2025, p. 464). The unintended consequence is the securitisation of neurodivergence that, like other popular stereotypes, may filter from biased public referral to the discriminatory mobilisation of counter-terrorism law enforcement (Haner *et al.*, 2022, p. 1081).

For children in particular, neurodivergence is significantly over-represented in institutional referrals, reflecting a broader risk-oriented, rather than needs-oriented, approach. The UK government's review of Prevent revealed that a "significant number" of referrals involve "complex needs [including] young people on the autistic spectrum" (Shawcross 2023, para. 4.96). Similarly, a review of children's social care in the UK found that almost all children and young people referred for risk of radicalisation are male with underlying vulnerabilities including ASD and other neurodivergent learning needs, such as attention deficit hyperactivity disorder (ADHD), Obsessive-Compulsive Disorder (OCD), and language and communication difficulties (Langdon-Shreeve, Nickson and Bright, 2021, p. 28). Heath-Kelly (2024) warns that children are being referred to Prevent inappropriately in the hope of fast-tracking access to mental healthcare, which risks criminalising their vulnerability rather than providing genuine support. A recent Amnesty International report similarly found that in addition to a disproportionate number of referrals, interaction with Prevent and parallel criminal investigation affects neurodivergent children in specific ways. This includes securitising or even suspending access to vital support services, resulting in heightened mistrust of figures and institutions of authority, further stigmatisation, and barriers to support (2023, p. 37).

Neurodivergent individuals are more likely to be "misunderstood or misperceived by other people", including public sector staff subject to the Prevent duty and counter-terrorism practitioners (Mitchell, Sheppard and Cassidy, 2021). While it is reported that individuals with "a suspected diagnosis" of ASD account for one quarter of those receiving deradicalisation support through the Channel programme (Warrell, 2024), Walter *et al.* (2021, p. 409) caution that "there is no specific reference to ASD in the criteria used by Channel, and [...] no publicly available training exists for professionals working with people with ASD who might be susceptible to radicalisation". Similarly, while UK counter-terrorism police face a high proportion of neurodivergent children and youth in their caseload (Warrell 2024), training for officers has yet to catch up. Only 48 per cent of 238 surveyed police officers in England and Wales feel knowledgeable about ASD, with 29 per cent reporting that they feel "poorly equipped" to work or manage interactions with individuals with ASD (Crane *et al.*, 2016, p. 2035). Failure by police to recognise ASD "will most likely result in the incorrect treatment of the individual and the use of excessive force" (Hepworth, 2017, p. 214). Indeed, Smith (2022. p. 103) finds that neurodivergent individuals become "entrenched as a suspect" on account of police misinterpretation of behaviours as suspicious or criminal, as well as the impact of investigatory powers, criminalisation, and interactions between officers and suspects. How this manifests in the context of custody and questioning for terrorism offenders is discussed in further detail below.

In some cases, diagnosis of neurodivergence is only made as a result of criminal justice processing, often in the context of court-directed psychiatric and psychological assessment to inform conviction and sentencing (Woodbury-Smith *et al.*, 2022, p. 3). Neurodivergent behavioural differences have been found to influence the perceptions of judges and juries about the defendant's criminal intent and potential for violence and aggression (Berryessa, 2021). Judges consider on a case-by-case basis whether a diagnosis of neurodivergence may negate the required elements to establish criminal liability, intent, and responsibility (Woodhouse *et al.*, 2024, p. 6). However, upon review of convicted cases of juvenile terrorism offending, the significance of neurodivergence to radicalisation was applied inconsistently, as both a mitigating and aggravating factor. While for some, associated differences served to explain and reduce culpability for offending behaviour, one boy's impressionable character related to ASD was judged as "not a condition from which you will recover", thereby justifying a life sentence to ensure "some sort of supervision for the rest of your life" (Vale and Rose, 2025, p. 11).

The severity and frequent exceptionalism of terrorism and violent extremism should not frame neurodivergence as justification for securitisation over safeguarding. Indeed, in light of high Prevent referrals and terrorism convictions of neurodivergent children, Jonathan Hall KC (2021, p. 3) explicitly questions: "is the criminal justice outcome the right one in all cases?". While neurodevelopmental conditions can have diverse manifestations and influences on radicalisation, recent scholarship has called for a rebalancing of risk management and rights protection to ensure neuro-inclusivity in counter-terrorism legislation (Dinesson, 2022). Similar arguments have been made for multi-agency practitioner collaboration to enable more sensitive detection, reporting, and support for alleged and convicted offenders (Allely and Faccini, 2019, p. 78). Rather than re-invent the wheel, perhaps the solution lies in existing youth justice policy.

9.4 The Promise and Practice of Child First in Policing

The convergence of these calls for reform suggests that established youth justice frameworks may offer viable pathways for addressing the complex intersection of neurodivergence and violent extremism. The systematic application of existing welfare-oriented principles to cases involving neurodivergent youth and violent extremism could address concerns about appropriate responses whilst maintaining necessary safeguarding measures. This approach's emphasis on developmental understanding, proportionate responses, and multi-agency collaboration aligns closely with the neuro-inclusive principles advocated by scholars such as Dinesson (2022) and the collaborative frameworks proposed by Allely and Faccini (2019). Rather than developing parallel systems, established youth justice frameworks provide a practical foundation for operationalising the theoretical rebalancing between risk management and rights protection that recent scholarship has identified as essential.

Central to this is the "Child First" strategy, which represents a significant shift in approach from risk-oriented models to more welfare-oriented perspectives on children who come into contact with the justice system (Case and Haines, 2015). The roots of the Child First approach can be traced back to academic discussions for shifting youth justice away from risk-management processes towards a more participatory approach. Such discussions predate recent policy shifts (Haines and Drakeford, 1998). However, the significant move towards a more explicit Child First approach came following the "Youth Justice Review" in 2016, which recommended that those aged under 18 should be understood as "children first, and offenders second" (Taylor, 2016). This review led to the Youth Justice Board's (YJB) (2021a, 2021b) formal adoption of the Child First strategy, replacing more punitive, risk-oriented approaches with welfare-oriented principles. Nevertheless, the roll-out was patchy and inconsistent despite the creation of national standards (Ministry of Justice/YJB, 2019; Case, Browning and Hampson, 2024). In addition, the continued use of the "AssetPlus" risk assessment tool alongside the Child First objectives is illustrative of the layering of youth justice policies over each other, rather than replacing earlier practices (Cohen, 1985). The question, then, is can these two approaches—the welfare, child-driven approach and the risk assessment and intervention approach—work together?

As articulated by the Youth Justice Board, the guiding principles of the Child First strategy are:

1. Prioritise the best interests of children and recognise their particular needs, capacities, rights and potential. All work is child-focused, developmentally informed, acknowledges structural barriers and meets responsibilities towards children.
2. Promote children's individual strengths and capacities to develop their pro-social identity for sustainable desistance, leading to safer communities and fewer victims. All work is constructive and future-focused, built on supportive relationships that empower children to fulfil their potential and make positive contributions to society.
3. Encourage children's active participation, engagement and wider social inclusion. All work is a meaningful collaboration with children and their carers.
4. Promote a childhood removed from the justice system, using pre-emptive prevention, diversion and minimal intervention. All work minimises criminogenic stigma from contact with the system. (YJB, 2021b, pp. 10–11).

The police, as frequent gatekeepers to the criminal justice system, play a crucial role in implementing the Child First strategy, but this means that the strategy is always mediated through the lens of discretionary practices and the political direction dictated by the Police and Crime Commissioner (PCC) through the Chief Constable. Indeed, the National Police Chiefs' Council (NPCC) (2015) endorsed a child-centred approach to policing in 2015, predating the Youth Justice Board's formal adoption of the strategy. However, the decentralised nature of policing in England and Wales presents significant challenges to consistent implementation. In addition, the governance structure of policing, whereby each police force area is overseen by its own PCC—a politically motivated form of administration introduced in 2012—creates a patchwork of approaches to youth justice, with some areas demonstrating stronger commitment to Child First principles than others (Case, Browning and Hampson, 2024). This inconsistency is particularly problematic for neurodivergent children, whose needs require specialised understanding and consistent approaches regardless of geographical location.

The NPCC's strategic document on policing children and young people acknowledges that policing this population is "an incredibly important part of the service we deliver" and that "the way in which we police this population now will affect attitudes and culture long into the future" (2015, p. 12). However, the motivation for adopting this approach is framed primarily in strategic terms—to reduce future demand on services rather than as a rights-based or welfare-oriented imperative. The document states that "getting it right WILL make a difference and reduce demand in the future" (Ibid). This strategic, rather than principled, framing may explain some of the implementation gaps observed. Her Majesty's Inspectorate of Constabulary (HMIC, 2015) identified that a key failure in attempts to shift stubborn ideologies—such as treating children as mini-adults prone to crime—is the difficulty in achieving whole-organisation buy-in. Where Child First principles might be accepted in theory, training often does not follow or is only targeted at specific officers rather than being embedded throughout the organisation (Case, Browning and Hampson, 2024).

As Case, Browning and Hampson (2024) have argued, there are many different actors involved in the implementation of the Child First strategy and that national strategies do not always fit with local cultures or priorities. This can result in police forces creating specific child-centred roles for select officers, particularly those involved in custody. While well-intentioned, this approach can have the perverse effect of concentrating Child First principles in the work of a few specialists rather than transforming the culture of the entire police service. The result is a fragmented implementation that fails to deliver consistent experiences for children encountering the justice system. For neurodivergent children, these inconsistencies are particularly problematic. Neurodivergent children, including those with ASD, ADHD, or other developmental conditions, require consistent, predictable, and appropriately adapted approaches from justice professionals. When the implementation of Child First principles varies between force areas or even between individual officers within the same force, neurodivergent children face additional barriers to fair treatment.

In the context of counter-terrorism policing, there are notable developments that signal greater consideration or awareness of children's duality of vulnerability and risk—at least in theory. In September 2024, the "Five Eyes"[3] alliance published its first ever public-facing paper calling for a "whole-of-society approach" to the radicalisation of children towards violent extremism (2024, p. 2). Echoing scholarship (Allely and Faccini 2019), it advocates for collective action combining "mental health, community initiatives, social services, and education" as *upstream* intervention "before security and policing responses are required", and further "acknowledges that unique characteristics of adolescent development require agencies to factor in additional considerations when dealing with minors" including in relation to "determining intent" (Five Eyes, 2024, p. 2). Similar framing has filtered down to the new Met Police "Children's Strategy"—a document positioned explicitly in reference to a Child First approach. One section of the strategy is dedicated to the prevention of children's radicalisation, with the acknowledgement of "complex needs" of those "vulnerable or susceptible to being drawn into terrorism" (2024, p. 26). However, whilst the language reflects a victim-first "prioritis[ation of] the best interests of the child", the suggested action point of appropriate management is to enact a "Prevent intervention, alongside an investigation" (Ibid). This does not elaborate on how such interventions—originally designed for neurotypical adults—can and should be tailored to meet such needs, and also implies the continued intention of pursuing juvenile prosecutions as standard. Moreover, the connection between the promise and practice of a Child First approach to countering extremism is unclear. Scotland's Prosecution Service (2022) published an extensive guidance document on the detention, treatment, and questioning of persons under terrorism legislation, and dedicated specific guidelines and recommendations for cases of children and vulnerable persons. No similar public-facing guidance for police in England and Wales is known to the authors. While the absence of evidence is not evidence of absence, it is striking.

9.5 Challenges in Police Custody for Neurodivergent Children

Police custody represents a particularly challenging environment for neurodivergent children. Custody processes can inadvertently discriminate against neurodivergent children in various ways (Kemp *et al.,* 2023). Standard communication methods may not be accessible, risk assessments may not account for neurodivergent differences, and the custody environment itself may exacerbate anxiety and distress (Parsons and Sherwood, 2016a, 2016b; Holloway *et al.*, 2020; Sowerbutts *et al.*, 2021). The Child First principle of prioritising children's best interests and recognising their particular needs is especially difficult to implement in custody settings that were not designed with neurodivergent children in mind.

Kemp *et al.* (2023) found that custody was often seen as part of the punishment by both children and police officers, who frequently operated on an assumption of "guilty until proven innocent". This punitive mindset directly contradicts Child First principles and can be particularly harmful for neurodivergent children who may not understand why they are being treated as wrongdoers or may struggle to effectively communicate their experiences. Rose and Vale (2023, pp. 33–35) found that the majority of juvenile terrorism convictions relate to possession or collection of information and documents relating to terrorism. Terrorism legislation is "designed in view of what an 'average' person committing a given act may seek to achieve" (Al-Attar, 2018, p. 326), without consideration of neurodivergent circumscribed interests that may have no operational or violent intention (Dinesson, 2022). Mere possession of documentation may thus not be understood to be a criminal offence by the detained child. In current practice, Woodhouse *et al.* (2024, p. 6) find that "the onus is on the defendant's legal team to instruct experts to assess the individual and determine their understanding of the offence". As such, Al-Attar (2018, p. 326) calls for police interviewers to explain the "rules" and social context for how justice is determined for terrorism offending, in order to reorientate custody into "an orderly and rule-driven" experience that neurodivergent children can navigate and process more easily.

Notably, 56% of non-terror-related cases in Kemp *et al.*'s (2023) study resulted in "no further action", suggesting that many children, including neurodivergent children, experience the trauma and distress of custody unnecessarily. There is a similarly high number of "no further action" outcomes for those arrested on terror charges. Home Office statistics (2025) reveal that while 39 children were arrested for terrorism-related activity in 2024, only three children were charged, and no juvenile convictions were registered. This reality stands in stark contrast to the fourth principle of the Child First strategy, which aims to "promote a childhood removed from the justice system" and "minimise criminogenic stigma from contact with the system" (YJB, 2021b, p. 11).

The treatment of neurodivergent children in custody also raises serious questions about their access to justice. Communication difficulties may affect the ability to understand their rights, participate effectively in interviews, or make informed decisions about legal advice (Sowerbutts *et al.*, 2021). Research on procedural justice in police custody (Savigar-Shaw *et al.*, 2022) suggests that perceptions of fair treatment are crucial for legitimacy; yet, neurodivergent children may experience procedures differently and require adaptations that are not consistently available.

A growing body of research over the past decade indicates negative and unsupportive experiences with the police for neurodivergent adults and juveniles (Woodhouse *et al.*, 2024, p. 5). Bagnall and Maras (2025) problematise understandings of vulnerability in police custody, beginning with screenings and risk assessments during "booking-in" procedures. They argue that "risk and vulnerability are often assessed subjectively, with decision making driven by custody officers' professional experience and knowledge" without clinical training and in the context of "complex, unpredictable, and often under-resourced working environments" (2025, p. 198). Moreover, screening tools currently in use in custody fail to recognise or adequately capture the scope of vulnerabilities for adults and juveniles (Farrugia, 2021; Holland, Hutchinson and Peacock, 2023). The "consequences may be that vulnerability is not properly accounted for at the investigative interview stage" (Bagnall and Maras, 2025, p. 198). Indeed, neurodivergent (adults and) children in custody may face heightened anxiety resulting in less detailed testimony than neurotypical suspects (Bagnall *et al.*, 2023), and provide false confessions due to weakened resilience under pressure (Gudjonsson *et al.*, 2016). This may create or crystallise appraisal of concerning or non-compliant behaviours that overshadow underlying vulnerabilities. The introduction of the Registered Intermediaries (as outlined in the Youth Justice and Criminal Evidence Act 1999) offers a platform for adaptations to be made for interviews with neurodivergent victims and witnesses, including a bespoke assessment, recommendations, and communication facilitation during the interview process. However, Woodhouse *et al.* (2024, p. 5) highlight the specific exclusion of provision for police suspects, further embedding the exceptionalism of cases of vulnerability *and* risk.

The context of terrorism and violent extremism presents further and unique challenges. The Counter-Terrorism Act 2008 allows for police questioning after charge, making "terrorism interviews the most protracted forensic interviews undertaken within the British CJS" (Al-Attar, 2018, p. 322). Prolonged questioning, combined with the complexity of unpicking actions, intentionality, and ideology in interviews, places a high cognitive load on the suspect, the effects of which may not be visible or obvious to the interviewer, legal representative, or mental health professional (Ibid).

Misinterpretation of social communication styles associated with neurodevelopmental conditions, such as ASD, may feed into the reading of neurodivergent children as "suspect". For example, discussion of ideology in very graphic and matter-of-fact terms or volunteering substantial detail may self-incriminate or be mistaken as evidence of strong ideological commitment, or trying to invoke fear or shock from an interviewer (Al-Attar, 2018, p. 327). Allely *et al.* (2024, p. 184) note that these behaviours "may confound the 'terror' that others may appraise—such as a threat or a risk assessment professional". In their recommendations for practitioners, Salman and Al-Attar instead encourage interviewers to "consider blunt, detailed or efficient responses as indicators of good communicative engagement", whilst also "offering explicit, matter-of-fact explanations of the consequences of disclosure to individuals whose understanding may be impacted by their cognitive profile" (2023b, p. 13). Professional values of honesty and candour sit in contrast to those adopted by violent extremist groups, and thus put CJS practitioners in an influential position to model more inclusive and respectful communication in forensic settings (Al-Attar *et al.*, 2018, p. 11).

These challenges underscore the gap between Child First principles and custody practices, particularly for neurodivergent children. While the YJB's strategy emphasises child-focused, developmentally informed approaches that acknowledge structural barriers, the reality of police custody often falls short of these ideals.

9.6 Innovations and Adaptations in Custody

In a participative walkthrough of the custody process, Holloway *et al.* repeatedly highlight communication barriers that negatively impact both police custody officers and detainees with ASD. One recommendation made by a participant was for more accessible forms of information such as "visual prompts of what was gonna happen", "a visual timetable", and "a booklet outlining the custody process" (2020, p. 6). Similarly in order to reduce stressors in the context of protracted counter-terrorism detention, Salman and Al-Attar (2023b, p. 13) repeatedly recommend visual imagery or representations, as well as sensory stimulation aids, to facilitate communication and engagement with the custody and investigation processes.

Some police forces have implemented innovations to meet these needs and better support vulnerable children, including those with neurodivergence, in custody settings. One such innovation is the video-book project, which aims to provide accessible information and support to children in custody. Video-books are tablet-like devices without network functionality, pre-loaded with videos that provide information about the custody process and potential pathways to support services. These devices can be tailored to reflect children's characteristics, including age, gender, and disclosed neurodivergence. Of course, in many cases neurodivergence may not be a diagnosed condition, but the content could be designed so that different delivery methods can be chosen by the detainee, such as visual, written, symbols or aural presentations (Parsons and Sherwood, 2016a, 2016b; Sowerbutts *et al.*, 2021). There are several pilot schemes across England and Wales; the exact number is not known. However, the authors are working with 14 police force areas that have expressed interest in adopting the technology, in addition to at least one police force that uses fixed screen terminals in custody cells (Skinns, 2025). The video-books currently in use have varied content, with videos outlining the custody and regulatory processes that need to be followed. This is typically done using animation with a voice-over, although a version used by the Metropolitan Police used actors to represent detainees. In addition, videos that try to encourage detainees to remain calm, such as showing relaxation breathing techniques, have also been created. The version used by the Metropolitan Police also directed detainees to a website run by a third-sector organisation that specialises in mentoring children and young people to find training, education or employment, as well as routes to mental and physical healthcare. By providing information in visual and auditory formats, video-books may be particularly helpful for neurodivergent children who process information differently. However, at present, such devices remain under-developed due to lack of resources. This technology has the potential to be a game-changing addition to custody, or other criminal justice settings, where complex legal information needs to be delivered under stressful and challenging conditions.

Innovations like video-books have the potential to demystify and streamline custody processes, with benefits for detainees and officers. For example, clear, age-appropriate, and bite-sized informational videos on staff roles, investigatory processes, and welfare services can ensure children are informed of their rights and responsibilities and may also support diversion from further offending. For neurodivergent children in particular, the structured, visualised, and asynchronous content may offer a more accessible means of understanding their rights and the custody process than traditional written or verbal explanations, whilst also relieving boredom, anxiety, and cognitive overload (Al-Attar, 2018, p. 322). At the same time, engagement with the video-book has the added benefit of reducing the workload of custody staff, potentially compensating for gaps in officer training or awareness of neurodivergence (Crane *et al.*, 2016; Hepworth, 2017). As such, video-books can embed Child First principles and equality, diversity, and inclusion values through their content and accessibility. As Her Majesty's Inspectorate of Constabulary (HMIC) (2015) identified, systemic failures to change police culture to reflect crime-reduction strategies like Child First require pragmatic solutions. Technologies like video-books can "carry" these principles in the absence of widespread cultural adoption.

For counter-terrorism policing, such tools can ease tensions or misunderstandings concerning neurodivergent cognitive and communication styles that are frequently read as "suspect" or evidence of ideological or violent motivation (Smith, 2022). Alongside a more nuanced reading of detailed or enthusiastic accounts relating to extremist interests (Al-Attar, 2020, p. 937), professional values of honesty and candour—communicated accessibly through videos concerning, for example, the consequences of information disclosure and self-incrimination—sit in contrast to those adopted by violent extremist groups, and thus put criminal justice practitioners in an influential position to model more inclusive and respectful communication in forensic settings (Al-Attar *et al.*, 2018, p. 11). Moreover, the protracted period of pre-charge detention and post-charge questioning for terrorism offending—while broadly contrary to Child First principles—does provide an opportunity for more robust assessment and multi-agency support referrals for neurodivergent children and vulnerable persons with suspected links to violent extremism. While we strongly echo Heath-Kelly's (2024) concerns over the misappropriation of the counter-terrorism apparatus to fast-track access to healthcare, the ability for a video-book to be tailored to highlight and connect to appropriate services may provide a critical diversionary pathway from prosecution to support the underlying vulnerabilities that contextualise the child's extremist engagement.

However, the implementation of such innovations faces similar challenges to the broader implementation of Child First principles. The decentralised nature of policing means that promising practices developed in one area may not be adopted in others. Political considerations, resource constraints, and cultural resistance can all impede the spread of effective approaches. In addition, technological solutions should complement, not replace, essential changes in police culture and practice. The risk of relying too heavily on technological fixes is that they may reduce pressure for more fundamental reforms in how police interact with neurodivergent children. Without addressing underlying attitudes and systemic issues, the benefits of such innovations may remain limited.

9.7 Conclusions and Recommendations

This chapter has examined the criminal justice response to neurodivergent children suspected of violent extremism, focusing on the gap between the promise of Child First principles and their practical implementation. Our analysis reveals a system struggling to reconcile competing demands: the need to address legitimate security concerns whilst protecting children who may not fit the "typical" profile of an extremist or themselves understand the criminal nature of their actions. The duality of vulnerability and risk that characterises neurodivergent children's involvement in violent extremism challenges traditional binary thinking in both youth justice and counter-terrorism practice. These children simultaneously represent potential threats requiring security responses and vulnerable individuals needing protection and support. The Child First strategy provides a framework for navigating this complexity; yet, its implementation remains patchy and inconsistent across England and Wales.

The decentralised governance structure of policing, with politically motivated Police and Crime Commissioners overseeing individual force areas, exacerbates these implementation challenges (Case, Browning and Hampson, 2024). What emerges is a postcode lottery of responses, where neurodivergent children's experiences depend more on geographical location and local political priorities than on their individual needs or the complexity of their alleged offences. This inconsistency is particularly problematic given that neurodivergent children require predictable, specialised approaches regardless of where they encounter the justice system (Smith and Dehaghani, 2025). The sensory overwhelm of custody suites, extended detention periods permitted under terrorism legislation, and "atypical" cognitive and communication styles create conditions that can exacerbate distress and compromise fair treatment (Kemp *et al.*, 2023; Holloway *et al.*, 2020; Parsons and Sherwood, 2016a). As Bevan (2022) notes, following Sykes (1958), the "pains of police custody" for children create conditions particularly detrimental to neurodivergent individuals who struggle with environmental changes and sensory processing. The tendency for custody officers to interpret neurodivergent behaviours as non-compliance, deception, or threat poses particular risks in the counter-extremism context where security concerns may override welfare considerations.

Innovations such as video-books demonstrate the potential for technological solutions to support neurodivergent children in custody (Parsons and Sherwood, 2016b). However, these remain limited in scope and implementation, highlighting the broader challenge of translating promising practices into systemic change. The securitisation of neurodivergence through Prevent referrals and counter-terrorism practice represents a concerning trend that requires careful examination, reflecting complex interactions between neurodivergent cognitive styles, online environments, and extremist content rather than inherent predisposition to violence. Moving forward, significant systemic reforms are required to address these challenges comprehensively. The establishment of mandatory national standards specifically addressing the custody and interview procedures for neurodivergent children suspected of violent extremist engagement or terrorism offending represents a crucial first step. These standards should be developed collaboratively between relevant agencies, ensuring that political considerations do not override evidence-based practice, with national oversight monitoring compliance across all force areas.

The current exclusion of suspects from the Registered Intermediary Scheme represents a significant barrier to fair treatment for neurodivergent children (Dehaghani and Smith, 2024; Woodhouse *et al.*, 2024). Extending this provision to include child suspects with diagnosed or suspected neurodivergence would provide independent assessment of communication needs and ongoing support throughout the custody process. Given the extended detention and questioning periods possible under terrorism legislation, up to 14 days without specific provisions for children, the need for appropriate communication support becomes even more critical. Terrorism-specific custody resources should be developed for neurodivergent children, explaining the unique aspects of terrorism detention and addressing the specific confusion that may arise for children who engage with extremist content as a circumscribed interest without understanding its criminal nature (Dinesson, 2022). The over-representation of neurodivergent children in Prevent referrals requires reform of upstream referral pathways, establishing neuro-inclusive assessment protocols within Channel panels with mandatory training for all members (Walter *et al.*, 2021). Dual-track approaches should be developed where children can access mental health and educational support without default labelling as "suspect" (Smith, 2022).

The current binary approach of either pursuing prosecution or taking no further action fails to address the complex needs of neurodivergent children. Graduated response protocols should be developed that consider neurodivergent factors in charging decisions, including mandatory and neuro-inclusive psychological pre-charge assessment (Al-Attar *et al.*, 2018), and alternative education programmes specifically designed for neurodivergent children. Enhanced multi-agency collaboration through dedicated teams combining counter-terrorism policing, child protection services, educational psychology, neurodiversity specialists, and youth justice workers is essential to ensure coordinated and nuanced responses. The theoretical frameworks that underpin our analysis point to fundamental questions about the purpose and nature of youth justice in cases involving violent extremism. The Child First strategy's emphasis on diversion, minimal intervention, and recognition of children's developmental needs offers a promising alternative to purely punitive approaches (Case and Haines, 2015). However, realising this promise requires acknowledging that terrorism cases need not be exceptional to the extent that they bypass welfare-oriented youth justice principles.

As Skinns *et al.* (2017) argue, the custody suite is uniquely placed to provide a "teachable moment", where detainees may be more receptive to positive messaging and support; yet, this potential is currently undermined by inadequate understanding of neurodivergent needs that contextualise extremist engagement. Future research should focus on longitudinal outcomes for neurodivergent children who experience different types of criminal justice responses to violent extremism, alongside comprehensive investigation into professional perspectives across different forces, crime types, and international contexts. We need systematic research into the insights from custody officers, counter-terrorism policing, appropriate adults, and other professionals regarding specific challenges they face, their training needs, and examples of best practice. The development of validated assessment tools specifically designed to identify neurodivergent children's support needs in terrorism contexts represents another important research priority, building on work by Kemp and Watkins (2022) on children's understanding of legal rights. Technological innovations, particularly the video-book system, require significant development to realise their potential for supporting neurodivergent children in custody. The video-book system could be enhanced to provide adaptable content with specific modules designed for neurodivergent children facing terrorism allegations. These devices could help keep children calmer by providing familiar, predictable content that reduces anxiety and sensory overwhelm, whilst facilitating structured avenues for communication between children and police. This enhanced communication capacity could significantly aid the interview and evidence collection process by helping neurodivergent children better understand what is being asked of them and providing alternative methods for conveying information when verbal communication proves challenging.

Ultimately, the criminal justice response to neurodivergent children suspected of violent extremism must be grounded in evidence-based understanding of both neurodivergence and radicalisation processes. This requires moving beyond stereotypes and assumptions towards a nuanced appreciation of neurodiversity and individual circumstances and needs. The promise of the Child First strategy lies in its recognition that children—including those involved in the most serious offences—remain children first. For neurodivergent children suspected of violent extremism, this principle offers hope for responses that acknowledge their developmental stage, whilst addressing legitimate concerns about public safety. Realising this promise requires sustained commitment to reform, adequate resources for implementation, and courage to challenge entrenched attitudes that see punishment as the only appropriate response to violent extremist engagement and terrorism-related offending. The path forward demands recognition that security and welfare need not be mutually exclusive, that vulnerability and risk can coexist, and that protecting children's rights enhances, rather than undermines, national security.

Notes

1 A note on terms used in this chapter. "Neurodiversity", coined by Singer (2016), refers to the range of natural diversity in human neurodevelopment. Traditional conceptions construct "neurotypicality" as the "correct" or "normal" manner of thinking and processing information or within the typical range of the majority of the population, while "neurodivergence" is characterised by difference from the putative norm, and is an umbrella term for a variety of neurodevelopmental conditions including autism spectrum disorder (ASD), attention deficit hyperactivity disorder (ADHD), and learning and communication difficulties. This chapter draws from the neurodiversity paradigm, which rejects the view that neurodivergence is a deficit, and instead advocates for the value of diversity in neurodevelopment (see Walker, 2012; Pellicano and den Houting, 2022).

2 We echo criticism of the legal and social uses of the term "vulnerable", which can be perceived as disempowering (Peacock and Hutchinson, 2025, p. 443). However, we acknowledge that this terminology is used as standard in the field across scholarship and practice.

3 The "Five Eyes" is an intelligence alliance comprised of the UK, US, Canada, Australia and New Zealand, established in 1946 following World War II. It functions as a global surveillance mechanism to understand and respond to threats such as international terrorism, cyberattacks, and contemporary regional conflicts.

References

Al-Attar, P. and Zainab (2018) 'Interviewing terrorism suspects and offenders with an autism spectrum disorder', *International Journal of Forensic Mental Health*, 17(4), pp. 321–337. Available at: https://doi.org/10.1080/14999013.2018.1519614.

Al-Attar, Z. (2020) 'Autism spectrum disorders and terrorism: How different features of autism can contextualise vulnerability and resilience', *The Journal of Forensic Psychiatry*

& Psychology, 31(6), pp. 926–949. Available at: https://doi.org/10.1080/14789949.2020.1812695.

Al-Attar, Z. and Worthington, R. (2025) 'Online terrorism offenders with ADHD: In what ways can ADHD create contextual vulnerabilities and risk?', in S.J. Macdonald and D. Peacock (eds) *The Routledge handbook of disability, crime, and justice*. Abingdon: Routledge, pp. 137–156.

Al-Attar, Z. *et al.* (2018) *Ethical guidelines for applied psychological practice in the field of extremism, violent extremism and terrorism*. British Psychological Society. Available at: https://doi.org/10.53841/bpsrep.2018.inf313.

Allely, C.S. and Faccini, L. (2017) '"Path to intended violence" model to understand mass violence in the case of Elliot Rodger', *Aggression and Violent Behavior*, 37, pp. 201–209. Available at: https://doi.org/10.1016/j.avb.2017.09.005.

Allely, C.S. and Faccini, L. (2019) 'Clinical profile, risk, and critical factors and the application of the "path toward intended violence" model in the case of mass shooter Dylann Roof', *Deviant Behavior*, 40(6), pp. 672–689. Available at: https://doi.org/10.1080/01639625.2018.1437653.

Allely, C.S. *et al.* (2024) 'Autism spectrum disorder, extremism and risk assessment', *Criminal Behaviour and Mental Health*, 34(2), pp. 182–196. Available at: https://doi.org/10.1002/cbm.2330.

Amnesty International (2023) *"This is the thought police": The Prevent duty and its chilling effect on human rights*. London. Available at: https://www.amnesty.org.uk/files/2023-11/Amnesty%20UK%20Prevent%20report%20%281%29.pdf?VersionId=.hjIwRZuHiGd1_lECXroFwg25jyBtwur (Accessed: 27 November 2024).

Anthony, L.G. *et al.* (2013) 'Interests in high-functioning autism are more intense, interfering, and idiosyncratic than those in neurotypical development', *Development and Psychopathology*, 25(3), pp. 643–652. Available at: https://doi.org/10.1017/S0954579413000072.

Awan, I. (2012) '"I am a Muslim not an extremist": How the prevent strategy has constructed a "suspect" community', *Politics & Policy*, 40(6), pp. 1158–1185. Available at: https://doi.org/10.1111/j.1747-1346.2012.00397.x.

Bagnall, R. and Maras, K. (2025) 'Autism and police interviewing: An individual, interpersonal, and environmental model of vulnerability', in S.J. Macdonald and D. Peacock (eds) *The Routledge handbook of disability, crime, and justice*. Abingdon: Routledge, pp. 197–217.

Bagnall, R. *et al.* (2023) 'Police suspect interviews with autistic adults: The impact of truth telling versus deception on testimony', *Frontiers in Psychology*, 14, pp. 1–12. Available at: https://doi.org/10.3389/fpsyg.2023.1117415.

Berryessa, C.M. (2021) 'Defendants with autism spectrum disorder in criminal court: A judges' toolkit', *Drexel Law Review*, 13(4), pp. 841–868. Available at: https://doi.org/10.2139/ssrn.3730822.

Bevan, M. (2022) 'The pains of police custody for children: A recipe for injustice and exclusion?', *The British Journal of Criminology*, 62(4), pp. 805–821. Available at: https://doi.org/10.1093/bjc/azab107.

Borum, R. and Patterson, T.D. (2019) 'Juvenile radicalization into violent extremism: Investigative and research perspectives', *Journal of the American Academy of Child & Adolescent Psychiatry*, 58(12), pp. 1142–1148. Available at: https://doi.org/10.1016/j.jaac.2019.07.932.

Bronner, S.J. (2014) '"The shooter has Asperger's": Autism, belief, and "wild child" narratives', *Children's Folklore Review*, 36, pp. 35–54.

Browne, D. (2018) 'Children as agents of terrorism and political conflict', in A. Silke (ed) *Routledge handbook of terrorism and counterterrorism*. Abingdon: Routledge, pp. 135–148.

Case, S., Browning, A. and Hampson, K. (2024) 'The child first strategy implementation project – Translating strategy into practice', *Youth Justice*, 24(2), pp. 204–230. Available at: https://doi.org/10.1177/14732254231191978.

Case, S. and Haines, K. (2015) 'Children first, offenders second positive promotion: Reframing the prevention debate', *Youth Justice*, 15(3), pp. 226–239. Available at: https://doi.org/10.1177/1473225414563154.

Cohen, S. (1985) *Visions of social control: Crime, punishment and classification*. Cambridge: Polity.

Corner, E., Gill, P. and Mason, O. (2016) 'Mental health disorders and the terrorist: A research note probing selection effects and disorder prevalence', *Studies in Conflict & Terrorism*, 39(6), pp. 560–568. Available at: https://doi.org/10.1080/1057610X.2015.1120099.

Crane, L. *et al.* (2016) 'Experiences of autism spectrum disorder and policing in England and Wales: Surveying police and the autism community', *Journal of Autism and Developmental Disorders*, 46(6), pp. 2028–2041. Available at: https://doi.org/10.1007/s10803-016-2729-1.

Davies, G., Wu, E. and Frank, R. (2021) 'A witch's brew of grievances: The potential effects of COVID-19 on radicalization to violent extremism', *Studies in Conflict & Terrorism*, 0(0), pp. 1–24. Available at: https://doi.org/10.1080/1057610X.2021.1923188.

Dehaghani, R. and Smith, T. (2024) 'Neurodivergence, autism and the appropriate adult safeguard in police custody', *Northern Ireland Legal Quarterly*, 75(4), pp. 690–719. Available at: https://doi.org/10.53386/nilq.v75i4.1138.

Dinesson, K.E. (2022) '(Un)reasonable excuses – On R v Dunleavy, R v Copeland, and Section 58', *The Modern Law Review*, 85(6), pp. 1550–1561. Available at: https://doi.org/10.1111/1468-2230.12721.

Dresser, P., Rowe, M. and Harding, J. (2025) 'Unintended consequences of public-facing counter-terrorism training and vigilance campaigns on minority groups', *Critical Studies on Terrorism*, 18(2), pp. 450–477. Available at: https://doi.org/10.1080/17539153.2025.2479912.

Druitt, F. *et al.* (2023) 'Do autism spectrum disorders (ASD) increase the risk of terrorism engagement? A literature review of the research evidence, theory and interpretation, and a discussion reframing the research-practice debate', *Journal of Policing, Intelligence and Counter Terrorism*, 18(3), pp. 307–332. Available at: https://doi.org/10.1080/18335330.2022.2158361.

Farrugia, L. (2021) 'Identifying vulnerability in police custody: Making sense of information provided to custody officers', *Journal of Forensic and Legal Medicine*, 80, p. 102169. Available at: https://doi.org/10.1016/j.jflm.2021.102169.

Five Eyes (2024) *Young people and violent extremism: A call for collective action*. Available at: https://www.counterterrorism.police.uk/wp-content/uploads/2024/12/Unclassified-Five-Eyes-CT-minors-paper.pdf (Accessed: 29 May 2025).

Forrest, D.L., Kroeger, R.A. and Stroope, S. (2020) 'Autism spectrum disorder symptoms and bullying victimization among children with autism in the United States', *Journal of*

Autism and Developmental Disorders, 50(2), pp. 560–571. Available at: https://doi.org/10.1007/s10803-019-04282-9.

Georgiou, N. *et al.* (2024) 'People with autistic traits are more likely to engage with misinformation and conspiracy theories in a simulated social media context', *Cognitive Neuropsychiatry*, 29(4–5), pp. 286–305. Available at: https://doi.org/10.1080/13546805.2024.2443576.

Gray, S.M. *et al.* (2024) 'An exploration of diagnostic identity for autistic individuals: A systematic review of existing literature', *Research in Autism Spectrum Disorders*, 114, p. 102394. Available at: https://doi.org/10.1016/j.rasd.2024.102394.

Gudjonsson, G.H. *et al.* (2016) 'A national epidemiological study investigating risk factors for police interrogation and false confession among juveniles and young persons', *Social Psychiatry and Psychiatric Epidemiology*, 51(3), pp. 359–367. Available at: https://doi.org/10.1007/s00127-015-1145-8.

Haines, K. and Drakeford, M. (1998) *Young People and Youth Justice*. London: Macmillan.

Hall, J. (2021) *What is the threat to the UK today?* Independent Reviewer of Terrorism Legislation. Available at: https://terrorismlegislationreviewer.independent.gov.uk/wp-content/uploads/2021/07/July-2021-What-is-the-threat-to-the-UK-today.pdf (Accessed: 14 May 2025).

Haner, M. *et al.* (2022) 'When do Americans "see something, say something"? Experimental evidence on the willingness to report terrorist activity', *Justice Quarterly*, 39(5), pp. 1079–1103. Available at: https://doi.org/10.1080/07418825.2021.1942162.

Heath-Kelly, C. (2024) *Unhealthy liaisons: NHS collaboration with the Counter Terrorism Clinical Consultancy Service*. London: Medact. Available at: https://stat.medact.org/wp-uploads/2024/07/Unhealthy-Liaisons-WEB-final-2.pdf (Accessed: 27 November 2024).

Hepworth, D. (2017) 'A critical review of current police training and policy for autism spectrum disorder', *Journal of Intellectual Disabilities and Offending Behaviour*, 8(4), pp. 212–222. Available at: https://doi.org/10.1108/JIDOB-06-2017-0011.

Her Majesty's Inspectorate of Constabulary (HMIC) (2015) *The-welfare-of-vulnerable-people-in-police-custody.pdf*. Available at: https://assets-hmicfrs.justiceinspectorates.gov.uk/uploads/the-welfare-of-vulnerable-people-in-police-custody.pdf (Accessed: 6 June 2025).

Holland, C., Hutchinson, P. and Peacock, D. (2023) 'The importance of screening for speech, language and communication needs (SLCN) in police custody', *The Howard Journal of Crime and Justice*, 62(3), pp. 295–312. Available at: https://doi.org/10.1111/hojo.12514.

Holloway, C.A. *et al.* (2020) 'Exploring the autistic and police perspectives of the custody process through a participative walkthrough', *Research in Developmental Disabilities*, 97, pp. 1–12. Available at: https://doi.org/10.1016/j.ridd.2019.103545.

Home Office (2025) *Operation of police powers under TACT 2000, to December 2024*. Available at: https://www.gov.uk/government/statistics/operation-of-police-powers-under-tact-2000-to-december-2024 (Accessed: 15 May 2025).

Inderberg, A.M.S. *et al.* (2019) 'Autism, intellectual disabilities and additional psychosis, and affiliation to groups with violent ideology: Short communication', *Journal of Intellectual Disabilities and Offending Behaviour*, 10(1), pp. 1–7. Available at: https://doi.org/10.1108/JIDOB-09-2018-0010.

Kapp, S.K. (2016) *Social justice and autism: Links to personality and advocacy*. PhD. University of California. Available at: https://www.proquest.com/openview/97a411d

021ee551061d8c51e50425151/1?pq-origsite=gscholar&cbl=18750 (Accessed: 28 May 2025).

Kemp, V. *et al.* (2023) *Examining the impact of PACE on the detention and questioning of child suspects*. University of Nottingham. Available at: https://www.nuffieldfoundation.org/wp-content/uploads/2021/07/Kemp-Examining-the-impact-of-PACE-on-the-detention-and-questioning-of-child-suspects.pdf (Accessed: 4 June 2025).

Kemp, V. and Watkins, D. (2022) 'Exploring children's understanding of the legal rights of suspects in England and Wales', *Youth Justice*, 22(3), pp. 320–338. Available at: https://doi.org/10.1177/14732254211030597.

Langdon-Shreeve, S., Nickson, H. and Bright, C. (2021) *Safeguarding and radicalisation: Learning from children's social care*. Department for Education. Available at: https://dera.ioe.ac.uk/id/eprint/38118/1/DfE_Safeguarding_in_CSC.pdf.

Langman, P. and Straub, F. (2019) *A comparison of averted and completed school attacks from the police foundation averted school violence database*. Washington, DC: Office of Community Oriented Policing Services. Available at: https://www.policinginstitute.org/publication/a-comparison-of-averted-and-completed-school-attacks-from-the-police-foundation-averted-school-violence-database/.

Lowe, P. (2021) 'Young people and violent extremism in the Covid-19 context', in L. Close and D. Impiombato (eds) *Counterterrorism yearbook 2021*. Australian Strategic Policy Institute, pp. 101–105. Available at: https://s3-ap-southeast-2.amazonaws.com/ad-aspi/2021-03/ASPI%20Counterterrorism%20YB2021-v2.pdf?qRIjpA0b0aLaWsvXREMAf8yo8I.uyWxN.

Metropolitan Police (2024) *MPS children's strategy*. Available at: https://www.met.police.uk/SysSiteAssets/media/downloads/force-content/met/about-us/children-strategy/the-children-strategy-a4-final.pdf (Accessed: 29 May 2025).

Ministry of Justice/Youth Justice Board (2019) *Standards for children in the youth justice system 2019*. Available at: https://assets.publishing.service.gov.uk/media/6363d2328fa8f50570e54222/Standards_for_children_in_youth_justice_services_2019.doc.pdf (Accessed: 6 June 2025).

Mitchell, P., Sheppard, E. and Cassidy, S. (2021) 'Autism and the double empathy problem: Implications for development and mental health', *British Journal of Developmental Psychology*, 39(1), pp. 1–18. Available at: https://doi.org/10.1111/bjdp.12350.

Moskalenko, S. *et al.* (2022) 'Predictors of radical intentions among incels: A survey of 54 self-identified incels', *Journal of Online Trust and Safety*, 1(3). Available at: https://doi.org/10.54501/jots.v1i3.57.

Murphy, D. (2018) 'Interviewing individuals with an autism spectrum disorder in forensic settings', *International Journal of Forensic Mental Health*, 17(4), pp. 310–320. Available at: https://doi.org/10.1080/14999013.2018.1518939.

National Police Chief's Council (NPCC) (2015) *National strategy for the policing of children & young people*. Available at: https://www.npcc.police.uk/SysSiteAssets/media/downloads/publications/publications-log/local-policing-coordination-committee/national-strategy-for-the-policing-of-children-young-people.pdf (Accessed: 6 June 2025).

Palermo, M.T. (2013) 'Developmental disorders and political extremism: A case study of Asperger syndrome and the Neo-Nazi subculture', *Journal of Forensic Psychology Practice*, 13(4), pp. 341–354. Available at: https://doi.org/10.1080/15228932.2013.817890.

Paolini, A. (2015) 'School shootings and student mental health: Role of the school counselor in mitigating violence', *American Counseling Association*, 90, pp. 1–17.

Parsons, S. and Sherwood, G. (2016a) 'A pilot evaluation of using symbol-based information in police custody', *British Journal of Learning Disabilities*, 44(3), pp. 213–224. Available at: https://doi.org/10.1111/bld.12140.

Parsons, S. and Sherwood, G. (2016b) 'Vulnerability in custody: Perceptions and practices of police officers and criminal justice professionals in meeting the communication needs of offenders with learning disabilities and learning difficulties', *Disability & Society*, 31(4), pp. 553–572. Available at: https://doi.org/10.1080/09687599.2016.1181538.

Pawlowski, N.S. (2023) 'Suspicious cities: An analysis of the securitisation of urban everyday life in London and Brussels', *Critical Studies on Terrorism*, 16(2), pp. 305–327. Available at: https://doi.org/10.1080/17539153.2023.2176408.

Peacock, D. and Hutchinson, P. (2025) 'A critical realist analysis of communication and engagement barriers for "vulnerable" suspects in the police station', in S.J. Macdonald and Peacock (eds) *The Routledge Handbook of Disability, Crime, and Justice*. Abingdon: Routledge, pp. 443–458.

Pellicano, E. and den Houting, J. (2022) 'Annual research review: Shifting from "normal science" to neurodiversity in autism science', *Journal of Child Psychology and Psychiatry*, 63(4), pp. 381–396. Available at: https://doi.org/10.1111/jcpp.13534.

Regehr, K. *et al.* (2024) *Safer scrolling: How algorithms popularise and gamify online hate and misogyny for young people*. University College London and University of Kent. Available at: https://www.ascl.org.uk/ASCL/media/ASCL/Help%20and%20advice/Inclusion/Safer-scrolling.pdf (Accessed: 14 May 2025).

Rose, H. and Vale, G. (2023) *Childhood innocence?: Mapping trends in teenage terrorism offenders*. London: International Centre for the Study of Radicalisation. Available at: https://icsr.info/2023/11/15/childhood-innocence-mapping-trends-in-teenage-terrorism-offenders/.

Rose, H. and Vale, G. (2025) 'Childhood innocence project live dataset'. International Centre for the Study of Radicalisation. Available at: https://icsr.info/childhood-innocence-project/.

Salman, N. and Al-Attar, Z. (2023a) *A systematic review of neurodivergence, vulnerability, and risk in the context of violent extremism*. Crest Advisory. Available at: https://crestresearch.ac.uk/resources/a-systematic-review-of-neurodivergence-vulnerability-and-risk-in-the-context-of-violent-extremism/#:~:text=The%20review%20indicated%20that%20in,stressors%20that%20uniquely%20combine%20in.

Salman, N. and Al-Attar, Z. (2023b) *Autism and extremism: The questions that operational practitioners should be asking*. Crest Advisory. Available at: https://crestresearch.ac.uk/resources/autism-and-extremism-practitioner-report/ (Accessed: 25 October 2024).

Savigar-Shaw, L. *et al.* (2022) 'Procedural justice as a reward to the compliant: An ethnography of police–citizen interaction in police custody', *Policing and Society*, 32(6), pp. 778–793. Available at: https://doi.org/10.1080/10439463.2021.1960332.

Shawcross, W. (2023) *Independent Review of Prevent*. Available at: https://assets.publishing.service.gov.uk/media/63e26968d3bf7f17385a3421/Independent_Review_of_Prevent.pdf

Singer, J. (2016) *NeuroDiversity: The Birth of an Idea*. Self-Published.

van Schalkwyk, G.I. *et al.* (2017) 'Social media use, friendship quality, and the moderating role of anxiety in adolescents with autism spectrum disorder', *Journal of Autism and*

Developmental Disorders, 47(9), pp. 2805–2813. Available at: https://doi.org/10.1007/s10803-017-3201-6.

Scotland's Prosecution Service (2022) *Lord Advocate's guidelines on the detention, treatment and questioning of persons under Section 41 and Schedule 8 of the Terrorism Act 2000, and Section 23 of the Counter-Terrorism Act 2008.* Crown Office and Procurator Fiscal Service. Available at: https://www.copfs.gov.uk/publications/lord-advocate-s-guidelines-detention-treatment-and-questioning-of-persons-under-terrorism-legislation/.

Shane-Simpson, C. *et al.* (2016) 'Associations between compulsive internet use and the autism spectrum', *Research in Autism Spectrum Disorders*, 23, pp. 152–165. Available at: https://doi.org/10.1016/j.rasd.2015.12.005.

Skinns, L. (2011) *Police custody: Governance, legitimacy and reform in the criminal justice process*. Abingdon, Oxon U.K. New York: Willan.

Skinns, L. (2025) *'Good' police custody: Influencing police custody policy and practice, University of Sheffield.* Available at: https://sheffield.ac.uk/law/research/good-police-custody-influencing-police-custody-policy-and-practice (Accessed: 18 August 2025).

Skinns, L. and Wooff, A. (2021) 'Pain in police detention: A critical point in the "penal painscape"?', *Policing and Society*, 31(3), pp. 245–262. Available at: https://doi.org/10.1080/10439463.2019.1706506.

Skinns, L. *et al.* (2017) 'Police legitimacy in context: An exploration of "soft" power in police custody in England', *Policing: An International Journal*, 40(3), pp. 601–613. Available at: https://doi.org/10.1108/PIJPSM-06-2016-0077.

Smith, T. (2022) 'Caught in the net: Police powers of investigation and the risks for autistic individuals'. Available at: https://uwe-repository.worktribe.com/output/8688572/caught-in-the-net-police-powers-of-investigation-and-the-risks-for-autistic-individuals (Accessed: 29 May 2025).

Smith, T. and Dehaghani, R. (2025) *Submission to the independent review of the criminal courts – Written evidence on neurodivergence, vulnerability and the criminal courts.* Techical Report. Bristol: The University of West England. Available at: https://uwe-repository.worktribe.com/output/13662705 (Accessed: 6 June 2025).

Sowerbutts, A. *et al.* (2021) 'Supporting young offenders to communicate in the youth justice system: A scoping review', *Speech, Language and Hearing*, 24(2), pp. 87–104. Available at: https://doi.org/10.1080/2050571X.2021.1899571.

Spaaij, R. (2012) *Understanding lone wolf terrorism: Global patterns, motivations and prevention.* Dordrecht: Springer Netherlands (SpringerBriefs in Criminology). Available at: https://doi.org/10.1007/978-94-007-2981-0.

Speckhard, A. and Ellenberg, M. (2022) 'Self-reported psychiatric disorder and perceived psychological symptom rates among involuntary celibates (incels) and their perceptions of mental health treatment', *Behavioral Sciences of Terrorism and Political Aggression*, 0(0), pp. 1–18. Available at: https://doi.org/10.1080/19434472.2022.2029933.

Sykes, G. (1958) *The society of captives: A study of a maximum security prison.* Princeton, NJ: Princeton University Press.

Taylor, C. (2016) *Review of the youth justice system in England and Wales*. London: Ministry of Justice. Available at: https://assets.publishing.service.gov.uk/media/5a7ffc81ed915d74e622bcdb/youth-justice-review-final-report-print.pdf (Accessed: 6 June 2025).

'The work of the Home Office - Oral evidence' (2025). Available at: https://committees.parliament.uk/event/23982/formal-meeting-oral-evidence-session/ (Accessed: 4 June 2025).

Vale, G. and Rose, H. (2025) 'Firm convictions?: Unpicking framings of child terrorism offenders', *Terrorism and Political Violence*, 37(7). Available at: https://doi.org/10.1080/09546553.2025.2502402.

Walker, N. (2012) 'Throw away the master's tools: Liberating ourselves from the pathology paradigm', in The Autistic Self Advocacy Network (ed) *Loud hands: Autistic people, speaking*. Washington, DC: The Autistic Press, pp. 225–237.

Walter, F. *et al.* (2021) 'Characteristics of autism spectrum disorder and susceptibility to radicalisation among young people: A qualitative study', *The Journal of Forensic Psychiatry & Psychology*, 32(3), pp. 408–429. Available at: https://doi.org/10.1080/14789949.2020.1854831.

Warrell, H. (2024) 'Home Office to review autism cases in anti-extremism unit', *Financial Times*, 21 December. Available at: https://www.ft.com/content/4218b9c3-8d60-4354-96fe-8a947e93d0b7 (Accessed: 7 March 2025).

Woodbury-Smith, M. *et al.* (2010) 'Circumscribed interests and "offenders" with autism spectrum disorders: A case-control study', *The Journal of Forensic Psychiatry & Psychology*, 21(3), pp. 366–377. Available at: https://doi.org/10.1080/14789940903426877.

Woodbury-Smith, M.R. *et al.* (2022) 'Vulnerability to ideologically-motivated violence among individuals with autism spectrum disorder', *Frontiers in Psychiatry*, 13. Available at: https://doi.org/10.3389/fpsyt.2022.873121.

Woodhouse, E. *et al.* (2024) 'Identification and support of autistic individuals within the UK Criminal Justice System: A practical approach based upon professional consensus with input from lived experience', *BMC Medicine*, 22(157), pp. 1–30. Available at: https://doi.org/10.1186/s12916-024-03320-3.

Youth Justice Board (YJB) (2021a) *Business plan 2021–2022*. London: The Youth Justice Board for England and Wales. Available at: https://assets.publishing.service.gov.uk/media/6062ea05e90e072d8f8b864d/YJB_Business_Plan_2021-22.pdf (Accessed: 6 June 2025).

Youth Justice Board (YJB) (2021b) *Strategic plan 2021–2024*. London: The Youth Justice Board for England and Wales. Available at: https://assets.publishing.service.gov.uk/media/603f6d268fa8f577c44d65a8/YJB_Strategic_Plan_2021_-_2024.pdf (Accessed: 6 June 2025).

Chapter 10

Neurodiversity, the Criminal Justice System, and Mutual Aid Theory

Mel Jordan, Anne-Marie Day, Andrew Forrester, Jane McCarthy, James Tangen, Emma Joyes, and Eddie Chaplin

10.1 Introduction

This chapter focuses on mutual aid theory and what it might be able to bring to our criminal justice system, with reference to people who are neurodivergent and have convictions or are under investigation. It does this by firstly providing context about neurodivergence as a form of vulnerability in the criminal justice system, then explains mutual aid theory itself, and then discusses how this could be applied to the context of neurodivergence and our criminal justice system. To use mutual aid theory permits us to reimagine social life, plus our organisation of, and organisations therein; including our criminal justice system. Within this chapter we refer to the services of police, court, prison, and probation within the discussions; our writing embraces multiple elements of the criminal justice system and switches often between the services without preamble. We end the chapter with our critical reflections on the use of mutual aid theory and anarchist studies in this context.

The neurodiversity work that is occurring within our universities and frontline services currently is complex, cross-disciplinary, and uncompleted. Divergent stages of the criminal justice system are undergoing different changes (e.g. neurodiversity *support* in prisons, neurodiversity *screening* in police custody, neurodiversity specialist *approaches* in courts, and new neurodiversity *training* for magistrates). This body of work also includes disputed definitions, is evolving rapidly, traverses multiple settings (e.g. forensic sites and police custody suites), and embraces diverse standpoints (e.g. service users, legal practitioners, psychologists, social workers, psychiatrists, prison and probation staff, academics, reformers, and non-governmental organisations). Importantly, neurodiversity scholarship is also legitimately, but problematically, bringing into question major underpinnings of our criminal justice system (e.g. criminal intent and questions of capacity).

A brief introduction to neurodiversity might be: neurodiversity refers to the different ways in which our brains interpret information, and that there are *social expectations* built-in to this variety of brain functioning, hence the terms neurotypical and neurodivergent. Neurodiversity includes conditions such as autism spectrum disorder (ASD), attention deficit hyperactivity disorder (ADHD), and

DOI: 10.4324/9781003638742-11

speech, language, and communication needs (Day, 2022a). This chapter also includes comorbidity alongside neurodiversity, and this is because people with neurodivergence can experience multiple health issues within the criminal justice system. As a prison example, male prisoners with neurodevelopmental difficulties, in comparison to neurotypical male prisoners, are significantly more likely to have thought about self-harm and suicide in the last month, and to have significantly higher rates of concurrent mental disorders, including psychosis, anxiety, depression, personality disorder, and substance dependency disorders (McCarthy et al., 2020). Neurodivergence is a convoluted field of research, practice, and experience, wherein knowledge production is ongoing and our understanding continues to evolve.

In terms of language and our overall position in this chapter, we adopt the terminology of neurodiversity. Where we paraphrase others' work we often use this standardised wording too, to provide coherence for the chapter. We recognise that language and terminology are influential in this realm. For example, Revolving Doors (2022) are working with the Ministry of Justice and those who identify as neurodivergent and state: 'neurodivergence is a form of multiple *disadvantage*' (p. 1, emphasis added). The term disadvantage is emphasised, and so it is important we clarify our meaning and usage. Our position in this chapter is that the disadvantages experienced by vulnerable people who are neurodivergent are the responsibility of our *societal* structures, including our criminal justice system, that can exclude, ostracise, misunderstand, misrepresent, and subjugate. Therefore, any deficit-style narratives, labels, or definitions that are sometimes levelled at people with neurodivergence are misguided, and we do not support such terminology which problematises *individuals.* Labels are important.

Goldson (2013) highlights how our social and statutory constructions of children who are in conflict with our law have an important impact upon responsibilisation; making it very clear that how we narrate and conceptualise people within our criminal justice system is powerful and has consequences (not always good ones). For example, the language within Allely's (2022) neurodivergence work is noteworthy: where features of neurodiversity are discussed alongside offending behaviours, this is conceptualised as the context of vulnerability to engaging in [the behaviour]. Allely's (2022) approach is, at least according to our reading, thoughtful, understanding, and compassionate. Within this chapter, we too attempt to adopt this approach. However, we recognise that negotiating the boundaries between understanding, awareness raising, normalisation, search-for-justice, support, empowering, advocacy, and infantilisation are not simple. For us, we support a move towards a compassion-, rapport-, and relationship-orientated criminal justice system, that prioritises the needs of justice-involved individuals. Nahouli et al. (2022) argue rapport-based supervision in probation is linked to positive behavioural change and reduced reoffending for probation service users, and eminent Professor Rob Canton's (2024) contemporary essence of probation is: treat people with kindness, concern, compassion, warmth, and respect, to help them to be their best. We support this view that compassion within the criminal justice system is not misplaced.

There is also a need in this introductory section to briefly detail why neurodiversity in the criminal justice system is important now. Conceptually, a moral, academic, and activist response might be: there is existing vulnerability and persistent inequality, and a search for social justice demands that this be addressed. A practical response might be: the existing system is failing neurodivergent people. For example, there are problems at all stages with identification, problems with compliance expectations at police interview, and prisons not designed for neurodivergence. As such, there is unmet neurodiversity need across our criminal justice system despite substantial evidence that vulnerability is common; for example, 'there is a consensus that approximately one third of people in prison self-identify as having a learning difficulty or disability' (Revolving Doors, 2022, p. 3). In addition, where decision-making across our criminal justice system *does* take account of neurodiversity, decisions can be negatively affected by stigmatising misunderstandings. For example, the behaviours of neurodiverse people when defendants within court can be misinterpreted and perceived negatively by court-based decision-makers, affecting the notion and conduct of a fair trial (Allely, 2022). Collins et al. (2023) conclude that some of the social behaviours exhibited by suspects (e.g. eye contact) may add to risk perceptions and thus contribute to a custodial sentence decision. In the court context, some behaviours may be unfairly considered to be disruptive, disrespectful, or perceived as wilful non-engagement with the court process. For neurodivergent people, distress can manifest as so-labelled disruptive behaviour, and this is not just within the courts. Disadvantage as a result of an absence of neurodivergence understanding occurs during police and probation contact too, especially where license conditions are involved (Revolving Doors, 2022). A 2021 roundtable attended by government ministers, NHS leaders, policymakers, prison governors, researchers, GPs, and psychiatrists agreed that if ADHD were diagnosed and managed appropriately in our prisons, the result would be a significant reduction in criminality (Takeda, 2022). If the quarter of the prison population who meet the diagnostic criteria for ADHD received appropriate treatment and multi-agency liaison, recidivism outcomes could be improved (Young et al., 2018).

This is an issue across the life-course too, which is another perennial concern for social scientists; the cradle-to-grave concern. 'Children defined as 'neurodivergent' are over-represented in the English and Welsh criminal justice system' (Day, 2022a, p. 1). Day (2022a) shows us how our system is disabling and criminalising neurodivergent children via processes that isolate, neglect, label, stigmatise, and harm. To be blunt, our criminal justice system is currently failing those who are neurodivergent. Indeed, this was acknowledged by the Criminal Justice Joint Inspection (2021) on neurodiversity which found that 'provision is patchy, inconsistent and uncoordinated, and that too little is being done to understand and meet the needs of individuals' (p. 4). To refer back to one of our earlier comments regarding disadvantage, this failure to support vulnerability is a matter of social justice. Revolving Doors argue 'neurodiversity should be considered as core to multiple disadvantage, rather than as a peripheral issue' (2022, p. 4) and we support this highlighting of neurodivergence as important for our criminal justice system today. It is also a current government concern, with recent Ministry of Justice funding for specialist neurodiversity officers into public prisons (Ministry of Justice, 2024). Therefore, it is timely to consider theory, policy, and practice change in the realm of neurodiversity and the criminal justice system now.

10.2 Neurodiversity and the Criminal Justice System

Issues of definition and inclusion/exclusion are complex within the evolving field of neurodiversity. Prior to engaging with definitions, we would add a word of caution about over-reliance on clinical diagnoses as both basis for defining neurodivergence and as an explanation for vulnerability/need in the context of criminal justice. First, such definitions emphasise deficit and impairment, rather than the social-structural causes of vulnerability. Undoubtedly, neurodivergence – however defined – can be disabling for some in some circumstances. People who are neurodiverse may require sensory, education, or socio-communicative support. Adults with neurodivergence may experience difficulties associated with communication and social interactions, restricted and repetitive behaviours, or speech and sensory sensitivities (Chaplin et al., 2020). However, clinical definitions – by their nature – do not highlight *built-up* disadvantages such as disabling environments, language, and processes that pervade various *socially-constructed* contexts (including criminal justice services).

Second, over-reliance on diagnoses for practical actions (like identification and access to support) is problematic. For example, many children will not have been assessed and diagnosed, or they may have levels of need that do not meet the criteria for a diagnosis (Hughes, 2015). Notably, waiting lists in England and Wales for state-funded assessment across a range of neurodivergent conditions often run into several years, so undiagnosed and unsupported people are present in the criminal justice system. Further levels of complexity are added when we consider the impact of early childhood trauma, and comorbid conditions such as mental ill-health and/or poor physical health. Additionally, current diagnostic criteria are said to under-diagnose groups of neurodivergent individuals (an example being women and girls with autism spectrum disorder). Whilst we consider it necessary to outline how common neurodivergences are defined via diagnostic criteria, we hope this context will be borne in mind.

Autism spectrum disorder (ASD) and attention deficit hyperactivity disorder (ADHD) are, for clinical purposes, defined as neurodevelopmental disorders with behaviours described in terms of impairment. For example, the ICD-11 characterises ASD as involving persistent deficits in the ability to initiate and to sustain reciprocal social interaction and social communication, and by a range of restricted, repetitive, and inflexible patterns of behaviour, interests or activities; whilst ADHD is described as a persistent pattern of inattention and/or hyperactivity-impulsivity that has a direct negative impact on academic, occupational, or social functioning (World Health Organisation, 2022). Several other diagnoses are included in the umbrella term of neurodivergence, including traumatic brain injury, non-traumatic acquired brain injury, communication disorders, intellectual disability, and specific learning difficulties such as dyslexia, dyspraxia, and dysgraphia (Clasby et al., 2022). Tic disorder is also included within the motor disorder strand of neurodevelopmental disorders (McCarthy et al., 2020), and – collectively – the initialism NDD (Neurodevelopmental Disorders and Difficulties) is also seen in the literature (McCarthy et al., 2015). Neurodivergence is lifelong and defined by emergence in early development (for example, ASD – even in adulthood – requires onset in childhood (Chaplin et al., 2020)). For policy making purposes, the Ministry of Justice defines neurodivergence as an umbrella term used to describe an inclusive list of difficulties, differences, conditions and disorders included, but not exclusive to, learning disabilities, learning difficulties, ADHD, Autism, and Acquired Brain Injury (MoJ, 2022).

Literature on neurodivergence and criminal justice highlights several correlations. Some research suggests certain categories of offending are associated with different forms of neurodivergence and age brackets. For example, Rutter et al. (2022) found around a third of male *adolescents* diagnosed with ASD were convicted of a sex offence, whereas among male adolescents diagnosed with ADHD, charges for non-violent property offences were more common. Into *adulthood*, where people with ASD do offend, offences can include stalking, computer offences, violent offences, sexual offences, and arson. However, this list of offences can of course equally be reported in relation to people without ASD, and as such we would highlight the delicacy with which correlations between neurodivergence and other elements of human personality, environment, motivations, and actions should be handled. Indeed, it should be noted that people with an ASD diagnosis are not more likely to engage in offending behaviours than the general population, are not more violent, and indeed individuals with ASD are more likely to be the victims of crime (Allely, 2022). Similarly, Collins et al. (2023) find evidence that autistic people who encounter the criminal justice system often have a previous history of victimisation.

Fairness and support within the courts service is brought into question. Neurodivergent individuals drawn into the criminal justice system as suspects and defendants face significant challenges due to the stressful, complex, and specialised nature of criminal proceedings (Clinks, 2025). Collins et al. (2023) argue adults with autism who encounter the criminal justice system have specialist needs; for example, despite already having prior experience of the courtroom process, trial proceedings can be difficult to understand and follow. McCarthy et al. (2021) explore neurodiversity across three international jurisdictions and conclude that these vulnerable defendants within the legal system do not receive equal treatment and that this variation requires consideration, specifically in terms of early identification and safeguarding the rights of defendants during court proceedings, 'and an emphasis on the least restrictive disposal options' (p. 709). Further, it is important that the system does not prioritise a risk paradigm with neurodivergent young people, as the consequences can be negative and long-term, too deficit-focused, and ignore needs – the system can cause harm when it should support and provide care-based responses (Day, 2022a). Indeed, Hughes (2015) highlights how our youth justice system can disable and criminalise, and that institutional processes can hamper positive work with young people with neurodivergence. Within our court system, neurodivergence deserves a forensic assessment because of its potential impact on criminal responsibility (Gómez-Durán, 2022, based on Spanish system). Clasby et al. (2022) debate procedural fairness in (New Zealand) courts, for young adults who have neurodivergence, and argue that individual support is required, plus system-wide neurodiversity screening and training.

The literature on imprisonment and neurodiversity is in its infancy but increasing. In 2015 McCarthy et al. recorded 70 persons within a male prison who met the diagnostic criteria for ID, ASD, or ADHD – importantly, most of these people with this *new* neurodivergent diagnosis were previously *unrecognised* in the prison estate, evidencing there is unmet neurodiversity need in prisons. Young et al. (2018) argue that 'ADHD remains both mis- and under-diagnosed and consequently inadequately treated' (p. 1) in our prisons, which is regrettable as 'appropriate diagnosis and treatment can be a critical intervention to improve outcomes' (p. 1). Chaplin et al. (2022) explored ADHD across two prisons in London, with 22.5% of prisoners meeting the diagnostic criteria for ADHD. McCarthy et al. (2020) 'found prisoners with neurodevelopmental difficulties showed greater vulnerability to mental disorder and thoughts of suicide and suicide-related behaviours' (p. 309) than neurotypical men in the same prison. Adult men in prison with NDD form a disproportionately *vulnerable* group in terms of risk of other disorders including mental illness, personality disorders, and substance misuse disorders (McCarthy et al., 2020). His Majesty's Prison Service is beginning to respond in this realm – for example, Neurodiversity Support Manager roles now exist in English and Welsh prisons. Allely (2022) explores ASD in the prison environment and finds that the setting is more challenging due to vulnerability to coercion within the prison, experiences of isolation, routine disruptions, and communication difficulties with staff and fellow prisoners – further, in terms of the sensory sensitivities: 'individuals with ASD may not be able to habituate to all the noise in the prison environment, making it perpetually overwhelming' (p. 257). Allely (2022) recommends community-based sanctions, not prison, where low-level offending behaviour permits.

Based on extant evidence, we argue that there is now a moral and practical imperative for neurodiversity support to play a more significant role in the day-to-day workings of our criminal justice system. This might include more training for staff to raise awareness, recognition and acceptance of behaviours, more screening and diagnosis leading to more support for neurodiverse people in custody, and medication, for example for ADHD, where desired by clinician and patient. In order to make the criminal justice system as a whole more inclusive and fair, the design of processes, environments, and interactions should intentionally support the needs of people who are neurodivergent. Prevalence dictates attention. There is a supply and demand call-to-action here. Day's (2022b) work demonstrates between 60% and 90% of young people in custody met the diagnostic criteria for communication disorders. Much of the neurodiversity literature champions and values neurological differences; however, our criminal justice system has not kept pace with these wider developments in neurodivergence theory and practice. We recognise this might be considered ambitious; however, we believe that a monumental shift in this realm is required. Whilst the criminal justice system is our purview here, there are links between neurodivergence and poor educational achievements, poor employment opportunities, multiple convictions/imprisonments, and homelessness (McCarthy et al., 2016), hence a call for change within and beyond the criminal justice system is what is required. Judge Greenaway argues 'justice cannot be done' (Volkmar et al., 2021, p. vi) if players in the justice system do not understand autism, and that 'our societal treatment of those with autism is checkered at best' (p. v). In the following section, we propose a different approach to neurodivergence in the criminal justice system, using mutual aid theory.

10.3 What Is Mutual Aid Theory?

The concept of mutual aid is present in anarchist studies and so a brief introduction to anarchism is required. The work of the celebrated British anarchist Ward frames anarchism as striving to improve society via the related concepts of community endeavour, social ties, dynamic activity, association, social connectedness, vibrant participatory communities, person-to-person contact, and reciprocity (Honeywell, 2011). In terms of law and order Ward's ([1973] 2018) anarchism makes it clear that societies host coexisting yet divergent social attitudes, and so conflict and anti-social acts will occur, and that there will always be people with a desire to maintain our punitive machinery and an urge to punish. Therefore, it becomes the task to explore methods of containing such anti-social acts, with human dignity and responsibility, via social groups with strong social ties, to avoid being victims of our current authoritarian and punitive solutions. Anarchist ideas critique the barbarity of the penal system, the fatuity of the legislature, policing methods, and the fallibility of the courts (Ward, [1973] 2018). Anarchism is a call to revolution and reform. Ward's anarchist thinking centers on a sociological approach, actual experiences, and *practical* examples (Wilbert and White, 2011). Ward's work is an appeal to imagine, invent, and *action* alternatives to small problems, in the first instance; to avoid authoritarian solutions and being powerless victims in big affairs (Wilbert and White, 2011). This is especially relevant for this chapter, where justice-involved people with neurodivergence can be considered a vulnerable social group.

Mutual aid is a strand within anarchic ideas that promotes meeting social needs via mutuality. Mutuality and 'mutual aid' is collective coordination to meet each other's *needs*, usually from an awareness that the systems we have in place are *not* going to meet them' (Spade, 2020, p. 7, emphasis added). The theory of mutual aid is, originally, from Kropotkin. Both Ward and Kropotkin are practical anarchists who emphasise the need to create alternative forms of social organisation based on mutual aid, even under contemporary capitalism (Morris, 2013). Kropotkin's mutual aid work places *cooperation*, not competition, as 'the most powerful force in the advancement of species' (Marsh, 2012, p. 314). Mutual aid is a powerful force (Spade, 2020). Mutual aid theory 'makes a virtue of the pluralism of human life' (Honeywell 2011: 77) and depends on reciprocal emotional and social relationships. Although mutual aid discussions are often theory-heavy, mutual aid is a definable, workable, *active*, and 'concrete practice' (Preston and Firth, 2020, p. 5). Examples of mutual aid projects include coordinated letter-writing to prisoners and community emergency medicine training in areas where ambulance response is poor (Spade, 2020). Mutual aid theory demonstrates that cooperative behaviour creates satisfaction, joy, and pleasure. Human mutual aid embraces empathy, evaluation of needs, aversion to inequality, detection of emotions, and compassion (Servigne and Chapelle, [2017]2022). Servigne and Chapelle ([2017]/2022) helpfully distinguish between 'action (mutual aid) and intention (altruism)' (p. 169); mutual aid is always active. Mutual aid involves acts of giving and resultant reciprocity. Reciprocity is performed diligently, akin to an obligation. Human mutual aid supports social cohesion via this performance of reciprocity. (It is not charity.) Mutual aid 'helps to break stigma, shame, and isolation … see the *systems*, not the people suffering in them, as the problem' (Spade, 2020, p. 13). Mutual aid theory is suited to our consideration of neurodivergence in the criminal justice system as it holds systems, not individuals, to account.

10.4 How Might Mutual Aid Theory Be Considered alongside Neurodiversity and the Criminal Justice System?

When operationalised, mutual aid theory is *active* and pragmatic. If the interactions across our criminal justice system were based on the social norms of kindness, generosity, and compassion then, we argue, we might better serve stakeholders, including those with neurodiversity. (We are not naive, and we recognise prisons, mental health hospitals, and likewise institutions have long been critiqued for their institutionalisation, loss of liberty, perpetuating stigma, loss of autonomy, plus depersonalisation, and low material standards (Jones and Fowles 1984, p. 200).) However, mutual aid is based on anarchist principles and can be used as a force for *change* (Preston and Firth, 2020). Ward, the British anarchist, shows how anarchism more generally can be relevant when addressing public dilemmas and how it can be constructive, reasonable, and *pragmatic* (Honeywell, 2011). Anarchism conceptualises people as innovative and effective at providing for their needs via creative and reciprocal associations. Mutual aid projects 'meet people's survival needs, and are based on a shared understanding that the conditions in which we are made to live are unjust' (Spade, 2020, p. 7). This awareness of justice and injustice makes mutual aid theory relevant and useful for social scientists, especially those with an interest in vulnerable social groups such as persons with neurodivergence in the criminal justice system. In addition, mutual aid is action-orientated and can, thus, be utilised to facilitate change, so it is not a social theory alone which might stymie action.

Mutual aid theory is relevant because it embraces interdependence between people and facilitates supportive actions between people. 'The strength of human beings comes from their vulnerability and their interdependence with others … All well-functioning societies require mechanisms that coordinate action and prevent exploitation' (Servigne and Chapelle, [2017]/2022, p. 163 and p. 169). Mutual aid theory reveals our inescapable interdependence, connections, and interactions; so much so that, for Servigne and Chapelle ([2017]/2022), the very concept of the individual begins to lose some of its meaning. Kropotkin's original mutual aid theory considers our human sociality to be rooted in duty and justice (Boas, 1925). This argument is timely as, in June 2022, the Ministry of Justice submitted an Action Plan and fully committed to one recommendation and partly agreed to five others; the time is now to push with this neurodiversity agenda across our criminal justice system. Theoretically, combining social theory with contemporary neurodiversity work is achievable. For example, Reeves et al. (2023) interconnect (a) the concept of belonging, (b) the lives of people labelled with intellectual and developmental disabilities, and (c) social inclusion theory. We acknowledge that mutual aid theory and social inclusion theory are different, but our point here is that theories from the social sciences can be brought into the neurodiversity world to good effect: 'to reimagine inclusion' (p. 1) and to renegotiate wellbeing and community participation (Reeves et al., 2023).

Mutual aid theory embraces intentional cooperation to address needs. In the face of such a hostile system which is not fit for purpose, 'mutual aid – where we choose to help each other out, share things, and put time and resources into caring for the most vulnerable – is a radical act' (Spade, 2020, p. 8). Kropotkin's theory of mutual aid prioritises harmony and mutual support, and not divisive individualism. Indeed, Kropotkin observes how 'unsocial species decay' (1902/2019, p. 75). Cooperative and altruistic groups survive well, and prosper. Human mutual aid and 'for the good of the group' service by individuals within a cooperative group occurs where members of the group experience a sense of security, group identity, equality and fairness across the group, feelings and practice of trust, confidence in the future of the group, and shared group *purpose* (Servigne and Chapelle, [2017]/2022, p. 161, emphasis added). An agreed group purpose might be a site for criminal justice system reflection, and dare we say, in the spirit of mutual aid, system revolution. What is the end goal of our work with people with neurodiversity who perform acts labelled as harmful, deviant, or criminal? Is it the Prevent Another Victim agenda, wherein the aim is to prevent reoffending within a supportive framework? We argue intentional *collective work* to reduce reoffending is worthwhile. This contrasts with the tendency of the criminal justice system to hold individuals wholly responsible.

Mutual aid structures tend to be organic and changeable; reflection and learning are important facets of mutual aid and its helpful ability to be flexible and responsive, and so let's move towards a system wherein more frequent cooperative interactions occur *intentionally*. The repertoire of mutual aid includes action (Firth, 2020). Specifically, it is action against control and domination, and the uprising and 'expression of an authentic outside' (Firth, 2020, p. 58); authentic outside, in this case, meaning the lived experience and needs of vulnerable people in the criminal justice system who are neurodivergent. We argue it is time for our criminal justice system to bring in the developing evidence on neurodiversity, so that it is no longer on the outside or the periphery, but central to our understandings and work regarding offending and justice sanctions. Fortuitously, mutual aid is apt for consciousness raising and has the potential for robust structural critique of the criminal justice system. Mutual aid can help 'build shared understandings about why people do not have what they need' currently (Spade, 2020, p. 9), and so directing our responses to reducing reoffending in terms of future needs (not re-highlighting past faults).

Kropotkin remarks upon humankind's 'ever-living tendency for mutual aid' across societies and across periods in history (1902/2019, p. 151). Intentional cooperation is a key facet of mutual aid. Such a community favours cooperation and social harmony (Marsh, 2012). Social harmony here implies multiple elements of a whole engaging in mutual support (Marsh, 2012). Mutual aid presumes a shared empathy and humanity (Preston and Firth, 2020). Kropotkin's mutual aid 'works with, not against, individualistic tendencies' (Marsh, 2012, p. 320). Mutual aid practice 'is the surest means for giving to each and to all the greatest safety' (Kropotkin, 1902/2019, p. 76). Keating et al. (2023) discuss preferred language use from the perspective of individuals with an ASD diagnosis and note that 'there is no universally accepted way to talk about autism' and that personal preferences should prevail. This links up with language in practice. For example, an intentional cooperative could be marked by an exploration of, and *commitment* to, personal preference; wherein justice-involved persons with neurodivergent diagnoses are asked, as individuals, about their preferred language usage. Such a commitment may initially be received as yet another action on a busy practitioner's to-do list, which we acknowledge it is, but the actual time required is, in reality, minimal and the effects are significant. Contemporary examples from analogous settings exist.

Successful moves towards more person-centred and compassionate care in the NHS have occurred recently; for example, the 'Hello, my name is …' campaign and NHS-wide action, and the accompanying 'No decision about me without me' mantra. Contemporary police research is also promising in this realm. Millie and Hirschler (2023) study UK police recruits and report empathetic policing. 'The recruits emphasise an inclusive empathy and greater compassion for others – often irrespective of what those others have done' (Millie and Hirschler, 2023, p. 777). These new recruits also prioritised a need for kindness and giving others a voice. Those who are entering the police are bringing renewed moral judgements regarding 'doing the right thing'. It seems an ideal time, therefore, for neurodiversity and related inclusion work to be brought into police early career training. It is important to note that this work of Millie and Hirschler (2023) is not an artefact of naivety, as most new police had previous policing experience as PCSOs or special constables. However, empathy was not always easy to practise, and these police officers list drink driving and domestic violence alleged perpetrators as those falling into this challenging response realm. The general desire to treat others fairly, however, was strong, with the police service being labelled *a caring profession.* As there is no non-authoritarian equivalent for police personnel, and because 'it is scarcely possible for us to re-define the police, the agents of law enforcement, in a way that is shorn of authoritarian connotations' (Ward, [1973] 2018 p. 148), frontline policing could be conceptualised as intentionally upscaling community action, intentional cooperation between stakeholders, support for vulnerable persons, and embracing inclusion (broadly defined and including neurodiversity).

His Majesty's Courts & Tribunal Service may be a site for improvement, via the collective decision-making inherent therein. In terms of our courts, judicial decisions are often made cooperatively, through twelve-person juries or a bench of three magistrates. Within this existing model of group decision-making, perhaps through new Sentencing Council guidance and training among the judiciary, there could be a prompt to 'Think Neurodiversity' when reviewing the sentencing options, post-conviction, for the specific defendant with neurodiversity. However, this relies on identification by justice-involved professionals, or self-awareness and self-report by the alleged/convicted offender, which is problematic as we know formal diagnosis levels are low. The Sentencing Council does have a related document wherein guidance applies 'when sentencing offenders who at the time of the offence and/or at the time of sentencing have any mental disorder, neurological impairment or developmental disorder' (2020); the contents of this document could be typified as a nod towards ensuring neurodiverse people understand the setting, rather than a setting overhaul for, and by, neurodiverse people. Here is an example excerpt: 'Courts should always be alive to the impact of an impairment or disorder on an offender's ability to understand and participate in proceedings. Courts should ensure that offenders understand their sentence and what will happen if they reoffend and/or breach the terms of their licence or supervision. Courts should also ensure that any ancillary orders, such as restraining orders, are capable of being understood and fulfilled by the offender'. At present, individuals with autism can experience considerable difficulties in being able to understand court demands, whilst also simultaneously struggling to be understood by staff therein (Mattison and Allely, 2022).

Whilst the ultimate aim is greater inclusivity for neurodivergent people within the courts service, it may, for a finite period, be appropriate to focus on a neurodiversity strand for awareness raising and supportive problem-solving within the courts service. Positive results have arisen previously from courts that are able to think and work more flexibly regarding the complexities of what constitutes criminality and non-custodial ways of sanctioning within these cases. Specific problem-solving courts for some criminal case types have arisen – whereby in place of the adversarial process, they provide court-supervised treatment – and are called drug courts, mental health courts, domestic violence courts, veterans' courts, and homeless courts (Castellano, 2011). However, concerns have been raised 'about the possible net widening effects of treatment programmes in the criminal justice system, suggesting that they expand state power under the auspices of helping people' (Castellano, 2011, p. 962). Within this model of individualised response, issues can arise regarding (a) constrained choice for justice-involved persons and (b) therapeutic control. Problem-solving courts also promote accountability through judicial monitoring, improved compliance with court orders, and a procedurally fair environment (Centre for Justice Innovation, 2015), which is once again about minor edits to court processes, not an overhaul to embrace neurodiverse court users. Mutual aid, in contrast, advocates for community and compassionate responses. There is a strong *collective* element to mutualism, which could be applied to local Magistrates' Courts specifically. Human *solidarity* exists within the conscience of society (Kropotkin, 1902/2019), and court proceedings for low-level civil or non-violent offences might further embrace intentional compassion and recommend social inclusion support services in the community within non-custodial sanctions. 'Mutual aid is a practice of community helping' (Firth, 2020, p. 57), which is important. Mutual aid is not charity, but instead is based on reciprocal relationships and services, which lends itself well to community sanctions. Magistrates' Courts should note, however, that for mutual aid to flourish its practice must (a) avoid private enterprise instead of public service and (b) distinguish between deserving and undeserving (Spade, 2020).

Mutual aid theory might assist us in improving the point of arrest and police settings for accused persons with neurodiversity. Autistic people in police custody report:

> how the combined impact of not being able to understand their arrest and detention as suspects and having to cope with the demands associated with being detained in the custody environment, adversely affected their participation in the custody process. They referred to experiencing a desire to escape police custody which influenced how they made key decisions and engaged in the police interview.
>
> (Holloway-George, et al., 2025, p.1)

There are elements from mutual aid theory that could be brought into being here to support people who are neurodivergent in police settings. Individual-deficit models could be superseded by intentional compassion to prevent exploitation of the vulnerable. To use some Kropotkin (1902/2019) with added emphases: the mutual aid tendency of the public and its constructive genius is *interwoven* into evolution and humankind due to our '*need* of mutual support' (p. 216) and our knowledge that 'narrow-minded individualism' (p. 218) is to be *avoided*. Facing forward, with one example: where neurodiverse people are questioned in police settings, it should be recognised that these individuals may have difficulty in making or maintaining eye contact and may avert their gaze, and that this should be increasingly accepted as a valid response to minimising sensory overload during questioning (Mattison and Allely, 2022). Indeed, the Clinks (2025, p. 24) report asks criminal justice professionals to accommodate 'emotional and sensory needs', including body language, eye contact and allowing for 'regulatory behaviours (e.g. stimming)'.

Kropotkin (1902/2019) argues we have an 'everworking tendency for association and mutual support' (p. 262), and this support for the vulnerable is important for police settings, where the powerful legal system is at play. Communication in police settings should be viewed as *between interdependent* individuals. Notably, there can be significant differences in how neurodiverse and neurotypical people experience and process the world around them, and a lack of reciprocal understanding between the two groups can arise (Pearson et al., 2022). The double empathy problem can occur, which refers to a breakdown in understanding when differing dispositions attempt to interact (Milton et al., 2022). However, any communication deficits implied by a medical approach to neurodiversity should, instead, be considered a deficit of the community/setting/interaction, and not the individual (Pearson et al., 2022). Milton et al. (2022), whilst not anarchists nor mutual aid enthusiasts, do appeal for conceptualising neurodiversity as a broad range of developmental differences and embodied experiences, and that society should enact humility in the face of difference and intentionally build rapport.

To use some mutual aid theory here, consideration should be given to the 'mechanisms… [of] coordinated action' and communications for those within the system (Servigne and Chapelle, [2017]2022, p. 163). It has been argued that interventions in this realm of communications have historically focused on improvements in communication for neurodivergent individuals; however, more contemporary approaches have focused on increasing understanding of neurodivergence for neurotypical people (Jones et al., 2021). This would represent dynamic activity and intentional association, which are hallmarks of mutuality. Looking to the future, when questioning neurodiverse people, professionals 'should allow time to build rapport and to establish trust', 'actively check understanding by asking the person to explain in their own words', 'support the individual to stay on topic by being clear about exactly what you need to know', and 'adopt an accepting and understanding response to unexpected or unusual repetitive forms of verbal and non-verbal communication' (Mattison and Allely, 2022, pp. 60–61). Beyond questioning, practitioners might consider adapting their communication style into: 'clear, non-abstract wording; avoiding idiom/metaphor; short, discrete points; avoiding multi-part concepts/sentences; closed questions', as well as checking for understanding as suggested above (Clinks, 2025, p. 25). All of these responses would enact elements from mutual aid theory, for example accepting our inescapable interdependencies, and embracing reciprocal associations and forms of communication among people.

In terms of probation, we propose increased clinical support and a focus on *active* community inclusion. 'Anarchism in all its guises is an assertion of human dignity and responsibility' (Ward, [1973] 2018, p. 166). If you bring anarchy into being within the probation realm, determined and practical reform would: increase the autonomy, roles, and responsibilities of people with convictions, whilst the service operated a model based on human dignity, a community feel, and inclusion of offenders, and where the reform also included a reduction in overt oppression, punitiveness, commercialisation, and risk as foci. This is where the cradle-to-grave and life-course recognition is important too. ADHD is a lifelong neurodevelopmental condition with a global prevalence of 2.5% to 6.7% among adults (Yang et al., 2025). Linked to this, the probation service often works with people for long periods of time. As part of professional development, practitioners are encouraged to increase their knowledge and understanding of neurodiversity, via a 'variety of sources', including the individual themselves (Clinks, 2025, p. 24).

To better support neurodivergent people within the probation service, perhaps more joined-up working between the justice and health services might be fruitful (as commissioning and provision of related support services, where they exist, can occur in unhelpful silos). For ADHD, a combined response of prescription medication and psychotherapy can provide long-term benefits for adults (Do et al., 2024). Non-pharmacological interventions have demonstrated effectiveness both as standalone responses and adjuncts to pharmacotherapy in managing adult ADHD (Yang et al., 2025). And so multimodal responses for ADHD might be embraced within community custodial sanctions, *with offender-patient informed consent* (and the knowledge and agreement of the neurodivergent person is key here), plus at no financial cost to the offender-patient. Where a clinical response is desired by the person with neurodivergence: cognitive behavioural therapy may be the most effective intervention for adults with ADHD and associated emotional disorders, while Mindfulness-based Cognitive Therapy is recommended as a preferable option for those without comorbidities (Yang et al., 2025). Crucially, non-pharmacological responses are worthy of consideration as evidence and expert opinion is divided on the use of ADHD medication; for example, a review of the evidence on ADHD medication for adults across jails, prisons, and correctional settings finds stimulants as first-line prescription *and* stimulants as prescription of last resort (Byrne and Guenter, 2023). A purely-medicalised and individual-deficit response to neurodiversity across the criminal justice system is neither effective nor just. Currently, whilst a punitive approach often pervades practice across the criminal justice system, contemporary approaches which, conversely, adopt a strengths-based ethos mark a positive attempt to shift towards a rehabilitative focus – towards a mode of response that encourages a move beyond the focus of the 'risky individual' and towards an understanding of an individual's strengths, albeit not without its tensions (Tomlin and Jordan, 2022). However, a strengths-based approach must also consider individual variations in the conceptualisation of abilities, strengths, and values, which would mean expanding normative conceptualisations of what is meant by 'thriving' or 'a good life' in which human needs are met (Tomlin and Jordan, 2022). In the realm of children and young people who are neurodivergent and in contact with the youth justice system, 'a holistic, individualistic, and tailored approach based on their welfare needs, that focused on their strengths and future aspirations' is recommended (Day, 2022, p. 7). To return to Firth (2020), mutual aid is about the helpers and the helped working together; we support intentional cooperation between people who are neurodivergent and their reducing reoffending and harm prevention practitioners in the community.

However, it is important to resist the temptation to immediately accept all non-pharmacological responses to neurodiversity and offending simply because they are not clinical. Recent developments in the delivery of talking therapies have established a digital modality that purports to promise further insights and opportunities for responding to neurodiversity, whilst simultaneously expanding the predictive capabilities of Artificial Intelligence (AI) and *states' usage* of such within security, *surveillance*, and social order services (Nellis, 2022) (italics added for emphasis). Following the course set by China and the US, all sectors of our governance, including prisons and probation, are becoming digital-first and data-driven, in terms of their interactions with the public (Nellis, 2022). An automated, AI-driven future for probation is a possibility, with smartphone-linked supervision, personal data extraction, and probation via apps (Nellis, 2022). Virtual reality and role playing with avatars, for immersive correctional practice, are also underway, and versatile chatbot probation officers are not a nonsensical possibility (Nellis, 2022). Nellis's (2022) work here is a warning against techno populism, and we extend that warning to our work with neurodivergent people involved in the criminal justice system too; such an approach risks dehumanising neurodivergent people, undermines efforts for active community inclusion, and ignores the merits of intentional reciprocity and mutuality afforded by active relationships among people (and recommended by mutual aid theory).

On to where custodial sanctions occur: our prison environment requires neurodiversity improvements, particularly *because* the route into prison, and the prison itself, is not just for housing, and certainly not designed for neurodivergent people. Across our criminal justice system at present 'stressful and formulaic environments, compounded by practitioner misunderstandings of neurodivergence, can result in a higher likelihood of being arrested, charged, convicted and receiving harsher (and less appropriate) sentencing decisions' (Clinks, 2025, p. 23). This leads to imprisonment for neurodivergent people. Whilst there may not be examples of mutual aid practice in prisons at present in England and Wales, there are practices that are collaborative, reciprocal, that aim to diminish hierarchy, and honour lived experiences as valuable knowledge with which to co-create better prisons. For example, through participation in a prisoner council or peer-to-peer (prisoner to prisoner) schemes, such as being a Samaritan Listener. Listeners are volunteer prisoners who provide 'confidential emotional support to other prisoners with the aim of reducing feelings of distress' and the reduction of suicide risk (Samaritans, 2020, p. 7). Prison peer support work can be beneficial, providing meaning and increasing positive relationships for prisoners (Einat, 2017). And yet, peer-to-peer roles are not a panacea. They are subject to the wider dynamics of prison and state power, and their use can be motivated by cost savings to the provider (Buck, 2020; Nixon, 2020). There are further concerns about the emotional labour prisoners provide for free, often in 'dangerous, distressing situations with minimal support' (Buck et al., 2023, p. 15). Therefore, we are cognisant of the limitations of these examples and yet maintain a belief in the potential of these sites of mutuality.

For the final theme, we turn to the nature of research. Our research processes and the steps in knowledge production should increasingly involve persons with neurodiversity. *Intentional cooperation* from mutual aid theory is worthy of note here. Our academic research design and practice models might further embrace mutual aid: strive for dignity, creativity, connection, and belonging (Spade, 2020). The person is the expert in their neurodiverse experience, 'but may need support from others to convey this' (Clinks, 2025, p. 24). Indeed, the development of assessment tools has also been conducted in which participatory research involves individuals with neurodiversity (Cassidy et al., 2021). It has also been argued that the avoidance of tokenistic involvement is imperative for the authentic improvement of society (Keating, 2021). From here to end of paragraph I am awaiting refs from co-authormode_commentThe limited literature on research methods with neurodiverse adults points to a mistrust of (Gowen et al., 2020) and disconnect with researchers (Pickard et al., 2021), and the importance of developing cooperative, participatory approaches to research design and delivery (den Houting et al., 2022; Fletcher-Watson et al., 2019). Co-production and creative approaches have been increasingly used with children in justice settings (Smithson and Jones, 2020) and neurodivergent adults (Leadbitter et al., 2021) in recent years, but such approaches are rare with neurodivergent children (Lewis et al., 2023).

Despite this, co-production and creative approaches have been used in disability studies since the 1960s with the principle 'nothing about us without us' at its core (Lewis et al., 2023). Further, according to The Committee on the Rights of the Child, children (and adults) with justice experience should be involved in research and evaluation of the justice system (United Nations Committee on the Rights of the Child, 2019). Holloway-George recently used participatory approaches to consider adaptations to the police custodial processes and environment for autistic children and adults, to great effect (Holloway et al., 2020). Research leaders might take note of how leadership that prioritises cooperation and enacting mutual aid theory embraces: joint decision-making, seeking others' opinions, willingness to admit mistakes, good listening, openness to influence, fostering inclusivity, reliability in terms of main value/goal, and interest in what can be learned from discomfort and transforming conditions (Spade, 2020).

10.5 What Are Our Mutual Aid Theory Reservations?

Anarchist writings and scholars are, in differing ways, anti-authoritarian, and whilst we enthuse about some elements of Kropotkin's work, we admittedly do not utilise others. Kropotkin's (1924/2012) mutual aid includes a sense of *equity* and equalitarian self-restraint, which supports the enactment of justice. This could be conceptualised as observing a natural solidarity among humans. We support these community and inclusion elements. However, we should be clear here that Kropotkin was also an anarchist and rejected centralised governments (Marsh, 2012) and criticised the growth of the nation state (Honeywell, 2011). 'Kropotkin believed that the acquisitive, devisive nature of centralised governments was antithetical to the processes of mutual aid' (Marsh, 2012, p. 325). Centralised government is considered to foster inequalities among, and isolation between, citizens (Marsh, 2012). For us in this chapter, we do not espouse such an overt critique of statehood. We recognise that our amount of, or our professed commitment to, wider anarchist thought and a stateless society could be critiqued.

We agree there is an absence of working-class uprising, confrontation, capitalism criticism, state reconstruction, class war, the market, and Marxism within this chapter. These are not the elements of anarchist thought or mutual aid that we've elected to embrace to explore our topic. It *is* important to recognise here, however, that social change endeavours in the presence of state arbitration may result in silenced or repressed perspectives (Preston and Firth, 2020), thus the aforementioned issue of equity must be considered during any process of system change. Thus, all stakeholders' voices within our justice services, including neurodivergent individuals, should be included. We accept that operationalising the concept of equalitarianism within a criminal justice system – which is constructed to be an arbiter of law and social order, with dominating agents and agencies and thus subjugated peoples – is challenging, but reconceptualising these actions as small frontline acts of mutual aid and inclusion makes it more achievable, we suggest.

Secondly, Kropotkin himself recognised that mutual aid practice may receive criticism that it is utopian when considered for frontline action (Marsh, 2012). For example, as highlighted by Preston and Firth (2020), we are aware that Kropotkin supports horizontal social logic and is against hierarchical social relations mediated by the state. Kropotkin is critical of state power; indeed, the rejection of the legal system, the law, and law enforcement is a stalwart anarchist position (Ward, [1973] 2018). This chapter, however, is not aiming for a stateless society, neither justice provision via anarchy. We accept that our criminal justice system will have overarching policies, decision-makers, commissioners, providers, and governance. We are, however, arguing for, and stemming from mutual aid, a 'proliferation of everyday connections' (Preston and Firth, 2020, p. 7), and intentional cooperation to better support those with neurodiversity and all those impacted by our system of justice's responses, interactions, outcomes, successes, and failures.

Thirdly, we also accept that extreme mutual aid could facilitate questionable actions. Servigne and Chapelle ([2017]2022) remind us that it is 'unnecessary and dangerous to deny' that humans can 'act selfishly and aggressively' (p. 157) but that the opposite should not also be denied: 'the human species also possesses very powerful cooperative and altruistic capacities' (p. 157). Human beings are 'simultaneously capable of extreme altruism and cruelty' (Servigne and Chapelle, [2017]2022, p. 168). We are aware, of course, that a full understanding of mutual aid recognises that mutual aid is not necessarily a morally good act; indeed, extremely powerful collective ecstasies can lead to 'the worst' in human collective action and othering (Servigne and Chapelle, [2017]2022, p. 161). However, it is not to this most extreme form that we refer in this chapter. A more standard example of mutual aid is given by Spade (2020) where the Sylvia Rivera Law Project builds solidarity via a law collective that provides free legal help 'to trans and gender-nonconforming people who are low income and/or people of color' (p. 13) who experience issues with the police, immigration, prison, and care system. Mutual aid in practice reveals, and can support, the complex realities of injustice in a proportionate manner.

10.6 Conclusion

The context for this chapter is our criminal justice system. The concern is that people who are neurodiverse and justice-involved face disadvantages, which raises issues with fair access to justice, harmful experiences, unmet needs and vulnerabilities, and appropriate responses from the police, court, prison, and probation services. Our current system is stigmatising, disabling, and criminalising, via (a) settings designed for neurotypical people and (b) processes that isolate, neglect, and negatively label. The contribution of this chapter lies in embracing intentionally collective, cooperative, and inclusive responses for, and with, neurodiverse people within the criminal justice system (and also a move away from an individualised/impairment/deficit model).

We propose a new approach to neurodivergence in the criminal justice system, using mutual aid theory. Mutual aid theory comes from practical anarchism. Kropotkin ([1924] 2012) argued mutual aid was a predominant fact of nature, which: (a) offers immense advantages to all who practise it, (b) disrupts the balance of power to the disadvantage of predatory beings, and (c) assists with adaptations to ever-changing conditions of existence. Ward shows how this form of anarchism can be relevant when addressing public dilemmas and how it can be constructive, reasonable, and pragmatic (Honeywell, 2011); as, although mutual aid discussions are often theory-heavy, mutual aid is an *active* and 'concrete practice' (Preston and Firth, 2020, p. 5). Mutual aid theory facilitates us to enliven and encourage intentional compassion, reciprocal association, exploitation prevention, and system accountability. Mutual aid is a radical act, representing caring for the vulnerable in a hostile system. Mutuality is a concept we use, and this espouses active aversion to inequality. The practical anarchism utilised in this chapter highlights our inescapable interdependencies as humans, and how dynamic and collective action can address vulnerabilities experienced by a subjugated group of people within a given system. Mutual aid 'helps to break stigma, shame, and isolation … see the *systems*, not the people suffering in them, as the problem' (Spade, 2020, p. 13). Mutual aid theory is suited to our consideration of neurodivergence in the criminal justice system as it holds systems, not individuals, to account.

We acknowledge that the vulnerability of neurodiverse people creates a challenging environment for criminal justice system staff and alleged/convicted offenders, but mutual aid can strengthen group collectivity. Mutual aid theory teaches us that external challenges can be utilised to strengthen a collective: 'mutual aid acquires its power in a hostile environment' (Servigne and Chapelle, [2017]2022, p. 165). Whilst we do not intend, not at all, to paint neurodiversity as a negative challenge to the criminal justice system in a denigratory fashion to those with neurodiversity, it *is* the case that neurodiversity literature is constructing challenging questions for our criminal justice system, for example regarding criminal intent. Where conflicts arise, mutual aid encourages *debate* and then resolution by determined and involved persons (Preston and Firth, 2020). Kropotkin repeatedly insisted on the importance of multiple points of contact between people, knowing others in-depth, and more closely knit groupings as a means to contain anti-social acts (Ward, [1973] 2018). We argue that the challenges being presented to the criminal justice system by the developing field of neurodiversity theory and practice be wielded to improve our services that respond to neurodivergent people who offend, to support their needs and their rights, plus concurrently embrace a non-punitive approach to reducing reoffending.

To use mutual aid theory permits us to reimagine social life, plus our organisation of, and organisations therein; including our criminal justice system. Whilst negotiating the boundaries between awareness raising, normalisation, search-for-justice, empowering, advocacy, and infantilisation are not simple, we support a move towards a compassion-, rapport-, and relationship-orientated criminal justice system, that prioritises the needs of justice-involved neurodivergent people. Due to the nature of neurodiversity, this is an issue across the life course, an important cradle-to-grave concern. Mutual aid is about the helpers and the helped working *together* (Firth, 2020); we support intentional cooperation between people who are neurodivergent and their reducing reoffending and/or harm prevention practitioners. Canton's (2024) contemporary essence of probation is: treat people with kindness, concern, compassion, warmth, and respect – to help them to be their best. We support this view that compassion within the criminal justice system is not misplaced. After all, 'anarchism in all its guises is an assertion of human dignity and responsibility' (Ward, [1973] 2018, p. 166).

References

Allely, C. (2022) *Autism Spectrum Disorder in the Criminal Justice System: A Guide to Understanding Suspects, Defendants and Offenders with Autism*. London: Routledge.

Boas, George (1925) Ethics: Origin and Development. *Journal of Philosophy*, 22(9): 245–248.

Buck, G. (2020) *Peer Mentoring in Criminal Justice*. Oxon, United Kingdom: Routledge.

Buck, G., Tomczak, P., Harriott, P., Page, R., Bradley, K., Nash, M., and Wainwright, L. (2023) Prisoners on prisons: Experiences of peer-delivered suicide prevention work. *Incarceration*, 4. https://doi.org/10.1177/26326663231172023.

Byrne, C. and Guenter, D. Treatments for ADHD in adults in jails, prisons and correctional settings: A scoping review of the literature. *Health Justice*, 11: 36. https://doi.org/10.1186/s40352-023-00234-9.

Canton, R. (2024) Probation as social work1. *Probation Journal*, 71(3): 214–233. https://doi.org/10.1177/02645505241241588.

Cassidy, S. A., Bradley, L., Cogger-Ward, H., and Rodgers, J. (2021) Development and validation of the suicidal behaviours questionnaire-autism spectrum conditions in a community sample of autistic, possibly autistic and non-autistic adults. *Molecular Autism*, 12: 1–22. https://doi.org/10.1186/s13229-021-00449-3.

Castellano, U. (2011) Problem-solving courts: Theory and practice. *Sociology Compass*, 5: 957–967. https://doi.org/10.1111/j.1751-9020.2011.00422.x.

Centre for Justice Innovation (2015) Problem-solving courts: An evidence review. Available at https://justiceinnovation.org/publications/problem-solving-courts-evidence-review (Accessed: 26/11/25).

Chaplin, E., Rawat, A., Perera, B., McCarthy, J., Courtenay, K., Forrester, A., Young, S., Hayward, H., Sabet, J., Underwood, L., Mills, R., Asherson, P., and Murphy, D. (2022) Prisoners with attention deficit hyperactivity disorder: Co-morbidities and service pathways. *International Journal of Prisoner Health*, 18(3): 245–258. https://doi.org/10.1108/IJPH-03-2021-0020.

Chaplin, E. et al. (Eds.). (2020) *A Clinician's Guide to Mental Health Conditions in Adults with ASDs: Assessment and Interventions*. London: Jessica Kinglsey.

Clasby, B., Mirfin-Veitch, B., Blackett, R., Kedge, S., and Whitehead, E. (2022) Responding to neurodiversity in the courtroom: A brief evaluation of environmental accommodations to increase procedural fairness. *Criminal Behaviour and Mental Health*, 32(3): 197–211. https://doi.org/10.1002/cbm.2239.

Clinks (2025) Working with neurodivergent people in contact with the criminal justice system. Available at https://www.clinks.org/sites/default/files/2025-05/Working%20with%20neurodivergent%20people%20in%20contact%20with%20the%20criminal%20justice%20system_1.pdf (Accessed: 26/11/25)

Collins, J., Horton, K., Gale-St. Ives, E. et al. (2023) *A systematic review of autistic people and the criminal justice system: An update of King and Murphy (2014). Journal of Autism and Developmental Disorders*, 53: 3151–3179. https://doi.org/10.1007/s10803-022-05590-3.

Criminal Justice Joint Inspection (2021) Neurodiversity in the criminal justice system: A review of evidence. Available at https://cloud-platform-e218f50a4812967ba1215eaecede923f.s3.amazonaws.com/uploads/sites/43/2024/09/2021-07-15-Neurodiversity-in-the-Criminal-Justice-Sustem-a-review-of-evidence.pdf (Accessed: 26/11/25).

Day, A.-M. (2022a) Disabling and criminalising systems? Understanding the experiences and challenges facing justice experienced, neurodiverse children in the education and youth justice systems. *Forensic Science International: Mind and Law*, 3. https://doi.org/10.1016/j.fsiml.2022.100102.

Day, A.-M. (2022b) Autism and ADHD: The youth justice system is harming neurodivergent children. *The Conversation*, November 24. Available at https://theconversation.com/autism-and-adhd-the-youth-justice-system-is-harming-neurodivergent-children-188776 (Accessed: 26/11/25).

Do, D., Lee, T., Bably, M., Inneh, I. A., and Patel, U. (2024) Prevalence and predictors of multimodal treatment among U.S. adults newly diagnosed with ADHD. *American Journal of Preventive Medicine*, 66(4): 707–716.

Einat, T. (2017) The wounded healer: Self-rehabilitation of prisoners through providing care and support to physically and mentally challenged inmates. *Journal of Crime and Justice*, 40(2): 204–221.

Fletcher-Watson, S., Adams, J., Brook, K., Charman, T., Crane, L., Cusack, J., Leekam, S., Milton, D., Parr, J.R., and Pellicano, E. (2019) Making the future together: Shaping autism research through meaningful participation. *Autism*, 23(4): 943–953. https://doi.org/10.1177/1362361318786721.

Goldson, B. (2013) 'Unsafe, unjust and harmful to wider society': Grounds for raising the minimum age of criminal responsibility in England and Wales. *Youth Justice*, 13(2): 111–130. https://doi.org/10.1177/1473225413492054.

Gómez-Durán, L. E., Marti-Agustí, G., and Martin-Fumadó, C. (2022) People with intellectual disabilities and borderline intellectual functioning in the Spanish criminal justice system. *Criminology & Criminal Justice*, 25(2): 549–568. https://doi.org/10.1177/17488958221128131.

Gowen, E., Taylor, R., Bleazard, T., Greenstein, A., Baimbridge, P., and Poole, D. (2020) Guidelines for conducting research studies with the autism community. *Autism Policy & Practice*, 2: 29–45.

Holloway, C. A., Munro, N., Jackson, J., Phillips, S., and Ropar, D. (2020) Exploring the autistic and police perspectives of the custody process through a participative walkthrough. *Research in Developmental Disabilities*, 97. https://doi.org/10.1016/j.ridd.2019.103545I.

Holloway-George, C. A., Munro, N., Jackson, J. et al. (2025) Experiences of autistic people in police custody: The need for adjustments to improve participation in the custody process. *Journal of Autism and Developmental Disorders.* https://doi.org/10.1007/s10803-025-06952-3.

Honeywell, C. (2011) Colin Ward: Anarchism and social policy. *Anarchist Studies*, 19, 2: 69–83.

den Houting, J., Higgins, J., Isaacs, K., Mahony, J. and Pellicano, E. (2022) From ivory tower to inclusion: Stakeholders' experiences of community engagement in Australian autism research. *Frontiers in Psychology*, 13: 876990. https://doi.org/10.3389/fpsyg.2022.876990.

Hughes, N. (2015) Neurodisability in the youth justice system: Recognising and responding to the criminalisation of neurodevelopmental impairment, Howard League working paper. Available at https://howardleague.org/wp-content/uploads/2016/04/HLWP_17_2015.pdf (Accessed: 26/11/25).

Jones, K. and Fowles, A. (1984) *Ideas on institutions: analysing the literature on long-term care and custody*. London: Routledge & Kegan Paul.

Jones, D. R., Morrison, K. E., DeBrabander, K. M., Ackerman, R. A., Pinkham, A. E., and Sasson, N. J. (2021) Greater social interest between autistic and non-autistic conversation partners following autism acceptance training for non-autistic people. *Frontiers in Psychology*, 12. https://doi.org/10.3389/fpsyg.2021.739147.

Keating, C. (2021) Participatory autism research: How consultation benefits everyone. *Frontiers in Psychology,* 12. https://doi.org/10.3389/fpsyg.2021.713982.

Keating, C. T., Hickman, L., Leung, J., Monk, R., Montgomery, A., Heath, H., and Sowden, S. (2023) Autism-related language preferences of English-speaking individuals across the globe: A mixed methods investigation. *Autism Research,* 16(2), 406–428. https://doi.org/10.1002/aur.2864.

Kropotkin, P. (2019) *Mutual Aid: A Factor Of Evolution*. Great Britain: Read Books [Original work published 1902].

Kropotkin, P. (2012) *Ethics: Origin and Development*. New York: Dial Press [Original work published 1924].

Leadbitter, K., Buckle, K.L., Ellis, C., and Dekker, M. (2021) Autistic self-advocacy and the neurodiversity movement: Implications for autism early intervention research and practice. *Frontiers in Psychology*, 12: 635690. https://doi.org/10.3389/fpsyg.2021.635690.

Lewis, K., Hamilton, L., and Vincent, J. (2023) Exploring the experiences of autistic pupils through creative research methods: Reflections on a participatory approach. *Infant and Child Development*, 33: https://doi.org/10.1002/icd.2467.

Marsh, C. (2012) Converging on harmony: Idealism, evolution, and the theory of mutual aid. *Public Relations Inquiry*, 1(3): 313–335. https://doi.org/10.1177/2046147X12448583.

Mattison, M. and Allely, C. (2022) Questioning autistic people: Police and courts, in Taylor, N. and Sheeran, A. (Eds.), *Working with Autistic People in the Criminal Justice and Forensic Mental Health Systems*. Abingdon: Routledge, pp. 55–67.

McCarthy, J., Chaplin, E., Underwood, L., Forrester, A., Hayward, H., Sabet, J., Young, S., Asherson, P., Mills, R., and Murphy, D. (2015) Screening and diagnostic assessment of neurodevelopmental disorders in a male prison. *Journal of Intellectual Disabilities and Offending Behaviour*, 6(2): 102–111. https://doi.org/10.1108/JIDOB-08-2015-0018.

McCarthy, J., Chaplin, E., Underwood, L., Forrester, A., Hayward, H., Sabet, J., Young, S., Asherson, P., Mills, R., and Murphy, D. (2016) Characteristics of prisoners with neurodevelopmental disorders and difficulties. *Journal of Intellectual Disability Research*, 60: 201–206. https://doi.org/10.1111/jir.12237.

McCarthy, J., Chaplin, E., Forrester, A., et al. (2020) Prisoners with neurodevelopmental difficulties: Vulnerabilities for mental illness and self-harm. *Criminal Behaviour and Mental Health*, 29: 308–320. https://doi.org/10.1002/cbm.2132.

McCarthy, J., Chaplin, E., Hayes, S., Søndenaa, E., Chester, V., Morrissey, C., and Forrester, A. (2021) Defendants with intellectual disability and autism spectrum conditions: The perspective of clinicians working across three jurisdictions. *Psychiatry, Psychology and Law*, 29(5): 698–717. https://doi.org/10.1080/13218719.2021.1976297.

Millie, A. and Hirschler, S. (2023) Police recruits, moral judgements and an empathetic policing. *Criminology & Criminal Justice*, 777–797. https://doi.org/10.1177/17488958221146142.

Milton, D., Gurbuz, E., and López, B. (2022) The 'double empathy problem': Ten years on. *Autism*, 26(8): 1901–1903. https://doi.org/10.1177/13623613221129123.

Ministry of Justice (2022) A response to the criminal justice joint inspection: Neurodiversity in the criminal justice system. *A Review of Evidence*. MoJ_Neurodiversity_Action_Plan_30_06_2022__001_.pdf.

Ministry of Justice (2024) Greater support for neurodivergent offenders in bid to cut crime. Available at https://www.gov.uk/government/news/greater-support-for-neurodivergent-offenders-in-bid-to-cut-crime (Accessed: 26/11/25)

Morris, B. (2013) Colin Ward and Kropotkin's legacy, in Levy C. (Ed.), *Colin Ward*. London: Lawrence & Wishart.

Nahouli, Z., Mackenzie, J.-M., Aresti, A., and Dando, C. (2022) Rapport building with offenders in probation supervision: The views of English probation practitioners. *Probation Journal*. https://doi.org/10.1177/02645505221137448.

Nellis, M. (2022) From electronic monitoring to artificial intelligence, in Burke, L. et al. (Eds.), *Reimagining Probation Practice: Re-forming Rehabilitation in an Age of Penal Excess*. Oxon: Routledge.

Nixon, S. (2020) The emotional labour of prison listeners, in Phillips, J., Waters, J., Westaby, C., and Fowler, A. (Eds.), *Emotional Labour in Criminal Justice and Criminology*. Oxon, United Kingdom: Routledge, chp. 15.

Pearson, A., Surtees, A., Crompton, C. J., Goodall, C., Pillai, D., Sedgewick, F., and Au-Yeung, S. K. (2022) Addressing community priorities in autism research. *Frontiers in Psychology*, 13. https://doi.org/10.3389/fpsyg.2022.1040446.

Pickard, H., Pellicano, E., den Houting, J., and Crane, L. (2021) Participatory autism research: Early career and established researchers' views and experiences. *Autism*, 23: 477–493. https://doi.org/10.1177/13623613211019594.

Preston, J. and Firth, R. (2020) *Coronavirus, Class and Mutual Aid in the United Kingdom*. Cham, Switzerland: Springer.

Reeves, P., McConnell, D., and Phelan, S. K. (2023) The (radical) role of belonging in shifting and expanding understandings of social inclusion for people labelled with intellectual and developmental disabilities. *Sociology of Health & Illness*, 45(2): 317–330. https://doi.org/10.1111/1467-9566.13574.

Revolving Doors (2022) Exploring the links between neurodiversity and the revolving door of crisis and crime. Available at https://revolving-doors.org.uk/wp-content/uploads/2022/09/Revolving-Doors-neurodiversity-policy-position.pdf (Accessed: 25/11/26).

Rutten, A. X., Kempes, M., Bongers, I. L., Vermeiren, R. R. J. M., and van Nieuwenhuizen, C. (2022). Offence type and neurodiversity: A comparison of 12-17-year-old boys charged with a criminal offence by diagnosis of autism spectrum disorder, attention deficit hyperactivity disorder or both. *Criminal Behaviour & Mental Health*, 32(6): 404–420. https://doi.org/10.1002/cbm.2267.

Samaritans (2020) *Pilot of Postvention Support in Prisons – Evaluation Report*. Available at https://media.samaritans.org/documents/Samaritans_Postvention_in_prisons_FINAL_pdf.pdf (Accessed: 26/11/25).

Sentencing Council (2020) Sentencing offenders with mental disorders, developmental disorders, or neurological impairments. Available at https://sentencingcouncil.org.uk/guidelines/sentencing-offenders-with-mental-disorders-developmental-disorders-or-neurological-impairments/ (Accessed: 26/11/25)

Servigne, P. and Chapellle, G. (2022) *Mutual Aid: The Other Law of the Jungle*. Cambridge: Polity [Original work published 2017].

Smithson, H., Gray, P., and Jones, A. (2020) They really should start listening to you': The benefits and challenges of co-producing a participatory framework of youth justice practice. *Youth Justice*, 21: 147322542094159. https://doi.org/10.1177/1473225420941598.

Spade, D. (2020) *Mutual Aid: Building Solidarity During This Crisis (and the next)*. London: Verso.

Takeda (2022) ADHD in the criminal justice system: A case for change. Takeda. https://www.adhdfoundation.org.uk/wpcontent/uploads/2022/06/Takeda_ADHD-in-the-CJS-Roundtable-Report_Final.pdf.

Tomlin, J. and Jordan, M. (2022) Strength- and recovery-based approaches in forensic mental health in late modernity: Increasingly incorporating a human rights angle?. *Social Theory & Health*, 20: 398–415. https://doi.org/10.1057/s41285-021-00169-x.

Volkmar, F., Loftin, R., Westphal, A., and Woodbury-Smith, M. (2021) *Handbook of Autism Spectrum Disorder and the Law*. Cham, Switzerland: Springer.

Ward, C. (2018) *Anarchy in Action*. Oakland: PM Press [Original work published 1973].

Wilbert, C. and White, D. (2011) *Autonomy, Solidarity, Possibility*. Edinburgh: AK Press.

World Health Organisation (2022) *ICD-11: International Classification of Diseases 11th Revision*.

Yang, X., Zhang, L., Yu, J., and Wang, M. (2025) Short-term and long-term effect of non-pharmacotherapy for adults with ADHD: A systematic review and network meta-analysis. *Frontiers in Psychiatry*, 16. https://doi.org/10.3389/fpsyt.2025.1516878.

Young, S., Gudjonsson, G., Chitsabesan, P. et al. (2018) Identification and treatment of offenders with attention-deficit/hyperactivity disorder in the prison population: A practical approach based upon expert consensus. *BMC Psychiatry*, 18: 281. https://doi.org/10.1186/s12888-018-1858-9.

Index

For Product Safety Concerns and Information please contact our EU representative GPSR@taylorandfrancis.com Taylor & Francis Verlag GmbH, Kaufingerstraße 24, 80331 München, Germany